Moral Principles
and Nuclear Weapons

Moral Principles and Nuclear Weapons

Douglas P. Lackey

ROWMAN & ALLANHELD
PUBLISHERS

ROWMAN & ALLANHELD PUBLISHERS

Published in the United States of America in 1984
by Rowman & Allanheld, Publishers
(A division of Littlefield, Adams & Company)
81 Adams Drive, Totowa, New Jersey 07512

Library of Congress Cataloging in Publication Data

Lackey, Douglas P.
  Moral principles and nuclear weapons.

  Bibliography: p.
  Includes index.
  1. Atomic weapons—Moral and ethical aspects.
2. Atomic warfare—Moral and ethical aspects. I. Title.
U264.L33 1984   172'.42   84-11540
ISBN 0-8476-7116-X

ISBN 0-8476-7515-7 (pbk.)

    86 / 10 9 8 7 6 5 4 3 2

Printed in the United States of America

Contents

List of Tables

Glossary

ABM. Anti-ballistic missile.

ASAT. An anti-satellite weapon.

atomic bomb. An explosive device powered by atomic fission.

Categorical Imperative. Immanuel Kant's supreme moral principle: Always act in such a way that you could wish the maxim of your act to become a universal law.

CEP. Circular error probable: an approximate measure of missile accuracy and reliability; the smallest diameter of a circle within which half of the missiles directed at a certain point will land.

counterforce weapons. Weapons capable of destroying the strategic weapons of the opponent.

counterforce targeting. Directing of strategic weapons at military targets, especially the strategic weapons of the opponent.

countervalue targeting. Directing of strategic weapons at targets valued by the opponent, usually economic and industrial targets and urban centers.

conventional weapons. Non-nuclear weapons.

cruise missile. A small pilotless jet plane carrying a nuclear or conventional warhead.

detente (as used in this book). The policy of retaining nuclear weapons only for the purpose of deterring nuclear attack; also called Minimum Deterrence.

double effect, principle of. Rule of moral theology which holds that it is permissible to perform an act which has evil effects provided that (a) the act is not evil in itself, (b) the good effects outweigh the evil effects, (c) the agent does not desire to produce the evil effects, and (d) the evil effects are not the means by which the good effects are obtained.

EMT. Equivalent megatons: the destructive force of a nuclear weapon at ground level, which is the two-thirds power of the total megatonnage of the device.

expected death. A measure of risk, consisting of any product of probability and deaths caused by a policy equal to 1. For example, a policy which creates a 10% chance of killing 100 people causes 10 expected deaths. Also called: statistical death.

expected value. A measure of the value of a policy, calculated by adding together the value of the outcomes of the policy. The value of each outcome is measured by multiplying the value of the outcome by its probability.

first strike capacity. The ability to launch strategic weapons at an opponent with such effect that the opponent cannot inflict unacceptable damage in return.

flexible response. A nuclear strategy that permits a variety of strategic responses to conventional or nuclear attack.

hydrogen bomb. A explosive device powered by the fusion of hydrogen nucleii.

IAEA. International Atomic Energy Agency.

ICBM. Intercontinental ballistic missile.

IRBM. Intermediate range ballistic missile.

K-factor. A measure of the ability of a strategic weapon to destroy a reinforced target: the EMT of the weapon divided by the square of the CEP.

megaton. An explosive force equal to the explosion of one million tons of TNT.

Minuteman. A solid fueled American ICBM.

minimax rule. Principle of decision theory which holds that in the absence of information about the probabilities of outcomes, the policy which has the least disastrous worst outcome should be preferred.

MIRV. Multiple independently targeted re-entry vehicle: devices mounted on missiles that can direct several warheads to distinct assigned targets.

MIRVed missiles. Ballistic missiles carrying MIRVs.

non-possession. The policy of renouncing the possession of nuclear weapons.

nuclear fusion. The process of joining together nucleii of atoms, accompanied by a large releases of energy.

nuclear winter. A global drop in temperature caused by dust clouds generated by a nuclear exchange.

NSA. The National Security Agency.

Pareto principle. Rule that policy A is preferable to B if some persons prefer A to B and no person prefers B to A.

pastoral letter. Guidance on a moral problem from a council of bishops to priests and laypeople.

Poseidon. An American SLBM.

rad. A measure of radiation absorbed by tissue (100 ergs per gram of tissue).

rule of discrimination. Rule of the just war theory which says that military violence should not be directed at noncombatants. Also called: principle of noncombatant immunity.

rule of necessity. Rule of just war theory which says that the military force used in war must be the minimum needed to obtain the objective.

rule of proportionality. Rule of just war theory which holds that a war is just only if the damage expected from the war is less than the good that could be expected from winning the war.

SALT. Strategic Arms Limitation Talks.

SALT I. Treaty (1972) limiting the size of the missile forces of the U.S. and U.S.S.R.

second strike capacity. The ability to suffer a nuclear attack and still retain sufficient strategic weapons to inflict unacceptable damage on the attacker in return.

SLBM. Submarine launched ballistic missile.

strategic triad. Distribution of nuclear weapons among bombers, land-based missiles, and sea-based missiles.

strategic weapons. Long range nuclear weapons.

tactical nuclear weapons. Small nuclear weapons for battlefield use.

thermonuclear weapons. Weapons the energy of which is derived from nuclear fusion.

Titan. Liquid fueled American ICBM.

victory (as used in this book). A nuclear weapons policy in which nuclear threats are used to control all types of unwanted behavior in an opponent; also called Extended Deterrence.

Preface

As the title shows, this book draws on two fields: the study of ethics and the study of nuclear weapons. It presupposes no knowledge of either field. Those familiar with the study of ethics may wish to skip Chapter 1. Readers familiar with the history of strategic weapons may wish to skip Chapter 2.

People who have done some reading about strategy and nuclear weapons may be surprised to discover that certain familiar subjects are not discussed in this book. In particular, I do not discuss, in any detail, results from the theory of games concerning the Prisoner's Dilemma, Chicken, and other formal games that shed some light on the nuclear arms race and nuclear confrontations. I have avoided these topics (a) because there are numerous excellent discussions of these subjects already in print,* and (b) because I think that work on the theory of games is largely irrelevant to the moral evaluation of nuclear weapons policies. What the theory of games shows is how a prudent "player," whether a person or a nation, can obtain a certain minimal level of payoffs by making the prescribed strategic choices. Thus the theory of games is about self-interest, enlightened self-interest, perhaps, but self-interest all the same. There is a logical gulf between the demands of morality and the dictates of self-interest. Indeed, the conflict between duty and self-interest creates much of the interest and misery of our daily lives.

Many have helped me with this project, but special thanks are due to Dean Martin Stevens for released time, to Kenneth Shouler, Samuel Long, Harvey Goldman, and Gloria Goldman for assistance with the research, and especially to Mrs. Esther Guttenberg for her help and patience.

---

*See, for example, Schelling 1960, Rapaport 1964, Russett 1983, in the Bibliography at the end of this book. For important recent results see Axelrod 1980.

For an enduring universal peace by means of the so-called balance of power in Europe is a mere chimera, rather like Swift's house whose architect had built it in such perfect accordance with all the laws of equilibrium that a sparrow lighting on the roof made it promptly collapse.

I for my part put my trust in the theory that proceeds from the principle of justice, concerning how relations between individuals and states ought to be.

Immanuel Kant [Kant 1793 80–81]

Basic Moral Considerations

War and Non-War Uses of Nuclear Weapons

About a year ago I told my mother that I was going to a New Jersey college to give a speech about the morality of nuclear war. "What's moral about nuclear war?" my mother said, and sounded quite puzzled.

My mother was right. There's nothing moral about nuclear war. In a typical nuclear war millions and perhaps tens of millions of people will be killed, and there's nothing moral about *that*.

But this is not a book about the morality of nuclear war. This is a book about the morality of nuclear weapons, and the various uses to which nuclear weapons can be put. Making war is only one possible use. Indeed, it is a very rare use; of the fifty thousand or so nuclear weapons that have been produced since 1945, only two have ever been used in war. I am particularly interested in evaluating non-war uses of nuclear weapons, such as the use of nuclear weapons to make threats. Is it moral, for example, for a nation to use nuclear threats to prevent a nuclear attack on itself? Such uses are usually described as *nuclear deterrence*, and we cannot decide that nuclear deterrence is wrong simply by observing that nuclear war is wrong.[1]

There are, of course, connections between the war uses of nuclear weapons and the non-war uses. The production of nuclear weapons for any use creates a certain risk that they will be used in war. The development of the system of nuclear deterrence and the enunciation of nuclear threats may further increase the probability that a nuclear war will occur. Much of the debate about nuclear weapons is a debate about this risk. Some of the debate focuses on the empirical facts: do threats of retaliation increase or decrease the chance that an attack will occur? Some of the debate, however, is distinctly moral in nature. If we ask whether a nation's attempt to prevent nuclear attack, preserve national sovereignty, contain communism, or secure oil supplies from the Middle East justifies a given risk of nuclear war, we are dealing with a moral problem.

Suppose that you had to choose between two nuclear weapons policies, A and B. Policy A produces a 3 percent risk of nuclear war and a 10 percent chance that the United States will be intimidated by another nation through nuclear threats. Policy B produces a 2 percent risk of nuclear war, but the chance that the United States will be subjected to successful nuclear blackmail rises to 30 percent. You think that nuclear war is a bad thing, but you also think that submission to blackmail is a bad thing. Which policy does morality tell you to choose? Is a 1 percent decrease in the chance of nuclear war worth a 20 percent increase in the chance of nuclear blackmail?[2]

Saying that nuclear war is bad does not provide a clear verdict between A and B. Is nuclear war so bad that any decrease in the chance of nuclear war, however small, is worth any sacrifice, however great? If the answer is yes, we ought to choose A. If the answer is no, perhaps we should choose B. One would hope that ethics and moral theory would provide help with questions like these.

Moral Interest and the National Interest

Since this book will be wholly devoted to the moral evaluation of nuclear weapons policies, it is important at the outset to distinguish moral criticism from other forms of criticism.

Perhaps the most important distinction in this regard is between criticism of a policy as immoral and criticism of the policy as contrary to some particular interest. At the personal level, everyone understands what the distinction is. Every schoolchild recognizes that he or she may get ahead by cheating on a test, but that cheating on tests is morally wrong. At the level of nations, the same kind of distinction emerges: in this instance, between the national interest and the interests of morality. What is in the national interest is one thing; what is morally right may be another.[3]

To say that national interest and the interests of morality are not the same thing does not imply that they always conflict. Sometimes the national interest and morality coincide. It was in the interests of the United States to fight Hitler. It was also morally right to do so. The problem is that the national interest and the interests of morality do not *necessarily* coincide, and occasions will arise when the morally right thing will require national self-sacrifice. Some have argued, for example, that though it is in the national interest for the United States to keep building nuclear weapons, morality requires that the United States should stop.

Although the difference between morality and self-interest is universally understood, there is less agreement when it comes to recognizing the difference between morality and the national interest. Many people are simply incapable of believing that there could be a divergence between the interests of morality and the interests of the United States. They believe that the United States possesses certain spiritual qualities and sets a moral standard for the rest of the world. In this book, I will not pass judgment on whether or not the United States possesses such qualities. I will merely note that nearly everyone in the world believes this about his own country. Poles think that there is something special about Poland; Russians believe that Russia and the Slavs will redeem the West from spiritual degeneracy; many Israelis believe that Israel is of special interest to God, and so forth. If we are to judge a policy fairly, we must consider primarily what the policy is, not what nation happens to put such a policy into effect. We should judge nations just as we should judge individuals, on the basis of what they do, not on the basis of who they are.

There are others who, while capable of distinguishing between the national interest and morality, believe that morality should be ignored when the national interest is at stake. They believe that the interests of the United States are *more important* than moral interests. This view will be considered later in this chapter, under the heading "The Theory of Reasons of State." It is sufficient at this point to note that someone who says, "The interests of the United States should always prevail over those of other nations," is saying something very similar to the person who says, "*My* own interests should always prevail over the interests of other people." When someone says *that*, we call him an egoist. Perhaps extreme patriotism is simply national egoism.

Three Basic Moral Concepts

To criticize a national policy morally, then, is to do something different from saying that it is unwise, or contrary to the national interest. But what *is* a moral criticism? Here we will assume that a moral criticism is one of three things:

(a) It is a moral criticism to say that a policy is *contrary to the interests of humanity*;

(b) It is a moral criticism to say that a policy *violates human rights*; or

(c) It is a moral criticism to say that a policy is *unfair* or unjust.

In short, we will assume that there are three basic moral concepts: the common good, human rights, and fairness, and that there are three elementary moral principles: Do good, Respect rights, Be fair.[4]

To present a moral criticism is to present a moral reason against a policy. Unfortunately, it often happens that when there are moral reasons against a policy, there are also moral reasons for it. (There may be strong moral reasons against all the alternative policies). To make a moral case against a policy, one must show, *first*, that there are moral reasons against the policy; *second*, that the moral reasons against the policy are stronger than the moral reasons for it. The second part of making a moral case is often the most difficult part.

A further complication arises because different philosophers have different opinions about which moral reason should prevail. Those who feel that the interests of humanity should always prevail are called *utilitarians*. Those who feel that the preservation of human rights should prevail are called *rights theorists*.[5]

In this context, we are not attempting to settle the battle, now several centuries old, between utilitarians and rights theorists. Rather than assuming that either the interests of humanity or human rights must be the deciding factor, we will look at each policy as it comes, consider the moral reasons for it and against it, and try to judge which reasons weigh heaviest in that particular case. Let us now look a little more carefully at the three basic moral concepts.

(a) The Common Good

When American politicians talk about the common good, they have in mind the welfare of the American people. When philosophers talk about the *moral* concept of the common good, they have in mind the welfare of *everyone*, not just Americans. The common good, morally considered, is the sum of the interests of every person in every country, and every person in every future generation.[6]

It is often difficult to determine what a person's interests are. The simplest and most liberal approach is to identify a person's *interests* with his *preferences*. But it may also be difficult to determine what a person's preferences are. In this book, we will make some elementary assumptions about human preferences. We will assume that people prefer to be alive, not dead, well, not sick, to be uncontaminated rather than contaminated by radioactivity. People prefer to pay less taxes rather than more. They prefer to be governed by the political institutions with which they are familiar, unless they believe that those institutions are controlled by foreigners, or that those institutions hold them in contempt. People prefer to be out of jail, rather than in it, and prefer to live in a society in which the expression of their normal impulses does not carry the threat of jail.

On the basis of these attitudes towards life, welfare, freedom, and so forth, we assume that each person decides, given two weapons policies A and B, whether he prefers A to B, B to A, or whether he is indifferent between the two. This will provide us with the list of individual comparative preferences regarding weapons policies.

Once we have the individual preferences, we can go on to compare the two policies as regards the common good. Suppose it turns out that some people prefer A to B, and that no people prefer B to A. Then it is obvious that A serves the common good better than B. In short, we adopt the following rule:

> If A and B are two policies, and some people prefer A to B and no one prefers B to A, then A serves the common good better than B.

This is a variant of the Pareto principle, familiar to students of economics. A policy is judged to serve everyone if it hurts none and helps some.

Unfortunately it often turns out that given two policies, A and B, some people are better off with A, while others are better off with B. In that case, the A-supporters can try to bribe the B-supporters and the B-supporters can try to bribe the A-supporters. (Such bribes are usually called "compensation"). But suppose that there is nothing that A-supporters can offer B-supporters to persuade them to adopt A, and nothing that B-supporters can offer A-supporters to get them to adopt B. In such cases, the Pareto principle cannot be applied. We need a different decision rule, and the most reasonable rule is that the common good is best served when the greater number of preferences is satisfied. The common good, then, is what the majority of human beings prefer (including the human beings in future generations who are affected by the policies).

There are a number of technical difficulties in the idea of majority rule. We do not know how many votes to assign to future generations, since we do not know how many persons will be living in future generations. The procedure described gives no weight to intensity of preference; a mild favoring of A over B counts as much as an intense preference of B over A. If more than two policies are under consideration, inconsistencies may develop: the majority may prefer A to B, B to C, and C to A. With such "cyclical majorities" it is impossible to determine what the majority preference is.

In this study, we cannot attempt to deal with these technical problems. At the practical level, most of the technical difficulties can be eliminated by removing from consideration the *far* distant future, and by demanding that the majority who determine the common good be a *substantial* majority.[7] This leads to the *majoritarian rule*:

> If A and B are policies, and A is preferred to B by a substantial majority of persons in this and several future generations, then A serves the common good better than B.

By a "substantial" majority I have in mind something on the order of 80 percent.

Suppose that we have two weapons policies, A and B, and that A is supported by 60 percent of the people affected and B is supported by 40 percent of the people affected. Since A does not command a substantial majority, we cannot say according to the majoritarian rule that A serves the common good better than B. To distinguish A from B morally, we must look to the other moral considerations, considerations of rights or considerations of justice.

(b) Human Rights

It is obvious from the majoritarian rule that so far as the common good is concerned, a large number of preferences can overrule a small number of preferences. It is a distinctive feature of the idea of human rights that human rights cannot be so overruled. Ten preferences can overrule one preference, but ten preferences cannot overrule one right. In fact, ten rights cannot overrule one right.

It is not possible to discuss here all the different theories that can be proposed to provide a philosophical foundation for the idea of human rights.[8] We will simply assume that there are rights and that human beings have them. We will assume that all have a right not to be killed, confined or coerced by other people into adopting plans that are not their own. Traditionally, these are described as the rights to life, liberty, and the pursuit of happiness. We will assume that the right to life is more important than the right to liberty; in short, that it is morally permissible to use coercion to protect life and limb.

Two logical features of the idea of rights are especially important. First, it is always permissible for the holder of a right to *waive* the right. If I impose a risk of death on you, for example, I have not violated your right to life if you have freely consented to accept this risk. Second, it is always permissible for the holder of the right to take steps to *enforce* the right, provided that the steps taken to enforce the right do not violate rights of greater importance. This leads us to a general *principle of self-defense:*

> If a person P is about to violate a right R of person Q, then it is permissible to take any steps against P which are necessary to prevent the violation of the right, provided that these steps do not violate a right of P which is of greater importance than right R.[9]

The reader should inspect the principle of self-defense carefully. Note that the principle does not require that the defense of Q's rights must be undertaken by Q himself. The self-defense principle allows *collective* defense, in which other people assist P in the defense of his rights.[10] Note, furthermore, that the principle only allows steps to be taken against P, the aggressor who is trying to violate the right. Self-defense does not allow the violation of the rights of innocent persons, who are not involved in the threat to Q's rights. It follows that the principle of self-defense is *not* a general warrant for actions needed to guarantee personal survival.

Since rights cannot be summed together, the principle of self-defense permits actions against any number of aggressors. If twenty aggressors attack one victim, it is permissible for the victim to kill all twenty, if that is the only way he can save his life. Likewise, since rights cannot be summed together, it is not permissible, *on grounds of rights*, to take the life of a single innocent person no matter how many other lives happen to be at stake. Even if killing one innocent person will save twenty innocent persons from death, nothing in the notion of rights justifies killing the one to save the twenty.

It should be clear from the preceding that it is crucial to our understanding of human rights to be able to distinguish who is an aggressor from who is innocent. According to the principle of self-defense, an aggressor is anyone who by his actions raises a threat to the rights of someone else. It is not necessary that the aggressor realize that he is creating a threat, nor is it necessary that the aggressor desire to create the threat. He may create the threat by accident; he may create it unintentionally. If he creates the threat, he is nonetheless an aggressor, and it is permissible to violate his rights in self-defense. This will prove to be an important point in the moral analysis of nuclear threats. A nuclear threat which raises risks to innocent parties may have a noble purpose, but if it threatens the innocent, it is a violation of rights, not justifiable on the grounds that harm is not intended.

(c) *Justice*

Perhaps no concept has excited more theoretical work in recent ethics than the concept of justice. Nevertheless, our sense of justice needs little help from theory. Suppose that you are in line at the bank, waiting for a teller. Someone barges in and goes straight to the head of the line. Obviously, this person wants to get ahead of you, but would object to your getting ahead of him. We immediately recognize such conduct as unfair. If you heard that the bank rules *allow* this person to go first because he is a drinking buddy of the bank manager, you would declare that the bank rules are unjust.

The essential core of the idea of justice is the idea of fairness. In human life, there are many processes and procedures which generate benefits but also create burdens. We think it basic to fairness that those who enjoy the benefits should bear a proportionate share of the burdens. We think it unfair when someone seizes the benefits without bearing the burdens. In the case of queueing at the bank, the benefit is that everyone gets to the window; the burden is that you have to wait your turn. If someone goes to the window without waiting his turn, he seizes the benefit without paying the burden.[11]

A great many of the standard immoralities are offenses against justice. Most acts of cheating and deceit are acts against justice, since cheaters do not want to be cheated and deceivers do not want to be deceived. Most acts of exploitation are usually acts against justice, since exploiters usually do not enjoy being exploited. If a coal miner consents to a risk of death on the job, and the mine owner seizes the lion's share of the benefits from the mine while the coal miner bears the lion's share of the risks, the arrangement between the mine owner and the mine worker may be an offense against justice.

The idea of fairness in the distribution of benefits and burdens inevitably involves the idea of proportionality: people should obtain benefits in proportion to the burden they have assumed. But in most concrete cases it is difficult to determine whether a given distribution of benefits and burdens is proportional. In modern theories of justice, it is common to consider as fair or proportionate any procedure for distributing benefits and burdens to which *unanimous consent* has been obtained. The idea that fairness can spring from unanimous consent is the foundation of the *social contract theory* of justice.

In the social contract theory, we imagine that each social arrangement which distributes burdens and benefits is presented for a vote to all the people who will obtain a benefit or suffer a burden. If the arrangement is unanimously approved, the distribution of burdens and benefits is just.[12]

There are, however, two different interpretations of "unanimous consent." In one interpretation, each voter knows in advance what burdens and what benefits he will receive from the arrangement. Knowing what he will receive from the arrangement, he will approve it if, in his opinion, he gains more than he loses. Every just distribution must necessarily be a distribution which leaves everyone better off.

The standard of justice established by this version of the social contract theory is very severe. It is unlikely that very many social arrangements are such that they leave everyone better off, even if elaborate arrangements are made to compensate the losers with a share of the benefits that have gone to the winners. In addition, this version seems to interfere with the right to liberty, since it does not permit social arrangements which allow any member of society even to take a risk of a loss. These difficulties lead us to the second interpretation of unanimous consent, which might be called *unanimous consent with risk.*[13]

In the second version, no voter knows in advance what benefits or burdens he will receive from the social arrangement. He knows only that he has an equal chance of being *any one* of the persons who receive benefits and burdens. If the voter agrees to a social arrangement in which *some* persons get more benefits than burdens while *others* get more burdens than benefits, he is *gambling* that he will be among the winners with the benefits and not among the losers with the burdens. The bet, in his view, is a good bet.

Let us take a concrete example. Suppose that it takes 1,000 coal miners to produce enough coal to provide electricity to 200,000 people. The miners and the citizens are considering different levels of safety in the mine. Each improvement in safety produces a certain increase in the cost of electricity. What safety level is just? The 200,000 citizens (including the 1,000 miners) are presented with different safety levels, each with its corresponding price of electricity. The safety level is just if every voter approves it, knowing *only* that he has an equal chance of being any one of 200,000 people, and that he has a one in 200 chance of being a coal miner. The chance of being a miner is slight, but the risks of being a miner are great compared with the small burden of a higher electric bill. A rational person will choose his preferred safety level with care.

Decisions about safety levels in mines will be reached with a certain sobriety if everyone affected realizes that he stands some fixed chance of being a consumer and some fixed chance of being a miner. In the real life situation, what usually happens is that the miners are concerned with safety and not interested in electric bills, and the consumers are interested in electric bills and not concerned with safety in mines. Neither attitude is fair, and each side attempts to pass off its burdens on the other.

The passing off of costs to those who do not share the benefits is addressed in economics as "the problem of externalities." The problem of externalities makes a particularly poignant appearance on the international scene, when one nation attempts to pass off uncompensated burdens on another. The citizens of the nation that reaps the benefits will applaud the politicians that thought up the policy; those politicians are gratified by the thought that they have served their constituents. The citizens of the nation that suffers the burden will be angry, but in many cases they have no way to obtain compensation without going to war, which usually costs more than the compensation that is desired. Suppose, for example, that a certain nuclear weapons policy reduces the chance of a nuclear attack on the United States, but increases the chances that citizens in other nations will be exposed to massive releases of radioactive fallout should the United States respond to attack. Citizens in those nations may protest that it is not fair that they should bear the risks of a policy which is mainly beneficial to Americans. They may attempt to justify their protest by citing various versions of the social contract theory. If the citizens of these countries reject the policy, even at the price of losing all American aid, then the policy is unfair according to the principle of unanimous consent (without risk). If a rational person would reject the policy, knowing that he stood an equal chance of being a citizen in any of the nations involved, then the policy is unjust according to the principle of unanimous consent (with risk). Even in the absence of genuine international government, the social contact theory can be applied to questions of justice in international affairs.

The Principles of Just War

An understanding of the fundamental moral concepts—the common good, human rights, and justice—is essential to undertaking the moral analysis of nuclear weapons policies. But there is also a fourth concept which we will press into service in the analysis of nuclear war: the concept of *just war*.

The theory of just war is a set of principles that distinguish just wars from unjust wars and just means of making war from unjust means of making war.[14] In its present form, the theory is a mixture of distinctly moral considerations and considerations of enlightened self-interest.[15] Because of this mixed character, we cannot assume that a nuclear weapons policy that satisfies the principles of just war is necessarily a moral policy, or that a policy that fails to satisfy these principles is necessarily an immoral policy. Nevertheless, the contemporary principles of just war represent the accumulated wisdom of 2300 years of intellectual concern with war; they are attuned to the realities of international conflict and the problems of the battlefield in a way that abstract moral principles are not, and they are to some extent embodied in generally recognized principles of international law.

In the conceptual landscape, the theory of just war provides a middle path between two extreme attitudes towards war: the attitude of pacifism and the attitude of extreme nationalism. Pacifism asserts that all wars are unjust. Extreme nationalism asserts that no wars are unjust. The theory of just war asserts that some wars are just and some wars are unjust. Since many of those involved in the debate about nuclear weapons are either pacifists or nationalists, we will not simply assume, as we have with the concepts of the common good, human rights, and justice, that the principles of just war theory are valid. We will first consider whether there is any merit in pacifism or nationalism, and then examine the principles of just war as they developed over time.

Pacifism and Its Problems

In its standard form, pacifism is the view that it is always wrong to use violence to obtain any end. It follows that it is always wrong to deliberately kill a human being, and it follows that participation in war, on *any* side, is morally impermissible. The doctrine has been maintained by Jains, by Buddhists, by the early Christians, and by several modern Protestant sects.[16]

It is, of course, possible to accept pacifism as an article of religious faith, and to live according to its tenets without having any arguments to show that universal morality requires pacifism. But in a philosophical essay of this kind only the arguments matter, and indeed many pacifists have offered arguments that purport to show that morality requires pacifism.

We will consider three such arguments. The first is that each human life has infinite value, so that it always does infinite harm to kill a human being. The second is that every human being has a right to life, so every killing of a human being is a violation of human rights. The third is that killing violates the principles of justice, since the killer wants to kill others, but does not want to be killed himself.

In the first argument, the underlying assumption is plainly false, since no one sets an infinite value on life, not even his own life. Almost everyone, in the course of a day, takes some life-threatening risks. Every time, for example, a person drives a car, he takes a risk, a small risk, of death; he considers the convenience of driving his car more valuable than eliminating a small risk of death. Thus each person sets a large but finite value on his own life.

The second argument, that killing always violates human rights, runs head-on into the self-defense principle, which asserts that rights may always be defended against deliberate attack. Pacifists, to be sure, reject the self-defense principle. But what is the point of asserting that there are such things as rights unless one believes that rights may be defended?[17] The doctrine of human rights was created to define, around each person, a private space into which it was not permissible for other individuals or for society to intrude. There is little point in defining such a "barrier" without permitting the barrier to be defended.

The third argument, that killing is unfair because killers do not themselves wish to be killed, assumes that each person wants never to be killed, no matter what the circumstances. This assumption is false. Suppose that a group of persons gather together to choose the rules for a new social community. One rule that they consider is the rule that it is permissible for persons under unjust attack to use deadly force in self-defense. I think almost everyone would agree to such a rule. This implies that each person agrees that, should *he* ever mount an unjust attack, *his* attack be met with deadly force. It follows, from the social contract theory, that the rule of self-defense is a just rule, and acts of self-defense do not go against the idea of fairness.

Because of these difficulties with standard pacifism, a special sort of pacifism, which might be called anti-war pacifism, as opposed to general, anti-violence pacifism, has evolved. According to this view, while it is conceded that individuals have a right to self-defense and that individuals can use force against their attackers, nations have no moral right to make war, even in the event of unprovoked armed attack.[18]

The reasons offered for anti-war pacifism are various, but two stand out. One argument is that history teaches that wars always do more harm than good, even wars fought in self-defense. The other is that when nations go to war, it is inevitable that some innocent people will be killed.

The view that *most* wars have done more harm than good is one that nearly everyone, I think, would be willing to endorse. The view that *all* wars have done more harm than good will be rejected by nearly everyone because of the example of World War II. Possibly the world would have been better served if Hitler had been met everywhere only by passive resistance and non-violent action, but this does not seem likely.

The argument that, in war, the innocent will be killed as well as the guilty, stands on firmer ground. But is it always wrong to pursue a policy that one foresees will lead to the death of innocent people? If so, the Congress of the United States is guilty of mass murder, since it refused to set highway speed limits that would substantially reduce the number of fatalities. A speed limit of 25 or 30 miles per hour, for example, would save many innocent lives. Since we do *not* consider it murder if the government does not set the safest possible speed limit, we should not consider it immoral for the United States to go to war, simply on the grounds that some innocent people will inevitably be killed in the war.

Nationalism

(a) Extreme Nationalism and Its Contradictions

In some ways, extreme nationalism is even more radical than pacifism. Applying moral laws to war, the pacifist declares that all wars are unjust. The extreme nationalist maintains that the laws of morality cannot be applied to war: that war is *exempt* from moral judgment. For the extreme nationalist, wars can be successful or unsuccessful, wise or foolish, but not just or unjust.[19]

It is a cliché that "all's fair in love and war," and many people believe that when war begins, the laws of morality should fly out the window. But what arguments are there to prove the cliché? A review of the literature shows that the same two arguments are repeatedly cited. First, there is the argument that moral principles are meaningless when they cannot be enforced, and in the absence of world government they cannot be enforced on the international scene. Second, there is the argument that moral codes are the product of particular societies, and hence that there is no "objective" standpoint from which to judge moral issues when two societies with different codes come into conflict.

Both of these arguments are so weak that one can only assume that people who endorse them are exercising what William James called "the will to believe." The argument that moral laws cannot be applied where they cannot be enforced implies that anyone who successfully evades the police has done no crime. On the international scene, it would imply that if Germany had won World War II, the extermination of the Jews would not have been wrong. Nobody today believes *that*. The argument that there is no "objective" moral code with which to judge moral disputes between states would imply that if two individuals had different moral codes, there would be no way to judge a moral dispute between *them*. The argument from moral "subjectivity," in short, would destroy morality at the personal level as well as the international level, and few extreme nationalists want to destroy morality at the personal level. On the contrary, most extreme nationalists are strong sponsors of individual morality in their home states.[20]

(b) The Notion of "Reasons of State"

Extreme nationalism maintains that the *only* thing that matters in decisions about war is the national interest. We have rejected this view, but there is a milder doctrine that we should consider, since it is enthusiastically endorsed by most leaders of state. That doctrine is the doctrine that the national interest is *one* thing that matters—matters morally—in decisions about war. The President can acknowledge that he is bound by standard moral principles. But he can argue that he is *also* sworn to "preserve, protect and defend" the interests of the United States. It follows that in many situations the President is required—morally required—to favor the interests of Americans over the interests of non-Americans. Favoring American interests may require acts (acts of deception, for example) that would be immoral if performed or permitted by someone who did not have a special sworn responsibility to protect the United States. If the President supports policies that are contrary to the common good, human rights, or justice, but that nevertheless protect the interests of Americans, his support is justified—morally justified—on grounds of "reasons of state."

It is useful, in evaluating this notion of "reasons of state," to distinguish three different ways the President may set about "protecting American interests." The first way is to defend the United States and American citizens against acts which violate their rights. The second way is to improve the American position in the world, without injuring any other nation state. The third way is to improve the position of the United States in the world *at the expense* of other nation states, through various acts of coercion, deception, exploitation, or war.

Acts of all three types have been justified over the years as "required by the national interest." But an act that defends the moral rights of Americans is not justifiable *merely* in terms of the national interest: it is justifiable by the principle of self-defense. An act that improves the position of the United States without injuring any other nation is not justifiable *merely* in terms of the national interest: it is justified by the Pareto principle, and therefore serves the common good. On the other hand, acts of deception, coercion, exploitation, and war that injure other states but serve the interest of the United States are not justified on any moral grounds. In such cases, the appeal to the President's special responsibility to protect American interests is simply a cover-up.

Consider the following imaginary but instructive example. An American cruise missile gets loose, and the President's experts advise him that he has only two options (a) detonate the warhead over Michigan, killing many Americans, or (b) detonate the warhead over Ontario, killing an equal or greater number of Canadians. If the President has an overriding moral obligation to protect American interests, he would have a moral duty to let the warhead detonate over Ontario. But few people would say that the President has such a duty. Many would even say that it is not even *permissible* for the President to allow the warhead to detonate over Ontario. We conclude, then, that "reasons of state" are *either* disguised moral reasons, derivable from the concepts of common good, rights, and justice, *or* they are not moral reasons at all.[21]

Development of the Principles of the Just War

(a) Aristotle and Cicero

The theory of just war is a very old doctrine, but it has never been universally accepted and its influence has waxed and waned over the centuries. The history of the just war concept illustrates the difficulties of attempting to apply concepts like morality and prudence to situations that provoke intense passion. The story begins with Aristotle, who wrote in his *Politics*, "wars against men who are intended by nature to be governed, but who will not submit, are naturally just." (*Pol.* 1256b25) Fortunately there is more to Aristotle's theory of war than this single, rather depressing remark. Aristotle's signal contribution to the theory of war was to recognize that the condition of war is not an end in itself, and that therefore a decision to make war must be justified in terms of some end. "Peace is the end of war," he remarks (1334a15); and "There must be war for the sake of peace." (1333a35) Only in peacetime can people develop the arts and sciences, those distinctly human activities, which, more than anything else, provide human beings with a good life. War, then, is justified when it produces stable peace, and according to Aristotle there are three sorts of wars that produce such peace: (a) wars in self-defense, (b) wars that extend political rule over those who will benefit from it, and (c) wars that establish dominion over those who are slaves by nature (1133b37). All subsequent non-pacifist thinkers have followed Aristotle with regard to (a), wars in self-defense. The Christian tradition, as we shall see in the section on Augustine, accepts (b), wars undertaken for the benefit of the enemy. Few subsequent thinkers have accepted (c), wars of justifiable enslavement, although the text could serve as a warrant for the wars of colonial conquest from the 16th through the 19th century and for the Nazi wars against the Slavs, the Gypsies, and the Jews in the twentieth.

The Roman view of just war, surprisingly enough, seems to have been even more pristine than the Greeks. According to Cicero, "a lawful war is one which is waged to secure restitution of property or to repel an invader," (*de Rep.* III, xxiii)—a standard which limits just war to something close to self-defense. The distinctive contribution of the Romans to this subject, however, was the introduction of the notion of proper procedure in the course of war, an idea that is not to be found in Aristotle. According to Roman law, a war could not be lawfully waged without a formal declaration of war, and according to Cicero oaths made to an unscrupulous enemy nevertheless ought to be kept. Furthermore, after the victory, there is, according to Cicero, "a limit to retribution and to punishment. It is sufficient that the aggressor should be brought to repent of his wrong doing, in order that he might not repeat his offense and others may be deterred from doing wrong." (*de Off.* I. xi)

The Ciceronian standards are inspiring, and a good part of recent thought about just war can be viewed as the recovery of Ciceronian ideals from the theory of crusade, the doctrine of reasons of state, and other retrograde innovations that had all but displaced them by the 19th century.[22]

(b) Augustine

Early Christian thinkers, inspired by Christ's example and the explicit injunction to "resist not evil," were generally pacifists and rejected the notion of just war. Patristic writers like Origen felt that Christian belief was incompatible with military service, and several of the early saints were martyred for their refusal to fight for Rome. But in the fourth century Christianity became the official religion of the Empire, and a new breed of bishop, represented by Ambrose, felt that the Empire was worth preserving and worth fighting for. The intellectual problem of recounciling the use of violence with the Sermon on the Mount fell to Augustine, who downgraded the Roman notions of just cause and proper means and added the two further conditions of "right authority" and "right intention."

How can a Christian participate in war given Christ's explicit injunction to "resist not evil, but a person strike thee on the right cheek, turn to him the left also?" (*Matt.* v. 39) The answer, says Augustine, is that "what is here required is not a bodily action, but an inward disposition. The sacred seat of virtue is the heart." (*Epis.* XXII, 79) It follows that the use of violence is permissible provided that it is properly intended. The evils in war are not "the death of some who will die in any case, but love of violence, revengeful cruelty, fierce and implacable cunning, wild resistance, and love of power." (*Epis.* XXII, 75) In contrast to these wicked motivations, the proper and legitimate intention in war is a "certain benevolent severity,"

> For in the correction of a son, even with some sternness, there is no diminution of the father's love . . . If the commonwealth observe the precepts of the Christian religion, even its wars will not be conducted without some benevolent design, for the person from whom is taken away this freedom which he abuses in doing wrong is vanquished with benefit to himself. [*Epis.* CXXVIII, 14]

From this doctrine of "benevolent severity" Augustine deduces the causes of just war. The moral functions of violence are not merely to forestall attack or to right wrongs but to "bring under the yoke the unbridled lusts of war, and to abolish vices which ought, under a just government, to be either extirpated or suppressed." (*Epis.* CXXXVIII, 15)

It would seem to follow from these remarks that anyone can permissibly use violence provided that he has right intention and just cause. But Augustine, himself involved in the imperial suppression of heresy, took a dim view of private violence. The strictures of the Sermon on the Mount, lifted off the imperial shoulders, still bound the private Christian, and Augustine denied to private persons even the right of self-defense:

> For me the point to be considered is whether an onrushing enemy, or an assassin lying in wait, may be killed with no evil desire to preserve one's life or liberty or purity. How can I think that they act with no inordinate desire?
>
> Therefore the law is not just which grants to the wayfarer the power to kill a highway robber. I do not see how these men can be without fault, for the law does not force them to kill. How indeed are they free of sin before Providence, who for those things that ought to be held of less worth are defiled by the killing of a man? [*de Lib. Arb.* I, v]

A just war, then, can only be waged in obedience to God or some lawful authority, and the need for lawful authority is so stressed by Augustine that he argues that soldiers must obey unrighteous commands because "the position of a soldier makes obedience a duty." (*Epis.* XXII, 74) It was left to later commentators to provide rules for distinguishing a lawful authority from an unlawful one.

It is clear that Augustine enlarged the scope of just wars far beyond the limits envisioned by Cicero. According to Cicero, a war is just if it repels an injury; according to Augustine a war is just if it is a struggle against sin. For Cicero a war cannot be just without a prior injury and without an enemy identifiable as an aggressor. For Augustine a war can be just without a prior injury, and the enemy need not be an aggressor, provided that he is a sinner. For Cicero, just wars should terminate when the injury is repaired and safety restored. For Augustine just wars may continue beyond the requirements of safety, since a war is just if it *avenges* injuries ("Iusta bella ulciscuntur iniurias," *Quaes. in Hept.* VI, 10), and avenging injuries can go far beyond repairing them. After the sinner is defeated, he may be punished, provided that the punishment is motivated by the thought that punishment for the sinner is good for his soul. By introducing the notion of righteous intention, Augustine supplied Christianity with a moral rationale, not just for defensive wars, but for crusades, allegedly without abandoning the Christian commitment to universal love.[23]

(c) The Just War in the Middle Ages

The classical conditions for just war—right authority, right cause, right intention, and right means—were inherited and left largely unchallenged by the thinkers of the Middle Ages. At the start of the thirteenth century Lauretius Hispanus added a fifth condition—necessity—maintaining that a war is not just unless justice cannot be secured by any means but war. Perhaps of greater importance was the rehabilitation, by Aquinas, of the pre-Christian right to self defense. Aquinas's discussion of self-defense is delicate, since as a Christian he could by no means suggests that aggressors forfeit their status as fit objects of universal love. Instead Aquinas argued that universal Christian love, as well as natural impulse, implies that the Christian should love himself as much as his neighbor. If a Christian must kill in self-defense, his act is legitimate provided that he kills out of love for himself rather than hatred of his enemy:

> The act of self-defense may have two effects, one is the saving of one's life, the other is the slaying of the aggressor. Therefore this act, since the intention is to save one's own life, is not unlawful, seeing that it is natural for everything to keep itself in being.

So far Aquinas is at one with Aristotle. But he goes on to say:

> As it is unlawful to take a man's life, it is not lawful for a man to intend killing a man in self-defense, except for such as have public authority, who while intending to kill a man in self-defense refer this to the public good, as in the case of a soldier fighting the foe . . . although even these sin if motivated by private animosity. [ST II—II, 64,7]

In this passage, which is puzzling, Aquinas seems to retreat part-way towards the position of Augustine. If a private person may legitimately kill in self-defense in order to save his own life, obviously a soldier may also kill in self-defense to save his own life, and the reference to "the public good" is superfluous. The plain fact is that the natural tendency to self-defense is inconsistent with the "resist not evil" of the Sermon on the Mount and Aquinas's vacillation simply recapitulates the inconsistency. The second section of this passage, then, must be viewed as a vestige of Christian pacifism, perhaps the last vestige in an orthodox writer. Later authors in the tradition of natural law simply asserted the right to self-defense as a natural right, without reference to intentions. The distinction between killing with the intention to kill and killing to serve some better purpose, instituted here by Aquinas to justify the killing of aggressors, was transformed by these later authors into the "double effect procedure" for justifying the killing of the innocent.

In the same passage, Aquinas introduces another consideration that in several centuries was elevated into the sixth and last condition for just war—the condition of proportionality. "And yet, though proceeding from a good intention, an act can be rendered unlawful, if it is out of proportion to its end . . . It is lawful to repel force with force, provided that one does not exceed the limits of blameless defense."

The idea of proportionality suggested here is that the force exercised should be proportional to the value of the end sought. Proportionality implies that there may be some just ends that are not valuable enough to fight for, especially when one considers the losses that will be engendered by the fighting. Aquinas did not draw this conclusion, but the seventeenth century, staggered by the horrors of the Thirty Years War, did draw it, and declared that a war is not just if the damage forseen from the war exceeds the value of the just end secured.

But the most striking innovation in medieval thinking about war was the development of an elaborate code of rules for proper conduct in war. In Cicero, proper conduct in war consisted simply in observing standard moral rules—like the keeping of oaths—even in times of war. In the Middle Ages, proper conduct in war consisted of obedience to special rules applicable only to warriors and wartime. By the fourteenth century, the rules of conduct had become so elaborate that the theory of just war was divided in two branches: *jus ad bellum*, the rules indicating the proper occasions for war, and *jus in bello*, the rules indicating proper conduct after war has begun.

The sources of the new *jus in bello* were the canon law of the Church and the chivalric code of the knights. From the eleventh century on, the Church proclaimed that Sundays and other holy days fell under the Truce of God and were not permissible days for the waging of war. The ban on days of the year was extended by the Second Lateran Council in 1134 to a ban on the use of cross bows (at least in wars of Christians against Christians)—the first time in history that a particular weapon was singled out as immoral. By the thirteenth century, the Peace of God, the origin, perhaps, of all future doctrines of non-combatant immunity, had been elaborated in canon law. The Peace of God forbade attacks on clerics, monks, friars, pilgrims, travelers, merchants, and peasants cultivating the soil, on the grounds that since these classes do not make war, war should not be made against them. The goods of the merchants and the animals and lands of the peasants also fell under the protection of the Peace.

Conspicuously absent on the church's list of protected persons were other groups of noncombatants such as women, children, the sick, and the aged. One can only infer that these groups did not need explicit protection, as they were already protected from attack by the customs and code of chivalry. The chivalric virtues of prowess and glory were hardly consistent with the massacre of women and children, and obedience to such restrictions was facilitated by the lack of any military usefulness in attacks of this kind. Pursuits of the knightly virtue of courtesy led to the elaboration of a battlefield code, including the obligation to give quarter, protection, and the opportunity for ransom.

These courtesies, however, were extended only from knight to knight, not to common men at arms, who were slaughtered with great gusto by knights on all sides, even after they had lain down their arms. The knights' affection for this system of courtesy led to knightly complaints of foul play at Crecy, when the men on foot retaliated against the men on horse with showers of arrows fired from a prudent distance.

Throughout the Middle Ages the rules of *jus ad bellum* and *jus in bello* were more often honored in the breach than in the observance. Historians have observed that it is impossible to find a single battle that was delayed by a single day because of the rules of the Truce of God, and no medieval author ever suggested that the rules of war bound Christians in their wars against the Saracens. Nevertheless the refusal of states and individuals to obey the rules of war is no proof that the rules are invalid: murder does not become more legitimate as it becomes more frequent, and the frequent slaughters of hostages in the Middle Ages is no argument that the rules of non-combatant immunity generated in the chivalric and canon law traditions have no moral force. The real weakness of the medieval rules of war lies not in their failure to determine conduct but in their lack of universality, that universality or impersonality that all genuine moral rules must have. A rule that binds only Christians in their conduct with Christians or only knights in their conduct with knights is not a moral rule but something closer to a cultural taboo. Furthermore, the rules of chivalry lacked the overriding authority that genuine moral rules must have. For example, if a knight failed to give quarter, he was judged to be unchivalric but not wicked in any moral sense: he had failed as a knight but not as a moral being. Finally, it must be noted that the main rules of war from Augustine to Aquinas were derived from religious postulates, but, as Grotius cautiously observed in the seventeenth century, a just war should be just even if there is no God, and an unjust war should be unjust even if there is no God. The history of post-medieval thinking about just war is a history of attempts to purge the medieval theory of its theological elements and the parochial biases of the chivalric code.[24]

(d) Just War Theory in the Renaissance

The first steps towards the universalization of the medieval tradition were taken by Erasmus and Vitoria in the sixteenth century. In "Dulce bellum" (1514) Erasmus describes the horrors of war and the psychological pretensions of chivalry in terms so persuasive that future attempts at the glorification of war can only read like exercises in self-serving delusions. "War is sweet," he wrote, "to those that do not know it." Those who do know it know too well

> The furious shock of battle, and then wholesale butchery, the cruel fate of the killers and the killed, the slaughtered lying in heaps and the fields running with gore, the rivers dyed with human blood, the trampled crops, the burnt out farms, the villages set on fire, the cattle driven away, the girls raped, robbery, pillage, confusion, contempt of duty, indifference to law.

Nevertheless, Erasmus's attack on war remains couched in religious terms: "Can we say that Christ is of no consequence among men? . . . Why does his urging to mutual benevolence not deter them from the madness of war?" (Querela Pacis, 180)[25]

Responding to Spanish abuses in the conquest of the Americas, the Dominican theologican Francisco Vitoria argued eloquently in "The Indians Recently Discovered" and "The Law of War Made by the Spaniards on the Barbarians" (1532) that Indian princes and nations had rights and that mere difference in religion is no ground for just war. These assertions implied the equality of all nations before moral law and rejected the thousand-year tradition of Christian holy war. Equally eloquent was Vitoria's affirmation that the rights of non-combatants are moral rights, and not mere knightly gifts: "Even in a war with Turks it is not permissible to kill children. This is clear because they are innocent. Yes, and the same holds true for women among the unbelievers. This is clear, because so far as the war is concerned, they are innocent." (Vitoria 1917, *De jure belli*, 36)

The work of Vitoria was carried forward in the early seventeenth century by the Jesuit theologican Suarez, who deduced the basis of international law not from theological assumptions but the natural sociability of peoples and the interdependence of the human race:

> The human race, through divided into different peoples and realms, still has a certain unity, not only as a species, but, as it were, politically and morally, as is indicated by the precept of mutual love and charity which extends to all. [Suarez 1944, *On the Laws of God as a Legislator*, II, 19, 9]

If the principles of international law are deducible from such natural facts, then the principles of just war are deducible from similar natural facts, without reference to religious differences: "There are no grounds for war which are so exclusively reserved to Christian principles that they do not have some basis in natural law." (*De bello*, V, 6) From this it would seem to follow that if it is permissible for Christians to make war on Moslems because they are Moslems, it is permissible for Moslems to wage war against Christians because they are Christians. Since no Christian was prepared to accept the permissibility of *anti*-Christian crusades, the logic of the holy war was dead, and the theory of just war became a subdivision of the science of natural law.

The process of secularization took a giant step forward in the work of Grotius, the first non-theologian after Cicero to contribute significantly to the theory of just war. As the Thirty Years War raged, Grotius wrote his comprehensive treatise, *On the Law of War and Peace* (1624), which exhibits a thorough separation of natural and divine law. Following Aristotle, Grotius derives the natural law not from the fact that God is the author of nature but from the empirical proposition that man is a social animal. Though Grotius was a Protestant, there is hardly a line in his massive treatise that is prejudicial to the Catholic Church, and demands for holy war are replaced by pleas for mutual respect. It follows that Christians are bound to respect the treaties they make with pagan heretical princes, even if they are Saracens. As regards *jus in bello*, Grotius argues for the rights of prisoners and hostages, and for respect for the liberty and property of a vanquished enemy, even if the cause of the enemy was unjust. The decisive turn away from holy war suggested by Vitoria, Suarez, and Grotius seems to have had little effect on the course of the Thirty Years War.[26] Nevertheless when Catholics and Protestants left off fighting in 1648, the legitimacy of religious difference was written into the terms of the peace.

(e) Just War and the Modern Nation State

The decades and centuries following Grotius's great work witnessed the steady development of international law, particularly in such areas as the law of the sea, the right of extradition, and so forth. But the one area of international law that languished after Grotius was the theory of just war. The secularization of international law begun by Grotius and his followers left the more burdensome rules and scruples of just war with insufficient authority to resist the ambitions of princes and the pressures of military necessity, i.e., convenience, once the war had begun. Certainly the more interesting theoretical observations about war in the seventeenth through nineteenth centuries were made not by Pufendorf, Wolff, Vattel, and the other natural law theorists who followed in Grotius's footsteps but by Hobbes, Rousseau, Hegel, Marx, Nietzsche and other philosophers who, one way or another, rejected the tradition of natural law. Indeed, the dominant political fact of that period is the decline in the power of the churches and the rise in the power of the modern nation state, which by the nineteenth century could be described by philosophers as God personified. It is hardly surprising that in these circumstances the theory of just war should have been at least temporarily submerged by the doctrine that responded more appropriately to the new political facts—the theory of reasons of state.

Grotius had already conceded in 1624 that if a war is declared on proper authority the belligerent parties have the right to inflict damage upon each other regardless of the justness of their respective causes. But Grotius did not have to make this concession, as he could have declared that the side that violates natural law has no right to take up arms. The real progenitor of the "reasons of state" doctrine is Hobbes, who in his *Leviathan* (1651) rejected the idea of "natural law," altogether, substituting instead unmitigated egoism. In Hobbes, the chivalric virtues disappear, the theological virtues disappear, and of the classical cardinal virtues, only prudence remains, interpreted by Hobbes as a drive for survival. Though Hobbes said next to nothing about international relations, the moral is obvious. Just as nothing forbids any individual person from taking steps to assure his own survival, nothing forbids any state from taking steps to assure its own survival. The principal difference between individuals and states is that individuals have an instrument of self-protection, the state, which protects them in return for loyalty and obedience to its laws. No such instrument of self-protection exists for the state, and so there is no bargain the state can strike by which it obtains security in return for obedience to international law. On Hobbes' assumptions, international law simply cannot bind the actions of states.[27]

In Hobbes, war is a regrettable necessity, guaranteeing national survival for the victor, but providing little in the way of positive benefits. Later authors with more pronounced nationalistic sentiments came to view war as a force for human progress, developing national spirit and destroying decadent institutions. Hegel, for example, wrote in 1802: "War preserves the ethical health of peoples and their indifference to specific institutions, just as the blowing of the wind preserves the sea from foulness which would result for peoples under continual or indeed perpetual peace." (Hegel 1802 93) After the Napoleonic wars Hegel wrote about war in less rhapsodic terms, but he still felt that war played some positive role in history: "War is not to be regarded as an absolute evil or as a purely external accident. It is to what is by nature accidental that accidents happen, and the fate whereby they happen is thus necessity." (Hegel 1820 209)

Carlyle and later writers picked up the Hegelian thread and further elaborated what Ernst Cassirer called "the myth of the state." We will not consider these authors here, since they made no contribution to the theory of just war; but it is important to remember that at all points in its modern history the theory of just war has rebuked such nationalism.

Those who believe that the just war theory is a force for morality in the world may be embarassed to note that as the just war theory declined in popularity in the late seventeenth century, the practice of warfare became progressively more humane. The dynastic wars of the eighteenth century, though fought for reasons of state, were on the whole less brutal than the religious wars of the seventeenth century. The professional armies of the Age of Reason, adopting the disciplinary reforms of Gustavus Adolphus, maintained better order than the armed mobs of seventeenth century religious wars. Enlightenment monarchs, recalling the fate of Charles I, took prudent steps to keep weapons out of the hands of their subjects and firmly in the grasp of professional soldiers directly beholden to the crown. Given the professionalization of armies and the decline of religious fanaticism, the wars of the eighteenth century were, for the most part, wars of army against army, and the distinction between soldier and civilian was fairly consistently observed.

Unfortunately, the line between soldier and civilian was no sooner drawn than history conspired to rub it out. The Napoleonic War in Spain (1808) pitted an army against a people; the British in 1812 shelled the American coast as if every American was an armed enemy of the crown. The revolutionary uprisings of 1848 pitted the police against the populace, and Sherman in the Civil War hardly distinguished between the residents of Georgia and the Confederate Army. As warfare became less discriminating, it also became larger in scale. The device of the mass levy, introduced by the French at Valmy in 1792, multiplied manyfold the numbers of troops involved in the typical battle. Improvements in artillery, the introduction of repeating rifles and eventually machine guns, increased the scale of carnage. On June 24, 1859, three hundred thousand French and Austrian soldiers fought each other at Solferino, and at day's end forty thousand men were dead, many of whom might have been saved if elementary medical care had been available on the battlefield. The need for some regulation of warfare, at least to eliminate useless death and gratuitous suffering, was apparent on all sides. The first step towards the modern attempt at the humanization of warfare came in 1863, when Abraham Lincoln issued his *Instructions for the Government of Armies of the United States in the Field* (written by Francis Lieber), the first written manual for the conduct of land warfare.[28] The just war theory had revived, and has remained at the center of discussions of the morality of warfare ever since.

(f) Just War in The Modern Era

In its classic period, the just war theory was developed principally by philosophers, theologians, and humanists, none of whom had any particular reason to hope that their recommendations would be adopted by those who held power. In its modern period, the just war theory has been articulated mainly by statesmen, diplomats, and specialists in international law, who developed the rules of war in a remarkable series of international conferences commencing with the First Geneva Convention of 1864.[29] The result has been a decrease in theoretical depth but an increased interest in practical detail. The 1864 conference established the Red Cross and proclaimed the "neutralization" of medical personnel on the battlefield. The Declaration of St. Petersburg (1868) banned certain types of inflammable artillery shells. The Hague Peace Conferences of 1899 and 1907 established various rights of prisoners of war and introduced a remarkable series of protections (1899 Annex Section II, Ch. I) for noncombatants who find themselves in the path of war:

> *Article 25*: The attack or bombardment, by whatever means, of towns, dwellings, or buildings which are undefended is prohibited.
> *Article 26*: The officer in command of an attacking force must, before commencing a bombardment, except in cases of assault, do all in his power to warn the authorities.
> *Article 27*: In sieges and bombardments all necessary steps must be taken to spare, as far as possible, buildings dedicated to religion, art, science, or charitable purpose, historic monuments, hospitals, and places where the sick or wounded are collected, provided that they are not being used at the time for military purposes. It is the duty of the besieged to indicate the presence of such buildings or places by distinctive and visible signs, which shall be notified to the enemy beforehand.

After the catastrophe of World War I, interest shifted, understandably, from *jus in bello* to *jus ad bellum*. In the Locarno Pact of 1925, France, Germany, and Belgium pledged themselves to a policy of mutual nonaggression. In 1928, Germany, the United States, Belgium, France, Britain, Italy, Poland, Czechoslovakia, and Japan signed the Kellogg-Briand Pact, renouncing war "as an instrument of national policy." From the text of the Kellogg-Briand Pact it is not clear whether the contracting parties renounced all war or only certain kinds of war. In fact, the intent of the Kellogg Pact was to ban aggressive war only; the right to self-defense was considered so unimpeachable that the signatories did not see fit to mention or define it in the pact. Thus the door was left open in the 1930s for the plea of anticipatory self-defense as a justification for armament and preemptive attack. These were the pretexts cited by the Axis powers when they initiated World War II.

World War II dwarfed all previous conflicts in scale and scope. It was also unprecedented in the death and destruction it inflicted upon noncombatants. The concepts of total war and collective responsibility, the ideological and racial motives of the Axis powers, and the widespread use of aerial bombardment, made millions of civilians the indirect or direct targets of the techniques of mass destruction. About half of the 35 million persons who died in World War II were civilians, most of them not even remotely connected with military activities or the production of war materiel.

Accordingly, in the postwar years, the two most pressing items on the agenda of international legislation were the formulation of a new standard for *jus ad bellum* and a reaffirmation of the protected status of noncombatants.

A new standard regulating the use of force in international relations is proclaimed in 1945 in Article 2(4) of the Charter of the United Nations:

"All members shall refrain in their international relations from the threat of use of force against the territorial integrity or political independence of any states, or in any other manner inconsistent with the purposes of the United Nations." The wording of this article is strikingly different from the Kellogg-Briand pact. The Charter forbids, not just "war," but the use of force of any kind. Furthermore, the Charter forbids the application of *threats* of force, which can be deployed without actually going to war. Article 2(4) then, can be violated without the explosion of a single bomb or the firing of a single bullet, a point to be kept in mind when evaluating nuclear deterrence.

The Kellogg-Briand pact did not mention or define self-defense. In the UN Charter, self-defense is defined with some precision in Article 51:

Nothing in the present Charter shall impair the inherent right of individual or collective self-defense if an armed attack occurs against a member of the United Nations, until the Security Council has taken the measures necessary to maintain international peace and security. Measures taken by members in the exercise of this right of self-defense shall be immediately reported to the Security Council and shall not in any way affect the authority and responsibility of the Security Council under the present Charter to take at any time such action as it deems necessary in order to maintain or restore international peace and security.

There is little doubt that the intent of Article 51 is to rule out anticipatory self-defense: nations must *wait* until suffering an armed attack before legitimately using unilateral force. Furthermore the article rules out reprisals; even if a nation is attacked it is entitled only to use as much force as is necessary to preserve its sovereignty. It is *not* entitled to punish the attacker. The rule is hard, but at least it is precise, and there are two loopholes that permit nations a freer hand in the use of force than a first reading might indicate. First, Article 51 permits collective self-defense. Second, Article 51 does not restrict the occasions of self-defense to attacks on national territory: an attack on ships, airfields, military equipment, or overseas personnel of Nation A provides a legal occasion for the use of force by A. If the United States places airfields, ships, and troops around the Soviet Union, any attack on these forces by the Soviet Union provides a legitimate occasion for "self-defense" by the United States.

The question of noncombatant immunity was taken up at a Geneva Conference in 1949. The resulting convention is principally concerned with abuses by occupying military powers:

In the case of armed conflict not of an international character occurring in the territory of one of the High Contracting Parties, each Party to the conflict shall be bound to apply, as a minimum, the following provisions:

(1) Persons taking no active part in the hostilities, including members of armed forces who have laid down their arms and those placed hors de combat by sickness, wounds, detention, or any other cause, shall in all circumstances be treated humanely, without any adverse distinction founded on race, color, religion or faith, sex, birth or wealth, or any other similar criteria.

To this end the following acts are and shall remain prohibited at any time and in any place whatsoever with respect to the above-mentioned persons:

(a) violence to life and person, in particular murder of all kinds, mutilation, cruel treatment and torture;

(b) taking of hostages;

(c) outrages upon personal dignity, in particular humiliating and degrading treatment;

(d) the passing of sentences and the carrying out of executions without previous judgment pronounced by a regularly constituted court, affording all the judicial guarantees which are recognized as indispensable by civilized peoples. [Friedman 1972 525]

In 1977, a lengthy Protocol to the Fourth Geneva Convention was drafted and opened for signature. Given a strict reading of this Protocol (discussed further in Chapter 8), most strategic bombing, using either conventional or nuclear weapons, is contrary to the Fourth Geneva Convention. Aside from this Protocol, signed but not yet ratified by the United States, little has been done in recent years to develop legal protections for noncombatants in times of war.

(g) Current Status of Just War Theory

After 2300 years of development, what is the current status of just war theory? I take the current version of the just war theory to be the sum of all the principles developed in previous centuries that have stood the test of time. Most authorities recognize seven such rules:[30]

(i) The war must be declared by a *competent authority*; that is, by some authority recognized as legitimate by the citizens of the nation who find themselves at war

(ii) The war must be fought for a *just cause*. According to Article II(4) of the United Nations Charter the sole just cause is defense against armed attack. Many contemporary theorists also recognize as a just cause the prevention of serious and ongoing violations of human rights.

(iii) The war must be fought with a *proper intention*; it must be fought for the establishment of justice, not for some other reason for which the establishment of justice serves as a pretext.

(iv) It must be fought with proper means: means which are *proportionate*, not inflicting more damage than is necessary for victory, and *discriminate*, preferring the injury of soldiers to the injury of civilians.

(v) There must be some *chance of victory*; the resort of force must not be suicidal.

(vi) The war as a whole must be *proportional*. The costs of the war must not be a greater evil than the evil that would result if the injustice were not rectified.

(vii) The war must be undertaken as a *last resort*, after all peaceful means of resolution have failed.

The proliferation of rules of war from 1864 to the present seems to have done little to prevent the outbreak of war, and in the many wars since 1864 most rules of just war have been violated countless times. The contrast between the solemnity of the international declarations and the intensity of contemporary violence would be a fit subject for satire were it not so obvious. But the Convenants and Declarations probably have some civilizing effect, and there is no reason to think that there would have been less violence and less brutality had there been no rules of war. Explicit international agreements provide useful points of coordination that are often respected because both sides on some issues prefer cooperation to conflict. There is no substitute for the slow process of international negotiation, proclamation, codification, and legislation. The Law of War may not work well, but little else works better.

Consequences Unforseen and Undersired: The Assessment of Risk

The standard moral theories and the theory of just war deal with actions that have consequences that are desired or at least forseen. But what about acts which have consequences that are neither desired nor forseen, for example acts which create small risks of big disasters? Should these be omitted from moral analysis? Obviously not. The person who drives home drunk and runs over a child neither forsees the accident nor desires to run over a child. We hold him responsible nevertheless. Indeed, we consider it reprehensible when a man drives around drunk, even if he does *not* hit a child. By what moral principles do we reach such judgments? The drunk driver who gets home safe has not, apparently, violated anyone's rights, nor does it seem, at first glance, that he has damaged the common good. On what grounds, then, do we consider drunk driving to be immoral? What moral principles are relevant to assessment of risk as such?

The answer that we give to this question has immediate implications for the assessment of nuclear weapons policies. Frequently the crucial element in the assessment of a weapons policy is a consequence neither intended nor desired. Suppose that we are considering two weapons policies A and B, that A presents a 1 percent risk of nuclear war over the next 20 years and that Policy B presents a 5 percent risk of nuclear war over the next 20 years. How should we assess this 4 percent increase in the risk of nuclear war? A person who supports policy B obviously does not desire a nuclear war; nobody does. Nor does the person who supports policy B forsee that B will produce a nuclear war; after all, there are 19 chances out of 20 that the policy will *not* produce a nuclear war in the next 20 years. We need a rule to assess the increase of risk, regardless of what is desired or forseen.

The reader will take a step towards the relevant principles once he recognizes that *the risk of an evil is itself an evil*. The proof of this is the fact that, in our daily lives, we accept small evils in order to avoid the risk of greater evils; for example, we go to the dentist (a small evil) in order to decrease the risk of tooth decay (a greater evil). If we did not take the risk of tooth decay to be a real evil, we would never accept another evil in order to avoid it.

The mental calculations that we make to assess the evil of risk all have the same pattern. We always assume that a risk of some evil Y is equivalent to a sure chance of some lesser evil Z. In general, the greater the probability of evil Y, the greater the lesser evil Z must be before we acknowledge that it is equivalent to the risk of Y. The particular rules of conversion from probable greater evils to definite lesser evils differ from person to person, but every person accepts the general idea of converting possible greater evils into actual lesser evils. Accordingly, in this book we will always treat the infliction of a risk as morally equivalent to the infliction of some real lesser evil.

We will use two different methods for converting possible evils into actual evils. The first method, the *collective method*, simply multiples the probability of the greater evil by the magnitude of that evil. For example, by the collective method a 10 percent chance of killing 100 people is rated as equivalent to a 100 percent chance of killing 10 people, i.e., to ten actual deaths.

The collective method provides a useful approximation of the evil inherent in risks. But the method has its limitations. Sometimes the evil risked is not divisible, so that multiplication by a percentage will not be possible. Furthermore, the results obtained by this method may differ substantially from the way conscientious individuals would rate the risk. Most people, for example, given a choice between inflicting a 10 percent risk of death on 100 people and actually killing 10 people, would prefer to inflict the risk rather than kill the 10, but the collective method rates these options as equally undesirable.

For this reason, we will on occasion use a second method of calculating the evil in risk, the *individual method*. With this approach, each victim of risk is asked to consider how much he would be willing to sacrifice in order to remove himself from risk. The sum of the suggested sacrifices of all the victims of the risk constitutes the evil of the risk. For example, if we inflict a 10 percent risk of death on 100 persons, we should ask what each of these 100 people would be willing to sacrifice in order to avoid a 10 percent risk of death. The sum of these sacrifices is the evil done in inflicting a 10 percent risk of death.

If the infliction of a risk is equivalent to the infliction of actual evil, the same moral considerations that apply to the infliction of actual evil apply to the infliction of risk. When we observe one person inflicting harm on another, we can ask whether this infliction of harm violated human rights, transgressed the canons of fairness, or damaged the common good. Likewise, when one person inflicts risks on others, we can translate this risk into some equivalent actual evil and then ask whether the infliction of the equivalent evil would violate human rights, or go against justice, or damage the common good. This conversion of risks into equivalent actual harms will help forestall the common fallacy that attends the moral assessment of risk, namely, the fallacy of thinking that, if worst does *not* come to worst, no harm was done.

Summary

This completes our survey of basic moral concepts. It remains to apply them to nuclear weapons policies. The question to be addressed to each policy are:

(i)   Does the policy serve the common good best: or is there some alternative policy that better serves the common good?

(ii) Does the policy violate human rights, especially when risks are converted into equivalent harms?

(iii) Is the policy just, or does it inflict unfair burdens on some in order to benefit others?

(iv) Does it violate the canons of just war?

Unfortunately, such questions cannot be answered by philosophical reflection alone. To assess which of two policies better serves the common good, one must know something about the costs and benefits of the policies. In short, to assess weapons policies morally, one must know the facts about the policies first. Only then can informed moral judgment proceed. The purpose of the next two chapters is to supply that factual background. Then we will present the weapons policies, and proceed to judgment.

Notes

1. The idea that the best use of nuclear weapons is not to wage war but to prevent war seems to have been first stated by Bernard Brodie in 1946: "The first and most vital step in any American security program for the age of atomic bombs is to take measures to guarantee to ourselves in case of attack the possibility of retaliation in kind. The writer in making this statement is not for the moment concerned about who will win the next war in which atomic bombs are used. Thus far the chief purpose of our military establishment has been to win wars. From now its chief purpose must be to avert them. It can have almost no other useful purpose." (Brodie 1946 80–81)

The last three sentences of this quotation are frequently cited. But the first sentence is ominous. Any Soviet leader accepting the first sentence in 1946 would reject the Baruch Plan for the internationalization of atomic weapons and immediately start developing atomic weapons on his own. That is in fact what the Soviets did, a result quite bad from the standpoint of American security. From the beginning the idea of deterrence has had its paradoxes.

2. In the choice between a decreased chance of nuclear war or an increased chance of nuclear blackmail, the probabilities in the example are subjective probabilities, that is, they represent what the chooser considers credible on the basis of the evidence. Throughout this book, in discussing the probabilities of singular historical events like "a large scale nuclear war in the next fifty years," the probabilities involved are and must be such subjective probabilities. The two other standard interpretations of probability statements, the frequency interpretation and the a priori interpretation, cannot be easily applied to singular historical events, but are more properly suited to situations, like flips of a coin, in which a type of event is repeated or the range of outcomes is clearly determined. In the present example, what is crucial is that the chance of nuclear war is small but not vanishingly small in both cases, and that the chance of nuclear war is greater in the situation in which the chance of nuclear blackmail is smaller.

3. The classic argument for the separation of the moral point of view from any particular interest is found in Kant 1785. A good modern presentation is Baier 1958.

4. A nice introduction to basic ethics with some discussion of the problem of the relative weights of the three basic moral concepts is Feldman 1978.

5. For the battle between Utilitarians and their opponents, see Smart and Williams 1973 and the essays in Sen and Williams 1982.

6. The classic exposition of the common good as the fundamental moral concept is given in Bentham 1793 and Mill 1861. The clearest expositions of utilitarianism in its classic form are Moore 1912 and Russell 1910. A good and detailed exposition of modern utilitarianism is Narveson 1967.

7. The problem of cyclical majorities is at the core of Kenneth Arrow's famous proof of the impossibility of forming the idea of "the common good" out of the set of individual preferences: see Arrow 1951. Despite the importance of this theoretical result, I see no harm in assuming that what a very large majority prefers does constitute the common good, unless very large majority preferences turn out to be inconsistent.

8. The classic development of the theory of human rights is Locke 1690. Good contemporary expositions are Feinberg 1973, Nozick 1974, Dworkin 1978 and Fried 1978.

9. The idea that possession of a right implies the permissibility of defending that right with force against attack is accepted by all rights theorists except extreme pacifists. In the presence of a system of laws, however, rights theorists caution that the force with which the right is defended must be legally sanctioned force. A sophisticated study of self-defense is in Fried 1979 42–53.

10. The permissibility of collective self-defense is gradually achieving recognition in criminal law. In England, the right to use deadly force to aid someone under unjust attack was restricted until recently to close relatives of the person attacked. Now it is extended to almost any passer-by. See Ryan 1983 508–524.

11. The idea that injustice consists in passing off a burden while simultaneously seizing a benefit is developed as the basis of ethics in Kant 1785. In Kant, it is the essence of immorality to impose rules on others that you do not impose on yourself.

12. The social contract notion of justice is given classic exposition by Thomas Hobbes in his *Leviathan* (1651). But in Hobbes the decision procedure to which everyone agrees is very crude: everyone agrees that one person should decide everything!

13. The most magisterial presentation of a social contract theory of justice in modern times is Rawls 1971. In a sense Rawls' theory combines the two interpretations of "unanimous consent" presented here. In Rawls' theory, the social contractors make their choice of fundamental social arrangements in ignorance of their social position, race, sex, personal skills and other "morally irrelevant" factors, but they choose rules so conservatively that no person will accept any distribution in which the lowest person is worse off than he is under some other distribution. One wonders why Rawls didn't lift the veil of ignorance imposed on the contractors and simply impose a requirement of unanimous consent without risk.

14. There is no primer on the theory of just war. Two distinguished and relatively advanced expositions are given by Paul Ramsey (Ramsey 1961), who develops the theory from a set of Christian duties, and by Michael Walzer (Walzer 1977), who develops the theory on the basis of a more secular notion of rights. What I have called "extreme nationalism," Walzer calls "realism," far too honorific a title for the theory denoted.

15. One example of a rule in the theory of just war that is based on a mixture of morality and prudence is the rule that prisoners of war should never be killed. Since the killing of prisoners of war in most cases serves no useful military purpose, in most cases the killing of prisoners is recognizable as plain murder. But the motivation here is also prudential: if one side slaughters its prisoners, the other side is likely to, and both sides end up worse off than if the slaughtering had not started. If the principle is accepted, it is not clear whether it is accepted on moral grounds or prudential grounds. (Lackey 1982a)

16. The best known advocates of pacifism in the modern era are Tolstoy and Gandhi. For Tolstoy see especially Tolstoy 1890 and Tolstoy 1909. For Gandhi, see Gandhi 1971. For a brilliant but perhaps too strident attack on pacifism see Anscombe 1961.

17. The point that rights inherently imply the permissibility of defense with force is made in Narveson 1965.

18. A good modern presentation leaning in the direction of anti-war pacifism is Wells 1967.

19. Because of his persuasive critique of the natural law tradition and his view that each person has obligations only to himself, Hobbes must be viewed as an extreme nationalist by implication. In the absence of an international sovereign, each nation state has no reason to favor anything but its own national interest. The most philosophically developed presentation of extreme nationalism via moral historicism is Hegel, who sees in the customs and laws of the state and service to the state the highest possible expression of moral consciousness: "The State is the actuality of the ethical idea . . . the mind of a nation is the divine, knowing and willing itself." (Hegel 1820 257) It must be remarked in Hegel's favor that in his system art, religion and philosophy are exempted from national service.

20. For a different set of arguments against extreme nationalism than those given here, see Walzer 1967 ch. 1.

21. The notion that "reasons of state" might form a separate class of moral reasons is discussed and dismissed in Hare 1973 9–27. Thomas Nagel suggests that national leaders can legitimately weigh utilitarian considerations more heavily than common folk, because their actions have such sweeping effects on the common good. See Nagel 1979 75–91. For a sophisticated "realism" which favors actions taken for reasons of state over actions undertaken for "ideological" reasons see Morgenthau 1949 and the moral critique of Morgenthau in Paskins and Dockrill 1979.

22. For the history of just war thinking to the Renaissance, see Russell 1975. For the Renaissance to the present see Johnson 1981. No systematic secondary source in English on the just war in Aristotle or Cicero seems to exist.

23. For early Christian thought on war, see Bainton 1960. For some of the texts presenting Augustine's views on war, see Paolucci 1962 162–184. For the political background of Augustine, see Van der Meer 1961. For secondary commentary on Augustine's theory of war, see Ramsey 1961 Ch. 2.

24. For the period preceding Aquinas see Russell 1975 41–257 and Brundage 1969. For Aquinas, see Russell 1975 258–291, Tooke 1965, and Walters 1971. For the later Middle Ages, see Keen 1965 and Johnson 1981 121–172.

25. The quotations from Erasmus are from Sowards 1975 ch. 5; see also Bainton 1969.

26. For secondary commentary on Vitoria, Suarez, and Grotius, see Walters 1971.

27. For Hobbes' political theory, see Hobbes 1651. Classic secondary works include Warrender 1958.

28. For an assessment of Francis Lieber's General Orders No. 100, see Johnson 1981 49–50. For Lieber on guerilla warfare see Johnson 1981 246–47.

29. The history of late nineteenth century and twentieth century conferences regarding the regulation of war is related in Nussbaum 1954 215–232. One illuminating essay on this subject is Best 1979.

30. A concise summary of the implications of the U.N. Charter for the legality of national resort to force is given in Akehurst 1982. For the current status of the laws of *jus in bello* see Bindscheler-Robert 1981.

31. The principles as stated here largely follow the Orthodox Catholic presentation: see McCormick 1967.

31. The ambiguities in the notion of "intention" and "intentional" are discussed in Lackey 1984. The relation between desire and moral character is interestingly discussed in Nagel 1980 129–135.

32. The attempts of the law and legal philosophy to deal with consequences neither forseen nor desired are presented in Austin 1869, Terry 1915, and Williams 1953, all reprinted in Morris 1961 section 5.

33. The field of risk is surveyed by Nicholas Rescher in Rescher 1982.

34. The divergences in judgments reached by "collective method" and the "individual method" correspond to the divergence between policy choices designed simply to maximize expected gains and policy choices designed to reflect empirically given psychological tendencies to avoid sure losses and to seek possible gains. These divergences have been explored in Kahneman and Tversky 1979, Kahneman and Tversky 1981, and Kahneman and Tversky 1982. The subject was investigated first by Allais in Allais 1953.

2

Nuclear Weapons, Politics and Strategy: A Short History

The Dawn of the Nuclear Age

(a) Bequerel and Radioactivity

The story of atomic weapons begins with the discovery of radioactivity by Bequerel in 1896.[1] Bequerel discovered that certain chemical elements seemed to emit radiant energy all by themselves. To the laymen such a discovery was mildly interesting; to a chemist it was earth-shattering. It was an axiom of nineteenth century chemical theory that radiant energy could be released only after the interaction of two different chemical elements. Carbon and oxygen, for example, release heat when they combine during the burning of wood; but carbon and oxygen, by themselves, can radiate no heat. Now in 1896 chemists were confronted with solitary "radioactive" elements that nevertheless produced energy. How could energy be created without chemical interaction? What was the source of this energy? The excitement of the scientific community intensified when it was discovered by the Curies in that same year that the quantity of energy released by radioactive elements was very much larger than the energy, per unit of mass, that could be produced by any known chemical reaction.[2]

(b) Einstein and the Special Theory of Relativity

In 1905 Einstein suggested that the new source of energy was none other than matter itself. The route by which he reached this conclusion deserves to be traced. Early in 1905 Einstein published his great paper "On The Electrodynamics of Moving Bodies," which laid the foundations of what came to be called the *special theory of relativity*.[3] The cardinal notion of the special theory is that light always travels at the same speed, regardless of the speed of its source. If you toss a pebble forward from a moving automobile, then the speed of the pebble equals the speed of the automobile plus the speed with which the pebble was thrown. But with light the situation is different. If you turn on the headlights of a speeding car, the velocity of the light from the headlights relative to the ground does not consist of the speed of the light plus the speed of the car. According to the special theory of relativity, the speed of the light from the moving headlights is exactly the same as it would have been if the car had not been moving at all. This simple idea that the speed of light is constant relative to every (unaccelerated) frame of reference changed physics, and changed the world.

Consider the consequences. If the speed of light is constant in every reference frame, then nothing can catch up with a beam of light. If my car is going 99 percent of the speed of light and I turn my headlights on, the light from my car travels ahead of me just as fast as if the car were standing still. It follows that no object can be accelerated to the speed of light. This crucial result is puzzling at first sight. If we exert force on an object, the object will go faster. There is no limit to the amount of force we can bring to bear on an object, so there seems to be no limit to the speed that an object can reach. But Einstein insisted that there is a limit, and suggested, as an explanation, *that as an object moves faster, it gains in mass.* In other words, the faster an object moves, the more massive it becomes, and the harder it becomes to move it a bit faster. At speeds approaching the speed of light, an object will become very massive indeed, and immense quantities of force are required to impart even the smallest increases of velocity. Since 1905, the hypothesis of this increased "relativistic" mass has been repeatedly confirmed in laboratory experiments.

In late 1905 Einstein published a three page meditation on the relationship between the mass of an object and energy contained in it. He reasoned that if the expenditure of energy needed to accelerate an object resulted in an increase in the mass of an object, then a decrease in velocity must produce a decrease in the mass of an object. The exact mathematical relationship between the mass of an object and the energy it contained flowed directly from the equations of the special theory, and was expressed in the famous formula:

$$E = mc^2$$

that is, that the energy of a body is proportional to the mass of the body multiplied by the square of the speed of light.[4] In 1908 physics and chemistry joined hands when Max Planck took note of Einstein's equation and suggested that the phenomenon of radioactivity could be explained as the direct transformation of matter into energy.

(c) The Idea of an Atomic Bomb

In the years immediately following Einstein's proposals, physicists and journalists amused themselves with calculations that a teaspoon of matter contained enough energy to power an ocean liner around the world. But even in the relatively pacific years before World War I the military implications of radioactivity and atomic energy did not go unnoticed. Fired by reports of the immense energies emitted by radium and uranium, H.G. Wells in his novel *The World Set Free* (1914) projected a mid-twentieth century world powered totally by atomic energy, a world in which the economic dislocations caused by atomic energy lead nations to war, and ultimately to the development of atomic bombs. A character in the novel remarks:

> This little bottle contains about a pint of uranium oxide; in the atoms in this bottle there slumbers at least as much energy as we could get by burning 160 tons of coal. If in one instant I could suddenly release that energy, it would blow everything around us into fragments. [Wells 1914 35]

Wells not only had the idea of the atomic bomb in 1914, he also guessed that the bomb would be delivered by air, guessed that a single bomb could destroy an entire city, guessed that areas subjected to atomic bombing would be contaminated by radioactivity and would be permanently uninhabitable, and guessed that nations suffering atomic attack would retain the ability to launch an atomic counterattack of their own.[5] The first city destroyed in the novel is Paris. The description prefigures Hiroshima:

> She had the impression of a great ball of crimson flame like a maddened living thing that seemed to be whirling about amid a chaos of falling masonry, that seemed to be attacking the earth furiously, burrowing into it like a blazing rabbit. [Wells 1914 102]

After the destruction of Paris, Berlin is next, since the French have retained their second strike capacity: "There's nothing on earth to stop us from going to Berlin and giving them tit for tat. Two men would be enough for what we have to do." (Wells 1914 35.) For in the age of atomic bombs

> Every sort of passive defense, armour, or fortification and so forth was being outmastered by the tremendous increase on the destructive side. Atomic destruction had become so facile that every little body of malcontents would use it. . . . a man could carry about in a handbag an amount of energy sufficient to wreck half a city. [Wells 1914 165]

and the result of the development of atomic weapons is that it is impossible for any side to win; war as a rational instrument of policy has become obsolete: "Nothing could have been more obvious to the people of the early twentieth century than the rapidity with which war was becoming impossible. They did not see it until the atomic bombs burst in their fumbling hands." (Wells 1914 113)

(d) Nuclei and the Energy of Fission

Einstein had shown how much energy was locked within the atom, but he provided no clues as to how to get it out. Extraction of energy from the atom required the elaboration of the modern theory of atomic structure. In 1897

Thomson discovered that atoms emitted particles called electrons, and soon thereafter Rutherford demonstrated that the interior of the atom consisted largely of empty space. By 1913 Bohr had produced an atomic model with positively charged protons at the center of each atom and negatively charged electrons revolving at the periphery. A new force was invoked to explain why the positively charged protons did not fly away from each other, and in 1919 Aston provided the first calculations of the quantity of energy involved in the binding force that held the nucleus of the atom together.

In the Bohr model, atoms of different elements contained different numbers of protons. Throughout this period Rutherford and others were bombarding atomic nuclei with radiation in hopes of altering the proton number, achieving thereby the alchemical dream of transmuting one element into another. By 1932, the procedure of bombardment had been improved by Lawrence's invention of the cyclotron, and Cockroft and Walton succeeded in inserting an additional proton into the nucleus of a lithium atom, transforming a single atom of lithium into two atoms of helium. By the mid 1930s it was recognized that any significant release of energy by alteration of a nucleus required not the simple transmutation of a nucleus by proton addition but the splitting of a large nucleus into two smaller pieces. On 17 December 1938, the German physicists Otto Hahn and Felix Strassman bombarded a radioactive mixture with neutrons and discovered lathanum in the residue, a result, Lise Meitner suggested, that could only have been obtained if the nucleus of a uranium atom had split into a nucleus of barium and a nucleus of lathanum. Since the binding energies of the nuclei of barium and lathanum were jointly less than the binding energy of the original nucleus of uranium, the fission of the uranium nucleus by Hahn and Strassmann was accompanied by a sudden and enormous release of energy.[6] "Do you realize what his new discovery means?" the Russian physicist Igor Tamm commented in 1939, "It means that a bomb can be built that will destroy a city out to a radius of maybe ten kilometers." (York 1976 29)

The Atomic Bomb

Nevertheless, no bomb could be built if each divided nucleus had to be split by laborious bombardment with neutrons supplied by a cyclotron. Some automatic mechanism of bombardment was needed, and the required mechanism (using nuclei that generated free neutrons when split) had been described by Leo Szilard as early as 1934. After Hahn's success, Bohr noted that such free neutrons might be generated by fission of nuclei of U-235 (a variety of uranium). Fear began to spread among scientists outside the Third Reich that an atomic bomb would soon be built, and that Germany, building on the work of Hahn and Strassman, would get it first.

(a) Building the Bomb

On 2 August 1939, Szilard and Einstein sent a letter to Roosevelt warning him of this possibility and suggesting that secret experimental work be carried forward towards the development of an atomic bomb. In March of 1940 Enrico Fermi confirmed that fission of U-235 would indeed release a sufficient quantity of surplus neutrons to sustain a chain reaction. After Fermi's success the British MAUD committee had decided that it was feasible to construct an atomic bomb, and on the American side, on 1 December 1941, General Leslie Groves signed contracts for the construction of reactors to produce U-235. One year later in Chicago, Fermi succeeded in starting and sustaining the first artificial chain reaction, vindicating the ideas of Szilard and Bohr.[7] By 1943, thousands of workers around the United States were mobilized for the Manhattan Project (code name of the American project for the construction of an atomic bomb), under the administrative direction of Groves and under the scientific direction of J. Robert Oppenheimer.[8] The design for the bomb, involving the implosion of pieces of U-235 into a mass large enough to sustain a chain reaction, was proposed by Seth Nedderweger in April 1943. Difficulties in the separation of U-235 from ordinary uranium delayed the project through 1944, and work moved forward simultaneously on the construction of an atomic bomb using plutonium, an element chemically distinct from uranium and in some ways easier to obtain than U-235. On 16 July 1945, after a night of calculations verifying that a chain reaction in a fission bomb would not spread to the atmosphere of the earth, the first atomic bomb, called Trinity, exploded over the sands of Alamagordo, New Mexico. The flash was seen miles away in Albuquerque; the steel tower which held the bomb was vaporized, and the cloud from the explosion boiled up to a height of 40,000 feet. A month later, after the Hiroshima bombing, the War Department released a description of this first explosion, saying in part:

> The lighting effects beggared description. The whole country was lighted by a searing tiny sun. It was golden, purple, violet gray, and it illuminated the ridge of the nearby mountain range with a clarity that cannot be described but must be seen to be imagined. It was that beauty that great poets dream about but describe most poorly and inadequately. [Smyth 1945 254]

(b) Hiroshima and Nagaski

The first atomic bomb used in war exploded over Hiroshima at 8:15 in the morning of 6 August 1945. The U-235 type bomb detonated at a height of 2,000 feet and released energy equal to the energy of 13,000 tons of TNT. Objects engulfed by a fireball a half mile in diameter glowed and crumbled. The shock wave destroyed buildings over a mile from ground zero, and in an hour the city was ablaze in a firestorm sustained by self-generated winds of 50 miles per hour. The sky was darkened, and black oily rain fell from the sky. Few firemen survived to fight the fire. Few doctors survived to treat the sick. Those not dead and not too badly burned or wounded began to walk, in silent groups, away from a city that had ceased to be.

"When I came to I was pinned under the house," wrote a boy who was eight years old in 1945:

> At first I thought I wouldn't have enough energy to get out of there. But I had the feeling that someone was calling my name. Frantically I crawled toward an

opening and finally I was able to make my way outside. It was my mother who was calling me.

I was completely amazed. While I had been thinking it was only my house that had fallen down, I found that every house in the neighborhood was either completely or half-collapsed. The sky was like twilight. Pieces of paper and cloth were caught on the electric wires. In some places the wires were cut and dangling. I went out to the garden patch behind the house. Five or six neighbors came dashing out. For the first time I noticed that my hand was injured. This was probably where I had got caught on a nail or something when the house collapsed. I washed the wound at the pump beside the garden and together with my mother went out to the main street. On that street crowds were fleeing toward the west. Among them were many people whose hair was burned, whose clothes were torn and who had burns and injuries. We fled to the west with them. From the end of Kannoh Bridge we turned in the direction of Eba Park. Along the way the road was full to overflowing with victims, some with great wounds, some burned, and some who had lost the strength to move farther and were seated at the roadside with vacant faces.

Two day later I went with my father to look at the place where we had been living. But there was neither shadow not shape of the house. The fig tree and the burned skeleton of the sewing machine were the only reminders of our home. [Osada 1959 135–6]

And a boy who was eleven in 1945 left this story:

Suddenly from outside the front entrance an indescribable color and light—an eerie greenishwhite flash—came thrusting in. After a little while I regained consciousness. Everything around me was pitch dark. Somehow I managed to figure out that I seemed to have been blown down the hall to the back part of the inn. I was buried under the wreckage of the two-story building and although I struggled to free myself and crawl out, I couldn't move my body. Mother pulled aside the boards and beams which were already on fire and pulled me out to safety. But at once I was stunned by the completeness of the change which had taken place in my surroundings. Everything in sight which can be called a building is crushed to the ground and sending out flames. People who are burned so badly that the skin of their bodies is peeling off in red strips are raising shrieking cries that sound as though the victims would die the next minute. There are even some people who are already dead. The street is so covered with dead people and burned people stretched out and groaning, and with fallen houses and things, that we can't get through. While we are trying to think what to do next we notice that the flames are steadily coming closer to the west of us. I walked over the roof of a fallen house that wasn't burning yet and escaped in the direction where there were no flames.

I came out at the river bank on the shore opposite Kyu Sen Tei. There for the first time I realized that I had become separated from Mother. At the side of the Kyobashi River burned people were moaning, "Hot! Hot!" and jumping into the river, and since they could not move their bodies freely, they would call for help with the voices of those facing death, and then drown. The river became not a stream of flowing water but rather a stream of drifting dead bodies. No matter how much I might exaggerate the stories of the burned people who died shrieking and of how the city of Hiroshima was burned to the ground, the facts would still be clearly more terrible and I could never really express the truth on this piece of paper; on this point I ask for pardon. [Osada 1959 218–19]

Three days after the atomic bomb fell on Hiroshima, a second atomic bomb, this time a plutonium device, fell on Nagasaki. At Hiroshima, 118,661 people were killed by the bomb and 30,524 were severly injured, 47 percent of the population of the city. At Nagaski, 73,884 were killed and 74,909 were severly injured. In the months and years that followed, tens of thousands more died from the lingering effects of the atomic explosions.[9] Years later, President Truman told a national magazine that he never lost a night's sleep over Hiroshima and Nagaski. But in 1945, even Truman was shaken by what the United States had done. He gave orders that plans for use of a third atomic bomb be postponed, because he wanted to "stop killing all those kids." (Herken 1982 21.)

Development of the Cold War

After V-J day, American troops by the millions returned to civilian life, and one of the greatest armies and certanly the greatest navy that the world had ever seen virtually melted away into thin air. The American troops were tired of fighting, and, so far as the general population was concerned, no serious threat to American interests existed anywhere in the world. The remaining military powers were all allies of the United States; future international tensions were to be settled before the United Nations, and if the United Nations failed, the United States could fall back on a weapon that it alone possessed and which was universally regarded as invincible.

Nevertheless, within a year of V-J day, the American leadership and a considerable fraction of the American population had come to believe that the United States was confronted in the world by a powerful antagonist whose interests were so diametrically opposed to the interests of the United States that disputes between them could be resolved only by the threat or use of force.

It would be fruitless to fix a date for the commencement of the Cold War.[10] One could say that it began with Stalin's refusal in 1945 to recognize the government-in-exile in London as the legitimate government of Poland, or one could say that it began when Truman and Churchill decided to make an issue of this refusal. One could date it from Churchill's "Iron Curtain" speech in Fulton, Missouri in March 1946, or from the Soviet rejection of the Baruch Plan for the internationalization of atomic weapons the following summer. Surely the wartime alliance between the United States and the Soviet Union was viewed as a marriage of convenience by many of the American power elite, and the American anti-Communist reflex, abetted by the rivalry that naturally develops between two great powers, simply reestablished itself as the dominant force in American foreign policy no later than 1946. By early 1947, an abstemious Congress was ready to appropriate $300 million for the defeat of the Communists in Greece. In July 1947, Congress passed the National Security Act, establishing the Department of Defense, the CIA, the National Security Council, and most of the *apparat* of the American national security state. The Cold War was on in earnest.

(a) The Birth of SAC

In the late 1940s, the principal visible expression of the resurrected anti-Communist posture was economic and military aid to war-devasted Western Europe. But the anti-Communist stance required military power as well, and in 1946 Congress established the Strategic Air Command,[11] which had, among other things, the responsibility of delivering, on command, a nuclear strike against the Soviet Union. The core of SAC in 1946 was the 509th composite group, which included the squadron of B-29s involved in the attacks on Hiroshima and Nagasaki. By the end of 1946, SAC had 148 B-29s; by the end of 1947, that number had increased to 369. In 1948, the SAC force was complimented by the B-50, a more powerful version of the B-29, and by the B-36, the last and largest of the piston driven bombers.

The B-29 was not capable of two way intercontinental missions, and the B-36, though long range, was slow, vulnerable to fighter attaack, and mechanically unreliable. To make atomic threats against Russia credible, the planes had to be moved closer to Russia, and in 1946, a SAC base was constructed in Alaska. By 1950, SAC bases had been constructed all around the Soviet periphery, where reliable allies were willing to allow them, and the United States, which in 1940 had been an isolationist nation with a small standing army, had become a world power capable of intervening virtually anywhere at any time.

(b) Atomic Diplomacy, 1945–1949

Though SAC in the 1940s had a respectable number of planes, only a small fraction of them (33 in 1948) were capable of carrying atomic weapons. The small number of nuclear-capable planes reflected the small size of the American nuclear arsenal, one of the best kept secrets of the post-War period. In 1946, Truman confessed that he had no idea how many atomic bombs the United States possessed, and the best unclassified estimates are that the American stockpile consisted of a mere half dozen bombs in 1946, and no more than 300 bombs in 1950.[12] But short of actually dropping the bombs, the main military function of nuclear weapons is to create the fear that they may be used, and this fear can be generated regardless of how small the stockpile actually is. The world was reminded of the bombs by a series of tests on Bikini atoll in 1946, and the B-29, known to be capable of carrying atomic weapons, began to appear on the international scene in situations in which President Truman wished to make a particularly memorable display of American power. In November 1946, when two U.S. army C-47's were downed over Yugoslavia, six B-29s were promptly dispatched to Germany and flew along the border. In 1947, Truman sent bombers assigned to SAC to South America, where they celebrated the inauguration of the new President in Uruguay. (The impression the B-29s made on the Uraguayans is not recorded.) In January, April, and June of 1948 nuclear capable SAC B-29s were sent to England during the various stages of the first Berlin crisis. During the same year the United States conducted another round of atomic tests, exploding three atomic bombs in the course of "Operation Sandstone." As the Cold War deepened through 1948, the carrot and the stick, the Marshall Plan and the threat of the bomb, were equally visible American presences on the world scene.[13]

(c) The Soviet Equalizer

By the summer of 1949, the United States had enjoyed a monopoly on nuclear weapons for four full years. But what had been called "the winning weapon" had not prevented the absorption of the Baltic States, the establishment of pro-Soviet regimes in Bulgaria, Roumania, Hungary, and Poland, the subversion of Czechoslovakia, or the collapse of Chiang Kai-shek. West Berlin had survived the blockade of 1948, but the defeat of the blockade was due to the efficacy of the Western airlift, and it could scarcely be demonstrated that American possession of atomic weapons had shortened the blockade by a single day.

Nevertheless, the illusion that the bomb provided political and military power persisted in Washington and London, and the failure of the Truman administration to obtain any real success (Berlin aside) in the Cold War was attributed not to a lack of power but to a lack of resolve. Many people inside and outside the American government pleaded with Truman to overcome his doubts and use the bomb to roll back the Communist tide.[14] But even the illusion of power was shattered by the explosion of the first Soviet bomb in August 1949.

The explosion of the Russian bomb caused consternation across America. General Groves, who had supervised the Manhattan Project, had assured the public in 1945 that the Soviets would not have the bomb for another twenty years, and the government's chief science advisor, Vannevar Bush, had reassured the public in early 1949 that the Russian bomb was a long way off. Conspiratorially minded Americans attributed the Russian success to spies, a view that touched off a series of witch hunts concluding triumphantly in 1953 with the execution of Julius and Ethel Rosenberg, two hapless left wingers who hardly knew enough physics to boil an egg. The only people not surprised by the turn of events were the atomic scientists, who knew that there were no deep secrets in atomic weapons production and that it was hardly surprising that Russian scientists, who commenced research into atomic weapons in 1943, should achieve in six years what American scientists had achieved in four. The real problem for the Administrative was not to find out how the Soviets had built their bomb. The problem was deciding what should be done about it. In particular, the administration had to decide whether or not to build a new type of atomic weapon—the fusion bomb.

(d) The Decision to Build the "Super"

It had been known since the 1930s that energy could be obtained by forcing free protons (hydrogen nuclei) to bind together in a single nucleus. The reason is that two protons bound together in a nucleus weigh less than two protons floating freely, and according to Einstein's formula any such loss in mass must be compensated for by a large gain in energy. In 1933 Hans Bethe suggested that the process of fusion accounted for the radiant energy of the stars, and he was right. At that time, however, there was no prospect of obtaining fusion energy on earth. Protons are primarily susceptible to two forces, the electromagnetic force, which pushes them apart, and the nuclear force, which pulls them together. The electromagnetic force dominates at great distances; the nuclear force dominates only at very small distances. Thus, to bind free protons together, the protons must be pushed against the electromagnetic force until they are close enough for the nuclear force to operate. In the 1930s no power existed strong enough to overcome the repulsive strength of the electromagnetic force. But by 1949, the necessary power could be obtained by using the standard fission bomb as a starter.

The physical theory behind the hydrogen bomb was the same as the theory behind the fission bomb. But there was one significant practical difference. The explosion of the fission bomb resulted from the implosion of small pieces of radioactive material into a single piece of critical size, capable of sustaining a chain reaction. There was a limit to the number of pieces that could be successfully imploded, and this set limits on the size and energy of the fission bomb. The hydrogen bomb suffered from no such limitations. The fission starter, in effect, ignited the hydrogen fuel, and the more fuel ignited, the larger the explosion. The fusion bomb could be made virtually any size. The atomic scientists called it the "Super."

In the fall of 1949, debate raged within the American government about the wisdom of building the Super. Oppenheimer and many of his associates from the Manhattan project argued that fission bombs were powerful enough and that the fusion bomb would only make a bigger hole in the ground, pulverizing dust that had already been pulverized. George Kennan in the State Department argued that such a unilateral escalation of the arms race would be immoral, and that the containment of Communism was more a political than a military problem. Other atomic scientists, led by Edward Teller, pleaded for the Super and argued that it would be folly to permit the Soviet Union to develop such a weapon first. In January 1950 Truman decided to build the Super.[15] Oppenheimer plunged from favor and in 1954 was deprived of his security clearance.

Missiles and the Bomb

(a) The Korean Years

The sudden invasion of South Korea by North Korean forces in June 1950 diverted public attention away from nuclear weapons to warfare of the conventional sort. Indeed, the war provided yet another lesson in the difficulties of translating nuclear force into usable military strength. Early in the war, Omar Bradley maintained that there was no military use for the atomic bomb in Korea, a view soon seconded by the Air Force.[16] Though MacArthur asked for the bomb and though the National Security Council recommended that the atomic bomb be used in Korea if negotiations broke down, no situation ever arose in which use of the atomic bomb could do more military good than harm. Nevertheless in the wartime atmosphere, work on the American nuclear arsenal pressed forward. In 1950, American aircraft carriers for the first time began carrying atomic weapons on a regular basis, and in 1951, components for nuclear weapons were placed in Britain— the first exportation of American nuclear devices. The Strategic Air Command received its first deliveries of the B-47, a long range all-jet bomber that was to be the mainstay of SAC in the middle 1950s, replacing the B-29 (phased out in 1954) and the B-36 (phased out in 1959). Work proceeded on the Super, with a major breakthrough in February 1951, when Teller and Stanislaw Ulam hit upon a new design for the bomb, successfully tested during Operation Greenhouse in May 1951. Another technical breakthrough in warhead design permitted the construction of very small fission bombs with weights of 3,000 pounds, one third the weight of previous nuclear devices. The practicality of equipping battlefield troops with these new "tactical" nuclear weapons was allegedly established by Project Vista in late 1951.

The same year brought a landmark in the development of American guided missiles. Though the theoretical basis for rocket development had been laid by an American, Robert Goddard, in 1919, and though Goddard by 1930 had actually built rockets reaching speeds of 3,000 miles per hour, none of the Allies had shown any interest in the interwar period in the use of rockets as weapons of war. Research and development fell to the Germans by default, and the Third Reich constructed, under Werner von Braun, a major center for rocket research at Peenemunde, near the Baltic sea. The fruits of German reserach were the jet-propelled V-1 "buzz bomb" and the rocket-propelled V-2, which obtained a top speed of 5,000 miles an hour. In 1944 and 1945, 2,500 V-1 bombs fell on London, and between 8 September 1944, when the first V-2 hit London, and the German surrender in May 1945, over 4,000 V-2 rockets struck behind Allied lines.

With the collapse of Germany, Russian forces occupied Peenemunde. Many German rocket scientists felt that the United States provided a more hospitable haven than occupied Germany or Soviet Russia, and in the summer of 1945, 82 scientists, including von Braun, came to the United States, pledging to work on American rocket and space research. Samples of V-2 rockets were brought over for study; the White Sands Proving Ground was established in 1945, the Pacific Missile Range in 1946, and the Atlantic Range in 1949.

The military significance of rockets in the atomic age could hardly go unnoticed. As early as September 1945, *Aviation Week* magazine suggested that a fearsome weapon could be constructed by placing an atomic bomb on the head of a V-2 rocket, and a classified report given to the President in December 1945 claimed that the construction of military rockets with intercontinental range was technically feasible. Nevertheless, the armed services at first showed little interest in rockets. Despite a drill on 16 May 1947 showing that half of SAC could not get airborne, the famous 1948 Finletter Report, "Survival in the Nuclear Age," recommended that the missile program be cut back in favor of the expansion of SAC. Budgets for missile research averaged only about $70 million per year through 1950. But the war conditions of 1951, coupled with the discovery that the Russians had put Peenemunde back into operation, swung opinion in favor of missile development, and the budget for missiles in 1951 (including the first contracts for the Atlas long range missile) was upped to $800 million, a six-fold increase over 1950. Inevitable interservice rivalries erupted about the disposition of the new money for missiles, and Secretary of Defense Wilson placed development of intercontinental range ballistic missiles (ICBMs) in the hands of the Air Force, the development of intermediate range ballistic missiles (IRBMs) in the hands of the Air Force and the Navy, and the development of surface to surface missiles (range, 200 miles) in the hands of the Army.

With new diffusion techniques for the isolation of U-235 and new demands for tactical nuclear weapons and nuclear missile warheads, the American stockpile of nuclear weapons grew rapidly through 1951 and 1952 to a total of perhaps 1,500 weapons. The new bombs needed testing, and the Atomic Energy Commission exploded 18 atomic bombs above the Nevada sands in 1951 and 11 more atomic bombs in 1952. The atmosphere received yet another suffusion of radioactivity with the explosion of the first British atomic bomb in October 1952. The nuclear club now had three members. But the biggest and most ominous test of all came at Eniwetok in the South Pacific. On 1 November 1952, a fission starter ignited the first fusion explosion and the atoll of Elugalab vanished from the face of the earth.

(b) Eisenhower and the "New Look":

By November 1952, American forces invading North Korea had been repulsed by fresh Chinese troops, and the war had settled into a bloody stalemate. Demanding "No More Koreas," a tired and frustrated public voted for Eisenhower, who had promised to go to Korea and who seemed pledged to ending the war. American troops had paid a stiff price for preserving Korea and Syngman Rhee from Communism, and it was doubtful that the public would tolerate similar sacrifices of American lives for the abstract ideals of overseas anti-Communism. The atomic bomb once again seemed an attractive alternative to foot-soldiering on foreign soil. Although Eisenhower was enough of a military man to recognize the weakness of strategic weapons, he was willing to give atomic diplomacy another try. The move to technology was called the "New Look."[17]

In the months following the Republican victory, Congress appropriated funds for research in no less than six major missile programs: the Air Force had its Atlas, Titan, Thor, and Minuteman; the Navy had Polaris; and the Army, which refused to be shut out of the intermediate range missile race, insisted on developing its Jupiter missile for deployment in Europe. The

CIA, under its new director Allan Dulles, greatly expanded its operations, and the AEC tested 15 more bombs in Nevada, some of them large enough to throw radioactive dust into populated parts of nearby Utah. NATO, which in 1952 had contemplated expanding to 90 ground divisions, backed off on proposed increases in conventional forces and accepted its first nuclear armed weapon, the 25-mile-range solid-fuel Honest John missile. But all this apparent stategic progress was nullified by the news that the Soviets had exploded their first hydrogen bomb on 12 August 1953. To make matters worse, American intelligence sources informed the government that the Soviet bomb had a more advanced design than the "Mike" device that had exploded at Eniwetok, and that the Soviets were making considerable progress in the development of missiles with ranges long enough to reach the United States.

By fall 1953 the Administration found itself increasingly hemmed in by events and by its own priorities. A significant expansion of American ground and conventional forces was unthinkable so soon after the frustrations of Korea. The technological edge enjoyed by the United States over the Soviets seemed to be dissolving, and the new administration was commited to fiscal prudence and a balanced budget. The government had apparently painted itself into a corner, but something of a solution was perceived to be at hand. While continuing to invest in the nuclear end of the weapons spectrum, the United States would escalate the rhetoric of the Cold War, attempting to convince its opponents that there was a real chance that the new American nuclear weapons would be used if the events of the Cold War took a sufficiently anti-American turn. The task of raising the diplomatic ante fell to the State Department and new Secretary of State, John Foster Dulles.

In January 1954 Dulles addressed the Council on Foreign Relations on "The Evolution of Foreign Policy." Before an audience that must have been astonished to hear a public presentation of American policy for the use of nuclear weapons, Dulles paid the usual homage to the continued need for conventional weapons, but went on to say:

> Local defense will always be important. But there is no local defense which alone will contain the mighty manpower of the Communist world. Local defenses must be reinforced by the further deterrent of massive retaliatory power. A potential aggressor must know that he cannot always prescribe battle conditions that suit him. Otherwise, for example, a potential aggressor, who is glutted with manpower, might be tempted to attack in places where his superiority is decisive.

Thus the administration had decided to "depend primarily upon a great capacity to retaliate, instantly, by means and at places of our own choosing." (U.S. Dept of State 1954 108)

Now, if the United States was to retaliate "instantly, by means and at places of our own choosing," it needed hydrogen bombs and the means to deliver them. The hydrogen bombs came first. On April 1954, the AEC set off at Eniwetok the first full fledged American hydrogen bomb. The "Bravo" bomb released the energy equivalent of 15 million tons of TNT and was more than one thousand times as powerful as the bomb that destroyed Hiroshima. The explosion lifted debris into the stratosphere, and when the wind took an unexpected turn, nearby populated islands in the Marshall cl contaminated with radioactive fallout. Eighty miles away, fisherman on Japense fishing boat *Lucky Dragon* succumbed to acute radiation poisoning, and the catch from 683 Japanese tuna boats was found to be contaminated by a single explosion of a single bomb. Massive retaliation with such weapons could be very massive indeed.

Encouraged by the development of gyroscopic stablizers that significantly improved missile accuracy, new missile programs went forward. By 1955 the Air Force had the Matador/Mace cruise missiles forward based in Europe, and a few 5,000-mile-range Snark missiles stood poised at Presque Island in Maine. In 1956, the Navy deployed the submarine launched Regulus cruise missile, and the Army successfully flew a Jupiter C over a 700-mile course. In 1957, Air Force intermediate range Thors made their appearance in Britain, Spain, and Turkey, and Jupiter C's were put in Italy. In November 1958, after a year of failure, the Air Force successfully tested its Atlas, the first American intercontinental range ballistic missile. By 1959, six Atlas missiles were operational and the Air Force had successfully tested the Titan, an intercontinental range ballistic missile in some respects more versatile than the Atlas. By 1960, over 100 intermediate-range American ballistic missiles could be found in Italy and Turkey alone, and the Navy had launched the first Polaris, an underwater launched submarine based missile which defied detection and which was as invulnerable as it was lethal.[18]

In addition to the intermediate-range ballistic missiles placed on NATO soil, NATO ground forces in these years were at least partially nuclearized. In addition to its Honest John missile of 1953 and its Matador missiles of 1954, NATO ground forces in February 1954 received 280-millimeter atomic cannon. NATO formally agreed to the use of tactical nuclear weapons in that year, and in late 1954, General Montgomery went so far as to say "We at SHAPE (Supreme Headquarters Allied Powers Europe) are basing all our planning on using atomic and thermonuclear weapons." Despite NATO war games in 1955 that indicated that a typical European war fought in these terms would result in 171 atomic explosions over Europe and several million civilian casualities, NATO document MC 14/2 called for a nuclear response to any Soviet intrusion, even local, if it persevered. Atomic cannon were eventually deployed worldwide, and made their appearance in 1958 on the islands of Quemoy and Matsu during the Formosa crisis.

The bulk of American firepower, however, still lay in the manned bombers of SAC, and the size of the bomber fleet was rapidly increased to meet the perceived requirements of massive retaliation. The B-47 fleet increased from 329 in 1953 to 795 in 1954, peaking at 1,367 in 1959. In 1955, the Air Force received its first deliveries of the B-52, an eight-engine intercontinental-range bomber capable of carrying four nuclear weapons. Starting with a first wing of 35 B-52's in 1956, the B-52 fleet increased to 100 in 1957 (when a B-52 flew nonstop around the world), 255 in 1958, and 588 in 1959. In its peak year of 1959, SAC had 1,854 large bombers. Every day a fraction of this immense force took off from bases in Spain, Morocco, and the United States, and flew towards the Soviet Union, returning only after reaching designated "fail safe" points within striking distance of their Russian targets. All these planes and all the new missiles required warheads, and the American nuclear stockpile kept pace, increasing from 1,500 weapons in 1953 to over 10,000 weapons in 1957. Between 1954 and 1960, the total megatonnage in the American arsenal increased twenty-fold.

The development of the new Polaris missile submarines, combined with the tremendous expansion of SAC during the Eisenhower years, led to rivalry in the late 1950s between the Air Force and the Navy. The Navy argued that the new Polaris was invulnerable and that Polaris submarines by themselves sufficed for the requirements of massive retaliation. In the Navy's view, atomic attacks by strategic bombers were "overkill" that contributed nothing to deterrence. The Air Force countered that the Navy's "finite deterrence" strategy was a "bluff" strategy that "lacked the capacity for victory" if deterrence failed.

A study completed in 1959 determined that the United States should retain both air borne and sea borne deterrent forces. A Joint Strategic Target Planning Staff was formed to determine which targets should be assigned to the Air Force and which to the Navy, and a National Strategic Target List was prepared. On the basis of the target list, the Joint Chiefs and Secretary of Defense in 1960 adopted the first *Single Integrated Operational Plan* (SIOP) for the deployment of American strategic forces in the event of nuclear war.

Brinksmanship: Nuclear Diplomacy, 1953–1960

The development of the New Look weapons systems would have been pointless if Eisenhower and Dulles did not intend that these systems be used, either as weapons of war or as vehicles for threats. As it turned out, Eisenhower and Dulles were prepared to exercise the nuclear threat, and did exercise it, at least eight times in eight years.

(a) Korea

Eisenhower had been elected in 1952 on the promise of ending the Korean stalement. Even before assuming office, Eisenhower and Dulles had decided that threats of nuclear attack might revitalize the stalled peace talks and bring the war to an end. (Eisenhower 1963 179—81) The first nuclear "signal" was dropped in February 1953 and further warnings were conveyed through Nehru in May. To the delight of the new Administration, the peace talks were reactivated and peace was concluded in July. Having waved the nuclear wand once, Eisenhower was prepared to wave it again. In August 1953, worried that the North Koreans might not have sufficient incentive to keep to the July agreement after the withdrawl of U.N. forces, Eisenhower allowed General Clark to issue the "Delaration of Sixteen," which spelled out in detail the consequences of violating the peace:

> We affirm in the interest of world peace, that if there is a renewal of the armed attack, challenging the principles of the United Nations, we should again be

united and prompt to resist. The consequences of such a breach of the armistice would be so grave that, in all probability, it would not be possible to confine hostilities within Korea. [Fleming 1961 648]

which was another way of saying that the United States would retaliate "at times and at places of our own choosing."[19]

The apparent success of nuclear threats in 1953 lent plausibility to the massive retaliation doctrine when Dulles announced it in January 1954. But Dulles had hardly finished speaking when the massive retaliation doctrine was faced with perhaps its greatest challenge.

(b) Vietnam

Through 1953 and into 1954, the French had been steadily losing control of their colony in Indochina to forces of the Viet Minh under the Communist leader Ho Chi Minh. In January, attempting to reverse a deteriorating military situation, the French General Navarre parachuted 20,000 troops deep into Viet Minh territory, in the valley at Dienbienphu. The French were promptly surrounded, and despite constant reinforcements it appeared that they would have to surrender, ensuring the loss of at least half of Vietnam to Ho Chi Minh. The American government had misgivings about the moral weight of French claims in Indochina, but the prospect of a Communist victory quelled all objections and American aid to the French by 1954 was costing $1 billion per year.

As April 1954 proceeded and the Dienbienphu siege turned into a nightmare, the possibility of American support, including support with nuclear weapons, was under discussion. Though Dienbienphu was a distant target, the new AJ Savages (piston driven carrier based planes converted for nuclear weapons delivery in 1951) could be flown from Japan to American carriers and from carriers to Dienbienphu. On 7 May 1954, however, Dienbienphu fell, and the atomic bombs went back on the shelf. There was no strong evidence that atomic bombs could have helped the French garrison against the Viet Minh and there were no other suitable targets for nuclear punishment; the Chinese had scrupulously avoided sending troops into Vietnam, and the Soviets were even less involved than the Chinese. Since there was no one against whom to direct a threat, no threat was made. As a later President would discover, deterrence was not a useful approach against Ho Chi Minh.

The inapplicability of massive retaliation in Vietnam did not break the nuclear faith. Rattled by the fall of Dienbienphu and upset by the unveiling, on Mayday 1954, of the first Soviet long range bombers, members of the National Security Council prepared a document calling for an all-out pre-emptive nuclear strike against the Soviet Union. "If at one blow the threat of America's destruction from atomic attack would be removed, then the blow should be struck,"[20] the document said, but Eisenhower had seen enough of war to know better, and apparently tabeled discussion of the proposal. Nevertheless, Eisenhower, in that same month of May 1954, ordered strategic bombers to Nicaragua and moved an aircraft carrier task group off the coast of Guatamala to protest the decision of the Arbenz government in Guatamala to accept military aid from the Soviet bloc. The bombers stood by, and the CIA managed to bring down the regime.

(c) The Formosa Straits

In the summer of 1954 the Chinese Communists began building up forces opposite several offshore islands still in the hands of Chiang Kai-shek and the Chinese Nationalists. In August, Eisenhower ordered strategic bombers into the Western Pacific to express American support for. Chiang. Apparently unimpressed, the mainland Chinese, in January 1955, began shelling the Tachen Islands, assaulted and captured nearby Yikiang, and gave evidence of their intentions to claim the islands of Quemoy and Matsu, 30 miles off the Chinese coast.

The United States was publicly committed to Chiang, but whether or not that commitment involved the defense of Quemoy and Matsu was not clear. In late January, Eisenhower demanded and got from Congress a blank check to construe the understanding however he saw fit, and in the months that followed Dulles did all he could to commit Eisenhower to the defense of Quemoy and Matsu. An arrangement was suggested whereby Chiang would evacuate Tachen if the United States agreed to defend Quemoy. But Eisenhower wavered and Chiang refused to withdraw, At this point, the nuclear threat was played as a trump card against the mainland Chinese.

Dulles went on national radio to warn the American public of the grave dangers ensuing from the fall of Quemoy. He warned the Communists that the United States was no "paper tiger" and that Communist attacks on the islands would be met with "new and powerful weapons of precision, which can utterly destroy military targets without endangering civilian centers," i.e., tactical atomic bombs. Eisenhower affirmed that tactical A-bombs would be used "just exactly as you would use a bullet or anything else." The Chinese, undisturbed, continued building cannon opposite Quemoy and airfields opposite Matsu. To many Americans, it appeared that American atomic bombs would be pitted against a nation of 600 million people.[21]

But there was no war. The Chinese shelled the islands, but did not attack them, and as the Chinese interest in attacking declined, so did the interest of the Administration in defending them to the death. There would be no war, and instead of war the Big Four convened at the summit conference in Geneva in 1955. It is possible that atomic threats had deterred the Chinese from the invasion of Quemoy. It is also true that American allies in the West were appalled at the thought of atomic war over some inconsequential offshore islands, and the diplomatic costs of issuing the nuclear threats had been immense. By the time of the summit, the United States found itself alone in its support of Chiang, and it was clear that the United States would not and could not support Chiang in any attempt to reconquer the mainland. But if in fact the United States had conceded mainland China to the Red Chinese, there was no point in the defense of Quemoy. If the atomic threats had succeeded, they had succeeded in a cause which was progressively becoming meaningless.

(d) Evaluating the Use of Nuclear Threats

The hair-raising confrontations of the Formosa crisis, coupled with growing evidence of Soviet strategic bomber strength, produced sobriety and discretion in the use of nuclear threats in the remaining Eisenhower years. In the Suez crisis of October 1956, the Lebanese intervention of July 1958, and the Berlin crisis of July 1959, nuclear-capable Sixth Fleet aircraft carriers were brought forward in the Mediterranean, with the intention of deterring the Soviets from overt military action. But these maneuvers were not accompanied by verbal threats of attack of the sort that Dulles had hurled against the mainland Chinese in February 1955. Likewise, when the Quemoy-Matsu crisis erupted with Red Chinese shelling of the islands in 1958, strategic aircraft were brought forward, atomic cannon were installed on the islands, but no verbal threats were issued.[22] The Dulles game of taking the world to the brink of war had fallen out of fashion.

In Korea, in the Taiwan straits, in Suez, in Lebanon, and in Berlin, nuclear threats had been issued and the objectives of these threats had been achieved. At least in the case of Korea, Eisenhower was convinced that nuclear threats had been essential to American success (Adams 1961 48–49). But in all these cases, Korea included, it is difficult, perhaps impossible, to verify that nuclear threats had done the trick. In Korea, by the spring of 1953, the futility of attempting to win the war on this ground should have been apparent to both sides, and it is possible that the North Koreans had already decided to accept the peace by June 1953, in which case the "success" of deterrence was no success at all. Did fear of nuclear war prevent the Soviets from entering the Suez crisis? Perhaps the Soviets, who wanted the British and French out of Egypt as much as Eisenhower did, felt that there was a better chance of achieving British withdrawal if they did not intrude their presence on the scene.

In grappling with the evaluation of massive retaliation it should be noted that Dulles judiciously refrained from making nuclear threats if there was a reasonable chance that the threats would fail. Ho Chi Minh would not be deterred and no nuclear threats were made against him. Likewise when the Hungarian Revolution was crushed by Russian tanks in August and September of 1956, no threats were made against Khruschev and the Soviets.

The case of Hungary is instructive, since the Eisenhower administration had far more at stake in Hungary than it had in Quemoy and Matsu. Indeed, in his first address as Secretary of State, Dulles had ringingly repudiated the Truman/Acheson doctrine of "containment" and had inaugurated the era of "rolling back" the Communist tide: "To all those suffering under Communist slavery . . . let us say, you can count on us!" (Fleming 1961 812.) Nevertheless, when the crunch came, the Hungarians could count on nothing but Russian tanks rolling through the streets of Budapest. Eastern Europe was construed as a Russian sphere of interest, and the United States was prepared to leave it alone; it would not threaten atomic war if it believed the enemy sufficiently motivated to call the bluff. But if massive retaliation would not be used to interfere in matters that the enemy took seriously, it followed that, if it deterred at all, massive retaliation only deterred the enemy from things in which he took little interest.

(e) Soviet Weapons Development and American Fears

The development of American strategic forces in the late 1940s and 1950s could hardly be ignored by the Soviet Union, which found itself, from 1946 on, the chief target of American strategic threats. Nevertheless, since the Soviet military tradition emphasized ground assaults and control of the land, Soviet responses to the growing power of SAC were modest at first. Shortly after the war, the Soviets introduced the TU-4 "Bull" bomber, a carbon copy of the American B-29. A certain number of Bull bombers were modified after 1949 to carry the new Soviet nuclear weapons, but since the Soviets possessed no overseas bases, the TU-4's could only be used against Europe and Asia; they posed no nuclear threat to the United States.

The first genuinely strategic bomber introduced by the Soviets was the TU-16 "Badger," an all-jet bomber with a range of 3,800 miles and a top speed of 600 miles per hour, roughly equivalent to the American B-47. First seen in 1952 (five years after the introduction of the B-47), the Badger became operational in 1954, and could reach the United States on a one-way mission. For the first time, the continental United States was open to nuclear attack.

In 1954, the Soviets exhibted the TU-20 "Bear," a turbo-prop jet with an 8,000-mile-range, capable of two way missions against the United States. Shortly after the Bear, the Soviet flew the Mya-4 "Bison" bomber, which is useful mainly in reconnaissance roles. In November 1955, the Soviets successfully tested an atomic bomb from these planes, the first aerial drop of an atomic weapon since Nagasaki.[23]

The Bear and Bison bombers are still in use, and still form the backbone of the Soviet strategic bomber force. Because of their low cruising speeds and cruising altitudes, the Bears and Bisons are no match for the American B-52. Neverless, if a single Badger, Bear, or Bison succeeded in reaching the United States, the resulting devastation would far exceed anything in previous American experience. It is not surprising that in the Cold War atmosphere of the mid-1950s the appearance of the Soviet Badgers, Bears, and Bisons provoked hysteria in the United States. I remember, in 1955, being told in school air raid drills to hide under my desk, cover my eyes and "come out after hearing the all clear." Millions of children did the same. Starting in 1954, Nike-Ajax anti-aircraft missile stations began sprouting from coast to coast, and in the summer of 1955, the United States began constructing a series of radar stations across Canada. This "Distant Early Warning" line was completed in 1957, and linked to the SAGE jet interceptor system in 1958.

Despite a ten-to-one advantage in strategic bombers, American worries about the Soviet bombers had grown so much by 1956 that the Air Force proclaimed that a "bomber gap" was developing between the Soviet Union and the United States.[24] To keep watch on Soviet developments, Eisenhower ordered the new, high-altitude American U-2 planes to begin reconnaissance flights over Soviet territory. But the fears of 1956 were nothing compared to the trauma of 1957. Two years before, in 1955, the Killian report had described great strides made by the Soviets in the development of long-range rockets. In August 1957, the Soviets successfully tested the world's first ICBM and in October they used the new rocket to launch Sputnik, the world's first artificial staellite. With the new ICBM, the Soviets could apparently destroy at will any city in the United States. The main American military reply to such an attack would be a bomber attack against Russian territory, an attack that might be blunted by the immense numbers of surface to air missiles the Soviets were installing between themselves and SAC. It was 1949 all over again. The illusion of superiority produced by the growth of SAC dissolved, and the sense of vulnerability felt by Americans, accustomed to the protection of the seas, was acute. Two months after Sputnik, civil defense director Val Petersen asked the government for $30 billion to construct fallout shelters. Ministers across the country began debating the moral course Christians should take if war came and unprotected neighbors begged for admission to overcrowded fallout shelters.

Weapons, Strategies, and Competition: 1961–1972

(a) Kennedy, McNamara and Flexible Response

The Presidential campaign of 1960 revolved around national security issues. Defending the Eisenhower policies, Nixon could point to the growth of SAC and the development of a variety of missile programs, some already operational. Kennedy could point to Sputnik and the Soviet ICBM, and to an alleged "missile gap" growing between the U.S. and the U.S.S.R., and to several strategic mishaps of the late Eisenhower years, especially the 1960 downing of a U-2 spy plane over Russian soil. Kennedy was elected by a hair; a small plurality agreed with Kennedy that "American prestige has never been lower."

In 1961 Kennedy and the new Secretary of Defense, Robert McNamara, conducted a review of strategic programs. McNamara's preliminary survey, as summarized by Ted Sorenson in 1965, found that U.S. military policy was characterized by:

1. A strategy of massive nuclear retaliation as the answer to all military and political aggression, a strategy believed by few of our friends and none of our enemies and resulting in serious weaknesses in our conventional forces.

2. A financial ceiling on national security, making military strategy the step-child of a predetermined budget.

3. A strategic nuclear force vulnerable to surprise missile attack, a nonnuclear force weak in combat-ready divisions, in airlift capacity and in tactical air support, a counterinsurgency force for all practical purposes nonexistent, and a weapons

inventory completely lacking in certain major elements but far oversupplied in others.

4. Too many automatic decisions made in advance instead of in the light of an actual emergency, and too few Pentagon-wide plans for each kind of contingency. [Sorenson 1965 603]

To solve the problem of strategic vulnerability, and the challenge raised by new Soviet air defenses, McNamara proposed to cut back on bombers and cruise missiles while stepping up solid fueled missile programs. To solve the problem of conventional weakness and over-reliance on atomic threats, he proposed a substantial increase in expenditures for conventional forces. To solve the puzzles of insurgency he inaugurated counterinsurgency programs and the development of special counterinsurgency forces.

The effects of these decisions were dramatic and traumatic, especially for the Air Force. McNamara phased out the Snark, the Mace, the Matador, and the Regulus cruise missiles. He began a phaseout of the B-47, ordered no new B-52s beyond those already in the pipeline, requested only limited quantities of the new supersonic B-58 bomber, and cancelled altogether the new B-70 long-range bomber. He cancelled the Atlas missile and limited the Titan missile force. On the other hand, he called for a vast expansion of the Polaris fleet, and gave high priority to procurement of the new Minuteman missile, which could be fueled and housed in an underground silo. The solid-fuel Minuteman was successfully tested in 1961, and soon became the mainstay of the American ICBM force.

The new balance of strategic forces created by McNamara needed its own operating plan, and McNamara's staff set about revising the Single Integrated Operational Plan. According to Henry Rowen, the new McNamara SIOP

differentiated more clearly between attacks on military targets and attacks on cities . . . [It] distinguished more clearly among . . . attacks on (1) nuclear threat targets, (2) other military forces, (3) urban industrial targets. It also provided options for withholding attack by country and for withholding direct attacks on cities. [Rowen 1979]

The flexibility afforded by the revised SIOP represented the first step away from the all-or-nothing strategy intimated by Dulles all through the fifties. McNamara went public with the new strategic concepts in his speech at Ann Arbor in June 1962:

The US has come to the conclusion that to the extent feasible basic military strategy in a possible general nuclear war should be approached in much the same way that more conventional military operations have been regarded in the past. That is to say, the principal military objective, in the event of a nuclear war stemming from a major attack on the Alliance, should be the destruction of the enemy's military forces, not of his civilian population.

The very strength and nature of the Alliance forces make it possible for us to retain, even in the face of a massive surprise attack, sufficient reserve striking power to destroy an enemy society if driven to it. In other words we are giving a possible opponent the strongest possible incentive to refrain from striking our own cities. [McNamara 1962]

The new strategy, which came to be called "flexible response," had two features that sharply distinguished it from massive retaliation. First, the strategy provided the President with the ability to destroy enemy military installations without necessarily destroying his cities, i.e., with "counter-force" as opposed to "countervalue" options. Second, the strategy, as presented by McNamara, implied that American strategic forces *for the most part* would only be used in the event of a nuclear attack on the United States. (I say "for the most part" because the McNamara strategy still allowed the use of strategic forces to repel a large ground assault in Europe. It should also be noted that nothing in the doctrine excluded a "first use" of tactical nuclear weapons.) The main function of strategic forces, from McNamara on, would be to deter a nuclear attack on the United States by threatening to destroy the nation imprudent enough to launch the attack. In short, massive retaliation was a first-strike doctrine; flexible response was, by and large, a second-strike doctrine. The days of waving the nuclear wand to achieve Cold War objectives were over.[25]

(b) Civil Defense and Mutual Assured Destruction

One thing that McNamara did not stress in his Ann Arbor speech was civil defense. In the early days of the New Frontier, civil defense and fallout shelters had been a Kennedy enthusiasm, and in July 1961, Kennedy submitted to Congress a plan to identify, mark, and stock some 50 million fallout shelters. But by 1962, Administration interest in fallout shelters was on the wane, and not only because there was a public outcry against them. The "Soviet threat," which had loomed so large in the Presidential campaign of 1960, was shown by the new SAMOS spy satellites to have been greatly exaggerated: as near as could be determined the Soviets had no more than a few dozen ICBMs in place in 1961, hardly the occasion for 50 million fallout shelters. Reviewing the shelter issue in 1962, McNamara's staff calculated that the Soviets could nullify every three dollars spent on civil defense by adding merely one dollar to their offense. This made civil defense look like a very bad buy. Finally, the kind of nuclear attack that the Soviet Union could mount by the late 1960s would be so devastating that inhabitants of shelters would not have a liveable environment into which they could emerge. In short, in the early 1960s shelters were not needed, and by the late 1960s would be useless.

There was another argument against civil defense, propounded by Herbert York, Jerome Wiesner, and other scientists who had been involved in strategic programs over the years.[26] The argument was that civil defense, by limiting damage caused by a Soviet strike, denied the Soviets their ability to deter an American first strike with a second strike of their own, thus raising (in Soviet eyes) the possibility of an American first strike. McNamara never subscribed to the York/Wiesner arguments, but he did concede that the nuclear age was an age in which the offense totally dominated the defense. The shelter program perished from neglect. By foregoing defense against attack, McNamara had, intentionally or unintentionally, permitted the development of Soviet second strike capacity.* In the future, each nation that suffered a first strike would retain the ability to launch a devastating second strike, a state of affairs that deprecatingly came to be called Mutual Assured Destruction, or MAD. But MAD was never a strategic doctrine. It flowed from the technology itself, a fact of life in the nuclear age.

It is one thing to set a general target of assured destruction, another thing to define assured destruction precisely and achieve it within the constraints of the defense budget. As the Minuteman and Polaris programs surged forward in the early 1960s, McNamara's staff wrestled with the question, "How much is enough?"[27] In speeches in the late 1960s, McNamara revealed that "enough" was defined by his staff as being "Enough weapons to survive an all out Soviet first strike and still retaliate with a force sufficient to kill one quarter of the Russian people and destroy one half of Soviet industry." Staff studies also determined that, past a certain point, increases in numbers of Minuteman and Polaris missiles provided very little in terms of increased destruction on the Soviet side. The optimum strategic mixture, one that seemed to achieve assured destruction at the least cost, involved about 54 very large warheads, carried by Titan missiles, 1,000 smaller warheads, carried on the Minutemen, and about 656 submarine-launched ballistic missiles, carried by Polaris subs. The United States had 108 land based ICBMs in 1961; under McNamara there were 834 by 1964 and the assured destruction figure of 1054 was achieved by 1967. In 1961, the United States had 96 submarine-launched ballistic missiles: by 1964 there were 416, and by 1967 the assured destruction goal of 656 was attained.

In an innovation that went relatively unnoticed at the time, the submarine-launched missiles introduced in 1964, called Poseidon A3s, carried three warheads apiece. Though these warheads could not be separately targeted, the change from one warhead to three provided a substantial increase in destructive force per missile, and, for the first time, the number of warheads exceeded the number of missiles, a possibility that was exploited by both the United States and the Soviet Union in the SALT constructed arms race of the 1970s.

Concurrently with changes in strategic forces at home, McNamara initiated major changes in nuclear forces in NATO. The Thor and Jupiter C IRBMs proved on study to be vulnerable to sudden attack, and McNamara ordered a phase out of these missiles, completed in 1963. To the old Honest John nuclear missiles NATO added, in 1962, the MGM29A Sergeant (range 25 miles) and the MGM31A Pershing (range 450 miles), and to the older atomic cannon NATO added (in 1964) the M-110 atomic capable cannon. Though nuclear warheads for these weapons remained in American hands, the weapons themselves found their way into Belgium, Britain, Denmark, West Germany, Greece, the Netherlands, Norway and Turkey.

In the years in which all these new missiles were added to strategic forces, the fleet of B-47 bombers disappeared. In the 1950s, the United States Air Force had built the mightiest assault force in the history of the world. In the 1960s, that force was largely scrapped and an immense new missile force had replaced the nuclear bombs carried on manned bombers, decreasing the total megatonnage in the American arsenal. For those who felt that the passing of the manned bomber meant a decline in American strategic strength, McNamara could report in 1967 that the United States had 4,500 nuclear warheads and bombs ready for delivery against the Soviet Union.

(c) Nuclear Crises, 1961–1972

The Berlin crisis of 1958 flared again in 1961 with Khruschchev's announcement that a treaty deciding the disposition of Germany must be signed in six months; if not, Khrushchev threatened, the Soviet Union would sign a separate treaty with East Germany, a treaty that would surely deny Allied claims in Berlin. Since Kennedy was not about to concede Berlin and since the Soviets were not prepared to tolerate further East German emigration through the Berlin fissure, tensions mounted through the summer of 1961. As in 1958, American aircraft carriers began making dramatic flourishes around the Mediterranean Sea. On 13 August, Khrushshev suddenly decided to settle the emigration issue independently of the treaty issue, and the Soviets built an impenetrable wall along the line dividing East Berlin from West Berlin. Though the construction of the wall violated agreements between the Soviets and the West dating from World War II, the wall was not contested; the nuclear gun was not drawn. Sorenson later wrote:

> All agreed that the Wall was illegal, immoral and inhumane, but not a cause for war. It ended West Berlin's role as a showcase and escape route for the East, but it did not interfere with the three basic objectives the West had long stressed: our presence in West Berlin, our access to West Berlin, and the freedom of West Berliners to choose their own system. [Sorenson 1965 593-94]

The United States was unhappy about the Wall; the Soviets were unhappy about the absence of a treaty. Each side felt threatened; each side flexed its muscles in exhibitions of strategic strength. The world for several years had been spared the effects of atmospheric tests. On 1 September 1961, the Soviets exploded a hydrogen bomb in Siberia with a yield of 60 million tons of TNT, the largest bomb ever exploded on earth, before or since. The Soviets tested 30 more bombs in 1961 and 40 more in 1962. Not to be outdone, the United States tested 9 bombs in 1961, and 89 bombs in 1962. Thus in 18 months starting in September 1961, the United States and the Soviet Union tested 168 bombs, releasing more fallout than had been released by all previous tests.

The tensions of 1961, however, were as nothing compared to the tension generated by the major crisis of 1962, the Cuban missile crisis. To this day, no one knows why the Soviet Union chose to put medium-range ballistic missiles in Cuba. One hypothesis is that the Soviets wished to test the nerve of the new American President. Another hypothesis is that the Soviets wished to secure the removal of intermediate-range ballistic missiles for Turkey, and were setting out to arrange a swap. Neither hypothesis is satisfactory. The traditional pragmatism of Soviet policy is inconsistent with "testing of nerves" when nothing is at stake, and in fact the Soviets had little to gain and much to lose by testing Kennedy's nerve in 1962. The hypothesis that the installation of the missiles was a step towards a swap is inconsistent with the number of missiles installed (40 missiles, as opposed to 19 Jupiter C missiles in Turkey) and the long range character of the construction work on the Cuban sites.

The real background to the crisis was the deterioration of the Soviet strategic position as they perceived it in 1962.[28] From Sputnik in 1957 through the "missile gap" scare of 1960, the world perceived the United States to be losing strategic ground to the U.S.S.R. Perhaps the Soviets believed this themselves. But in the fall of 1961, the United States announced that the "missile gap" had never existed and that on the basis of new intelligence it was clear that the United States enjoyed a substantial and growing strategic superiority over the U.S.S.R. It is a mystery why the Soviets had failed to press the advantage in ICBMs they had established in 1957. Perhaps the explosion that killed 200 top Soviet rocket scientists in 1960 had paralyzed the Soviet ICBM program. Perhaps the budget crunch that reduced the Soviet Army by a million men in 1961 had made deployment of ICBMs economically impossible. Whatever the reason, by 1962 the Soviet Union had few ICBMs and was menaced by rapidly growing numbers of Polaris and Minuteman missiles and the ever ready fleet of giant B-52s. To make matters worse, the new American President employed Cold War rhetoric far more strident than Eisenhower's, and the new Secretary of Defense had just announced an American counterforce strategy that put the small stocks of Soviet strategic weapons at peril from an American first strike. Something had to be done to salvage the situation, and the course of action seized upon was the dispersion of Soviet forces, including the installation of nuclear missiles in Cuba.

The Soviets had some reason to think that the United States would tolerate the Cuban MRBMs. The Soviets had been supplying Castro with arms since mid-1960 without interference from the United States. In the spring of 1961 the United States had sponsored an invasion of Cuba by anti-Castro forces, but had failed to support the invasion with U.S. forces when the going got tough. Finally, the Soviets may have believed that the Administration would realize that MRBMs in Cuba made little difference to the strategic balance; what mattered was the number of missiles that could reach the United States, not the locations from which the missiles were fired.

The first Soviet MRBMs arrived in Cuba on 8 September 1962. Deployment of missiles began on 15 September, but the missiles were not quite operational when they were spotted by a U-2 reconaissance flight over Cuba on 14 October. The photographs were interpreted; the President was informed, and the crisis began in earnest on 16 October. The President formed an Executive Committee of the National Security Council to make recommendations, and it took three days of meetings for the Committee to make up its mind.

The representatives of the Joint Chiefs on the executive committee, especially General Curtis LeMay, strongly recommended an attack on Cuba aimed at destroying the missiles. This view was powerfully seconded by Dean Acheson, Truman's Secretary of State. Secretary of Defense McNamara and Attorney General Robert Kennedy recommended a naval blockade of Cuba, interrupting deliveries to Cuba and demanding removal of missiles already in place. The military representatives attacked the notion of the blockade on grounds that it could not guarantee the objective—removal of the missiles. Robert Kennedy argued that a surprise attack on a small nation was morally repugnant and that surprise attack might produce all-out war. The President decided for the blockade, preferring a lesser chance of removing the missiles to a greater chance of all out war.

On Monday, 22 October, the President informed leading members of Congress of the existence of the Soviet missiles and of his decision to institute a blockade. He was roundly criticized by the Congressional delegation, including Senators Long and Fulbright, for failing to take more drastic steps. But the decision on the blockade was already taken. That evening on television the President informed the nation that "unmistakable evidence has established the fact that a series of offensive missile sites is now in preparation on that imprisoned island." Kennedy went on to say:

> Neither the United States of America nor the world community of nations can tolerate deliberate deception and offensive threats on the part of any nation, large or small. We no longer live in a world where only the actual firing of weapons represents a sufficient challenge to a nation's security to constitute maximum peril. Nuclear weapons are so destructive and ballistic missiles are so swift that any substantially increased possibility of their use or any sudden change in their deployment may well be regarded as a substantial threat to peace. [Kennedy 1969 139]

The President invoked the spectre of appeasement

> The 1930s taught us a clear lesson: Aggressive conduct, if allowed to grow unchecked and unchallenged, ultimately leads to war. This nation is opposed to war. We are also true to our word. [Kennedy 1969 134–5]

and then announced the blockade:

> I have directed that the following initial steps be taken immediately:
> First: To halt this offensive build-up, a strict quarantine on all offensive military equipment under shipment to Cuba is being initiated. All ships of any kind bound for Cuba from whatever nation or port will, if found to contain cargoes of offensive weapons, be turned back. This quarantine will be extended, if needed, to other types of cargo and carriers. We are not at this time, however, denying the necessities of life as the Soviets attempted to do in their Berlin blockade of 1948.

Of the remaining points in the Kennedy plan, the most interesting is the threat of a "full retaliatory response" against the Soviet Union in the event of an attack from Cuba. McNamara's "controlled counterforce" doctrine enunciated at Ann Arbor was dissolving under the pressure of events:

> Third: It shall be the policy of this nation to regard any nuclear missile launched from Cuba against any nation in the Western Hemisphere as an attack by the

Soviet Union on the United States, requiring a full retaliatory response upon the Soviet Union. [Kennedy 1969 133ff]

On the Tuesday following Kennedy's speech, construction work proceeded at an increased pace on the Cuban sites and Russian ships continued steaming towards Cuba. Grocery stores in America reported increased sales of canned goods, and a number of urban Americans packed their possessions and headed for the hills. The first peak of the crisis came on Wednesday, when Soviet ships approached the quarantine line and 25 destroyers, two cruisers, and several American aircraft carriers waited on the other side.

As Robert Kennedy wrote: "One thousand miles away in the Atlantic Ocean the final decisions were going to be made in the next few minutes. President Kennedy had initiated the course of events, but he no longer had control of them." (Kennedy 1969 71) At 10:30 A.M. the first Russian ship reached the quarantine line and stopped dead in the water. Six other ships that approached the line turned around and steamed away. There was to be no battle on the seas. On Friday 26 October, U.S. ships stopped and boarded the *Marcula*, a Panamanian owned ship under Russian charter sailing from Riga to Cuba. No weapons were found and the ship was allowed to proceed.

But while the quarantine was functioning on the high seas, intelligence reports showed that work on the missile sites in Cuba had been stepped up. Russian advisors were also beginning to assemble Russian IL-28 Beagles, bombers with a range of 2,500 miles. The objective of removing the Russian missiles had not been achieved, and various preparations were made preparatory to an all out American military assault.

It was a war of nerves and on Friday evening Khrushchev's nerves buckled—or so it seemed. He sent a letter to Kennedy promising removal of the missiles in return for a pledge that American forces would not invade Cuba. The White House was elated, but hopes for immediate victory were dashed by the arrival of very different letter the following day (October 27). In the second letter Khrushchev proceed to swap removal of the missiles from Cuba for removal of American missiles from Turkey: "You are worried over Cuba," Khrushchev wrote:

You say that it worries you because it lies at a distance of ninety miles across the sea from the shores of the United States. However, Turkey lies next to us. Our sentinels are pacing up and down and watching each other. Do you believe that you have the right to demand security for your country and the removal of such weapons that you qualify as offensive, while not recognizing this right for us?

You have stationed devastating rocket weapons, which you call offensive, in Turkey literally right next to us. How then does recognition of our equal military possibilities tally with such unequal relations between our great states? This does not tally at all.

This is why I make this proposal: We agree to remove those weapons from Cuba which you regard as offensive weapons. We agree to do this and to state this commitment in the United Nations. Your representatives will make a statement to the effect that the United States, on its part, bearing in mind the anxiety and concern of the Soviet state, will evacuate its analogous weapons from Turkey. [Kennedy 1969 166]

The Khrushchev "swap" proposal could not be dismissed as unreasonable. In fact, Adlai Stevenson, one week before, had suggested just such a swap instead of the more aggressive approach of a naval quarantine around Cuba. The missiles in Turkey were obsolete, served no strategic purpose, and were slated for removal at some future date. A joint removal of missiles would provide Khrushchev with a way to satisfy American demands without excessive loss of face, and would provide the world with a useful example of bi-lateral cooperation for peace. On the other hand, any agreement with the Soviets at this advanced stage of the crisis would be denounced as appeasement and cowardice by opposition political leaders, and would jeopardize Democratic chances in the forthcoming election, less than two weeks away. There was little time for further maneuvering. The missile sites were nearing completion. Once again, the Joint Chiefs insisted on an air strike followed by an invasion on Monday, 29 October.

Kennedy chose not to accept Khrushchev's offer of a swap. But he did not reject it either. He ignored it, and wrote to Khrushchev accepting the original offer of removal of the missiles in return for pledges not to invade Cuba. That evening Robert Kennedy assured Ambassador Dobrynin that the missiles in Turkey would be removed, not immediately, but some time in the near future. Khrushchev gave in that Saturday night, and agreed to remove the Cuban missiles without simultaneous removal of American missiles from Turkey. Thus ended the worst crisis of the nuclear era, a crisis in which, in the opinion of leading participants, the odds were 50-50 that a nuclear war would begin.

The stresses and risks of the Cuban missile crisis produced a worldwide yearning for peace in 1963. Negotiations were opened between the U.S. and U.S.S.R. on the subject of banning nuclear tests. These discussions stumbled early in 1963 on the question of verificaion and on-site inspections, but in June 1963 a major step towards the reduction of accidental nuclear war was accomplished with the establishement of a "hot line" direct communications link between command centers in Moscow and in Washington. Also in June, Kennedy announced an American commitment to a negotiated ban on atmospheric nuclear tests, and a Partial Test Ban treaty banning atmospheric tests was signed in October 1963. Between 1945 and the signing of the treaty, France had conducted 3 atmospheric tests, Britain 23, the Soviet Union 124, and the United States 271, for a total explosive force equivalent to 511 million tons of TNT. In years since, the U.S. and the U.S.S.R. have conducted over 650 further tests, but all these tests have been underground.

In the late 1960s American attention was distracted from strategic problems by the agonies of the war in Vietnam. At first there seemed to be no role for nuclear weapons in Vietnam. The war was obviously a war for the hearts and minds of the South Vietnamese, and nuclear weapons are not prized for their ability to win hearts and minds. But a war that began as a conflict between pro-government and anti-government forces in South Vietnam in 1965 had by 1968 expanded into a war between American forces and forces from North Vietnam, supplied with Soviet arms and Soviet surface to air missiles. As increasing numbers of boys fell before North Vietnamese bullets, pressure mounted for a nuclear solution to the Vietnam impasse.

The pressure for use of tactical nuclear weapons in Vietnam peaked in March 1968 during the siege of Khe Sanh, the American replication of Dienbienphu. Once again, far north of Saigon, a large force of Caucasian soldiers was pinned down by Vietnamese troops. Just as Dulles had considered the use of nuclear weapons to extricate the French at Dienbienphu, General Westmoreland asked for tactical nuclear weapons to extricate American troops from constant shelling at Khe Sanh.

> Because the region around Khe Sanh was virtually uninhabited, civilian casualties would be minimal. If Washington officials were so intent on "sending a message" to Hanoi, surely small tactical nuclear weapons would be a way to tell Hanoi something, just as two atomic bombs had spoken convincingly to Japanese officials during World War II and the threat of atomic bombs induced the North Koreans to accept meaningful negotiations during the Korean War. It could be that use of a few small tactical nuclear weapons in Vietnam—or even the threat of them— might have quickly brought the war there to an end. [Westmoreland 1976 336]

But McNamara and Johnson thought otherwise and the request for tactical nuclear weapons was denied, leaving Westmoreland and others free to propound the view that in Vietnam the United States had fought with one hand tied behind its back.

After three years of failure in Vietnam the Democrats were defeated by Richard Nixon, who claimed during the campaign that he had a "secret plan" for bringing peace to Vietnam. Since after the election the plan was never revealed, it is idle to speculate on what was in Nixon's mind in the fall of 1968. Nevertheless, after he was elected, Nixon seems to have repeatedly considered threats of massive nuclear retaliation as a means of bringing North Vietnam to terms. In his memoirs, Nixon relates that less than six months after assuming office he had decided to threaten the North Vietnamese into surrendering:

> I decided to go for broke, in the sense that I would attempt to end the war one way or the other—either by negotiated agreement or by increased use of force. After half a year of sending peace signals to the Communists, I was ready to use whatever military pressure was necessary to prevent them from taking over South Vietnam by force. [Nixon 1978 393]

That "whatever military pressure was necessary" included nuclear weapons was vividly recollected by H.R. Haldeman, Nixon's White House Chief of Staff:

> When Nixon spoke of his desire to be a peacemaker, he was not just delivering words his listeners wanted to hear. Nixon not only wanted to end the Vietnam War, he was absolutely convinced he would end it in his first year. I remember during the campaign, walking along a beach, he once said, "I'm the one man in

this country who can do it . . . I call it the Madman Theory, Bob. I want the North Vietnamese to believe I've reached the point where I might do anything to stop the war. We'll just slip the word to them that, for God's sake, you know Nixon is obsessed about Communism. We can't restrain him when he's angry—and he has his hand on the nuclear button—and Ho Chi Minh himself will be in Paris in two days begging for peace."

As it turned out, it wasn't Bill Rogers, the future secretary of state, who slipped the word to the North Vietnamese, but a brilliant, impulsive, witty gentleman with an engaging German accent—Henry Kissinger. [Haldeman 1978 82–83]

Kissinger brought the nuclear message to the North Vietnamese at a secret meeting in Paris, 4 August 1969: "I have been asked to tell you, in all seriousness, we will be compelled, with great reluctance, to take measures of the gravest consequence." (Nixon 1978 396) These were words, which, in the nuclear age, even a child could understand. But the nuclear threat seems to have had no effect. Ho Chi Minh was no more intimidated by potential use of American nuclear bombs in 1969 than he had been at Dienbienphu in 1954. On 25 August, Ho wrote to Nixon: "The United States must cease its war of aggression and withdraw their troops from South Vietnam, respect the right of the population of the South and of the Vietnamese nation to dispose of themselves without foreign influence." (Nixon 1978 397.)

Perhaps the most frightening nuclear incident of the late 1960s, however, did not involve Vietnam or the United States. On 2 March 1969, Chinese and Soviet border patrols clashed on the island of Chenpao (Damansky) in the Ussuri river, on the Sino-Soviet border. The clash of 2 March was followed by a full fledged battle on 14 March. Further armed clashes followed. These battles, which left perhaps several hundred dead on each side, were the most serious military incidents to date between powers that possess nuclear weapons.[29]

After the Sino-Soviet split developed in 1960, the Soviets had approximately tripled their troop strength along the Chinese border. Ancestral Russian fears about the Chinese were exacerbated by the explosion of a Chinese nuclear device in 1964, and by evidence that the Chinese were developing an intermediate range ballistic missile that put Moscow within range of Chinese atomic bombs. After the March boarder clashes, Soviet forces along the boarder were beefed up. H.R. Haldeman later reported: "I am told that U.S. aerial photographs revealed hundreds of Soviet nuclear warheads stacked in piles." (Haldeman 1978 90–98)

The conventional skirmishes between the Russians and the Chinese ceased on 14 August, but the strategic situation remained grave. The Soviets now had special reason to worry about the new Chinese nuclear capability. To make matters worse, the United States had taken several steps in 1969 to ease Sino-American tensions, presenting the Soviets with the prospect of eventually being odd man out in the nuclear club. On 27 August, CIA director Helms reported that the Soviets seemed to be exploring the possibility of a pre-emptive conventional strike against Chinese nuclear facilities at Lop Nor in Sinkiang.[30]

On 5 September Under Secretary of State Elliot Richardson intimated in public that the United States could not stand by in the event of a pre-emptive Soviet strike again China: "Ideological differences between the two Communist giants are not our affair. We could not fail to be deeply concerned, however, with an escalation of this quarrel into a massive breach of international peace and security." (Kissinger 1979 184)

Despite this warning, rumors of a pre-emptive Soviet strike, perhaps a pre-emptive Soviet nuclear strike, persisted through the fall of 1969. According to Haldeman, in December the United States circulated two uncoded messages through its intelligence network:

> [Major General George Keegan] sent a message to the Secretary of Defense "in the clear" as if by accident. The message said that the U.S. had 1,300 nuclear weapons airborne—and named Soviet cities which were targeted for the bombs . . . [The second message] was to assure the Soviets that many thousands of Russian citizens in Siberia would also die as a consequence of nuclear fallout generated by a Soviet strike against China. [Haldeman 1978 93]

Whether things happened as Haldeman says and whether these messages had any real effect on Soviet plans is impossible to tell. The fact is there was no pre-emptive Soviet strike, and by the mid 1970s China was a full fledged and strategically independent member of the nuclear club.

(d) Soviet Developments and American Responses, 1964–72

Though Robert Kennedy wrote that his brother had done everything possible to avoid humiliating the Russians during the Cuban missile crisis, the outcome had embarassed the Soviets, and the agreements of 1963 convinced many in Russia, that Khrushchev was weak when dealing with the West. In October of 1964, Khrushchev was toppled from power and Leonid Brezhnev became First Secretary of the Party. The limited liberalizations and consumer concessions of the Khruschev era disappeared, and conventional and strategic forces were expanded.[31] The ICBM program, stepped up after 1962, went into high gear; the Soviets had 224 ICBMs by 1965, 570 in 1967, and 1,028 by 1969, only 24 short of the American total. The first generation of the Russian ICBMs, the SS-7 Saddler (1961), the SS-8 Sasin (1963) and the SS-9 Scarp (1965) were relatively inaccurate missiles, but they carried such enormous warheads (the SS-9 warhead may have a power of 25 megatons) that low accuracy detracted little from their strategic strength. In 1966 the Soviets introduced the more accurate SS-11 and in 1968 the equally accurate SS-13; the SS-11 was produced in particularly large numbers and provided the Soviet answer to the American Minuteman missile force.

The development of Soviet submarine-launched missiles was not as rapid as the development of the ICBM force; by 1967 the Soviets had only 107 SLBMs to compare with the American 656. But in 1968, the Soviets launched their first modern-class nuclear missile submarine, and the SLBM force grew slowly but steadily thereafter. By 1970 the Soviet SLBM force was nearly half the size of the United States force. The Soviets now had second strike capacity; they had achieved, for the first time, some sort of strategic parity with the United States.

The growth of Soviet missile forces was viewed with predictable apprehension in the United States. The news that the Soviets were constructing an anti-missile-missile (ABM) defense force around Leningrad and Moscow did not help calm these fears, since the growing numbers of Soviet missiles combined with the new ABM system had the potential—in nightmare scenarios where everything went wrong for the United States—of depriving the United States of second strike capacity.

If the Soviet ICBM force, in a first strike, could neutralize Minuteman and Titan, then the Soviet surface-to-air missiles *might* hold off the American B52s while the new ABM intercepted Polaris. Various remedies were proposed. One was to defend American land based ICBMs with an ABM system of their own. One was to improve the destructive force of those ICBMs surviving a first strike by multiplying the number of independently targeted re-entry vehicles (MIRV) on top of each missile. A third idea was to negotiate limits to strategic forces such that each side retained second strike capacity for an indefinite period.

All three remedies were explored. In September 1967 McNamara announced plans for the construction of the Safeguard anti-missile missile system to protect the Minutemen. In August 1968 the first tests of MIRV were conducted.[32] In November 1969 the first rounds of Strategic Arms Limitation Talks (SALT) were begun at Helsinki, with American scientists explaining to befuddled Soviet representatives, many of them career officers in the KGB, the distinction between zero sum and variable sum games and other fine points of American strategic science.

It took three years, and considerable "backdoor" maneuvering by National Security Advisor Kissinger, but the first SALT talks produced agreements limiting ABMs and limiting strategic missile forces on 26 May 1972.[33] The ABM agreement provided that each nation could install two ABM systems of 100 missiles each, one around the capital city, and one around a set of ICBM silos. The strategic missile force agreement called for a freeze in numbers of missile launchers, with the number of ICBM launchers restricted to the number in place in July 1972 and the number of SLBM launchers restricted to the number in place or under construction in May 1972. As Secretary of State Rogers explained, this meant that the United States was limited to 1,054 ICBM launchers and 656 SLBM launchers, while the Soviet Union was restricted to 1,618 ICBM launchers and 740 SLBM launchers. Furthermore, a number of restrictions were placed on the freedom of the U.S. and U.S.S.R. to convert "light" missile launchers into "heavy" missile launchers. For example, the U.S.S.R. was forbidden to substitute heavy SS-9 missiles for light SS-11 missiles within its total of 1,618 launchers.

The announcement of SALT limits giving the Soviet Union superiority in gross numbers of ICBM and SLBM launchers touched off a furor in the United States. To many it seemed obvious that the Soviets had gotten the best of it at SALT. On the other side, it could be argued that SALT had removed the main new threat to American second strike capacity—a widespread Soviet ABM defense—while it did nothing to limit the main new American threat to Soviet second strike capacity, the MIRV. On balance, a majority in the U.S. Senate was convinced that the United States lost nothing of strategic importance in SALT and the world had gained an increased chance for peace. SALT was ratified on 2 September 1972 by a vote of 88 to 2.

Negotiations between the U.S. and the U.S.S.R. continued through 1973 and 1974 on a variety of issues left unresolved by SALT. A second strategic arms agreement was announced in a communique issued from Vladivostock 24 November 1974. The communique was cryptic, but clarifying statements by members of the Administration showed that the U.S. and U.S.S.R. had agreed to a limit of 2,400 "strategic delivery vehicles" for each side; that is, a total of 2,400 ICBMs, SLBMs, and strategic bombers, the mix to be determined by each nation according to its lights. The Vladivostock accord set a limit of 1,320 MIRV launchers for each side and a limit of 313 very heavy missiles of the Titan or SS-9 type. Since the figures were equal for both sides, the Vladivostock accords generated little public controversy. Those opposed to the accords could complain that the United States had, for the first time, committed itself to a theoretical limit to the size of its bomber force. On the other hand, the Vladivostock restrictions on very heavy missiles mainly restricted the Soviets. But all sides would have to agree that the Vladivostock accords did not end the arms race. The agreement set no limits on qualitative improvements, and the quantitative "limits" were far in excess of the existing stockpiles of either side in 1974.

The Arms Race of the 1970s: Missile Accuracy and Warhead Proliferation

SALT I set limits on the number of missile launchers the U.S. and U.S.S.R. could possess. But it set no limits on the accuracy of these missiles nor did it limit the number of warheads each missile could carry. Since the U.S. and the U.S.S.R. remained intense competitors after SALT I, the SALT agreements, while choking off the arms race in missile launchers, spawned two new weapons competitions. By 1980, the warhead race and the accuracy race had transformed the strategic arsenals of both superpowers.[34]

(a) American Weapons Development

In the American ICBM force, the Minuteman I had been introduced in 1962 and the Minuteman II in 1966. The Minuteman I carried one warhead and had a Circular Error Probable (CEP) of 929 meters; the Minuteman II also carried one warhead and had a CEP of 630 meters. In 1970 the United States introduced Minuteman III; the Minuteman III carried three independently targetable warheads and had a CEP of only 220 meters. As the 1970s progressed, 500 Minuteman I missiles and 50 Minuteman II missiles were phased out and 550 Minuteman III missiles were put in their place, greatly improving the average accuracy of the American ICBM force and increasing the number of independently targetable warheads by 1,100. Corresponding changes on the Navy side produced an increase of 3,800 Navy warheads between 1970 and 1981.

In retrospect, historians may record that the American deployment of MIRVs in the early 1970s was one of the great blunders of the nuclear era. The MIRV had been developed as a response to the Soviet ABM, but when the Soviet ABM was curtailed by SALT I in 1972, deployment did not stop even though the rationale had disappeared. These deployments (a) threatened Soviet ICBMs and prompted a step-up in the production of Soviet ICBMs; (b) encouraged the Soviets to build their own MIRV; (c) made a first strike by either side more likely, since with MIRV a first strike may be so devastating that the attacking country may find the counter-strike tolerable; and (d) produced larger arsenals that would make nuclear war much more destructive if it ever did occur. Thus MIRV worsened the situation for both sides, and both would have been better off if limits on MIRV had been negotiated in SALT I. The destablizing effects of MIRV are now apparent to nearly everyone, and President Reagan's blue ribbon panel on strategic issues, headed by General Brent Scowcroft, recommended in April 1983 that the United States return to single warhead missiles in the 1990s (Scowcroft 1983).

SALT I said nothing about bombers, and as the 1970s progressed the American strategic bomber fleet was also transformed, without the introduction of a single new plane. Before 1972, American B52s and FB 111As had carried atomic bombs, which, in action, were to be released over their targets and were propelled to the target by gravity. Starting in 1972, B52s in the G and H series and FB 111As began to be equipped with short-range attack missiles (SRAMs), which propelled nuclear warheads to targets over 150 kilometers away from the plane. The principal advertisement for the SRAM was that it made American B52s and FB 111As less vulnerable to attack by Soviet anti-aircraft defenses, but at least as significant for the strategic balance was the fact that a regular B52 could carry only four nuclear bombs, but a B52 equipped with SRAM could carry 20 missiles with 20 nuclear warheads. Likewise a regular FB 111A could carry only two nuclear bombs, but as many as six SRAM. With these changes in American bombers, together with the MIRVing of American ICBMs and SLBMs, it is no surprise that the total number of deliverable warheads in the American strategic arsenal grew rapidly every year after SALT I. If we define a "force loading" as either a nuclear bomb or nuclear warhead available for attack or counterattack, the United States had about 4,000 force loadings in 1970 and about 9,200 force loadings in 1980. Perhaps more instructive is the increase in the number of independently targetable nuclear weapons in the American arsenal. In 1970 there were about 1,870 independently targeted American warheads. In 1980 there were over 7,000.

(b) Soviet Weapons Development

The Soviets were determined not to be left at the gate in the warhead race. In early 1974, defense officials annnounced (with exaggerated shock, as if the challenge of American MIRVs would go unanswered) that less than two years after SALT I, the Soviets were in the advanced stages of testing four new ICBMs. The main Soviet ICBMs of the 1960s had been the heavy SS-9 (introduced in 1965); the somewhat lighter SS-11 (introduced in 1966, CEP 1,400 meters), and the light and mobile SS-13 (introduced in 1969, CEP 1,900 meters). After SALT I, the SS-9 was replaced by the SS-18; numbers of SS-11s, were replaced with SS-17s and SS-19s; and the SS-13 was to be supplemented by the SS-16. All of these missiles carried greater payloads with more accuracy than their predecessors.

The first Soviet MIRV was the SS-19, introduced in 1974 and carrying six warheads. The SS-19 had an on-board computer to improve guidance, and had a CEP of about 900 meters. The SS-17, operational in 1975, carried only four warheads, but had a CEP of 480 meters. The big SS-18, introduced without MIRV in 1974, was deployed with eight MIRVs in 1976. In the late 1970s, the Soviets also introduced single warhead versions of the SS-17, SS-18, and SS-19; these late models had CEPs of 120 meters, 250 meters, and 250 meters respectively, the equal of their Minuteman counterparts and far more accurate than the American Titan II.

Though the Soviets made these and other improvements in their ICBM force in the 1970s, they made few comparable changes in their strategic submarine and manned bomber forces. The principal Soviet SLBMs—the SSN-5 and SSN-6—answered only to the Polaris A2 and Polaris A3, and though the Soviets tested one submarine launched MIRVed missile (the NX 17), they did not deploy it in a MIRV format. In the air, they continued to fly the old Bear and Bison bombers, which carried one nuclear bomb apiece. The new Soviet bomber, the supersonic Backfire, introduced in 1974 and the subject of much commentary on the American side, did not have the ability to reach the United States and return. Nevertheless, despite restraint in bombers and SLBMs, the number of Soviet warheads available for delivery did grow rapidly through the 1970s. In 1970, the Soviets had about 1,650 warheads; in 1981 they had about 5,300.

As the Soviet warhead totals grew and Soviet missile accuracy increased, the alarm was sounded in the United States by persons with a special interest in perceived Soviet threats. One obvious point of comparison was missile size, and the Soviet missiles in general were larger than their American counterparts. The SS-19, for example, carried a payload of 7,000 pounds; while the equivalent American missile, the Minuteman III, had a payload of only 1,200 pounds. As a result, the total megatonnage in the Soviet arsenal far outstripped the United States. By 1971, Soviet missiles could deliver 4,694 megatons, American missiles 3525 megatons. This disturbed those Americans who did not want to be behind the Soviets in anything.

It should be noted that gross megatonnage is not the index of strategic strength. Another index is "equivalent megatonnage," a measure of the destructive force of a bomb on the ground. There is also "lethality," a measure of the ability of a bomb to destroy a hard target. Lethality or "k," is a function of equivalent megatonnage of the warhead and the accuracy of the missile that carries it. Even on some of these more esoteric indices, however, by the late 1970s the United States seemed to be falling behind. The most lethal missile in the American arsenal, the Minuteman III, had a k-factor of only 34. This was exceeded by the Soviet SS-18 m4 (k = 35), the SS-17m2 (k = 71), the SS-18 m1 (k = 179), the SS-18m3 (k = 207), and the SS-19m2 (k = 255). It was 20 years after Sputnik, but Soviet land based missiles had finally come into their own.

(c) Alleged Vulnerabilities and the Move to Counterforce

As the new Soviet missiles came into service, a number of citizens' groups, most notably the Washington-based Committee on the Present Danger, sprang into action, issuing warnings to the American public about improvements in Soviet stragetic forces.[35] Improvements in the accuracy of Russian missiles, the Committee argued, produced missiles with k-factors so high that a massive Soviet launch towards the United States could destroy most Minuteman missiles right in their silos. With Soviet forces steadily improving, the Minuteman was in peril, and the other legs of the strategic triad were wobbly. The B-52 was obsolete, and the Poseidon was inaccurate. America needed a new bomber, the B-1; a new land-based missile, the MX; a new air-launched missile, the cruise missile; and a new submarine, the Trident. With these, the United States could match the lethality of the new Soviet missiles.

The B-1, the MX, and the Trident had, in fact been on the drawing boards since the late 1960s, Congress, however, still embroiled in Vietnam and increasingly sceptical of the usefulness of force in achieving foreign goals, had been reluctant to fund new strategic programs. It was widely felt that the American submarine force alone provided an assured destruction capacity for the indefinite future, and that further defense spending was a waste of money. In addition, each of the new programs had conspicuous technical flaws. The B-1 bomber was intended as the answer to the latest Soviet anti-aircraft defenses, but many defense analysts believed that a far better solution to Soviet anti-aircraft defenses was to mount the new air-launched cruise missile on the B-52, which could fire the missile towards Russia from far outside the range of Russian defenses. The MX missile was supposed to meet the challenge the new Soviet missiles raised against Minuteman, but technical specialists had difficulty devising a basing mode for the MX that provided appreciably more "survivability" than the Minuteman itself. The Trident program called for 24 SLBMs on each new submarine as compared to 16 SLBMs on each Polaris sub. Thus each Trident submarine risked a larger percentage of the American SLBM force than did each Polaris, and this diminished American second strike capacity.

Despite Congressional opposition, a determined band of weapons supporters managed to keep all these programs alive through the lean years before the election of Reagan in 1980. The cruise missile was saved by the personal intervention of National Security Advisor Henry Kissinger in October 1973. Though President Carter "cancelled" the B-1 bomber in 1977, the plane stayed alive in the research stage as a "launching platform" for the new cruise missiles. Carter retained the MX as penance for having cancelled the

B-1, and the Trident program moved forward on the general grounds that an entire decade should not pass without the introduction of at least one new strategic system by the United States.

But the new systems were not innovation for innovation's sake. The new weapons were more versatile, more accurate, and more lethal than their predecessors. The Minuteman III missile had a k-factor of 34; its replacement, the MX, had a k-factor of 204. The Poseidon C3 missile had a k-factor of 2; the Trident C-4 had a k-factor of 12; and the Trident II missile had a projected k-factor of 24. The cruise missile, equipped with sensors that "read" the terrain as the missile approached its target, had an astounding CEP of 30 meters and correspondingly astounding k-factor of 1,305.

Was there a strategic purpose behind these new lethalities? If the goal of the American stragetic arsenal was simply to prevent Soviet attack by threatening a counterattack against "soft" targets like Russian cities, then lethalities far less than these would suffice. The MX, the Trident missile, and the cruise missile were obviously designed to take out "hard" targets, like Russian missile silos, as well as the softer, non-military targets; in short, the old weapons were largely "countervalue" weapons while the new weapons were largely "counterforce" weapons. When the Soviets had introduced weapons with pronounced counterforce capacities in the 1970s, the Pentagon had labelled these weapons as steps towards a Soviet first strike. If this was true, it followed that the new American counterforce weapons were steps towards an American first strike. If the SS-18 threatened Minuteman, then the MX threatened the SS-18. In fact, since the Soviets kept a far higher percentage of their strategic forces in land-based ICBMs, the MX was a far more serious threat to Russia than the SS-18 was to the United States.

What was the strategic purpose of developing missiles that implied American first-strike threats, tempted Soviet pre-emption, and increased the chance of nuclear war? Logic dictated that the answer to any Soviet first strike threat was improved second-strike capacity, not a first strike threat from the United States. The explanation of the new affection for counterforce lies partly in little-discussed changes in American strategic doctrine in the 1970s. As we have seen, McNamara had proposed a flexible response counterforce doctrine as early as 1962. As more and more Soviet ICBMs were placed in hardened silos, however, the number of counterforce options available to the President dwindled, and by 1968 talk of flexible response had been all but replaced by talk of assured destruction. The doctrine of assured destruction (and nothing else) came in for considerable criticism during the first Nixon administration. First of all, exclusive reliance on threats of massive counterstrikes made it clear to all parties that American strategic forces would be used only in defense of the United States. Thus under assured destruction, strategic threats in support of American allies lost credibility. Second, the assured destruction posture did not help solve a lingering strategic problem, which for want of a better name could be called the "limited Soviet strike problem."

The limited Soviet strike problem had first been studied by limited war theorists in the late 1950s. As Bernard Brodie explained it in 1959:

Suppose, for example, the enemy attacked our retaliatory forces with great power but took scrupulous care to avoid major injury to our cities, a form of attack that has already been publicly proposed as a strategy we might adopt ourselves if we ever initiated the attack . . . If his attack is successful to any serious degree, we should be left with a severely truncated retalitory force while his remained relatively intact. These hardly seem propitious circumstances for us to initiate an exchange of city destruction which would quickly use up our remaining power, otherwise useful for bargaining, in an act of suicidal vindictiveness. Our hitting at enemy cities would simply force the greater destruction of our own, and in substantially greater degree.

Thus it is easy to imagine a situation where it would be of little use to hit the enemy's airfields and disastrous as well as futile to attack his cities. [Brodie 1959 292–93]

Brodie proposed no solution for the problem, but it was generally believed that a limited Soviet strike could be deterred by the threat of a limited American counterattack, and the problem was thought dispatched by the flexible response posture put into effect in 1962. With the ossification of flexible response in the late 1960s, the problem surfaced again. In June 1969 Kissinger briefed Nixon on the difficulty, and the President noted it in his February 1970 foreign policy address to Congress: "Should the President, in the event of a nuclear attack, be left with the single option of ordering the mass destruction of enemy civilians, in the face of the certainty that it would be followed by the mass slaughter of Americans?" (Nixon 1970 54–55.)

The remedy, as Kissinger and Nixon perceived it, was the development of new strategic forces and the redeployment of old ones. Nothing could be done, however, until the war in Vietnam was over. With the signing of the Vietnam Peace Agreement and the arrival of Schlesinger as Secretary of Defense in 1973, the development of counterforce options began in earnest.

Schlesinger called for the development of the MX, the Trident, the cruise missile, and the B-1, but all these programs ran into opposition in Congress. Congress could say nothing, however, about the redeployment of existing systems, and Schlesinger set about revising the Single Integrated Operational Plan, which had remained virtually unchanged since 1962. The changes in the SIOP were explained by Schlesinger in his report to Congress on 4 March 1974:

Threats against allied forces, to the extent that they could be deterred by the prospect of nuclear retaliation, demand both more limited responses than destroying cities and advanced planning tailored to such lesser responses. Nuclear threats to our strategic forces, whether limited or large-scale, might well call for an option to respond in kind against the attackers military forces. In other words, to be credible, and hence effective over the range of possible contingencies, deterrence must rest on many options and on a spectrum of capabilites (within the constraints of SALT) to support these options. [Schlesinger 1974 38]

Schlesinger went on to say:

Targets for nuclear weapons may include not only cities and silos, but also airfields, many other types of military installations, and a variety of other important assets not necessarily collocated with urban populations. We already have a long list of such possible targets; now we are grouping them into operation plans which would be more responsive to the range of challenges that might face us. [Schlesinger 1974 39]

Secretaries of Defense subsequent to Schlesinger—Rumsfeld, Brown, Weinberger—all reaffirmed Schlesinger's insistence on the development and maintenance of a large number of counterforce options. Carter's Presidental Directive #59, which caused such a stir in 1979, seems to have been little more than an implementation or elaboration of the Schlesinger doctrine.

The development of limited nuclear options under Schlesinger led to he prospect that a nuclear war might turn out to be a protracted affair, not the short spasm usually envisaged in popular accounts. If a key problem of the 1960s was preventing a nuclear war from starting, a key theoretical problem for the 1970s was preventing a nuclear war that had reached stage N from going on to stage N + 1. The solution required that, at every step, the enemy must be deterred from taking the next step, and this became known among strategists as the problem of escalation dominance. Fortunately for the supporters of new weapons systems, escalation dominance seemed to requre a wide variety of counterforce options. It also required a sophisticated system of command, communications, control, and intelligence. Defense budgets in the late 1970's contained appropriations in the hundred of millions of dollars to provide communications links that could survive Soviet attacks in the event of protracted war.

With the election of President Reagan in November 1980, the strategic views of the Committee on the Present Danger became semi-official doctrine. Reagan reaffirmed the Carter commitment to the MX, the cruise missile, and the Trident submarine, called for a revival of the B-1 bomber, and asked for substantial increases in the defense budget. Major increases were allotted to communications, commmand, and control; and in 1982 news leaks revealed that the Weinberger Pentagon was preparing studies of defense needs for extended nuclear wars.[36] Whether all the Reagan defense programs could get through a Congress battered by record deficits and the Great Recession of the 1980s remained to be seen. But one strategic innovation was certainly forthcoming regardless of the recession: the transformation of the B-52 force with air-launched cruise missiles. With a load of 20 cruise missiles, each with a range of 1,300 miles, every B-52 in the mid 1980s would boast the strategic power and versatility of a 1960s Polaris submarine. With the survivability of a mobile missile and the accuracy of an ICBM, the cruise missile was the model weapon for the counterforce doctrines of the post-Schlesinger era.

Into the 1980's: Arms and Allies

The SALT treaty imposed limits on strategic forces only; no limits were suggested for theater nuclear weapons or for tactical nuclear weapons. As a result, the arms races in these areas pushed forward, and tactical and theater nuclear weapons became a Cold War bone of contention. The main theater of tension was Europe. Both NATO and Warsaw pact had deployed nuclear weapons for decades:[37] NATO had its Honest John in 1953, its nuclear cannon in 1954, its Pershing (range 400 miles) and Sergeant missiles in 1962, and its Lance missile in 1972. Nuclear weapons were carried by British and French nuclear submarines, and by U.S. carriers on patrol in the Mediterranean. The Soviet Union had introduced nuclear cannon in the 1950s, the Scud and Frog short-range missiles in 1957, Scud B in 1965 and the Scaleboard (range 500 miles) in 1969. The Warsaw pact had no carriers, but in 1962 they deployed SS-4 IRBMs (range 1,200 miles), and in 1965 they added the SS-5 (range 2,300 miles). Thus, all cities in Eastern and Western Europe stood in peril of nuclear attack, even if the continental United States stayed clear of war.

Starting in 1977, the Soviets began replacing the old SS-4 and SS-5 IRBMs with the new SS-20. The SS-20 has a range of 3,000 miles and carries three 150 kiloton warheads: it is the first MIRVed IRBM. As increasing numbers of SS-20s were deployed in 1978 and 1979, several NATO capitals responded with alarm. In December 1979, after a heated debate, NATO ministers in Brussels decided to deploy 576 new weapons—108 Pershing II missiles and 468 cruise missiles—as a response to the deployment of the SS-20. Needless to say, the decision to deploy new NATO missiles did not slow the pace of SS-20 deployment, and in 1981 President Reagan offered to withold the new NATO missiles in return for the elimination of Soviet IRBMs. Since the Soviets regard their IRBMs as a balance against American carriers, NATO submarines, and other western forward based nuclear weapons systems, the Reagan "offer" was rejected forthwith. The decision to deploy new Pershings and cruise missiles throughout NATO led to widespread public protests in Europe, but it seems likely that the new weapons will be in place by the end of 1984.

The Four Arms Races of the Nuclear Era

If we review the development of strategic arsenals from the 1940s to the present day, it becomes clear that there has not been one strategic arms race involving the United States and the Soviet Union, but at least four different strategic races.

The first race (1940–1953) was the race for nuclear weapons themselves, the fission bomb and the fusion bomb. The race to create the fission bomb began with a multinational theoretical effort in the late 1930s and turned into national engineering races in the 1940s. The United States won the fission race in 1945, beating the Soviets by 4 years. The race for the fusion bomb was closer; the United States was first in 1952, beating the Soviet Union by a year.

The second race (1947–1959) was the race for a system to deliver these weapons, which turned into a race to develop and produce manned bombers. The United States introduced the first jet bomber in 1947; the Soviet Union produced a long-range bomber in 1954 and a truly intercontinental bomber in 1956. In all phases of this race the United States remained far ahead in terms of numbers. When manned bombers ceased to be of primary strategic importance because of the introducton of ICBMs, United States bombers still outnumbered the Soviet fleet of Bears and Bisons more than ten to one.

The third race—the missile race—began with Sputnik in 1957 and ended with the introduction of MIRV in 1970. The Soviets had a slight edge in missiles in 1958 and 59, but the United States forged ahead with the introduction of Polaris in 1960 and Minuteman in 1962. In the early 1960s the United States was far ahead in numbers of ICBMs and SLBMs. The Soviet Union closed the gap in the late 1960s, but when the race ended in 1970 the Soviets were still far behind.

In the 1970s and 1980s the crucial indices of strategic strength were numbers of warheads and the accuracy with which they could be delivered. The United States introduced MIRV in 1970, four years before the Soviet Union, and as a result the gap between the already superior American arsenal and the Soviet arsenal widened until 1975. For the remainder of the decade, the Soviets devoted themselves to narrowing the gap, but even by 1982 they were still several thousand warheads short of the American total. In the accuracy race, superior gudiance systems kept American missiles more accurate, in every year of the decade, than their Soviet counterparts. Even before the election of Reagan in 1980 and subsequent increases in budgets for strategic programs, the United States retained a margin of superiority in both quality and quantity of strategic weapons.

Notes

1. There are many histories of the pioneering years of atomic physics. One that indicates how each development in physics was a step towards the possibility of producing atomic weapons is Clark 1980.

2. The importance of Bequerel's work was described by Madame Curie in her *Traité de a Radioactivité* (1910), relevant portions of which are translated in Taton 1960 204. Other crucial ideas in the early history of atomic physics are presented in Rutherford and Soddy 1903 576–91, and Rutherford 1904.

3. Of the many books explaining the special theory of relativity, none surpasses Einstein's own *Relativity: The Special and General Theory* (1916). Einstein's exposition is exceedingly concise. A good exposition with more background information is Born 1924.

4. See Born, 1924 278–289.

5. Wells acknowledged that many of the ideas in *The World Set Free* are adapted from Soddy 1909.

6. Hahn's autobiographical account of the first splitting of an atomic nucleus is given in Hahn 1970.

7. A good bit of the physics needed to understand the chain reactions involved in the atomic bomb was released by the U.S. Government in 1945 in Smyth 1945. For Szilard's work on chain reactions see Szilard 1972, and Szilard 1968.

8. For the history of the Manhattan Project, see Hewlitt and Anderson 1939/46, Groves 1962

9. The most complete account of the physical effects of the atomic bombings of Hiroshima and Nagasaki was compiled for the Committee for the Complication of Damage 1981. For fatalities see 113–14. See also Hersey 1946 and Lifton 1968.

10. For the early history of the Cold War see Fleming 1961; Kolko 1968; Kolko 1972; Sherwin 1975; and Yergin 1977. All these books have their prejudices, but the prejudices are so apparent as to be neutralized by their visibility.

11. See Anderson 1976.

12. According to David Alan Rosenberg, recently declassified documents indicate that the American nuclear arsenal consisted of 2 bombs in 1945, 9 in 1946, 13 in 1947, 50 in 1948, at least 292 in 1950, and approximately 400 bombs in 1951. Rosenberg 1982 26.

13. For the early history of atomic diplomacy see Herken 1982, and Quester 1970. For a list of demonstrations of strength involving nuclear threats, see Blechman and Kaplan 1978.

14. Early American plans for atomic war against Russia are described in Rosenberg 1983, 3–71, especially pages 12–21; and Wells 1981 31–52.

15. For the decision to build the hydrogen bomb see Schilling 1961, 24–46; Herken 304–338; and Rosenberg 1979 61–87. The story of the "Super" controversy is told from Teller's side in Teller 1962. The controversy lingers on. In November 1982, Hans Bethe argued that on the basis of the best information available in 1950, Oppenheimer was right in declaring that the H-bomb was technically impossible using all known methods. See Broad 1982 769–772. It follows that Oppenheimer's opposition to the bomb was basically scientific, not political and that Teller's support was basically political, not scientific, the reverse of the usual description of the battle between the two physicists.

16. For the perceived difficulties in using nuclear weapons in Korea see Brodie 1959 319–21. Curtis LeMay is quoted as saying in 1954: "There are no suitable strategic air targets in Korea." See Rosenberg 1981–82 27. For the development of missiles, see Beard, 1976.

17. For continuities between Truman's and Eisenhower's ideas about the use of nuclear weapons, see Wells 1979 and Rosenberg 1983.

18. For the development of ICBMs see Beard 1976; Armacost 1977. For the development of the Polaris missile see Sapolsky 1972.

19. Eisenhower's confidence that nuclear weapons had forced the Communists to accept the peace in Korea is expressed in Eisenhower 1963 179–81.

20. The suggestion for a pre-emptive nuclear attack on the Soviet Union came from the Advance Study group of the Joint Chiefs of Staff and was presented to Eisenhower in a briefing in May 1954. Eisenhower did not denounce the proposal at the briefing, but he did explicitly approve NSC 5440 (28 Dec. 1954), which states, "The United States and its allies must reject the concept of preventive war or acts intended to provoke war." See Rosenberg, 1983 34.

21. The Formosa Straits confrontation is well described in Fleming 1961 707–737.

22. For the implied presence of nuclear weapons in the crises of the late 1950s see Blechman and Kaplan 1978, chs. 7 and 9.

23. The capacities of Soviet strategic aircraft in the 1950s are summarized in Polmar 1982 ch. 4.

24. For the response on the American side see Rosenberg 1983 46–61; and Quester 1970 145–97.

25. McNamara, "The U.S. has come to the conclusion," *The New York Times*, 17 June 1962. The story of the "Flexible Response" strategy is given in Kaufmann 1964. See also Quester 1970 205–53; and Halperin 1962.

26. The York/Wiesner argument that civil defense destabilizes the strategic balance is given in Wiesner 1964 35.

27. The problem of deciding how may weapons must be purchased to assure Soviet destruction in the event of Soviet attack is discussed in Enthoven and Smith 1971. See also York 1970 147–73, and Roherty 1970.

28. For the Soviet strategic situation and strategic thought before the Cuban missile crisis, see Berman and Baker 1982 38–50. Of the numerous books on the Cuban missile crisis, none will surpass Robert F. Kennedy, *Thirteen Days* (Kennedy 1969).

29. For accounts of the Ussuri river incidents, see Maxwell 1973 730–39; Kissinger 1979 171–73; and Haldeman 1978.

30. For Helms' report, see *The Washington Star*, 28 August and 29 August 1969.

31. For Soviet strategic developments in this period see Holloway 1983 39–70; Baker and Berman 1982 41–67; Polmar 1982 37–51.

32. For McNamara's response in the Johnson years, see McNamara 1968. For the debate on whether or not to build the "thin" anti-missile system, see Bethe and Garwin 1968 (anti); and Brennan 1969 (pro). For the debate on MIRV, see York 1969–1970; and York 1970 173–241.

33. For the SALT negotiations and Kissinger's "back door" efforts, see Kissinger 1979 112–150, 810–823, 1202–58. Other accounts include Newhouse 1973; and Wolfe 1979.

34. The arms race of the 1970s is chronicled in the yearly volumes issued by the Institute for Strategic Studies, London, under the title *The Military Balance*. For an analysis of the strategic effects of MIRV see York 1970 173–87.

35. A fraction of the American body politic was unhappy with SALT I from the day it was signed. On that day, the Senate voted 56–35 in favor of an amendment offered by Henry Jackson calling on the President not to enter into any agreement with the Soviet that provided the United States with "levels of strategic forces inferior to the Soviet Union." The story of the campaign against detente and arms control in the late 1970s is sketched in Cox 1982 29–120, and Scheer 1983. Many of the early arguments about detente and the alleged Soviet threat are presented with a tilt in the "threat" direction in Prager 1976. The virtues of the new counterforce approach are extolled and expounded in Holst and Nerlich 1977. Some new arguments why detente with the Soviets is an impossible idea are presented in Gray 1977, especially ch. 3, "Geopolitics and Soviet Power: Breaking Out of the Heartland." For a review of perceived threats in arms control agreements under negotiation in the Carter Administration see Nitze, Dougherty, and Kane, 1979.

Less technical articles capturing the flavor of Committee on the Present Danger thinking are Podhoretz 1976; Pipes 1977 and Rostow 1979. For responses to the Committee on the Present Danger position see Rosenfeld 1977 and Kaplan 1982 47–53. For technical and strategic analyses of the new counterforce weapons see Carter 1974; Scoville 1981; and Kaplan 1983 26–34.

36. The news that the Pentagon was studying plans for extended nuclear wars was leaked by Richard Halloran in "Pentagon Draws Up First Strategy for Fighting a Long Nuclear War," *The New York Times*, 30 May 1982. See also, "The Five Year War Plan," *The New York Times* 10 June 1982.

37. For background on nuclear weapons and NATO see Kissinger 1957, and Schilling 1973. For recent developments see Burt 1977; Hughes 1978; and Kissinger, 1979. For a general rebuttal, see Bundy 1982.

Appendix: Four Strategic Races

1. Total nuclear bombs	U.S.	U.S.S.R.
1945	2	0
1946	9	0
1947	13	0
1948	50	0
1949	100	5
1950	300	30
1951	400	50
1952	1500	150
1953	2500	150
1954	2500	350
1955	5000	500
1956	7000	2000
1957	10000	2500

2. Manned Intercontinental bombers	U.S.	U.S.S.R.
1950	10	0
1951	100	0
1952	250	0
1953	329	0
1954	795	0
1955	908	0
1956	1035	100
1957	1300	140
1958	1587	150
1959	1844	150

3. Strategic Missiles	U.S.	U.S.S.R.
1957	0	1
1958	0	5
1959	6	10
1960	57	20
1961	217	50
1962	438	150
1963	648	197
1964	1250	297
1965	1308	331
1966	1496	399
1967	1710	677
1968	1710	979
1969	1710	1224
1970	1710	1603

4. Independently Targetable Warheads[a]	U.S.	U.S.S.R.
1969	1710	1603
1970	1874	1722
1971	2938	1887
1972	3858	1996
1973	5210	2114
1974	5678	2222
1975	6410	2302
1976	6842	2758
1977	7130	3568
1978	7274	4427
1979	7000	5325
1980	7032	5920
1981	7032	6848
1982	7354	6911

[a]Does not include gravity bombs, or nuclear weapons carried by SRAM or cruise.

3

Present Risks and Plans for Nuclear War

The Nuclear Threshold

As the decade of the eighties began, at least six and possibly eight nations were in possession of nuclear weapons.[1] The vast and growing arsenals of the nuclear powers, manned by thousands of vigilant personnel and informed by hundreds of orbiting satellites, stood ready and faced each other across the Arctic Sea, the plains of North Germany, and the wastes of Sinkiang. The Americans had 52 Titan missiles, 1,000 Minuteman Missiles, 80 Polaris Missiles, 432 Poseidon missiles, 64 Trident missiles, 41 missile submarines, 348 B-52 bombers, 132 F-111 fighter bombers, 224 nuclear-capable fighter-bombers in England, 72 such fighter-bombers in Korea, 96 more on two carriers in the Mediterranean, and 144 more on three carriers in the Pacific. The Soviets had 470 SS-11 missiles, 60 SS-13s, 180 SS-17s, 311 SS-18s, 210 SS-19s, an assortment of 989 submarine-launched ballistic missiles on 84 missile submarines, 340 SS-4, 40 SS-5, and 230 SS-20 intermediate-range ballistic missiles, 140 intercontinental bombers, and large numbers of land-based strike aircraft capable of carrying nuclear weapons. The British had 4 submarines with 16 Polaris missiles each. The French had 5 nuclear submarines, with 16 M-20 missiles each, plus 18 intermediate range ballistic missiles. The Chinese had 4 CSS-3 intercontinental ballistic missiles, 75 intermediate-range ballistic missiles, and 50 medium-range ballistic missiles. NATO and Warsaw pact forces were equipped with a variety of nuclear cannon and short range missiles. The Indians had exploded a nuclear device; the South Africans might have, the Pakistanis were getting close, and the Israelis were widely believed to keep a disassembled stock of nuclear weapons as an ace in the hole. Yet there was no war between nuclear powers, and though there had been wars aplenty since 1945, for over 35 years no nuclear weapon had been used in war.

The restraint exercised by the nuclear powers since 1945 has had an effect. All nations, and all national leaders, have some sense that nuclear weapons are taboo. Like poison gas, they should not be used at all, or used only in cases of supreme national emergency. Any nation that resorts to nuclear weapons will be, in an instant, an outlaw among civilized nations; any nation that breaks the nuclear peace will be embargoed, blockaded, and stigmatized by the rest of the world. National leaders who contemplate the use of nuclear weapons must keep all this in mind. There is, in short, a threshold that must be reached before a nuclear power will break the nuclear peace, and since 1945, no nation possessing nuclear weapons has reached that threshold.

There are two ways of interpreting this uneasy nuclear peace. We can say that mutual deterrence, fear of nuclear war, the balance of power, and the developing nuclear taboo have preserved the peace; that with deterrence, war is not likely, and that if deterrence is preserved we will have continuing stability and lasting peace. Or we can say that nuclear war in the long run is likely to occur so long as nuclear weapons remain in the hands of hostile powers; that nuclear war has been probable since the resurrection of the Cold War, and that only luck or the grace of God has spared us thus far from the horrors of nuclear war. If the first interpretation is right, preservation of the *status quo* will prevent nuclear war. If the second interpretation is right, preservation of the *status quo* will eventually lead to nuclear war. One thing is certain: both interpretations cannot be right.

Seven Ways Across the Nuclear Threshold

Nuclear weapons can be used intentionally or they can be used by mistake. There are four ways they can be used intentionally: (a) if a national leader seeks to begin and win an aggressive nuclear war; (b) if a fanatic explodes a nuclear bomb as part of a campaign of terror; (c) if a national leader finds himself losing a conventional war and escalates to the nuclear level in hopes of avoiding defeat; and (d) if a nation is struck by a nuclear attack and uses its weapons to launch a nuclear counter-strike. There are three ways they might be used be mistake: (a) if a subordinate with control of nuclear weapons launches them without proper authority; (b) if a national leader orders a launch as a result of misinformation; or (c) if a nuclear weapon goes off by itself because of mechanical failure.[2] All seven possibilities deserve consideration.

(a) Aggressive Nuclear War

Nuclear weapons are exceedingly destructive and the radiation that they leave behind is as dangerous to the victor as to the victim. In considering the possibility of aggressive nuclear war, we have to imagine circumstances in which a national leader wants an enemy destroyed, not just conquered. This will happen if the enemy is viewed as a dire threat to national survival. It will also happen if the enemy is seen as a kind of demon.

In the nuclear era, the main threat to national survival is the threat posed by nuclear weapons. It is not surprising, then, that the situations in which pre-emptive nuclear strikes have been most discussed have been situations in which a potential enemy was on the verge of acquiring nuclear weapons or the means to deliver them. Pre-emptive American nuclear strikes against Russia were discussed in the late 1940s, before Russia acquired the bomb, and in 1954, before Russia acquired the ICBM.[3] The United States may have contemplated a pre-emptive nuclear strike against China in 1962, before China's first bomb, and Russia certainly considered one in 1969, before China's first ICBM.[4]

Though the possibility of a pre-emptive nuclear strike of this sort exists, the chance that one will occur in the coming decades appears slight. If the development of nuclear weapons is the threat that deserves pre-emption, then in most cases the pre-emption can be achieved by a conventional attack, which removes the nuclear threat without violating the nuclear taboo. The Soviet strike against China in 1969, if it had occured, would in all probability have been a conventional attack using high explosives to destroy the weapons plant at Lop Nor. Likewise, the Israelis only needed conventional explosives and daring to blow up the Osirak reactor in Iraq in June 1981, when the Israeli government suspected that the reactor would be used to produce materials for Iraqi atomic weapons.

The more likely source aggressive nuclear war is the belief that the opponent is some kind of devil, and that the destruction of this devil would be a service to the world. If Hitler had had nuclear weapons, he would have sought some way to use them against the Jews. In the United States, talk of pre-emptive nuclear strikes against Russia has, since 1945, gone hand in hand with a demonizing of the Soviet Union. When, in December 1945, Senator "Big Jim" Eastland reported to the U.S. Senate that "we find in Czechoslovakia savage, barbarian Mongolian hordes;" when, in 1946, Dr. Virgil Jordan announced that "Russia is a primitive, impoverished predatory Asiatic despotism . . . which rests today as it did in the time of Tamerlane or Attila on a vast pyramid of human skulls," the remedy was not hard to find. "We must be prepared," Jimmy Doolittle told the American people in 1948, "physically, mentally, and morally to drop atomic bombs on Russian centers of industry at the first sign of aggression."[5] Since then, talk of fighting a nuclear war has flourished in the presence of leaders like Dulles and Reagan, who see history as a struggle of light against darkness. It has declined in the presence of leaders like Kissinger, who view history as a struggle of darkness against darkness.[6] Fortunately, since 1945, there has been no national leader who simultaneously had a finger on the nuclear button and visions of a devil in his mind. This fact, however, is a contingency of history. There is no way of assessing the probability that some future decade will produce a nuclear Hitler. Certainly there is no international mechanism in place to prevent this from happening.

(b) Nuclear Terrorism

If a political leader contemplates a nuclear strike against another nuclear power, he must weigh the risks of nuclear reprisal. If he contemplates a nuclear strike against a non-nuclear power, he must weigh the costs of world-wide condemnation, and the possibility of reprisal by some nuclear power that happens to side with the non-nuclear victim. Unlike the political leader, the nuclear terrorist will not be affected by these considerations.[7] If a nuclear terrorist gets his hands on a bomb he is more likely to use it than the typical political leader. The main question is whether he can get his hands on a bomb. He has two options: he can make a bomb, or he can steal one.

The technical information for the construction of fission devices has been available in the open literature since 1958. Furthermore, the increasing numbers of nuclear specialists employed by the world nuclear power industry make it more and more likely that someone with the ability to make nuclear bombs will defect to a terrorist group. Perhaps the main obstacle to construction of nuclear weapons by terrorist groups will be the obtaining of fissionable material, which must be enriched uranium or plutonium, neither of which occurs in nature. Here, though, technology is on the terrorists' side. The old gas-diffusion methods for enriching uranium, which made the production of weapons-grade uranium expensive and monitorable, may be replaced by laser techniques that are simpler, cheaper, and more easily concealed. Weapons-grade plutonium is produced in uranium reprocessing plants, and by the mid-1980s at least 20 countries will have reprocessing plants, each one of which will produce enough weapons grade plutonium to make a dozen or so atomic bombs a year.[8] Whether all these plutonium stocks can be kept terrorist-proof remains to be seen.

On the theft side, the primary targets for terrorists are the tactical nuclear weapons in the hands of the U.S. Army in the United States and Europe. The Army regularly assures the public that these weapons are carefully watched, and no doubt they are. But there are over 4,000 tactical nuclear weapons in Europe alone, and the loss of one weapon in 4,000 may be difficult to spot.[9]

Should a terrorist obtain a nuclear weapon, he must find some way of using it that will serve his ends. This may prove difficult. The PLO, for example, can hardly use nuclear weapons against Israel, contaminating the land to which they hope to return. Likewise, the provisional IRA cannot use them in Belfast, nor can the FALN use them in New York. If the terrorist puts his bomb in Paris or London, he must convince the world that he has a bomb, and that he will indeed explode it if his demands are not met. He may not be believed on either count. If his demands are not met, he must consider whether he wishes to be a mass murderer, and whether this will serve his cause. Finally, if he decides to explode his bomb, the result will be a catastrophe, but there will be one explosion only, not a nuclear war.[10] Considering all these factors, we may judge that nuclear terrorism is an appreciable and slowly growing possibility, but, if it occurs, it is likely to cause less devastation than might be expected from a nuclear war between nations.

(c) Nuclear Escalation

Since the early 1950s, NATO forces have been supplied with tactical nuclear weapons, backed by intermediate-range nuclear systems, backed by strategic systems in the United States. There has never been any doubt that the presence of these weapons is designed to deter a Soviet attack on Western Europe. There has never been much doubt that at least some nuclear weapons would be used in the event of a major Soviet attack, even if the Soviets did not use nuclear weapons first.[11] Such first uses of nuclear weapons fall under the heading of nuclear escalation.

Any nuclear power, faced with the prospect of conventional defeat and a chance of success with nuclear weapons, will be tempted to escalate to the nuclear level.[12] The probability of such escalation depends on the perceived chance of success, the perceived costs of breaking the nuclear taboo, and the perceived costs of the impending conventional defeat. If the enemy is a nuclear power, the nation contemplating escalation must consider the prospect of a nuclear reprisal. If the enemy is a non-nuclear power the nation contemplating escalation must consider that a nuclear attack on a non-nuclear nation will appear to the world like the act of a bully. Nevertheless, the threat of conventional defeat can provide a strong incentive to run such risks, and what appears crazy or self-defeating in peacetime may take on a certain plausibility in times of war. Escalation must be seen as one of the most probable routes across the nuclear threshold, if the threshold is crossed at all.

Since maintaining the ability to make escalatory threats is one of the main reasons that states retain nuclear weapons, it would be nice to know, from case to case, how effective threats of nuclear escalation really are. Western statesmen from Churchill on down have been convinced that threats of nuclear escalation have deterred the Soviet Union from invading Western Europe. One could go on from there and say that threats of nuclear escalation deterred the Soviets from sending troops into North Vietnam, stopped the Soviets from invading China, discouraged the Chinese from invading Russia, stopped the Chinese from invading India, and so forth. But any student of logic knows that such claims are pure conjecture. To prove that the presence of NATO nuclear weapons has deterred a Soviet invasion of Western Europe, one must prove that if the nuclear weapons had *not* been there, Russia *would* have invaded Western Europe. To prove that India's nuclear "arsenal" has prevented Chinese attack, one must show that if India had not joined the nuclear club, the Chinese *would* have invaded India. What is the evidence that the Soviets would have invaded Europe if nuclear weapons had not been there? What is the evidence that China would have attacked India if India had not had a nuclear bomb?

The fact is that there is no evidence—no war plans drawn up on the Soviet side and then called off for fear of nuclear escalation; no Chinese documents showing plans for invasion of India suddenly shelved when the Indian blast went off in 1974.[13] Instead of evidence, what is presented as proof is the postulate that the other side is inherently aggressive, desiring to attack but holding back for fear of the nuclear club. The postulate is steadfastly maintained by both parties in the Cold War, the West claiming that Marxism-Leninism contains a plan for world conquest; the East claiming that capitalism leads to imperialism and imperialism leads to aggressive war. If one believes the postulate, one will believe that threats of escalation have prevented attacks in the past and will continue to prevent them in the future. If one does not believe the postulate, one will believe that the threat of nuclear escalation has not prevented past attacks, and will not prevent a future attack if a nation considers its vital interests sufficiently at stake to run the risk.

(d) Crossing the Threshold With a Second Strike

The main purpose of the weapons systems possessed by the superpowers is to deter nuclear attack through credible threats of a nuclear counter strike. Thus, if a nuclear nation is subjected to nuclear attack, its strategic systems have in fact failed to do their job, and in these circumstances it may be immoral and self-destructive to proceed with a second strike. Nevertheless, the probability that second strikes will follow on the heels of first strikes is high. If the threat of a second strike is to be effective, the opponent must believe that the second strike will indeed follow the first strike, and the only way to make the second strike believable is to make it *likely*. Furthermore, in most first strikes, great damage will be done to the nation that is struck. The desire for revenge after such an assault will be intense, and this natural desire will make a second strike irresistible. (National leaders who reflect that revenge is useless are likely to be replaced by more hot-blooded subordinates.) Finally, in the case of certain limited first strikes, a limited second strike may be perceived as the best means to prevent further attacks.

The world has been repeatedly threatened or reassured by comments from American officials that, if the United States suffers a first strike, a second strike is certain.[14] General George Seignious, former director of the staff of the Joint Chiefs of Staff, remarked in 1979:

> I find a surrender scenario irresponsible—for it sends the wrong message to the Soviets. We have not built and maintained our strategic forces—at the cost of billions—in order to weaken their deterrent impact by telling the Russians and the world that we would back down—when we would not. [Scoville 1981 82]

and in 1982 Robert McNamara told the *Los Angeles Times*

> To try to destroy the 1,054 Minutemen, the Soviets would have to plan to ground-burst two nuclear warheads of one megaton each on each site. This is 2,000 megatons, roughly 160,000 times the megatonnage of the Hiroshima bomb. What condition do you think our country would be in when 2,000 one-megaton bombs ground burst? The idea that, in such a situation, we would sit here and say, "Well, we don't want to launch against them because they might come back and hurt us" is inconceivable! [Scheer 1983 217–18]

(e) Unauthorized Nuclear Attacks

In Stanley Kubrick's brilliant film, *Dr. Strangelove* (1964), a crazed SAC wing commander, obsessed with Communist plots to fluoridate American water, sends his B-52s off on a nuclear attack against Russia. The Air Force at the time heatedly denied that the Strangelove scenario was possible, and later prints of the film included a disclaimer of factual accuracy. Since then, the American public has been repeatedly reassured that no American nuclear weapons can be used without direct authorization from the President. In the case of land based missiles, the further claim is made that it is physically impossible for aimed launches to occur without receipt of electronic codes sent along from higher authority. In the case of other nuclear weapons, an elaborate system of fail-safe and dual key devices guard against unauthorized use.[15] The effectiveness of these protections against unauthorized launch is evidenced by the occasional complaints of Army field commanders that by the time authorization arrives from the National Command Authority for the use of nuclear weapons against a Soviet assault, the Red Army will be sitting in Paris, or perhaps in Cleveland.

The confidence of the military services in the resistance of strategic and tactical systems to unauthorized launch is perhaps well founded. Nevertheless, there are several weak spots that are cause for concern:

(a) In the event of an overpowering conventional Warsaw pact attack on Western Europe, NATO field commanders might use tactical nuclear weapons without authorization, especially if they believe that this is the only way they can save themselves and their units and stem the red tide. Self-preservation is a natural instinct that orders from the top might not suppress.

(b) In the case of ballistic missile submarines, submarine commanders under present procedures have the physical ability to launch their SLBMs to assigned targets without receipt of electronic codes. The likelihood of an unauthorized launch from submarines, even in peacetime, is possible but hardly likely. (It would involve, apparently, cooperation among a crew gripped by mass psychosis). But the likelihood of an unauthorized launch from submarines in wartime is more than merely possible. Under conditions of nuclear war, submarines may be cut off from the surviving levels of command, and submarine commanders, under certain conditions, might launch their weapons even if the American authorities did not wish them to do so.

(c) Presidential control of land-based strategic forces in peacetime seems relatively secure. But one can question whether the control of these forces by authorized persons is secure under conditions of nuclear war. In the event of nuclear attack, present plans call for the evacuation of the President by helicopter to Andrews Air Force Base, where he is supposed to take off in a specially equipped plane and maintain control of strategic forces from the air. Given 9 minutes between the detection of incoming SLBMs and their arrival in Washington, one wonders whether the President will be able to get airborne in time. If he does not, it is doubtful whether the sequence of authority can be preserved. If one bullet in a President's side can cause the Secretary of State to forget the constitutional order of succession, it is hard to imagine what a nuclear attack might do to perceptions of legitimate authority, especially among those who have the physical ability to release strategic weapons.

All of these remarks apply to unauthorized uses of *American* nuclear weapons. The same problem exists for every nuclear power, and it is not known to what degree the safeguards installed in American strategic systems have been matched by the other nuclear powers. One might expect that the Soviets, given their general interest in controlling the points of power in their society, keep a tight lock and key on their nuclear weapons. But they may have overlooked something, as might we. Furthermore, their control procedures, like ours, might be totally disrupted under conditions of nuclear war.

(f) False Alarms and Mistakes

One of the favorite plots in fictional treatments of nuclear war involves nuclear war that begins by mistake.[16] In the usual story, the President receives misleading information, on this basis orders a nuclear strike, and then discovers the error too late to recall the attack. Since the late 1950s, there has been no lack of real incidents in which glitches have thrown strategic systems into higher stages of alert. In the early years, when the main fear was a Soviet air strike and the intelligence was provided by ground—based radar systems, there were reports of nuclear alerts triggered by radar beams bouncing off clouds, off flocks of geese, or off the moon. Hopefully, in the age of the surveillance satellite, errors of this sort are less frequent. Nowadays the main problem is not in the sensor end but in the processing of information by computer, and reports of computer failure seem to be on the rise. On 16 November, 1979, a computer error triggered a nuclear alert so serious that 10 American jet interceptors were scrambled to meet a nonexistent challenge. Then on 7 June, 1980, the Pentagon announced that the failure of a 69-cent computer chip had produced computer indications on June 3 and June 5 that a Russian ICBM and SLBM nuclear attack was headed towards the United States. In each case, the error was detected by human analysts in about three minutes. On 17 June, 1980, Assistant Secretary of Defense Gerald Geneen summarized the incidents of June 3 and June 5 and commented: "In a real sense, the total system worked in that even though the mechanical part produced false information, the human part correctly evaluated it and prevented any irrevokable reaction."[17] Later in June, reporters for the Chicago *Tribune* stated that the U.S. strategic forces went on alert at least 50 times a year in response to reports of trouble later diagnosed as benign. To round out the year, Defense Department sources testified to the House Armed Services Committee that warning system computers produced about 147 false alarms in 1979.

One can take these reports as good news or bad news. The good news is that despite all the false alarms no nuclear attack has ever been launched by mistake, nor does it seem that the United States has ever been close to launching a nuclear attack by mistake. The bad news is that there has been a continuing series of false alarms, down to the present day, and that if a single false alarm ever generates a nuclear attack, the result will be a terrible disaster. Should we infer from the past 35 years of success that war by mistake will not occur in the future? Or should we infer from 35 years of false alarms that sooner or later there must be a nuclear war by mistake? Should we take heart from the news that human analysts picked up the June 1980 computer errors in "only three minutes," or should we take note, given nine minutes lead time before the arrival of Soviet SLBMs, and assuming that the President would have ordered an attack if the error had not been detected, that the world in 1980 was six minutes away from nuclear war?

There is some reason to think that the bad news outweighs the good news. First of all, the factual situation may be worse than public news stories indicate. The Pentagon is under no obligation to reveal its blunders, and in addition to the natural desire to hide one's mistakes in a cloak of secrecy, public reporting of American computer blunders would put the Soviets on edge and undermine strategic stability. Second, there is the consideration that all these false alarms were detected at times when there was no reason to expect that a Soviet attack was forthcoming. It remains to be seen whether the correct interpretation of false alarms can be sustained if there is an increase in international tension and a heightened expectation that the United States might indeed be subjected to nuclear attack. Third, false alarms have triggered nuclear alerts, and nuclear alerts, by themselves, may cause nuclear war. A false alarm could trigger an American alert, which precipitates a Soviet alert, which triggers a higher American alert in response to the Soviet response, and so on up the ladder to war.[18] Finally, there is the consideration that the United States is one of six nuclear nations, any one of which might initiate a nuclear war by mistake.

(g) War By Accident

The idea that a nuclear war might begin as a result of a purely mechanical failure, unassisted by human hands, seems at first sight quite implausible. It is nearly impossible that a nuclear device should explode of itself, as if by spontaneous combustion. Furthermore, even if a nuclear weapon did explode of itself, that would create damage only in the nation in which it exploded. It is difficult to imagine how such damage could trigger a nuclear war. So students of the subject consider this sort of accidental nuclear war to be a bare possibility, hardly worth discussing. But this optimism may be unfounded.

There have already been a surprisingly large number of accidents involving nuclear weapons. Between 1950 and 1968 there were at least 33 publicly noted incidents in which an American nuclear weapons delivery system was destroyed and in which nuclear weapons were either destroyed or damaged.[19] In 1961, a B-52 from Seymour-Johnson Air Force Base, Goldsboro, North Carolina, crashed 15 miles north of the base. Examination of the wreck showed that five of the six safety switches had snapped on a multi-megaton bomb.[20] In 1966, a collision between a B-52 and a refueling tanker resulted in the loss of four hydrogen bombs, one of which landed in a ditch, two of which released radiation in populated areas, and one of which was retrieved after a desperate search in the sea. How many unreported accidents there have been since 1950, how many additional accidents there have been since 1968, and how many such accidents there have been in

Russia and China, is difficult to determine; but the total must be considerable.

Do incidents like these pose a risk of nuclear war? Considering the number of nuclear weapons, the frequency of accidents seems low, and the typical accident is not the kind of event that might plausibly produce nuclear war. Nevertheless, there are so many nuclear weapons in the world that small chances of accidents add up. When one hears, in the debate about nuclear power, that the probability of a core meltdown in a nuclear reactor is one in every 17,000 reactor years, the chance appears so slight that there is strong temptation to dismiss it. But when one realizes, with 65 nuclear reactors in operation in the United States in 1980, that this frequency of accidents implies a *one-in-10* chance of a meltdown in *some* reactor in the next 30 years, one recognizes that the chance of serious accident should not be dismissed.[21] As with nuclear reactors, so with nuclear weapons systems, and an accident that will not tip the scales in peacetime may suffice to create war in times of crisis and suspicion.

Proliferation

There are seven ways to cross the nuclear threshold, and there are six nations in possession of nuclear weapons. If we exclude nuclear terrorism as a policy of nation states, this leaves six times six, or 36 ways the nuclear nations could come to use nuclear weapons.[22] It seems a mere matter of multiplication that the more nations there are that have nuclear weapons, the greater the likelihood that nuclear weapons will be used.

Some have disputed this view, arguing that the universal spread of nuclear weapons will bring universal deterrence and universal peace. This view was implausible when it was advanced by Gallois in 1960, and it is implausible now.[23] Even if the spread of nuclear weapons diminishes the chance that a nuclear nation will wage an aggressive nuclear war, the spread of nuclear weapons increases the chance that nuclear war will occur as a result of escalation, miscalculation, accident, or what have you. Since it is hardly likely that the chance of nuclear war via aggressive first strikes outweighs the chance of nuclear war by all other means combined, we should conclude that nuclear proliferation increases the chance of nuclear war and presents a grave threat to world peace.

Since the techniques for producing fission bombs are widely known, it is surprising and encouraging that only six nations have developed nuclear weapons since 1945. Furthermore, the rate at which the nuclear club is expanding seems to be in decline: in the first 20 years of the nuclear era, five nations joined the club; in the next 19 years, only one nation has joined officially, and only two others, at most, have joined unofficially.

The reasons for the slow spread of nuclear weapons are disputed by the experts. Those who feel that nuclear weapons and deterrence provide real security argue that the major non-nuclear powers have not developed nuclear weapons because they feel safe under the nuclear umbrella of one nuclear superpower or the other. Those who feel that nuclear weapons breed only insecurity argue that the non-nuclear nations have simply shown good sense and have recognized that their security objectives cannot be obtained by the development of nuclear weapons. Whatever the reason, it provides no ground for a relaxation of concern over the proliferation problem. Because of the international development of the nuclear power industry, there is plenty of plutonium in the world and every year there is more.[24] Should Argentina or Brazil or Pakistan or South Korea or Taiwan or some other state decide that its security requires atomic weapons, it will be very difficult to prevent them from getting them. And once any one of these non-nuclear states acquires nuclear weapons, all of its rivals will want them too.

Summary: The Risk of Nuclear War in the Coming Decades

The existence of nearly 40 years of nuclear peace since 1945 has brought many experts to the conclusion that the chance of nuclear war in the coming decades is slight. Potential nuclear aggressors are kept in line by the threats of nuclear retaliation. The chance of escalation is kept low by continuing efforts of the nuclear powers to avoid armed confrontation at the conventional level. The threat of nuclear terrorism is being combatted by international efforts to monitor the spread of fissionable material and nuclear weapons technology. The chance of miscalculation, mistake, or nuclear accident is the subject of constant professional study, and devices like the Hot Line will help to keep small miscalculations from developing into big disasters. The proliferation problem has been kept under control. Caspar Weinberger summed up the optimistic case in a lecture to the Massachusetts Medical Society in May 1982:

> What, then, has deterrence done? Again, I must stress that it has worked and is working today. There have been 37 years of peace in Europe. Despite the threat of the Soviet Army, despite the threat of the Soviet's nuclear weapons, Western Europe has prospered. Its political freedoms have flourished, and its social institutions have grown stronger. Indeed, there has not been an equal period of uninterrupted peace on the European continent since the Roman Empire fell. At the risk of stating the obvious, the United States and the rest of the world have also avoided the scourge of nuclear fire. Deterrence thus is and remains our best immediate hope of keeping peace. [Weinberger 1982 767]

Nevertheless, in this book we will assume, on a variety of grounds, that the risk of nuclear war is large enough, and that the methods used to control the risk are questionable enough, to warrant careful consideration of radical changes in current methods of managing this risk. First of all, it is not proven that "37 years of peace in Europe" are the result of deterrence and nuclear weapons. Europe had even longer periods of peace in the nineteenth century (for example, 1815–1853, 1871–1914) without the presence of nuclear weapons, and the longest period of peace ended in the holocaust of World War I. Second, even if the risks of nuclear war from any one cause are small, there are so many different ways that a nuclear war might begin that these risks accumulate to an appreciable level. Third, even if the overall risk is small, the presence of the risk over an extended period of time makes it more and more likely that nuclear war will occur sooner or later. Fourth, even if the risk of nuclear war under current conditions is slight, the magnitude of the disaster that will result if these methods fail is perhaps much greater than the magnitude of the disaster that might result if other and perhaps only slightly more risky methods were employed. Fifth, even if current methods produce only a small risk of nuclear war, it might be that the current methods are not morally acceptable, while other, more morally acceptable means generate an equal or only slightly greater risk. Sixth, even if the numerical risk of nuclear war is small, nuclear war is such a terrible disaster that a quantity of risk which would be tolerable even in relation to a conventional disaster may be intolerable when it is a risk of nuclear war. Just what the effects of a nuclear war might be, is the subject of the following sections.

The Effects of Thermonuclear Weapons

In the preceding chapter, the effects of the Hiroshima bombing were described by children who endured it. The bomb that fell on Hiroshima had an explosive force equivalent of about 13,000 tons of TNT. The smallest warhead in the American strategic arsenal, the warhead on the Poseidon SLBM, has an explosive force of 50,000 tons of TNT. The warhead on the Minuteman II is rated at one million tons (one megaton) of TNT, and the Titan II warhead at nine megatons. On the Soviet side, most Soviet SLBMs, the SS-11, the SS-13, and the SS-17 have warheads rated at about 1 megaton each; the SS-19 can carry a five megaton warhead, and the SS-18 can carry a 24-megaton warhead. A one megaton warhead then, is about the average for strategic weapons.

If a one megaton warhead ever exploded above a populated area, here is what would happen. Thirty miles from ground zero, windows facing the blast would break. People in the open ten miles away would suffer second degree burns. Six miles away, 30 percent of the trees would be blown down. Five miles away, most wooden frame structures would be destroyed. Four miles away, most buildings would catch on fire. Three miles away, most wall-bearing multi-story buildings would fall down. At two miles away most reinforced steel buildings would collapse. At 1¾ quarter miles or less from ground zero, everyone not already burned or crushed would die from radiation poisoning. At one mile or less from ground zero, everything would be crushed or burned and everyone would be dead.

After the shock wave passed, everything flammable up to four miles from ground zero would be on fire. These fires might coalesce into a firestorm that creates its own draft and supplies itself with air. Those who survived the initial blast and radiation might die in this firestorm. Many of those who survive the blast, the heat, the radiation, and the firestorm, would die from injuries. What medical support there is that survives the blast would be too little and come too late.

If the warhead exploded near the ground, the fireball from the explosion would touch the earth, and a great cloud of dust, made radioactive from the explosion, would be kicked into the air. This radioactive dust, called fallout, would drift downwind from the explosion. If the prevailing winds were fifteen miles per hour, an area of 150 miles downwind from the explosion and 20 miles wide would become contaminated by radioactivity. Locations 150 miles downwind from the explosion would be uninhabitable for two years. Locations 50 miles downwind from the explosion would be uninhabitable for ten years.

These effects would be the effects of *single* one-megaton blast. An atomic attack, if it occurs, will consist of a coordinated sequence of such blasts.[25] Right now, the United States has detailed operational plans for nuclear attacks of various sorts on the Soviet Union. The Soviet Union, presumably, has detailed plans for nuclear attacks on the United States. We must consider what the effects of attacks would be if they ever occurred. To do this, we must have some information about the war plans themselves.

(a) American Plans for a Nuclear Attack on Russia: the 1940s and 1950s.

In the late 1940s, a certain amount of attention, inside and outside of SAC, was devoted to plans for a nuclear strike against the Soviet Union. Informed by studies of the effects of strategic bombing on Germany and Japan, the first plans concentrated on the destruction of the Soviet oil industry. By 1947, however, Soviet cities were increasingly picked out as targets for attack. The 1947 BROILER plan called for 34 bombs on 24 cities, the HARROW plan called for 50 bombs on 20 cities, the TROJAN plan (December 1948) called for 133 bombs on 70 cities, and the OFFTACKLE plan (October 1949) called for 220 bombs on 104 Soviet cities.[26]

By later standards, these were limited plans, restricted by the size of the stockpile, the relatively small size of fission bombs, and the limited delivery capacities of propeller driven aircraft.

By the middle 1950s, these impediments had been removed. The B-47 had been deployed, fission bombs were in mass production, and fusion bombs were being introduced. In the brave new world of nuclear plenty, it was possible to plan truly massive nuclear attacks. In a top-secret briefing at Offutt Air Base on 15 March, 1954, General A.J. Old, Chief of SAC operations, indicated that with proper deployment of tankers, SAC was prepared to send 585 B-47s and 150 B-36 bombers armed with 600 to 750 atomic bombs forward against Russia.[27] A Navy captain present at the briefing said that General Old gave the impression that "all of Russia would be nothing but a smoking radiating ruin at the end of two hours."[28] A recently declassified 1955 Weapons Systems Evaluation Group report provides further details of the attack plans of the mid 1950s: 645 Soviet airfields were to come under attack; 135 atomic bombs were to land on targets inside Central Europe, 40 bombs were to land on South Central Europe; and 118 of the 134 largest cities inside Russia were to be destroyed. The report goes on to say that the combined atomic offensive would cause a total of 77 million casualties within the Soviet bloc, of which 60 million would be fatalities. In a dazzling summation, the report concluded: "Such casualties, coupled with the other effects of the atomic offensives, may have an important bearing on the will of the Soviets to continue to wage war." (Rosenberg 1981-82 31) One would think so.

The SAC attack plans of the 1950s were determined largely by considerations of efficiency: the goal was to inflict as much damage as possible on the enemy with as little damage as possible to SAC. Nevertheless, there is a neat correspondence between the grisly details of SAC plans and the well publicized declaratory policy of these years—the policy of "massive retaliation." Were the attack plans of the 1950s designed for "massive retaliation", or were they plans for massive pre-emption?

Certainly there is nothing in the plans which prevents them from being used in a first strike mode. Furthermore, documents reveal that the highest priority objective assigned to SAC plans was the destruction of Soviet nuclear weapons, an objective that could only be confidently achieved if Soviet planes and weapons were destroyed on the ground by a SAC surprise attack. Curtis LeMay, the head of SAC, commented at the Offutt briefing in 1954 that it was his opinion, if the U.S. were "pushed in a corner" that we would not hesitate to strike first. [29]

The decision as to how American nuclear weapons would be used, of course, lay not with LeMay but with Dwight Eisenhower. Eisenhower was no opponent of nuclear weapons, and had supported the introduction of tactical nuclear weapons into NATO. The basic document containing the strategic policy of those years, NSC 162/2 (made public as part of the Pentagon Papers) stated "In the event of hostilities, the United States will consider nuclear weapons to be as available for use as other munitions."[30] Nevertheless an earlier NSC memorandum, NSC 68 (1950) had repudiated the idea of preventive war,[31] and Eisenhower himself believed that it would not be possible to get a declaration of war from Congress in support of a secret surprise attack. On balance, the most reasonable inference from these conflicting elements is that Eisenhower was prepared to launch a nuclear first strike against Russia in response to a Soviet attack on Western Europe, even if the Soviets did not use nuclear weapons first. The first blow had to be Russian, but the first nuclear blow was to be American.

(b) American Plans for Nuclear Attack on Russia: 1960—1983

The SAC plans of the 1950s had to be drastically modified in the 1960s. The manned bomber was progressively replaced by the ICBM, and the Polaris program gave the Navy an expanded role in strategic planning. Most importantly, Soviet ICBM capability required that all planning give serious consideration to a Soviet second strike. The first plan adjusting to these new factors, developed by Eisenhower in 1960, was SIOP-62. McNamara's revised "flexible" SIOP, developed in 1961, was SIOP-63. Schlesinger's SIOP, approved December 1975, was called SIOP-5. The changes in the

SIOP resulting from Jimmy Carter's Presidential Directive-59 (July 1980) have apparently produced SIOP 5-D.

All these SIOPs are top secret, but a certain amount of information about them has leaked out over the years. Considering the intensity of public controversy about nuclear weapons policies, it is remarkable that the SIOP does not appear to have changed radically since SIOP-63. What over two decades of planning have achieved is not a change in basic planning but the development of more and more options from which the President can choose.

According to Desmond Ball, SIOP-63 contained five attack options, with American strikes proceeding in order of priority, against

    I. Soviet strategic nuclear delivery forces;
   II. Soviet conventional military forces located away from cities;
 III. Soviet military forces located near cities;
 IV. Soviet command and control centers; and
  V. Economic targets including Soviet cities.[32]

Much of what we know about SIOP-5 was revealed in testimony before the House Armed Services Committee in March 1980. There are over 40,000 targets, or designated ground zeros, in SIOP-5, divided into four categories:

  I. Soviet Nuclear Forces
      ICBMs, IRBMs
      Nuclear weapons storage sites
      Airfields supporting nuclear-capable aircraft
      Nuclear missile-firing submarine bases
  II. Conventional Military Forces
      Supply depots
      Marshalling points
      Conventional airfields
      Ammunition storage facilities
      Tank and vehicle storage years
 III. Military and Political Leadership
      Command posts
      Key communications facilities
 IV. Economic and Industrial Targets
    (a) War supporting industry
      Tank factories
      Petroleum refineries
      Railway yards and repair facilities
    (b) Coal
      Basic steel
      Basic aluminum
      Cement
      Electrical power[33]

According to testimony, several classes of targets, including Soviet cities, territory of Soviet allies, and top command and control centers, are reserved for later phases of attack.

Nevertheless, Soviet cities still remain on the target list. In 1979, Secretary of Defense Harold Brown argued publicly for their inclusion:

> To have a true countervailing strategy, our forces must be capable of covering, and being withheld from, a substantial list of targets. Cities cannot be excluded from such a list, not only because cities, population, and industry are closely linked, but also because it is essential at all times to retain the option to attack urban-industrial targets—both as a deterrent to attacks on our own cities and as the final retaliation if that particular deterrent should fail. [Brown 1979 77]

(c) Effects of American Nuclear Strikes on Russia

Under current plans, then, the President has the option of attacking Soviet strategic forces while leaving all else aside. Suppose that the President did order such a strike, and suppose that this strike was an American second strike, using only American strategic forces that have survived a large Soviet counterforce first strike, and suppose that this strike was directed mainly at military targets.

Such a limited attack may not be as discriminate as it appears at first sight. Twenty-two of the 32 Soviet strategic air bases, three-quarters of the IRBM and MRBM fields, and 26 Soviet ICBM sites are located in European Russia, where the population is dense.[34] Unpublished estimates prepared by the Arms Control and Disarmament agency estimate that such an American strike would kill between 3.7 and 27 million people in the U.S.S.R., depending on weather conditions and the number of people who reached shelter before the attack.[35] In addition to these millions, many more would die as a result of radiation sickness, disease and perhaps from starvation due to the disruption of Soviet food supplies.

If the President proceeds down the target list beyond Category I, it will become increasingly difficult to distinguish a limited nuclear attack from a direct attack on cities. The public has been told that the targets are "Conventional Military Forces," "Command and Control Centers," and "Soviet Industry," but it is likely that many of these targets are located in or near populated areas. As Herbert York explained, the SIOP may target Moscow because it is a communication center, Kiev because it is a transportation center, Leningrad and Odessa because they are ports, and so forth. (York 1970 43)

Studies have shown that a pinpoint nuclear attack designed to destroy the Soviet oil industry would result in approximately 5 million Soviet casualties, of which about 1.5 million would be fatalities, even though much of the Soviet oil industry is located in remote areas.[36]

Given the immense damage that "limited" American nuclear strikes would cause in Russia, the delicate distinctions between types of nuclear attacks delineated in the current SIOP may be lost on the Soviet leadership. Indeed, the most likely hypothesis is that the Soviet leadership will probably perceive any nuclear attack on the Soviet Union as the beginning of an all-out war. Certainly we should not expect the Soviet leadership to show restraint in the face of millions of deaths among their fellow citizens. The most likely end result, then, of implementing any part of SIOP 5-D would be a massive Soviet attack on the United States, followed by an all-out American response in the opposite direction.

An all-out American nuclear attack on the Soviet Union, even if the attack were an American second strike with forces surviving a Soviet first strike, would leave the same "smoking radiating ruin" portrayed by SAC generals in 1955. At least 34 million people in the Soviet Union would die in the attack. Some estimates prepared by the Defense Department predict 100 million Soviet deaths. How long, if ever, it would take the Soviet Union to "recover" from such a strike, no one can say.

(d) Effects of a Soviet Nuclear Attack on the United States

Obviously we know even less about Soviet nuclear war plans than we know about American nuclear war plans. We do not know how the Soviets intend to use their weapons. But we do know what their weapons can do.

In 1979, on instructions from Congress, the Office of Technology Assessment (OTA) prepared several studies of the results of Soviet attacks on the United States. They considered the results of a 25-megaton attack on Detroit, a Soviet attack on American oil refineries, and a Soviet counterforce strike against American strategic weapons. They found that a 25-megaton attack on Detroit would kill 1,840,000 and injure 1,360,000 Americans,[37] that a 100-megaton attack on American oil refineries would kill 5,031,000 Americans, and that a Soviet attack on American ICBM bases, SAC airfields, and submarine support facilities which scrupulously avoided all other locations, would kill between 2 million and 22 million Americans, depending on the speed and direction of the winds after the attack. (The low figure assumes, quite unrealistically, that the entire American population takes to fallout shelters soon after the attack.)

The OTA concurred with earlier studies that a large-scale Soviet attack directed at economic and industrial targets would be totally catastrophic. In the absence of widespread use of fallout shelters, the Defense Department had estimated that 155 to 165 million Americans would die if all Soviet weapons were air burst. If half the Soviet weapons were ground burst, the Arms Control and Disarmament Agency had estimated that 105 to 131 million Americans would die. If widespread use of shelters were introduced, 76 million to 85 million Americans would die. The OTA study confirmed these ranges of deaths.

These figures are terrifying enough, but there is reason to think that they are underestimates. None of these studies attempted to estimate the number of wounded, nor what the survival rates of the wounded would be 30 days or longer after the attack. Recent studies by physicians and epidemiologists have concluded that after a large-scale nuclear attack millions will die from infection and communicable diseases, over and above those who are killed or made sick by radiation poisoning.[38] Furthermore, in evaluating the effects of fallout, these studies fail to take into account the impact of Soviet attacks on American nuclear power plants, which are likely targets in any large-scale Soviet attack. The United States has some 70 nuclear power plants in operation, each one generating about 30 tons of radioactive waste each year, waste which, for the time being, is accumulating in special pools underneath the power plants. A nuclear warhead detonated over a nuclear power plant will spew this radioactive waste into the atmosphere, creating a deadly cloud spreading over hundreds of square miles. A single warhead striking a single nuclear plant will kill everyone in an area of 500 square miles downwind from the plant, and will make an area of 64,000 square miles unsafe for human habitation. (An attack on a plant in Wisconsin, for example, could make Buffalo unsafe.)[39]

The bottom line in all these studies is that after a large-scale nuclear attack, the United States as we now know it would no longer exist.

Long-Term Effects of Nuclear War: Cancer and Nuclear Winter

Most of the studies of the physical effects of nuclear war consider only the immediate physical effects: effects that manifest themselves within 30 days after the nuclear attack. But a nuclear war will have some physical effects that will not appear for years or even for decades. Of these long-term effects, the most important are cancers and birth defects caused by radiation released in the war, radiation that is either lingering in the earth or drifting down in the form of fallout.

In the mid 1970s, the National Academy of Sciences and the Office of Technology Assessment made independent studies of the long-term effects of various nuclear wars, concentrating on the issue of cancer and birth defects.[40] The results of these two studies were remarkably consistent, and there is every reason to believe that these estimates are reliable.

(a) Suppose that the Soviet Union launched 77 missiles to attack the 80 largest oil refineries in the United States. In addition to 5 million deaths in the first 30 days, 2 to 5.5 million Americans would die from cancer caused by radiation released in the attack (assuming no special efforts to move the American population into shelters). Between 0.2 and 2.5 million American women would suffer spontaneous abortions because of chromosome damage caused to the fetus, and 0.9 to 9 million children would be born with birth defects due to increased radiation.

(b) In a limited nuclear war in which the United States and the Soviet Union attacked each other's missile silos but avoided striking cities, between 1.7 million and 13.1 million people would die from cancer, between 0.6 million and 7.2 million would suffer spontaneous abortions, and between 1.9 million and 19 million children would be born with birth defects. It is noteworthy that these studies show that the majority of cancers, abortions, and birth defects caused by a "surgical" counterforce strike by the United States against Russia would be suffered *outside* of the Soviet Union.

(c) In the event of all-out nuclear war between the Soviet Union and the United States, the number of long term victims increases, especially in neutral countries. If 6,500 megatons of Soviet nuclear weapons explode over the United States, and 1,300 megatons of American nuclear weapons explode over the Soviet Union, 3.1 million to 23.3 million people will die from cancer; 0.77 million to 19 million women will suffer abortions, and 2.9 million to 36.5 million children will be born with birth defects. Once again, most of the deaths caused by radiation released by American bombs will occur outside the Soviet Union.

But of all the long-term effects of nuclear war, the most devastating are likely to be changes in climate, and the ecological changes brought about by changes in climate.

That a nuclear war might have a substantial effect on climate has long been suggested. But, in 1983, new studies, using computer models of atmospheric mixing, provided the first clear and detailed argument that a nuclear war could produce a major climatic change, a change which has come to be called "the nuclear winter." (Peterson 1983, Turco 1983, Ehrlich 1983). The main culprits, the new studies showed, would be dust and soot tossed into the air by nuclear explosions.

In the event of a massive 5000 megaton counterforce exchange between the superpowers, the new studies showed that sufficient dust would be thrown into the atmosphere to block for days, weeks, or months, 95 percent of the sunlight that normally reaches the earths surface in the Northern Hemisphere. Temperatures in the Northern Hemisphere could drop during this period by as much as 70 degrees Fahrenheit. If the war comes in winter, most of the survivors of the war will freeze. If the war comes in summer, most of the plants will be destroyed, and many survivors will starve the following winter. A massive countervalue exchange will have virtually the same effects, caused not by dust thrown into the air, but by soot generated in large firestorms burning through urban areas. According to some studies dust and soot from the Northern hemisphere nuclear wars may work their way south, producing a nuclear chill in the Southern hemisphere. One need not be an ecologist in order to imagine what the effects of this nuclear winter will mean in terms of human casualties. In addition to the 250 million casualties expected from the short run effects of a major nuclear exchange, one must add several hundred million, or perhaps even several billion casualties resulting from nuclear winter, and most of these casualties will occur outside the United States and outside the Soviet Union.

The nuclear winter described here is the result of a 5000 megaton "baseline" nuclear exchange between the super-powers. There is some reason to believe that the most serious effects of nuclear winter can be generated by a nuclear exchange as small as 100 megatons, provided that the 100 megaton attack is directed at urban areas and produces large sooty fires. (Turco 1983 1285). It follows that the number of casualties caused by a "limited" exchange may be as great as the number of casualties in an all-out nuclear exchange. This is sobering news indeed. At the same time, it must be noted that there are many possible nuclear wars that will not generate a nuclear winter. Counter value exchanges of less than 100 megatons or involving less than 1000 nuclear detonations will not produce nuclear winter. Counterforce exchanges of up to 1000 megatons or more will not produce a nuclear winter, according to present models. Thus many "standard" sorts of nuclear war; for example, a nuclear terrorist attack, a one city nuclear attack, or a limited counterforce strike directed at ICBM silos, will not—so far as we know—produce a nuclear winter, provided that they do not escalate into all-out nuclear exchanges.

The End of the World?

The American hydrogen bomb test on 1 April, 1954, contaminated several thousand square miles of the South Pacific. A thousand such bombs could devastate millions of square miles. The scale of destruction caused by hydrogen bombs is so great that prominent scientists and philosophers in the 1950s, most notably Albert Einstein and Bertrand Russell, began to argue that nuclear war with these weapons posed a threat to the human race itself.[41] Since a number of writers have suggested that the possible extinction of the human species is the most important factor in the moral analysis of nuclear war, we must consider the possibility of "omnicide" carefully.[42]

In the large-scale nuclear exchange between the Soviet Union and the United States, in the worst case estimates, about 150 million people are killed immediately in the United States and about 100 million people are killed immediately in the Soviet Union. A total of 250 million dead is a catastrophe beyond all imagining, but 250 million people are only 5 percent of the human race. Millions more will die lingering deaths from cancer as a result of this war, millions more may die of starvation caused by the disruption of patterns of food supply and hundreds of millions more may die if the war provokes a "nuclear winter." Such a total of several hundred million dead, or even several billion, is beyond all imagining, but it does not appear that a nuclear winter would destroy the human species, which is the most widely diffused of all species in the history of the earth.

Could the radiation generated by a nuclear war extinguish the human race? The answer is: "Under present conditions, no; under future conditions, possibly." For a nuclear war to kill off the human species it would have to release enough radiation to subject every human being to a cumulative dose of about 100 rads. If all nuclear warheads in the world were evenly distributed around the world and exploded at once, this amount of radiation would not result. Consequently there is no way today that a nuclear war would destroy the human race, barring some side effect of nuclear war not presently known.

There are two ways that lethal worldwide levels of radiation could be reached in the *future* nuclear war. If the quantitative arms race continues, and if at some future date 100 thousand megatons of nuclear weapons are exploded, then everyone in the world will die (Feld 1976). Alternatively, if the nuclear power industry continues to expand and if radioactive wastes continue to accumulate beneath nuclear power plants, a nuclear attack on these reactors could produce enough fallout to kill everyone in the world. Neither of these scenarios is probable. Stockpiles in the 50 thousand megaton range are implausible since the total megatonnage in the world's stockpiles is declining, not increasing, as gravity bombs are replaced with precision warheads. (The U.S. megatonnage peak was reached in 1958). An attack on nuclear reactors is not probable because the resulting release of radioactivity would be so great that it would endanger the aggressor as well as the victim. There is also some reason to hope that in the coming decades some safer location will be found for the storage of radioactive waste.

The end of the world then, is not the principal result of nuclear war with which moral analysis should deal. It is, of course, *possible* that a nuclear war will destroy humanity, but it is also possible that humanity will be destroyed by creatures from outer space alerted to our presence by radio transmissions from the earth. If the human species destroys itself, it is far more likely that this destruction will come at the hands of some virus spawned in a biological weapons laboratory or some infection spawned accidentally during the course of research with recombinant DNA, than from nuclear weapons. Such killers are species specific, and spread from person to person. Fortunately, radiation sickness is not communicable.

What nuclear war *will* do is so bad that the news that it will not destroy the world provides little relief. A full scale nuclear exchange will kill hundreds of millions of innocent people and the survivors will face a world barely capable of supplying their elementary physical needs.[44] It is hardly likely that democracy could survive the shock or serve the needs of the survivors. As for the art and architecture destroyed by nuclear war, that will be gone forever. Those who speak optimistically of reconstruction after nuclear war should note that no one has ever reconstructed a Rembrandt or revived the dead.

Notes

1. The present six are: the United States, the U.S.S.R., Britain, France, China, and India. The possible two are Israel and South Africa. Likely candidates for future inclusion are Pakistan, South Korea, and Taiwan. For the Israeli nuclear capability, see Weissman and Krosney 1982 105–129.

2. Terminology about the origins of nuclear war is unstandardized and ambiguous, and the words "accidental" and "unintentional" are often mistakenly used as synonyms. A person who launches a nuclear attack because of a false warning launches intentionally but mistakenly. If a subordinate launches nuclear weapons without authorization, the attack is unintentional from the standpoint of the nation but intentional from the standpoint of the subordinate. The word "unauthorized" is preferable in such cases.

3. For American plans for pre-emptive war with Russia in the 1950s, see Rosenberg 1981–82 3–38.

4. The 1962 Air Force study on a pre-emptive strike against China is mentioned in Haldeman 1978 90. See also Ball 1981–82 42. Ball dates this idea to the late 1960s.

5. Quotations from Eastland, Jordan, and Doolittle in Fleming 1961 335, 393, 391.

6. For Dulles's Manichean world view, see Hoopes 1973. For Reagan's world picture, see the interview with Robert Scheer reprinted in Scheer 1983 232–60.

7. For a general survey of nuclear terrorism see Epstein 1979.

8. On the spread of fissionable materials see Wohlstetter, 1976–77. For an estimate on the number of present and future nuclear power plants worldwide, see "World List of Nuclear Power Plants," *Nuclear News* (February 1981), 75–94.

9. There are about 65 depots in Europe containing NATO tactical nuclear weapons, each one guarded, apparently, by only several dozen men at a time. See Lens 1977 238.

10. For some of the communication and credibility problems faced by the nuclear terrorist, see Schelling 1982 61–77.

11. For the zigs and zags of the Army's commitment to the use of nuclear weapons on the battlefield, see Rose 1980.

12. Perhaps the best general study of escalation is Smoke 1977. The best study of nuclear escalation in particular is Brodie 1966.

13. For a book which by inadvertent example shows the difficulty of finding sufficient evidence to support hypotheses about the effectiveness of deterrence, see George and Smoke 1974.

14. The pressure on the American President to act rather than exhibit patience can be overpowering. In the middle of the Cuban missile crisis John Kennedy remarked that if he had not acted, he would have been impeached (Kennedy 1969 67). What is interesting about this remark is not its truth but the fact that Kennedy believed it. Likewise, one suspects that President Carter ordered the rescue attempt of the hostages in Iran because of overwhelming external pressure that *something* be done. If missiles in Cuba and hostages in Teheran could force the President's hand, it is highly likely that a Soviet first strike would too.

15. The American command and control procedures for authorizing the use of nuclear weapons are diagrammed in Ball 1979.

16. The most thorough survey of the general problem is Frei 1983.

17. *Facts on File*, June 1980.

18. The pattern of alert-triggering alert is analyzed in Schelling 1960 Ch. 9.

19. The list of accidents from 1950 to 1968 is given in the Stockholm International Peace Research Institute *Yearbook of World Armaments and Disarmament* 1968–69, 266–68.

20. For the Goldsboro accident, see Ralph Lapp, *International Herald Tribune*, 6 March 1969.

21. The point about the accumulation of risks in multiple systems and the calculation of probabilities is made by Schrader-Frechette 1980 84.

22. For general studies of proliferation, see 1966, and Quester 1973.

23. See Gallois 1961. For another view of the relation between the number of nuclear powers and the chance of war, see Intriligator and Brito 1981.

24. For the relationship between the civilian nuclear power industry and its potential military implications, see Wohlstetter 1979, and Potter 1982.

25. The standard handbook for the effects of nuclear weapons is Glasstone 1977.

26. For the BROILER, HARROW, TROJAN, AND OFFTACKLE plans, see Rosenberg, 1983.

27. The briefing by General Old, summarized by Captain William B. Moore, USN, is printed as Document One in Rosenberg 1981 18–28. The Weapons Systems Evaluation Group briefing is Document Two in Rosenberg 1981 18–28.

28. Ibid., p. 25.

29. Ibid., p. 27.

30. NSC 162/2 30 Oct. 1953. Etzold and Gaddis 1978.

31. Etzold and Gaddis 1978 417.

32. The five Attack Options in SIOP-63 are described in Ball 1980 191.

33. The list of "designated ground zeros" is supplied by Ball in 1982/83 34. See also Leitenberg 1981.

34. The distribution of Soviet strategic forces is from Ball 1980b 167–70.

35. The estimates of casualties from an American counterforce strike from Office of Technology Assessment 1980 91–94.

36. The estimates for Soviet losses due to an attack on Soviet oil refineries are from Office of Technology Assessment 1980 75–80.

37. The figures for deaths in the attack on Detroit are in Office of Technology Assessment 1980 37. The fatalities for the strike against oil refineries are on p. 77, the Soviet counterforce strike fatalities are on p. 84. See also Sullivan 1979 for an estimate of 8 to 12 million fatalities (without warning), and 5 to 8 million fatalities (with warning).

38. See Abrams and von Kaenel 1981.

39. See Fetter and Tsipis 1981.

40. The National Academy of Sciences Study is *Long Term Effects of Multiple Nuclear Weapons Detonations* (Washington, D.C. National Academy of Sciences, 1975). See also *The Effects of Nuclear War* (Washington, D.C., U.S. Arms Control and Disarmament Agency, April 1975).

41. A widely publicized statement, written by Russell and signed by Einstein, was released by Russell on 9 July 1955. Part of the statement says: "Here, then, is the problem we present to

you, stark and dreadful and inescapable: Shall we put an end to the human race; or shall mankind renounce war? . . . If many hydrogen bombs are used there will be universal death— sudden only for the minority, but for the majority slow torture of disease and disintegration." The statement was signed by Russell, Einstein, Max Born, P. W. Bridgmen, Leopold Infield, J. F. Joliot-Curie, H. J. Muller, Linus Pauling, C. F. Powell, J. Rotblat, and Hideki Yukawa. The entire statement is reprinted in Russell, 1961 55–60.

42. One author who has developed the theme that omnicide is the main moral issue with regard to nuclear weapons is Jonathan Schell. See Schell 1982, especially Part II.

43. Paul Ehrlich and others in (Ehrlich 1983) write

In any large-scale exchange between the super-powers, global environment changes suffi- cient to cause the extinction of a major fraction of the plant and animal species on the earth are likely. In that event, the possibility of the extinction of the human species cannot be excluded. (Ehrlich 1983, 1299)

But to say that the extinction of the human species "cannot be excluded" merely indicates that the extinction of the species is a *possibility*. This is very far from claiming that a nuclear winter will kill off the human race. The same can be said of their earlier remark:

Coupled with the direct casualties of one billion people, the combined intermediate and long-term effects of nuclear war suggest that eventually there might be no human survivors in the Northern hemisphere. (ibid.)

which asserts that *possibly* the people in the Northern hemisphere will be wiped out.

44. The question of how long it would take the United States to recover from nuclear war is so controversial that is impossible to develop any figures that command a consensus. The leader of the optimists is Herman Kahn, who claimed in Kahn 1960 that the United States could recover from an all-out nuclear attack in three or four decades. Similar optimistic estimates have been echoed by authors inspired by the example of European post-war recovery in the 1950's. For pessimistic assessments which imply that the United States may never recover its pre-war levels of prosperity see Katz 1982 and Peterson and Hinrichsen 1982. The pessimist's case is strong since the European precedent is irrelevant. In a nuclear war, the most advanced powers go under; after World War II, the most economically advanced power emerged unscathed.

4

A Short Tour of Strategic Weapons Policies

In this chapter various weapons policies will be presented and considered strictly from the standpoint of the American national interest. We will say that a weapons policy serves American interests if it (a) diminishes the chance of an attack on the United States, (b) helps the United States resist illegitimate threats of force, (c) increases the chance of American victory in the event of war, and (d) preserves or improves the American standard of living.[1] In short, we define the national interest strictly in military and economic terms, and we reject any ideological component: we will not for example, consider the development of free markets overseas or the establishment of democratic regimes as relevant to the national interest, unless these changes demonstrably affect the military or economic concerns of the United States.

Because we have rejected the ideological component, we have not produced a definition of the American national interest that reduces to "America getting what America wants." The majority of Americans probably preferred Chiang Kai-shek to Mao Tse-Tung, but Mao's victory is not contrary to American interests as we have defined them, unless it can be shown that Mao's victory increased the chance of Chinese attack on the United States or somehow decreased the American standard of living. It seems hardly likely that it did. In short, we define American interests as America getting what it wants within its own borders, but not America getting what it wants elsewhere in the world.

Assessing how a particular weapons policy affects the American economy is a complicated business. One must consider not only the direct costs of the weapon and the effect of the purchase on private consumption, but also the effect of the weapons purchase on inflation, employment, investment, industrial innovation, and so forth. The study of these issues is a young science, and all conclusions are controversial. But it would be folly to ignore the subject.

Choice A: Possession or Non-Possession?

The basic decision that any nation must make regarding nuclear weapons is the decision whether or not to have them at all. The United States decided to develop atomic weapons out of fear that Hitler would get them first. After the war, the United States presented the United Nations with a plan for the internationalization of atomic weapons, a plan eventually rejected by the Soviets and abandoned by the United States around 1950. Since then the idea of a United States without nuclear weapons has been largely fantasy. Nevertheless, it is worth considering, at least as an exercise, what the United States gains and loses through the mere possession of atomic weapons.

(a) Diminished Risk of Attack

The principal alleged benefit that comes from the mere possession of nuclear weapons is a diminished risk of military attack. Nations considering whether to attack the United States must consider the possibility of an American nuclear reprisal, a possibility that they would not have to consider if the United States possessed no nuclear weapons at all.

One's assessment of this benefit, however, turns on one's estimate of what the chances of attack on the United States would be if it had no nuclear weapons. As we noted in the previous chapter, this assessment is largely a matter of conjecture. Suppose that, by a miracle, all American nuclear weapons disappear tonight. What is the chance that the United States would be attacked tomorrow, or the day after? If the chance of an attack on a United States without nuclear weapons is *nearly zero*, then nuclear weapons can hardly be said to *diminish* the chance of attack. As we noted at the start of the last chapter, estimates about what would happen if things were different are largely exercises in conjecture and prophecy.

If you believe that the Soviet Union desires war with the United States and is restrained from initiating war only by fear of American nuclear weapons; if you believe, as the famous yet secret National Security Council Memorandum 68 postulated in 1950, that

> The Soviet Union, unlike previous aspirants to hegemony, is animated by a new fanatic faith, antithetical to our own, and seeks to impose its absolute authority on the rest of the world...[Etzold 1978 385]

> The (Kremlin) design calls for the complete subversion or forcible destruction of the machinery of government and structure of society in the countries of the non-Soviet world...[Ibid. 387]

> There is no justification in Soviet theory or practice in predicting that, should the Kremlin become convinced that it would cause our downfall by one conclusive blow, it would not seek that solution...[Ibid. 394]

> We can expect no lasting abatement of this crisis unless and until a change occurs in the nature of the Soviet system...[Ibid. 389]

then you will rate the chance of a Soviet attack on a United States without nuclear weapons as high.

If you believe that the Soviet Union is basically a great nation state seeking to preserve its national interests, that based on its experience, in the last two hundred years, of being invaded or attacked by France (1812), England (1854), Austria (1914), Germany (1914), Britain and the United States (1918), and Germany (1941), the Soviet Union only desires the preservation of friendly governments around the Soviet periphery; if you remember that Soviet ideology predicts the collapse of the West without the intervention of military force; if you believe that neither country is burdened by overpopulation and that neither has natural resources essential to the other, then you will rate the chances of a Soviet attack on a United States without nuclear weapons as low.[2]

There is no doubt that nuclear weapons inspire fear, and fear may deter potential aggressors who would otherwise attack. But at the same time, fear inspires hostility, and hostility inspires aggression. Nuclear weapons may function to some extent like lightning rods, inviting attack, rather than as shields deterring attack. We may be confident that the aggressor will be destroyed if he attacks us, but the attacker may not believe this, or he may not care. All these considerations reduce the strength of the claim that nuclear weapons reduce the chance of attack on the Untied States.

Even if nuclear weapons diminish the chance that the United States will be subjected to a nuclear first strike, they certainly increase the chance that the United States will be subjected to a Soviet nuclear *second* strike. The United States may attack the Soviet Union in an act of madness, or it may attack Russia in the mistaken belief that it will obtain total victory through a first strike. It may attack Russia by mistake, or it may attack Russia by accident. In response to any of these events, the Soviet Union will probably launch a devastating second strike against the United States. The chance of such a *second* strike is rarely considered by those who are convinced that possession of nuclear weapons lowers the chance of nuclear attack.

(b) Increased Resistance to Threats

Many people believe that a United States without nuclear weapons would be helpless in the face of nuclear threats. Let us consider a hypothetical case. Suppose that the Soviet Union reinstitutes the Berlin blockade, demanding that West Berlin be placed under East German authority, and suppose that *this* time the Soviets threaten to shoot down American cargo planes if they attempt to supply the city. Since the United States possesses nuclear weapons, Soviet attacks on American planes run the risk of provoking an American nuclear attack. If the United States did not possess nuclear weapons, Soviet attacks on these planes would not run the risk of American nuclear reprisal, but any American defense of these planes runs the risk of a Soviet nuclear reprisal. It seems obvious to many people that the Soviets are more likely to take the initiative, make the threats, and successfully enforce their will in the absence of American nuclear weapons than in their presence. It is considerations like these that prompt people to say that nuclear weapons preserve the conventional peace.

As with the claim of "decreased chance of nuclear attack," the claim of "increased resistance to nuclear threats" can only be evaluated relative to what American resistance to nuclear threats *would* be *if* the United States did not possess nuclear weapons. If you feel that there is no chance that the United States could resist nuclear threats if it did not possess nuclear weapons, then you will think that nuclear weapons increase American will to resist by a great amount. If you feel that the United States would resist nuclear blackmail even if it did not possess nuclear weapons, then you will feel that nuclear weapons do not provide much in the way of increased resistance. There is some historical evidence that the ability of non-nuclear nations to resist nuclear threats is pretty good. American nuclear threats did not prevent the establishment of Communist Party control in Eastern Europe, the collapse of Chiang Kai-shek, the Chinese incursion into North Korea, the fall of Dienbienphu, the collapse of South Vietnam, or the seizure of the American embassy in Teheran. Soviet nuclear threats did not prevent the maintainance of political independence by Tito, the worker revolts in East Germany, the rebellion in Hungary, the Sino-Soviet split, the Prague Spring, the explusion of Soviet advisors from Egypt, or the rebellions in Poland. British nuclear threats did not prevent seizure of the Falkland Islands. The historical evidence does not even indicate that Japan surrendered in 1945 for fear of further nuclear attacks: the final blow that brought the ruling council to accept terms seems to have been the Soviet declaration of war against Japan, 8 August 1945.[3] To say that the United States could not resist nuclear threats when Russia, China, Hungary, Czechoslovakia, Vietnam, etc. have all resisted them would attribute to the United States a unique national cowardice.

In all these cases in which nuclear threats were made or implied, the outcome seems to have been mainly determined, not by the nuclear threats, but by the presence or absence of overwhelming strength in conventional weapons. Did Soviet ships turn back from Cuba in 1962 because Khruschev feared an American attack on Moscow? Or did they turn back because of the overwhelming strength of the United States Navy and the proximity of the engagement to naval bases in the United States? Did the Soviets give up in Berlin in 1948 because of the atomic bombs that may or may not have been in B-29s in England, or because of overwhelming American superiority in the air over Europe? Certainly a nation possessing nuclear weapons may collapse before threats, while a nation with no nuclear weapons may not collapse before threats, even nuclear threats.

(c) Increased Chance of Victory in War

It seems self-evident to many that if war breaks out between a nuclear nation and a non-nuclear nation, the nuclear nation must win. Certainly this is true in the case of an all-out war, in which one side seeks to annihilate the other. If annihilation is desired, then nuclear weapons are preternaturally suited to doing the job.

This model of all-out war captures the imagination so vividly that it takes an effort of concentration to realize that, in the history of war, all-out war is the exception, not the rule. Most wars are less than all-out contests; they are tests to see which nation is willing to sacrifice the most for a given objective. In such contests, annihilation of the opponent is not an objective; indeed, annihilation of the opponents may be extremely undersirable (The opponent may be for example, an important trading partner in peacetime.) It follows that in less than all-out struggles, possession of nuclear weapons may not provide a decisive advantage over a non-nuclear opponent.

Some will find proof of this assertion in the lesson of Vietnam. The maintenance of political control of South Vietnam was not something that could be achieved or even assisted with nuclear weapons, and when the conflict developed into a military struggle between the NLF, assisted by large North Vietnamese forces, and pro-Saigon troops, assisted by half a million Americans, it turned out that there was no decisive military advantage that could be obtained by the introduction of nuclear weapons, tactical or strategic. Certainly it was possible to bomb North Vietnam back into the stone age, as Curtis LeMay so memorably suggested. But the annihilation of North Vietnam was not an American objective, since such an act was likely to produce a war between the United States and China or Russia or both. Furthermore, any use of the larger nuclear weapons against supply routes or North Vietnamese cities would have produced fallout that could have contaminated Thailand, Cambodia, South Vietnam, China, or even Hong Kong, depending on the winds.

The Vietnam lesson—that it is very difficult to use nuclear weapons to achieve a limited objective—has been replicated on numerous actual and imaginary battlefields since the nuclear era began in 1945. The Air Force could find no use for tactical or strategic nuclear weapons in Korea. The Soviets did not use them against the Chinese in 1969. The Israelis could find no use for them in 1973, when only six tanks on the Golan Heights stood between Israel and disaster in the Yom Kippur War. In numerous NATO exercises in which NATO troops use nuclear weapons against invading Warsaw pact troops, estimates of civilian casualties in Europe run between two million and five million dead, results that may in the event of actual invasion lead most Europeans to prefer their conquerors to their defenders.[4] If the Iraqis or the Libyans or some other anti-Zionist power acquires nuclear weapons, they could not use them aganist Jerusalem without destroying the mosques they seek to liberate. Such examples could be multiplied indefinitely. What Bernard Brodie called "the absolute weapon" in 1946 has proven in practice to be considerably less than absolute.

In evaluating the relationship between the possession of nuclear weapons and the chance of military victory, one must consider not only the potential uses of nuclear weapons but also the effect that the possession of nuclear weapons has on the performance of troops on the battlefield. It can be argued that both tactical and strategic nuclear weapons have a negative effect on battlefield performance.

Tactical nuclear weapons have been integrated into U.S. Army combat procedures since the 1950s, and there are still over 5,000 tactical nuclear weapons with NATO forces in Europe. But battlefield training with these weapons in the 1950s was (fortunately) quite limited, and since the partial Test Ban treaty of 1963, battlefield training with nuclear weapons has been impossible.[5] The result is that Army troops depend on weapons that they do not know how to use and whose performance characteristics in battle are not well known. One does not have to be a military genius to recognize that this situation is a prescription for disaster on the battlefield.

The effect of *strategic* nuclear weapons on battlefield performance is considerable. First of all, strategic nuclear weapons cost money, and to some extent every dollar spent on strategic weapons is a dollar that could have been spent on the improvement of conventional weapons. The emphasis that strategic weapons have received since 1945 has twisted the budgets and procurements of all the services in the direction of high technology—"our one great advantage over the Soviets"—and as a result the services are now overstocked with complicated guns that won't shoot, complicated planes that won't fly, and complicated torpedoes that home in on the sound of their own engines. The whole idea that the nation's first line of defense is a set of spy satellites and missile silos is bound to affect the morale and performance of the Army and the Marines, and the decline in performance evidenced in the successively botched Son Tay, Mayaguez, and Iranian rescue attempts is too obvious to bear comment. In this light, it is not surprising that the last successful American military operation (Inchon, 1950) came before the rise of strategic weapons in the American arsenal. One might hypothesize that strategic weapons can become an addiction that saps the strength of conventional forces.[6] As the Israelis have demonstrated four times in 35 years, there is no substitute for spirit and skill on the battlefield, provided that victory, not Armageddon, is the objective. If so, the contribution that nuclear weapons make to the chance of victory in a typical war is open to debate.

(d) Economic Benefits of Strategic Weapons Development

Strategic weapons have cost the United States a great deal of money since the Manhattan Project began in 1942. But many people believe that the development and purchase of strategic weapons has helped, not hurt, the American economy.[7] There are three basic arguments for this view. (i) Though strategic weapons are expensive, they are not *very* expensive measured against other military purchases. In 1983, the costs of strategic weapons were only about 8.5 percent of the American military budget: 21.5 billion out of 249 billion dollars. (ii) Development of strategic weapons provides employment for thousands of highly trained scientists and engineers, who might otherwise be unemployed or underemployed. (iii) The development of strategic weapons leads to scientific discoveries and technological innovations that improve the American standard of living and help the United States compete effectively on the international scene. The Boeing 707 was nothing but a modified version of an Air Force cargo jet; integrated circuits were developed in important ways in the Minuteman II missile program; the spy satellite and the weather satellite go hand in hand, and so forth. There is some truth in all these assertions, but there are counter-arguments, point for point.

(i) Though it is true that strategic weapons are a small fraction of current military budgets, the expense of these weapons should not be underestimated. Current costs are low since the major strategic systems are in place, and present costs of these systems are limited to operation, repair, replacement. The fraction of the budget devoted to strategic weapons in previous years was far higher—in the 1950s *half* the budget went to the Air Force—and with the deployment of the Trident submarine, B-1 bomber and MX-missile, the fraction devoted to strategic weapons will rise once again. Furthermore, a substantial part of the cost of strategic weapons is tucked into the "research and development" section of the military budget, a section which consumes another 10 percent of current military budgets. If all research costs are added in, the total cost of strategic weapons since NSC-68 called for rearmament in 1950 approaches 700 billion 1983 dollars.[8] If this $700 billion provided, dollar for dollar, more security than purchases of other kinds, such a huge purchase might appear reasonable. But, as the preceding sections indicate, "more bang for the buck" does not necessarily mean more military power for the dollar.

(ii) At least 20 percent of the nation's scientists and engineers are supported by Defense Department purchases. If Defense Department purchases go down some of these scientists and engineers will be out of work. But in evaluating the overall impact of strategic weapons purchases on employment we must consider how many jobs would be generated if comparable sums were spent on other things. Studies show that a billion dollars spent on defense generates fewer jobs than a billion dollars spent on non-defense items. Strategic weapons purchases, which are "capital intensive" and involve high labor costs and generate even fewer jobs than the military average. A billion dollars spent on guided missiles will generate about 18,000 jobs, but a billion dollars spent on educational services generates about 61,000 jobs.[9] If government purchases are justified on grounds that such purchases reduce unemployment, the most efficient use of government funds dictates education purchases, not defense purchases. One does, to be sure, feel sympathy for the scientists and engineers who will lose jobs if defense spending is cut back, but scientists and engineers traditionally have low rates of unemployment. Government cut-backs are less likely to result in long-term unemployment among scientists and engineers than among any other occupational group.

(iii) In an age when economic success on the international scene increasingly means the ability to supply state-of-the-art technology, the case for the economic benefits of strategic weapons development seems strong. But in many ways the billions spent on strategic weapons research have not yielded the expected benefits in the civilian sector. The number of patents generated from Defense Department research is very low per research dollar, and time and time again the Pentagon has backed the wrong technological horse and has had to grudgingly admit that technology developed in the civilian sector is superior even for its own military purposes.[10] The reasons for this technological sterility are not well understood, but commentators have noted that (a) many military products, for example precision guided missiles, have no civilian applications or analogues; (b) the atmosphere of secrecy in which strategic weapons research is conducted is not conducive to creative thought; (c) the Defense Department spends a miniscule fraction of its research budget on basic research, the sort of research that yields real "breakthroughs"; (d) the Pentagon favors awarding contracts to large "tried and true" firms, not the smaller companies that are more likely to produce innovations; and (e) the "cost plus" system of accounting employed by the Pentagon does not encourage companies to produce cheap products that have a chance of competing in the private market.[11]

Whatever the causes, the Defense Department is no hotbed of technological innovation, and it is almost a rule that the deeper a firm is involved in defense production, the less capable it is of producing a product that can compete on the open market. For example, Lockheed has had to quit civilian production, McDonnell Douglas has had deep trouble with its DC-10; and even Boeing, the most "privatized" of the aircraft firms, is getting tough competition from the European Airbus.

Not all products inspired by the Defense Department are poor: the Boeing passenger jet is a notable counterexample. But the passenger jet would have been introduced sooner or later—defense research simply speeded up development by a year or two. There is, however, *one* product that might never have reached the domestic market without research assistance from the American government, and that is the nuclear power plant. Since 1942 a symbiotic relation has existed between nuclear reactors and atomic bombs: the reactors have supplied the fissionable material for the bombs, and the need for bombs has helped secure funds for the improvement of the reactors. Indeed, the push for nuclear power in this country is at least partially motivated by scientists trying to make amends for Hiroshima and a government trying to excuse the development of nuclear weapons on the grounds that "there are no evil atoms, only evil people." Given current safety and waste disposal problems, skyrocketing plant costs and stiff rate increases borne by consumers whose power companies have gone nuclear, the nuclear power plant is a spin-off from defense work that is a *very* mixed blessing.[12]

In calculating the opportunity costs of strategic weapons purchases, one must consider what the condition of the United States would have been if it had directed comparable monies and scientific talent into the development of technology for the civilian sector. Speculation about what might have happened can be guided in this case by the example of countries that took the civilian route, for one reason or another. In a study of 17 nations across 23 years (1960-83) the Council on Economic Priorities noted that the nation that devoted the smallest fraction of its Gross National Product to Defense—

Japan—was the nation with the highest rate of economic growth, and the highest growth in output per manufacturing hour. The two nations with the highest fractions of their gross national products devoted to defense, the United States and the United Kingdom, ranked 12th and 17th in real economic growth.[13] The Council noted that it found positive correlations between low economic growth and high military spending even when the cases of the United States and Japan were excluded, and that it did not find a positive correlation between low economic growth and increases in labor costs, between low economic growth and the degree of regulation in the economy, or between low economic growth and the size of transfer payments relative to the Gross National Product.

It would, of course, be rushing to conclusions to declare that Japanese economic success is due to low military spending while American economic stagnation is due to high military spending. Nevertheless, even the most isolated American is by now aware that Japanese products are displacing American products on the world market and on the home front. As he goes about buying Japanese cameras, Japanese cars, Japanese stereo equipment, Japanese video cassette recorders, and Japanese televisions, the average American may begin to wonder why all these products are now better made than their American counterparts, when "made in Japan" only 25 years ago used to signify that a product was junk. He might consider that if the Japanese had joined an arms race, the scientists and engineers who now make Nikons, Sonys, and so forth, would have been diverted to work on missiles and radars, like their American counterparts. With this in mind, he might reach a different conclusion from the one Secretary of Defense Harold Brown expressed in testimony in 1980: "our research suggests that military expenditures are beneficial in the long term to the civilian economy, since much of the additional spending promotes domestic production in our most capital and technology intensive sectors." (Degrasse 1983 55.)

Choice B: Tactical, Strategic or Both?

Once a nation decides to develop nuclear weapons, it faces the question of which sorts of nuclear weapons it will acquire. In particular, it must decide whether to acquire strategic nuclear weapons only, tactical nuclear weapons only, or both. A nuclear nation that loses on the conventional battlefield can always move up to strategic nuclear weapons. Why, then, should any nation acquire tactical nuclear weapons at all? Nuclear strategists suggest a reason. Some tactical nuclear weapons have explosive charges no larger than the explosive charges of large conventional weapons. Thus, it is psychologically easier for a nuclear nation to shift from conventional weapons to tactical nuclear weapons than from conventional weapons to strategic nuclear weapons. An opponent, considering whether or not to attack a nuclear nation N, will recognize that it stands a greater chance of evoking a nuclear response if N has tactical nuclear weapons than if N has strategic weapons alone. For example, a Soviet conventional attack in Europe is likely to be met with NATO tactical nuclear weapons, and the result may be an all-out nuclear war. Presumably, this thought prevents the Soviets from attacking in the first place.

According to this theory, tactical nuclear weapons bring both good news and bad news. The good news is that they help to prevent wars from starting in the first place. The bad news is that, once a war starts, they make it more likely that the war will become a nuclear war. But this theory may be too subtle for political or even military reality. Imagine that the Soviets are considering an invasion of Western Europe. They know that if they do so there is *some* chance of a nuclear holocaust. Do they calculate, in any precise way, what this chance is? Do they calculate how much *more* chance there is of a nuclear holocaust if NATO has nuclear weapons on cannons and not just in the bomb bays of F-111s? If they perform these calculations, how likely are these calculations to affect their behavior? Is there a "level of danger," and will the Soviets, finding themselves below this level, attack forthwith?

Certainly such models make a mockery of what we know about actual decision making in actual governments, and it attributes to the Soviets a decisiveness and boldness belied by the indecisiveness and timidity that characterize their post-war relations with the west.[14] In fact, the difference in the probability of nuclear response provided by tactical nuclear weapons may be imperceptible to the Soviets; if so, they fail to provide any strategic advantage. The strategic disadvantage of lowering the nuclear threshold and making nuclear war more likely (if war occurs at all) remains, regardless of how tactical nuclear weapons are perceived.

Choice C: Nuclear Aggression or Nuclear Defense

Once a nation has acquired nuclear weapons (of whatever kinds) it needs a policy to determine the circumstances under which these weapons will be used. In particular, the political leadership must decide whether they are to be used for aggressive purposes, or should be strictly confined to defense.

All of the nations that have so far acquired nuclear weapons have declared that they intend to use them only for defense. This is not surprising, since no nation, not even Nazi Germany, has ever confessed to aggressive purposes. The United States is no exception in this regard. As recently as February 1983, Secretary of Defense Weinberger affirmed: "Our strategy is defensive. It excludes the possibility that the United States would initiate a war or launch a pre-emptive strike against the forces or territories of other nations. (Weinberger 1983 32.)

It is commonly known that the Secretary's Annual Reports to Congress exhibit only the "declaratory policy" of the Defense Department; the real policy, the "action policy" may be quite different.[15] If the the Defense Department has taken steps to make it *physically impossible* for the United States to start such wars or launch such strikes, no such steps have been announced.

Certainly there are advantages in possessing a capacity for a successful pre-emptive strike, that is, a strike that annihilates the main military forces of an opponent. If the United States had this power, and if it discovered that the Soviet Union was preparing to launch a nuclear attack on the United States at 12 midnight, it could exercise its power and destroy all Soviet forces at 11:59 P.M., saving the lives of millions of Americans.

But there are also disadvantages in attempting to develop the capacity for a pre-emptive strike. (i) Under current conditions, it is technically impossible to develop the ability for a successful pre-emptive strike. Even if the United States destroyed most of the nuclear weapons of the Soviet Union, a few would probably escape, and those few could kill tens of millions of Americans. The search for pre-emptive "first strike" capacity could waste a great deal of money and still not succeed. (ii) American steps towards a pre-emptive strike capacity will hardly go unnoticed by hostile powers, who will realize that their forces will be put in jeopardy. There is no way to assure an opponent that our pre-emptive strike capacity will be used *only* if he considers an aggressive course of action. For all he knows, the new American strike capacity will be used to disarm his country, in preparation for conquest by the United States. With this in mind, he will do everything to counteract the American steps towards a first strike capacity. He might instruct the forces to strike at the first sign of American attack—the policy of "launch on warning"—in order to prevent his weapons from being destroyed on the ground. But a "launch on warning" posture is susceptible to accidents and mistakes. An American search for the capacity to launch a pre-emptive attack increases the chance that the United States will suffer an unintentional nuclear strike.

Choice D: First Use or No First Use?

Given the technical difficulties surrounding pre-emption, we can be confident that, at least for the present, the United States has no plans for a pre-emptive strike against anyone. Our present policy probably is, as Weinberger claimed, purely "defensive." But the notion of a "defensive" use of nuclear weapons is complex. Obviously nuclear weapons are not like shields or castle walls or other traditional modes of defense. They cannot stop a blow on its way to delivery: they can only discourage an opponent from launching a blow in the first place by promising a terrible retaliation in return. But what sort of blows should one seek to prevent with promises of nuclear retaliation? Blows of any kind? Or only nuclear blows? Notice that the nation that launches a nuclear counter-attack in response to a conventional attack will have broken the nuclear taboo, even if it did not start the war. To adopt a policy of never using nuclear weapons unless someone else does is to adopt a policy of "no first use." The United States has never publicly affirmed a "no first use" policy. Our implied declaratory policy, especially in the European theater, is to use nuclear weapons in response to conventional aggression. But declaratory policy does not matter as much as action policy. The United States could make a "no first use" declaration, and yet be prepared to use nuclear weapons first; it could refuse to make a "no first use" declaration, and yet be committed to not using nuclear weapons first.[16] Which action policy serves the interests of the United States best?

Obviously there is an advantage in having one's opponents believe that one is prepared to use nuclear weapons in response to a non-nuclear attack: it makes such non-nuclear attacks less likely to occur. But how can one create such a belief in an opponent? If the adversary has an intelligence network worth its name, he will only come to believe that the United States will use nuclear weapons in response to a non-nuclear attack if in fact the United States is committed to that course of action. In other words, a believable "first use" declaratory policy requires a genuine first use action policy.

But there are disadvantages to a genuine first use action policy. If the conventional attack is launched by an opponent that has nuclear weapons in reserve, then a nuclear reprisal may generate a nuclear counter-reprisal, and what started as a conventional conflict will be transformed into a nuclear war. This outcome does *not* serve American interests. If the conventional attack is launched by a non-nuclear power, then a nuclear response, though not leading to nuclear war, will nonetheless break the nuclear taboo and bring down the wrath of the civilized world. The original aggression will be forgotten in a general hysteria about nuclear weapons.

How dangerous would it be for Western Europe if NATO adopted a believable "no first use" action policy? Since the 1950s, it has been the belief of many experts that fear of a nuclear response from NATO has deterred a Warsaw pact invasion of Western Europe. But if this invasion is forthcoming, in the absence of NATO nuclear weapons, the Soviets must *want* to invade and they must believe that this invasion will succeed. But since the Berlin Wall went up in 1961 and since Soviet recognition of the partition of Germany in 1971, the Soviets have had no motive, short of madness, for invading Western Europe. Nor can they be confident of success, even on conventional terms: their vaunted superiority in numbers of tanks is neutralized by developments in anti-tank warfare, as evidenced by Israeli success in blowing up Soviet-built Syrian tanks in Lebanon in 1982. "No first use" has risks, but does not present a clear and present danger to stability in Europe.

Choice E: Commitment or Bluff?

Regardless of any decision reached regarding the use of nuclear weapons against conventional attacks, the primary function of American nuclear weapons is to deter *nuclear* attacks on the United States and its allies. Despite their awesome physical power, the objective of the American strategic weapons is mainly psychological: their job is to create in the minds of adversaries the unshakable belief that if they ever used nuclear weapons against the United States or its allies, they would surely come to regret it. Nuclear weapons, then, are a kind of propaganda designed to paralyze the will of opponents.[17]

How can we convince the Soviets that if they attack us we will surely issue a nuclear reprisal? One solution is to convince them that we find it in our interests to issue such reprisals. That is to say, we will convince them that we will counter-attack by showing that we would view such a counter-attack as a rational response to Soviet attack.

But *can* we convince the Soviets that an American nuclear counter-strike makes sense? Can we convince ourselves? Suppose that the Soviets launch a devastating nuclear attack against the United States, destroying most American cities, killing tens of millions of Americans, and totally disrupting the distribution of food, goods, and services in the United States. Under *those* circumstances, it is in the national interest to launch a nuclear counter-strike against the Soviet Union? What purpose would such an action serve? It will not revive the dead; it will not supply the survivors with food. It would inject more fallout into the atmosphere, perhaps making life more miserable for the Americans who have survived the attack. It might prompt the Soviets to use a few of their spare weapons to launch a nuclear counter-counter strike, polishing off the few American cities and factories that managed to ride out the first attack. And it would certainly cut off any chance of Soviet aid to the American survivors. No, a counter-strike in response to a massive Soviet strike does not seem like the sort of thing that a sane and self-interested nation would do.

Now, suppose that the Soviets launch a *limited* nuclear attack against the United States. Millions are dead, but most Americans and most American cities survive. Would it be rational *then* to launch a nuclear counter attack against Russia? If we do, the result may be the destruction of all the American cities that survived the first attack. This does not seem like the sort of thing a sane and self-interested nation would risk.

It appears, then, that there are many scenarios in which "striking back" would not be in our self-interest. We know this, and the Soviets, if they think about these things, know it too. It follows that we cannot count on the Soviets believing that we will issue a counter-strike because we believe that it is the rational thing to do. Those who think about nuclear deterrence have thought long and hard about this problem. Two solutions have been proposed, two methods for communicating to the Soviets the American intent to respond to attack.

One method is to *bluff*, to keep the Soviets guessing about what we would do. If the Soviets do not know what we will do, they will believe that there is at least a chance of American reprisal; and, recognizing how terrible this reprisal will be, they will call off any plans to attack. On this "bluff" strategy, if the Soviets attack, we will do *then* only what is rational. If it is counter-productive to issue an American reprisal, we will not issue it. Our bluff will have been called.

The alternative method is to *commit* American forces to reprisal, that is, to make an American response to a Soviet strike automatic, or at least semi-automatic. A present commitment to future action removes the element of choice at the time of a Soviet strike, that moment of decision that, under the bluff strategy, makes it possible for American leaders to call off the counter-strike should they find it irrational to proceed. If we make such a commitment, we will not be bluffing when we say that a Soviet nuclear attack will be met by an American nuclear reprisal. If the Soviets attack, we will have no choice but to respond: we will be bound, physically bound, by our automatic commitment to a second strike.[18] Which strategy serves American interests best, Commitment or Bluff?

(a) Commitment

In science-fiction style presentations of nuclear war situations, mechanical devices are often brought in as embodiments of the commitment strategy. In these stories, American strategic systems are usually hooked into a giant computer, programmed to issue a counter-strike in response to a certain input, no matter what the human beings who made the computer may desire to happen.[19] But we do not need these science-fiction devices to institute the commitment strategy. If enough persons are endowed with the power to launch strategic weapons once they decide a Soviet strike is in progress, it becomes a statistical certainty that one or more of these decision makers *will* issue a counter-strike in response to Soviet attack, even if the President should want to call off the strike. The more persons that have the physical ability to launch strategic weapons, the more likely it is that the reprisal will occur. So the commitment strategy can be enacted simply by widely distributing the power to launch strategic weapons.

The virtues of commitment are clear. There is no need for threats; no need to bluster. All one need do is explain the facts, explain that if America is attacked, there is no way that anyone can prevent an American reprisal from launching forth. If the conviction that a reprisal will occur is the best way to deter attack, then commitment seems the ideal strategy for creating this conviction.

The disadvantages of commitment are built into the strategy; if deterrence fails, one may be worse off with commitment than with some alternative strategy. Defenders of commitment do not consider this a serious problem, because they do not believe that with commitment deterrence will fail. But even with commitment, a nuclear attack on the United States may still occur. A psychotic enemy may not care about the counter-strike, a sane enemy might not believe that the strategy of commitment is actually in place. An accident or a mistake could trigger an unintentional attack on the United States. Furthermore, commitment increases the chances of an American first strike. Commitment requires that many Americans have the power to launch strategic weapons; and the more people who have this power, the more likely it is that some American controlling strategic weapons will make a mistake, go crazy, or decide to end the Cold War in one fell swoop. It seems that with commitment, the things that make deterrence likely to succeed are the very things that would make matters worse should deterrence fail. And deterrence may always fail, no matter what nuclear strategy is adopted.

(b) Bluff

Under the bluff strategy no irrevokable commitments are made to the launching of a second strike. True, high American officials *declare*, in solemn tones, that any nuclear attack on the United States will surely be met with a terrible reprisal. All the physical apparatus needed to mount these reprisals, no matter how severe the Soviet first strike, is installed and ready to fire. At the same time, control of American strategic systems remains in the hands of the President and the Secretary of Defense; and the President and the Secretary are free to decide whether to launch an American second strike or not. They retain this freedom even after a first strike has landed.

By concentrating the control of strategic systems in the hands of a few individuals, the bluff strategy minimizes risk of an unintentional attack on the Soviet Union. It leaves the President or his successor free to decide, in the event of a Soviet strike, on the course of action that best suits American interests. (It even leaves the President free to decide to do what is morally right.)

The disadvantage of the bluff strategy is that deterrence may fail if the bluff is found out. If the Soviets realize that the American President is free to choose his course of action at every point in time, they might devise a first strike such that an American counter-strike would be self-destructive. If the President acts rationally, he will not respond to such a strike.

To many, this potential failure of deterrence shows that the bluff strategy is defective, leaving the United States in peril of Soviet attack. But these fears may be grossly exaggerated. Even if the Soviets feel they could launch a first strike with impunity, it by no means follows that they *would* launch a first strike. There are many reasons for not launching a first strike besides fear of a second strike. A first strike against the United States means radioactive fallout blowing on the Soviet Union, means an end to purchases of American wheat, means an end to American credits, Pepsi-Cola, and so forth. Furthermore, even if the Soviets knew that the President retains the power to launch (or not to launch) strategic weapons, they cannot be sure what the President will do after America suffers a first strike. (Neither can the President.) They may know that they can launch a type of first strike that would make it irrational for the President to issue a second strike, but they cannot know that the President will act rationally, as he flies around in his National Emergency Airborne Commmand Post watching his nation suffering a nuclear attack. Since the President chooses freely, there is no way that this uncertainty can be removed. And this uncertainty about what the President will do can be almost as effective a deterrent as the certainty of a second strike.

Choice F: Counterforce, Countervalue, or Both?

In addition to deciding the circumstance under which nuclear weapons will be used, a nuclear nation must decide upon the targets at which nuclear weapons are to be aimed. There are three basic targeting policies. One can aim only at the military forces of the enemy: his missiles, airfields, submarine stations, weapons depots and so forth. This is called *counterforce* targeting. Alternatively, one can aim only at urban, economic, or industrial targets, leaving enemy forces aside. This is called *countervalue* targeting. Or one can adopt some mixture of counterforce and countervalue targeting. If we put moral consideration aside and consider only the *American* national interest, which targeting pattern is the most effective?

Questions about effectiveness cannot be answered without some specification of the objectives of the targeting plan. Unfortunately strategic weapons have been assigned multiple objectives, which makes the assessment of targeting plans difficult. In 1965, McNamara set as the basic objectives (i) deterrence of attack, and (ii) if deterrence fails, limitation of damage to the United States (McNamara 1965). In 1983, Caspar Weinberger set as the objectives (i) deterrence of war, and (ii) if deterrence fails, conclusion of the war "on favorable terms" (Weinberger 1983 32). It may turn out that the targeting pattern that serves the first objective well will not serve the second at all.

(a) Counterforce Targeting

In the age of the ICBM, counterforce targeting capacity implies the ability to find and destroy enemy missile silos. Since missile silos are small and heavily reinforced, the destruction of a silo requires highly accurate missiles. Since any missile that can hit a silo can also hit a city, it follows that counterforce ability implies countervalue ability (but not vice versa). Since counterforce ability entails countervalue ability, the decision to have an exclusive counterforce targeting pattern requires a voluntary renunciation of cities as targets. Thus, pure counterforce targeting requires voluntary restraints that may collapse in a crisis. Nevertheless, we will assume that the targeting pattern does not collapse.

The obvious and main advantage of counterforce targeting is that it limits damage to the United States should deterrence fail and war break out. Every enemy missile destroyed in its silo is one less missile that will land on the United States. Furthermore, the ability to destroy military targets without destroying enemy cities leaves those cities hostage to a subsequent American countervalue attack, a fact that may deter an enemy nation from issuing reprisals in response to an American counterforce attack. Finally, since counterforce targeting seeks to limit nuclear war, counterforce stratgey provides a believable deterrent to limit attacks on the United States: an opponent may think that the United States will not start an all-out war in response to a limited attack, but he may well believe that the United States is willing to risk a limited nuclear war in response to a nuclear strike.

Given these advantages, it is not surprising that the argument that counterforce targeting is "damage limiting" can be oversold. First of all, under current and forseeable future technology, no counterforce strike against the Soviet Union, no matter how massive, will destroy all Soviet strategic weapons, and the few surviving strategic weapons could destroy much of the United States. Secondly, counterforce targeting requires a technologically sophisticated offense, which provokes a technologically sophisticated defense, which prompts further development of the offense, and so on. In short, counterforce targeting generates a qualitative arms race. Thirdly, counterforce targeting is provocative, since the ability to issue a counterforce second strike implies the ability to issue an even more devastating counterforce *first* strike, one so effective that it might leave the enemy practically helpless, with his surviving cities serving as targets for irresistible nuclear blackmail.[20]

(b) Counterforce Targeting

A nuclear nation can adopt countervalue targeting by choice or by necessity. If it has precise weapons, it can adopt it by choice, deliberately avoiding targeting the military forces of the opponent. If it has only imprecise weapons, it will adopt it of necessity, targeting only objects it is sure to hit.

Countervalue targeting does not have the "damage limiting" advantages of counterforce targeting. But it has the advantages of technical simplicity: strategic weapons can easily destroy cities. Since it requires only the simplest strategic weapons, it does not provoke a technological arms race. It is not provocative; it does not threaten the opponent with the prospect of finding himself suddenly disarmed by a counter-force first strike.

Most of all, it produces terror, and terror provides an effective deterrent. An enemy may not believe that the United States will actually launch an attack that will destroy his cities, devastate his countryside, and kill tens of millions of people. But he cannot be sure about what the United States will do, and he can hardly afford to make a mistake.

Advocates of counterforce targeting reject the notion of deterrence through sheer terror. They argue that it is the *certainty*, not the *magnitude* of punishment that deters the criminal, and thus it is the certainty of punishment that will deter crimes by states. Furthermore, they will argue that the Soviet leadership may fear attacks on military forces *more* than attacks on cities, since military forces are the instruments by which they maintain political power. But the advocate of a countervalue strategy will note that a sufficiently determined criminal can deceive himself into thinking that he will escape punishment, no matter how likely it really is that he will be caught. It follows that no targeting strategy can convince a determined opponent that a second strike will come. As for the notion that Soviet leaders care more for guns than their own people, he will point out the psychological implausibility of Russian leaders not caring about the survival of Russia, and note that Soviet doctrine maintains that military forces can always be replaced if the industrial structure remains intact. If so, only a countervalue strategy can supply an effective deterrent.[21]

The different assumptions behind counterforce and and countervalue options are now clear. Those who favor counterforce targeting believe that a nuclear war can be voluntarily controlled. Those who favor countervalue targeting believe that once the nuclear threshold is crossed, control is impossible and sooner or later cities will be struck. The countervalue strategy keeps the nuclear threshold high, and this strategy, all things considered, is less likely to produce nuclear war. But if deterrence fails, the countervalue strategy leads straight to Armageddon. Under the counterforce strategy, if deterrence fails, we do not have Armageddon—at least not in the first two hours.

(c) Mixed Targeting Strategies

Since each targeting strategy has its supporters, it is not surprising that the targeting plan currently in force is a mixture of counterforce and countervalue targeting, with the United States starting out its second strike by attacking military targets, but moving on, if the war continues, to non-military targets. This mixed strategy combines the worst features of both targeting strategies while forfeiting the advantages of either. By starting out with counterforce targeting, it lowers the nuclear threshold, making the start of nuclear war more likely. By finishing up with countervalue targeting, it helps to guarantee that nuclear war will be a worldwide catastrophe if it occurs. Few theoreticians, for these reasons, have advocated a mixed strategy. Its persistance in action policy is the result of political compromise.

Choice G: Massive Retalition or Flexible Response?

Suppose that the United States is subjected to nuclear attack. If the President decides to respond at all, should he launch all his strategic weapons against the attacker, or should he limit his response and hold some weapons in reserve? This is the choice between massive retaliation and flexible response.

(a) Massive Retaliation

John Foster Dulles made massive retaliation the declaratory policy of the Eisenhower years. What are the advantages of massive retaliation as an *action* policy? (i) Massive retaliation is the most terrifying of all "rate-of-fire" responses.[22] If deterrence requires fear, massive retaliation will produce that fear. (ii) Massive retaliation is a believable strategy, in the sense that there is no technical impediment to carrying it out. (iii) Massive retaliation guarantees the most efficient use of American strategic weapons, since it protects strategetic weapons from being caught and destroyed on the ground. American strategic bombers cannot remain in the air forever, waiting for the correct stage of battle in which to go forward. American missiles, if not fired, may be destroyed in their silos, the locations of which are known to the opponent. American submarines, if they fire only some of their deadly cargo, will be destroyed with the remainder, since once an SLBM is fired, the location of the launching submarine is known. The only way to protect nuclear weapons is to use them all at once. (iv) Massive retaliation guarantees that strategic weapons will be fired according to the President's directive. If the nation waits before launching strategic weapons, the President may be dead, or he may be alive but out of contact with strategic forces. (v) Because of problems with command and control, a limited nuclear war is not very likely. If war begins, sooner or later all strategic weapons will be either used or out of commission. From the American point of view, it is better that they be used. (vi) Massive retaliation commits the United States to a massive strike against Russia or none at all. Not only should this deter the Soviet Union from attacking the United States, it should deter the United States from attacking the Soviet Union, since it forecloses the option of a limited pre-emptive strike against Soviet forces. Many have been tempted over the years by the idea of a pre-emptive strike against Russia. By eliminating the possibility of limited nuclear war, massive retaliation removes the temptation towards such pre-emptive strikes.[23]

(b) Flexible Response

Flexible or Controlled Response became declared policy in 1962, and there is no doubt that McNamara attempted to incorporate the notion of measured response into the operational plans from SIOP-63 on down.[24] Flexible response (if it works) has the advantage of permitting a nuclear reprisal that does not necessarily lead to all-out war, thus saving millions of lives, at least in the initial stages of a nuclear war. Since flexible response does not necessarily produce all-out war, it is a more believable strategy than massive retaliation, since opponents will recognize that the United States is more likely to use nuclear weapons for reprisals if there is a good chance that reprisals will not produce all out war. Furthermore, flexible response is a technically feasible strategy: all it requires is that a certain number of American missile submarines fire no missiles at all, even after a first strike lands on the United States. The surviving land ICBMs and surviving bombers can deliver a measured response, holding SLBMs ready for use at some later time.

Choice H: Strategic Defense or No Strategic Defense

The single most remarkable feature of the military situation in the nuclear era is the absolute predominance of offense over defense. Nuclear weapons can be produced in great numbers; a single weapon can produce terrible devastation, and the modes of delivery are supersonic and difficult to intercept. No one has yet devised, or even conceived, an effective phsyical defense against nuclear attack. They psychological device of "defense through deterrence" has had for almost 40 years to stand in for traditional defense.

Nevertheless, interest in a physical defense against nuclear attack seems never to die out. In the late 1950s and early 1960s, attention centered on protection through nuclear fallout shelters. The incongruity of the means compared with the immensity of the problem made shelters unpopular with the public, who were unhappy with the idea of crawling down into holes and unconvinced that there would be anything left to crawl back up to after a nuclear war was over. Beset by absurdities, the shelter idea fizzled out by the middle 1960s.[25] In the late 1960s, interest shifted to anti-missile missiles.

The Soviets built a small ABM system around Moscow, and the United States laid plans for a small ABM to protect the Minuteman against nuclear attack. It was never shown that either system had a chance of withstanding a nuclear attack, and technicians on both sides were probably relieved when the ABM Treaty of 1972 put a stop to ABM development. For 11 years both sides acquiesced in the idea of deterrence without defense. But hope springs eternal, and in his "Star Wars" speech of 23 March, 1983, President Reagan attempted to rehabilitate the notion of physical defense:

> But since the advent of nuclear weapons, those steps have been increasingly directed toward deterrence of aggression through the promise of retaliation.
> Over the course of these discussions, I have become more and more deeply convinced that the human spirit must be capable of rising above dealings with other nations and human beings by threatening their existence.
> If the Soviet Union will join with us in our effort to achieve major arms reduction we will have succeeded in stabilizing the nuclear balance. Nevertheless it will still be necessary to rely on the specter of retaliation—on mutual threat, and that is a sad commentary on the human condition.
> Wouldn't it be better to save lives than to avenge them?
> What if free people could live secure in the knowledge that their security did not rest upon the threat of instant U.S. retaliation to deter a Soviet attack; that we could intercept and destroy strategic ballistic missiles before they reached our own soil or that of our allies?
> I know this is a formidable technical task, one that may not be accomplished before the end of this century. Yet, current technology has attained a level of sophistication where it is reasonable for us to begin this effort. [Reagan 1983]

In his speech, the President acknowledged that these proposals involved great technological problems. Because of the technical difficulties, every proposal for strategic defense must face two challenges: first, can it be done? If it can be done, should it be done?

(a) Feasibility

Each superpower in 1983 possessed about 2,000 strategic delivery vehicles capable of launching about 7,000 independently targetable warheads. Given these resources a full-fledged "first strike" by either superpower against the other could involve a simultaneous launch of thousands of strategic weapons. Since 400 nuclear weapons striking vital points could destroy most of the United States, a strategic defense would have to be 95 percent effective to prevent total destruction and 99 percent effective to prevent mass death. No one involved in the development of anti-missile missiles really hoped that these percentages could be reached, and anyone who considers the prospects of trying to shoot down a bullet with another bullet will readily understand why.[26]

One of the principal difficulties with 1960s anti-missile missiles was that they were too slow to do their job. Ideally, interception devices should be much faster and much more maneuverable than their targets. Since few large physical objects travel much faster than ICBMs, the current search for a faster interceptor has concentrated, not on massive projectiles, but on electronic particles and laser beams.[27] Presumably it was laser or particle beam weapons that President Reagan was referring to in the "Star Wars" speech in March 1983.

A laser beam is simply a polarized beam of light. Since high energy lasers can cut through metal, the prospect of a laser defense against ICBM attack has intrigued many. A laser beam, however, cannot travel through the atmosphere without losing energy through absorption diffraction. An effective laser defense, it seems, must be located in outer space.

To interrupt Soviet ICBMs with a beam of sufficient force, the laser weapons would have to be 500 miles or less from their targets. If we imagine laser satellites carrying laser weapons orbiting the earth at a height of 500 miles, we need 50 satellites just to guarantee that one satellite will always be within range of attacking Soviet ICBMs. If 50 satellites are orbited with enough fuel to run the weapons (a task that would occupy the space shuttle for decades), each satellite would have to be capable of destroying approximately 1,000 ICBMs in the eight or so minutes that ICBMs are in space before reentering the atmosphere. This gives the laser about 1/2 second to find each ICBM, direct a laser beam towards it, verify that the ICBM was destroyed, and take a second shot if the first has missed. The odds that any mechanism could successfully perform such a task, 1,000 times over, are not good. To name one of many difficulties, the laser beam must strike the target directly in order to be effective, and no aiming mechanism now exists that can direct a beam at a target several hundred miles away.

Even if a laser weapon were devised that could destroy an ICBM at this range, there are many ways that a laser defense could be subverted. The fifty satellites carrying the weapons could be destroyed by "hunter-killer" satellites before the main ICBM attack begins. The missiles themselves could be protected by highly reflective paint and by rotating in flight (which diffuses the effect of the laser). Furthermore, the targeting task of the laser weapon could be made nearly impossible if each ICBM tossed off several dummy warheads.

Particle beam weapons are devices that direct streams of accelerated atomic particles at a target; they are the military equivalents of the cyclotrons and particle accelerators in the nation's physics laboratories. The accelerated particles travel at near light speed, and no ICBM can out maneuver them or outrun them.

Like laser weapons, particle weapons operate best in outer space. At least 50 satellites are required to keep Soviet ICBM fields constantly in range. Each weapon must be capable of destroying all Soviet ICBMs in a matter of minutes, a task requiring high operating speeds and a near perfect kill ratio. Like laser weapons, particle beam weapons cannot destroy a target without scoring a direct hit. Thus the particle beam must be tightly focused, and the nozzle that projects the particles must be capable of extreme accuracy. Moreover, there are special problems involved in aiming particle beams. If the particles are charged, the beam will be deflected by the earth's magnetic field; if the particles are neutral, it becomes difficult to focus the beam. As with laser weapons, the satellites are open to attack; the detection radar is subject to jamming, and the kill ratio may be degraded if attacking ICBMs throw off chaff and dummy warheads.

Particle beam weapons differ from lasers in that they can operate with some effectiveness at the earth's surface. This feature has prompted interest in a land based particle beam defense system surrounding American ICBM fields. Such deployments leave American cities unprotected, but they do preserve the American ability to retaliate, and they are not subject to the vagaries and vulnerabilities of satellite deployment. Particle beam weapons shooting from below, though, can be disrupted by a single nuclear blast. If one attacking ICBM gets through, the rest probably will too.

Since beam weapons and anti-missile missiles have different strengths and weaknesses, some engineers have suggested that a successful defense could be constructed from a combination of the two sorts of weapons. Recent discusssions have centered on the possibility of ground-launched lasers, followed by distant missile interceptors, followed by close-up interceptors to catch missiles that get through the first two defenses. Under current technology, there is little assurance that such systems will work. Costs are estimated at between 100 and 500 billion dollars, and deployment of the system would violate the spirit of the ABM Treaty signed by the United States and the Soviet Union in 1972.

(b) Desirability

The technical problems of strategic defense are formidable. But so were the problems of constructing the hydrogen bomb. Is it in the American interest to seek such defenses? At first sight, the question seems absurd. Security from attack is something that everyone desires. Even if one believes that the chance of Soviet attack under current conditions is slight, it is still not negligible, and an effective strategic defense would eliminate this small but terrifying possibility of national disaster.

Nevertheless, many persons strongly oppose the development of strategic defenses, arguing that such research is not in the nation's best interest. First of all, the development of these devices will cost a fortune, and there is no guarantee that they will work at the crucial moment. It is always possible that some new offensive development will leap over the defenses, the way the German blitzkrieg leaped the Maginot Line. Second, and perhaps more important, the development of strategic defenses will be perceived by the Soviets as a grave threat to their own national security. Currently, each side is confident that it can destroy the other after suffering a first strike. The development of an effective American strategic defense would deprive the Soviets of their ability to strike back; it would, in effect, render the Soviet Union helpless before an American nuclear attack, resurrecting the strategic situation of the 1940s and 1950s. The Soviets may take steps to prevent the clock from being turned back, and those steps might include a pre-emptive strike, a preventive war, or some other dangerous diversion. In short, the development of American defenses will threaten strategic stability.[28] A program to make America more safe in the far future may make America less safe in the near future. For many, this is a decisive consideration against proceeding with research into physical defenses against atomic attack.

Grand Strategies: Victory, Detente, Non-Possession

Every nation that is capable of developing nuclear weapons faces a succession of strategic choices: possession or non-possession, tactical and strategic or strategic devices only, first use or no first use, commitment or bluff, counterforce targeting or countervalue targeting, limited response or massive retaliation, strategic defense or no strategic defense. If a nation chooses non-possession, it has no further nuclear choices to make, except whether or not to build physical defenses against nuclear attack. If a nation chooses to develop nuclear weapons, it has six further choices to make—64 possibilities in all. Thus there are 65 different grand strategies for the use of nuclear weapons. If we tried to evaluate all 65 strategies in relation to the four moral considerations raised in the first chapter, this book would have 260 more chapters but no more readers. Fortunately, it is not necessary to consider separately each and every one of the 65 grand strategies. Certain patterns of choice among the strategic options are simply incoherent; other sets of choices make a certain overall sense. If one is interested in developing nuclear forces that will provide the United States with a greater capability for manipulating world events by force or by threats of force, and if one believes that the size and pattern of a nuclear war can be controlled, then one will choose (a) to possess nuclear weapons, (b) to possess as many kinds of nuclear weapons as possible, (c) to be prepared to use them first, (d) to be committed to using them, at least in limited quantities, when the chips are down, (e) to aim these weapons at all sorts of targets, including the enemy's strategic forces, (f) to arrange for every possible sequence of use, and (g) to build a physical defense against nuclear attack if possible. If one believes that nuclear weapons are needed to deter nuclear attack and to stop nuclear blackmail, but if one also believes that nuclear weapons are crude and dangerous weapons with which to attempt to influence world affairs, and that the size and pattern of a nuclear war cannot be controlled, then one will choose (a) to possess nuclear weapons, (b) to build only the few weapons needed to assure second strike capacity, (c) to commit the nation to "no first use," (d) to make it possible to back off from nuclear threats, (e) to aim nuclear weapons away from the opponent's strategic forces, (f) to arrange for minimum flexibility in the sequence of use, (g) to forswear any attempt to construct physical defenses. If one believes that nuclear weapons are simply not instruments that can usefully serve the national interest, then one will choose not to have nuclear weapons at all.

Let us call the first "grand strategy" (possession, first use, counterforce targeting, etc.) the *victory strategy*, since one assumption behind the strategy is that nuclear weapons can be used to obtain victories over opponents.[29] Let us call the second grand strategy (possession, no first use, countervalue targeting, etc.) the *detente strategy*, since the main purpose of this strategy is to prevent nuclear attack by permitting both sides to possess an effective nuclear deterrent. The third strategy, which eschews nuclear weapons, we will call the *non-possession strategy*. For a non-nuclear nation, the non-possession strategy requires abstention from nuclear weapons. For a nuclear nation, the non-possession strategy requires unilateral nuclear disarmament. It does not, however, require nations to give up weapons altogether (general and complete disarmament), only nuclear weapons. In fact, non-possession is consistent with increases in arsenals of conventional armaments.

The goal of the *victory strategy* is the ascendency of the United States; the means of ascendency is superior nuclear weaponry. Since the ascendency of the United States requires that the United States be protected from nuclear attack and preserved from nuclear blackmail, the victory strategy is committed to standard deterrence. But the victory strategy involves much more than the deterrence of nuclear attack. It includes the deterrence of conventional attacks with threats of nuclear reprisals. It does not preclude the use of nuclear threats in pursuit of United States foreign policy objectives. It implies a continuing search for offensive superiority and defensive invulnerability. In short, it seeks a first strike capacity against the Soviet Union and all other countries. It supports reductions in strategic arms only when such reductions are matched by other states and only if the relative position of the United States is stronger after the arms agreement than before.

The *detente strategy* assumes that nuclear weapons are weapons of the Apocalypse, that the notion of limited uses of nuclear weapons is absurd, and that the use of nuclear weapons, including the making of nuclear threats, to achieve limited policy objective is folly. With this strategy, the sole sensible use of nuclear weapons is the prevention of nuclear attack, and the best way to prevent nuclear attack is to guarantee that the attacker will be totally destroyed. If this threat of destruction guarantees that nuclear attacks will not occur, it will also guarantee that nuclear blackmail will not succeed, because any nation with a capacity for assured destruction knows that when the time comes, the blackmailer's bluff can be called. Since the detente strategy considers the mutual possession of second-strike capacity to be a stable stand-off involving little chance of war, it does not seek first-strike capacity, but only the preservation of second-strike capacity by the United States and by the other nuclear powers as well.

The *non-possession strategy*, equally concerned with the prevention of nuclear attack, considers that threats of nuclear counterattack are a poor long-term strategy to prevent nuclear war. It hopes to reduce the chance of nuclear attack on the United States (a) by reducing the nuclear arsenal of the United States, thereby reducing fear of the United States, and (b) by reducing the chance that the United States will be subjected to a second attack emanating from some other nuclear power. It assumes that so long as the United States possesses nuclear weapons, there is some chance that the United States will, intentionally or unintentionally, use these weapons to launch a nuclear first strike, and this first strike might produce a response that will destroy the United States.

It should be apparent from the discussions in the preceding sections that each of these three grand strategies in some ways serves the national interest, and in other ways fails to serve the national interest. In economic terms, non-possession causes the least, and victory the most, drain on the economic and scientific resources of the United States. In terms of the risk of war, opinion stands divided, but perhaps most observers will agree that detente generates the least chance of nuclear war in the short run, and non-possession the least chance of nuclear war in the long run. The victory strategy generates a higher chance of nuclear war in both the long run and the short run. But if we consider the magnitude of the nuclear war that will result if deterrence fails, it appears that the nuclear war generated by the victory strategy might well be smaller than the nuclear war generated by the detente strategy. (The nuclear war generated by non-possession, being one sided, would be smaller than either.)

It is difficult, therefore, to declare point-blank that one of these three policies serves America best, and that the other policies are necessarily suicidal folly. In all these discussions, we have consulted only the national interest, defined in very narrow terms. We have excluded moral considerations. It is time to bring them in.

Notes

1. I include as serving the national interest only the ability to resist *illegitimate* threats. Suppose that the Soviet Union has anti-aircraft units around Moscow and threatens to shoot down any American plane that threatens to drop nuclear weapons on their capital. I would not include the development of a jamming device that would neutralize these defensive measures as being in the American national interest.

The fact that national security cannot be considered apart from the effect of defense purchases on the economy must have been apparent to Truman in 1950. When the National Security Council presented him with NSC-68 calling for massive rearmament, "The President referred the report to the Secretaries of State and Defense . . . and requested that the National Security Council give a clear indication of the programs envisasged in the report, including estimates of their probable cost." (*Foreign Relations of the United States* 1950 I, p. 293-94)

2. The view of Soviet conduct expressed here resembles the views presented by State Department figures (after they retire!) in opposition to the NSC. See, for example, Kennan 1982, and Ball 1983.

3. On the reasons for Japan's surrendering when it did, see Feis 1966 66; and Craig 1967 106.

4. On the problems of using nuclear weapons in a European war, see Liddell-Hart 1960 74–82; and Zuckerman 1982 59–79. Zuckerman reports (p. 65) that in one NATO exercise restricted to 10,000 square miles and scrupulously avoiding cities as targets, 25 megatons of NATO tactical nuclear weapons killed 3½ million Europeans (air burst) or 1½ million Europeans (ground burst).

5. The miserable story of U.S. Army attempts to provide battlefield training with tactical nuclear weapons and its aftermath for the men irradiated is told in Wasserman and Solomon 1982 1–102.

6. The effect of high technology on battlefield performance is lucidly explored in Fallows 1981. See also Foster 1982.

7. Two important early studies of the impact of defense spending on the American economy are Cook 1964; and Melman 1974. Melman's lonely voice is now joined by the tables and arguments of the Council of Economic Priorities study; see DeGrasse 1983.

8. The figure of $700 billion is based on an assumption of an average of $30 billion per year for strategic weapons (1983 dollars) from 1950 to 1983. The standard estimates are usually much higher than this.

9. The figure for jobs created per billion dollars spent is developed from Bureau of Labor Statistics data in DeGrasse 1983

10. Some of the bad choices made by the military in the field of electronics are described in Braun and MacDonald 1978.

11. Many of the points about the adverse relationship between procurement policies and scientific development are described in Gansler 1980, especially chapter 4.

12. The political connections between the nuclear power industry and nuclear weapons are explored in Murphy 1982.

13. The data for the cross-national study of economic performance are in DeGrasse, 202–208.

14. For a study of the mixture of pragmatism and timidity that typifies Soviet decision-making, see Adomeit 1982.

15. On "declaratory policy" vs. "action policy," see Ball 1981 31–33.

16. The most recent plea for "no first use" declaratory policy is Bundy 1982. For a plea that goes beyond declaratory policy to action, see Sigal. For defense of "first use," see Hoffmann 1981–1982.

17. The development of the new idea of nuclear deterrence in place of the old military ideas of offense and defense is a long story. Some of the crucial steps in the development of the analysis of nuclear deterrence are: Brodie 1945; Viner 1946; Brodie 1946; Kaufmann 1954; and Amster 1956.

18. In the late 1950's the idea of commitment as the best way of communicating the intent to retaliate was developed by Schelling in a series of articles collected in Schelling 1960. See especially part III, "Strategy With a Random Element."

19. Two cinematic presentations on the automatic response theme (both negative) are Joseph Sargent's *The Forbin Project* (1970) and John Badham's *WarGames* (1983). For some reason, the top American leadership has never been receptive to the strategy of commitment. Perhaps top leaders do not like the idea of spreading power around. Or perhaps the idea that it might be good to render oneself powerless to obtain the satisfaction of some future desire seems devious to those accustomed to more forthright modes of thought. Nevertheless, commitment is a time-honored method for maximizing satisfaction: Odysseus uses it (successfully) when he has himself tied to the mast so that he can hear the Sirens without throwing himself in the sea. A more mundane example is the person who, while attempting to stop smoking, throws all his cigarettes away, so that he will find it impossible to smoke even if he feels an irresistable desire to do so.

20. In the controversy over the B-36 bomber in 1949, the Navy argued that the Air Force concept of blowing the Soviet Union to smithereens was contrary to basic principles of morality, a critique that apparently continued up until the moment that the Navy obtained the Polaris submarine with its relatively imprecise missiles. These criticisms must have had some impact, and in the mid-1950s, both active and retired Air Force officers responded with arguments that nuclear weapons need not be aimed at cities. The most prominently featured presentation was a nationally circulated article by Col. Richard S. Leghorn (Leghorn 1955). See also Walkowicz 1955. For current thinking about counterforce uses of nuclear weapons, see Davis 1981 42–64.

21. Countervalue strategy is usually associated with the later years of McNamara Secretary-ship, but it is not clear that McNamara's famed criteria of assured destruction were ever intended as action policy; they were, it appears, an analytical part of force acquisition policy. For a clear preference in favor of countervalue targeting, see the 1963 policy statement of the Committee for a SANE Nuclear Policy (described in Intriligator 1968 1145).

22. Most commentators concentrate on targeting policy to the exclusion of rate-of-fire policy. One who does not is Michael Intriligator. See Intriligator, 1967.

23. See Peeters 1959.

24. Kaplan 1959; Halperin 1962; Kaufmann 1964.

25. Except in Switzerland, which is honeycombed with fallout shelters, required by law.

26. For the problems of anti-ballistic missiles, see Garwin and Bethe 1968.

27. For laser weapons, see Tsipis, 1981. For particle beam weapons see Parmentola and Tsipis 1979. See also Karas 1983 chs. 6, 8.

For current work in high-technology ballistic missile defense and for attempts to outwit such defenses, see R. Jeffery Smith 1983.

28. Conditions for maintaining the strategic balance are described in Legault and Lindsey 1974.

29. I have named the first strategy "victory" after that memorable strategic treatise *Why Not Victory?* by Barry Goldwater (Goldwater 1962).

Appendix: Characteristics of the Grand Strategies

Policy Choice	Non-Possession	Detente	Victory
Possession?	Non-Possession	Possession	Possession
Weapons type?		Strategic	Tactical and strategic
Occasion of use?		No first use	First use
Rate of fire?		Massive retaliation	Flexible response
Targeting?		Countervalue	Counterforce
Posture?		Bluff[a]	Commitment[a]

[a] Detente involves a possible unsuccessful bluff of a massive strike; Victory involves a definite commitment to an appropriately sized strike.

5

Weapons Policies and the Common Good

In this chapter we will consider the three principal nuclear strategies in the light of the common good. In the first chapter, we defined the common good as that which is preferred by a substantial majority of persons in this and several future generations. Which of the three grand strategies—victory, detente, or non-possession—best serves the common good?

A World-Wide Poll?

At first sight, it appears that the logical way to attack this question is simply to poll everyone concerned about their preferences concerning American nuclear weapons. Such a poll, of course, must be hypothetical; for one thing, it is impossible to poll the members of future generations. We will have to settle for responsible estimates about what people would prefer if they had the chance to vote.

In the NATO countries the majority currently support either victory or detente and reject the option of non-possession. Polls taken in the United States show strong support for bi-lateral arms reductions (detente), but little support for unilateral nuclear disarmament.[1] In Britain the Labour Party's program for unilateral steps away from nuclear deterrence was one factor leading to their decisive defeat at the hands of Thatcher and the Conservatives in 1983. Polls in Holland, in which anti-nuclear demonstrations have been widespread, indicate that two-thirds of the Dutch population believe that a strong NATO deterrent is needed as a counterweight to the military strength of the Warsaw pact (Stoepel 1982).

NATO nations, however, have a combined population of about 600 million. This in 1983 was only 12 percent of the world's population. What would the other 88 percent of the people in the world say if asked about American weapons strategies? I believe that the policies of victory and detente would receive strong support in South Korea, Taiwan, Australia, Israel, and (perhaps) Spain and Pakistan, countries with a combined population of 185 million, or 4 percent of the world's population. Everywhere else, majorities would support the policy of non-possession; that is, the unilateral nuclear disarmament of the United States. Certainly the policy of non-possession would be favored in the Soviet Union and China, the principal targets of American weapons; in Japan, where nuclear weapons are perceived as a sort of poison; and in most Muslim countries, because of their prevailing anti-Americanism. Non-possession would be favored in Eastern Europe and the neutral European states, who wish to avoid getting caught in a crossfire between the superpowers. Non-possession would also command large majorities throughout Africa, South Asia, and Latin America, the populations of which feel that they have little to gain from American nuclear weapons but much to lose when American radioactivity comes floating in their direction. In our imaginary world-wide poll, then, non-possession comes in first, detente second, and victory third.

Does it follow that non-possession is the policy that serves the common good best, and that victory is the policy that serves the common good worst? Not necessarily. In considering policies with multiple and uncertain outcomes, we must consider the *outcomes* the majority prefers, not just the *policy* the majority prefers. To assess the relationship between the common good and nuclear weapons policies, we must consult, not just world opinion about the policies, but world opinion about the results the policies can be expected to produce.

When it comes to nuclear weapons, the "results" that people are most concerned about are negative results, such as the destruction of all-out nuclear war. In their minds, the key question is, "Which policy is the *least disastrous* for the human race?" Unfortunately, there are different ways of interpreting the idea, "least disastrous." If we focus attention on the *size* of the disasters that might happen, we will consider the "least disastrous" policy to be the one that produces the smallest possible disaster. In decision theory, this is called a "minimax" approach. If we focus attention on the probability of the disaster, we will consider the "least disastrous" policy to be the one with the smallest liklihood of disaster. This might be called a "disaster avoidance" approach. If we believe that both the size and the probability of potential disaster are important, then we will consider the "least disastrous" policy to be the one that produces the smallest combination of probability and destruction. Such an approach is usually described as "maximizing expected value." We will explore all three alternatives.[2]

The Minimax Rule

We have three weapons policies to consider. Each has several different outcomes, depending on how chance factors operate after the policy is chosen. The minimax approach to choosing among the policies works as follows:

> Consider the set of possible outcomes of each policy. Select the worst outcome from each set. Prefer the policy which has the best of these worst outcomes.

To apply this formula to decisions about the common good, we must interpret "the worst outcome" of each policy as "the worst outcome from the point of view of mankind." Thus, if we follow the minimax rule, a policy serves the common good best if the worst disaster that might be produced by the policy is better, from the point of view of mankind, than the worst disaster that might be produced by any alternative policy.

Now, the worst disaster that can be expected from the victory policy is an all-out nuclear war between the United States and the Soviet Union. Likewise, the worst disaster that might be expected from the detente policy is an all-out nuclear war between the United States and the Soviet Union. The worst disaster that might be expected from the policy of non-possession is a Soviet nuclear attack on the United States.[3]

If we took a world-wide poll as to which of these "worst" outcomes is the least of all evils, there is no doubt that a one-sided attack by the Soviet Union would be voted the best of the worst outcomes. It would be approved hands down in the Soviet Union, and the rest of the world would prefer this outcome because it will produce less fallout than an all-out nuclear war. The minimax rule declares that non-possession is the weapons policy that truly serves the common good.

The confidence one feels in this conclusion will be directly proportional to the confidence one feels in the applicability of the minimax rule to the problem at hand. One argument against the use of the minimax rule is that it ignores all information that we have about the probabilities of the outcomes. Some will argue that it is always a mistake to suppress information when trying to reach a rational decision. On the other hand, the minimax principle is most applicable to problems in which there is very great uncertainty or controversy about the probabilities of the outcomes, and in which some of the outcomes are so bad as to be catastrophic. Certainly this is the case in the choice of nuclear weapons policies.[4] One could imagine a perfectly reasonable person saying, "We don't have any real idea of what will happen in the future, but two of these policies *might* produce worldwide destruction, and the third certainly will not, so I prefer the third." If one reasonable person could say this, the majority of mankind would say it as well. The minimax principle, simple as it is, cannot be dismissed from the evaluation of nuclear strategies.

The Disaster Avoidance Principle

As a rule for rational decision making, the minimax rule expresses extreme prudence: it combines skepticism about the future with a desire to avoid disaster at all costs. But if one's highest goal is avoiding disaster, it is irrational to suppress *any* information that might be of help in avoiding disaster. Professor Kavka, of the University of California at Irvine, has devised a rule for rational decision making that embodies some of the prudence of minimax thinking while permitting some information about the probability of outcomes. Kavka's rule, which we could call the *disaster avoidance rule* is:

When choosing between potential disasters under two dimensional uncertainty*
it is rational to select the alternative that minimizes the probability of disaster
occurrence. [Kavka 1980 50]

Thus, while the minimax rule focuses on the size of potential disasters to
the exclusion of the probability of the disasters, the disaster avoidance rule
focuses on the probabilities of the disasters to the exclusion of their size,
provided, Kavka qualifies, that the disasters are "roughly equal in magnitude."[5]

In Kavka's analysis, the main disaster associated with victory or detente is
all-out nuclear war. The main disaster associated with non-possession is
Soviet world domination, resulting from Western strategic weaknesses after
the United States gives up nuclear weapons. These disasters are rated by
Kavka as "roughly equal in magnitude." But in Kavka's opinion the probability of Soviet world domination if the United States adopts non-possession is
greater than the probability of all-out nuclear war if the United States adopts
either victory or detente. It follows, from the disaster avoidance rule, that
victory and detente both serve the common good better than non-possession.

Once again, the persuasiveness of this conclusion depends on the strength
of the premises that produce it. Should we agree with Kavka that the
principal disaster associated with non-possession is Soviet world domination? Isn't a one-sided Soviet nuclear attack the principal disaster associated
with unilateral nuclear disarmament? And even if we agree that Soviet world
hegemony is an "outcome" of non-possession, should we agree that the
disaster of Soviet world domination is "roughly equal in magnitude" to the
disaster of all-out nuclear war? Given the catastrophic ecological effects of
all-out nuclear war, the mass of humanity might challenge Kavka's claim that
these disasters are "roughly equal in magnitude." If they are not equal, the
disaster avoidance rule cannot be applied to the choice between non-
possession, detente, and victory.

Kavka's rule, however, is helpful in comparing victory with detente. The
true disaster associated with detente is all-out nuclear war. The true disaster
associated with victory is all-out nuclear war. Obviously these disasters *are*
roughly equal in magnitude, so the disaster avoidance rule can be applied to
the comparison of victory with detente. According to Kavka's rule, the
common good is best served by that policy which is least likely to produce
disaster. Which of these policies is least likely to cause all-out nuclear war?

Supporters of the victory strategy claim that their policy is less likely to
produce all-out nuclear war than detente. First of all, their policy provides
for relatively moderate and therefore believable responses, which make for a
more believable deterrent to aggressive acts. Furthermore, if nuclear war
does occur, it is much less likely to develop into all-out nuclear war than
does a nuclear war produced under the detente strategy. Supporters of
detente point out that their policy is much less likely to produce a war by
accident or by mistake. Furthermore, since the detente policy is pledged to
"no first use" while the victory strategy is not, the victory strategy is much
more likely to cross the nuclear threshold than the detente strategy; and

once a nuclear war begins, it will be very difficult to keep it limited. All things considered, it seems to me that detente is indeed less likely to produce all-out nuclear war. If so, according to the disaster avoidance rule, detente serves the common good better than victory. But I am not a prophet. If you believe that the victory policy is less likely to produce all-out nuclear war than detente, then, if you apply the disaster avoidance rule, you reach the conclusion that the victory policy serves the common good better than detente.

Maximizing Expected Value and Minimizing Expected Deaths

The minimax approach emphasizes disaster size but not disaster probability. The disaster avoidance approach emphasizes probability but not precise size. It would be nice to have a system which gives equal weight to both. Such a system will require a unit that simultaneously measures the size and probability of disasters. In this book, that unit will be an "expected death," which is defined as "any combination of probability and real deaths equal to 1." For example, creating a 10% risk of death to 100 people creates 10 expected deaths, creating a 5% risk of death to 1000 people creates 50 expected deaths, and so forth. Given this unit, we can define *the policy which best serves the common good* as *the policy which creates the fewest expected deaths*.

The general idea of minimizing expected deaths sounds simple, but there is great controversy about the precise numbers and probabilities of real deaths that these policies might produce. Obviously it would be easy to get the "right" numbers of expected deaths for each policy by picking estimates that suit one's purposes. To avoid the charge of bias, we will not take any one particular estimate but rather work with ranges of estimates, where the ranges are generated by all parties in the debate.[6] In considering the number of deaths generated by a policy if worst comes to worst, we will use the high and low estimates of deaths submitted by reputable authorities. In considering the probability of disasters, we will consider the high and low chances of disaster as estimated by the opponents and by the supporters of each particular policy. The result will be a range of expected deaths associated with each policy, not a precise figure. But this range will be ecumenical.

Let us begin with estimates of the deaths that might be expected from possible results of these policies. The main sources of death will be all-out nuclear war, limited nuclear war, and nuclear attack on a non-nuclear United States.

(a) Deaths from All-Out War

In Chapter 3, the best estimates indicated that an all-out nuclear war would kill between 34 million and 100 million people in the Soviet Union, and between 105 and 155 million people in the United States. If we estimate that in addition to these deaths, 10% more deaths will be caused to persons living outside the U.S. and U.S.S.R. This gives us a high estimate of 225 million dead from all-out nuclear war and a low estimate of 153 million dead.*

(b) Deaths from Limited Nuclear War

Now, the most likely scenario for a limited nuclear war is a counterforce strike by each superpower against the other. A limited counterforce strike against the United States would kill, according to our estimates, between 2 and 22 million Americans. A limited counterforce strike against the Soviet Union would kill between 4 million and 27 million people in the U.S.S.R. This gives us a high estimate of 49 million persons killed in a two-sided nuclear counterforce war, and a low estimate of 6 million persons killed in a two-sided limited counterforce war.

(c) Deaths from Unilateral Nuclear Attack

Finally, we must consider what the effects of a one-sided nuclear attack on the United States would be, if the United States did not possess any nuclear weapons. We must imagine that the United States has done something so threatening that the Soviet Union or some other nuclear adversary is considering breaking the nuclear taboo and launching a nuclear attack on the United States. In this scenario, the United States has no strategic weapons with which to deter this attack. What sort of nuclear attack is the opponent most likely to launch? Obviously, the opponent is not going to launch a limited strike against American strategic forces, since the United States does not have any. The most likely forms of attack are (i) attacks on the ability of the United States to wage a conventional war, or (ii) terror strikes designed to make the United States submit to some demand.

Studies of strategic bombing indicate that the most efficient way to cripple the capacity of an opponent to wage conventional war is to attack his oil refineries. As indicated in Chapter 3, two-thirds of American oil refining capacity would be wiped out by 80 Soviet ICBMs, and in such an attack about 5 million Americans would die.

As for unilateral terror strikes, our only precedents are the bombings of Hiroshima and Nagasaki. The general idea in those cases seems to have been to destroy a city and then wait for surrender.* If that precedent holds, we can assume that a terror attack on the United States would involve a nuclear attack on a single large city, followed by a waiting period anticipating surrender, followed a second attack if surrender is not obtained, and so forth. If the city attacked is New York, such an attack could leave 10 million dead. Attacks on other large cities could each leave from 3 to 5 million dead. If we suppose that it is very unlikely that the United States would endure more than three such attacks without capitulating, we have a high estimate of 18 million dead from a nuclear attack on a non-nuclear U.S., and a low estimate of 5 million dead.

Now let us look at some estimates of the probabilities of these three catastrophes. Our procedure will be to assign to each policy the most favorable estimates of its supporters and the least favorable estimate of its opponents.

(d) Probability of war under the Victory Policy

Suppose that the United States adopts (or continues to pursue) the strategy that we have called "victory." What are the odds of all-out nuclear war under this strategy? What are the odds of a limited nuclear war?

Supporters of the victory strategy think that the chance of all-out war under this strategy is slight. Nevertheless, there is always a chance that something will go wrong. Supporters of victory, in a reasonable moment, would have to concede that even if their policy were followed to the letter, there is at least a 1 percent chance of all-out nuclear war in the next 40 years. The victory strategy, of course, generates a higher probability of limited nuclear war than all-out nuclear war. Suppose that we asked a supporter of the victory strategy what percentage of limited nuclear wars will escalate to all-out nuclear wars. On his theory, the odds are low; he might set the chance as low as 10 percent. Since the victory supporter concedes a 1 percent chance of all-out war in the next 40 years, it follows that he should concede a 10 percent chance of limited nuclear war, given the victory strategy, in the next 40 years.

Supporters of detente believe that the chance of limited nuclear war under the victory strategy is substantial. They also believe that limited nuclear wars are very likely to escalate into all-out nuclear wars. If victory supporters set the chance of limited nuclear war under victory at 10 percent (in 40 years), supporters of detente will want to set it at least at 30 percent. If victory supporters claim that one in ten nuclear wars will be an all-out war, supporters of detente will claim that one in two nuclear wars will be an all-out war. It follows that supporters of detente will set the chance of all-out war under victory at 15 percent in 40 years.

Supporters of non-possession believe that nuclear deterrence, to which both victory and detente are committed, is highly dangerous and carries a substantial risk of war. Thus supporters of non-possession will consider victory even more dangerous than supporters of detente. If supporters of detente put the odds of all-out war under victory at 15 percent, supporters of non-possession will want to set it at 30 percent. If supporters of detente set the odds of limited nuclear war under victory at 30 percent, supporters of non-possession will want to set it at least at 60 percent (over the next 40 years).

There is, under victory, one further possibility of war: the possibility of an unanswered American first strike. (Presumably the United States would not attempt a first strike unless the odds of Soviet response were negligible). If we assume that the chance of an American first strike is equal to the chance of a Soviet first strike leading to limited two-sided nuclear war, victory supporters will rate this chance at 10 percent, detente supporters at 30 percent, and non-possession supporters at 60 percent over the next 40 years.

(e) Chance of War Under the Detente Strategy

The supporter of Detente believes that the chance of all-out nuclear war is less under the detente strategy than under the victory strategy. Since the technological arms race has been eliminated by detente and since the chance of war by accident or mistake has been minimized, the supporter of detente may estimate that the chance of all-out nuclear war to be as low as 0.5 percent over the next 40 years, assuming that the detente strategy is adopted. The supporter of victory, of course, believes that the odds of all-out war under detente are higher than 0.5 percent. Nevertheless, he will not assign a very high chance of nuclear war to detente, since detente preserves the essential structure of nuclear deterrence. He may put the chance of all-out war under detente at 5 percent over the next 40 years.

The supporter of non-possession believes that detente is not a satisfactory long-run solution to the threat of all-out war. He will assign a higher probability of all-out war to detente than does the supporter of victory. On the other hand, he will probably think that the chance of all-out war under detente is less than under victory, which he set at 30 percent. If he believes that detente is half as likely to produce an all-out nuclear war as victory, he will judge the chance of all-out war under Detente to be about 15 percent over the next 40 years.

Under detente, the chance of a two-sided limited nuclear war is negligible. But since the detente strategy is partially bluff, there is the possibility that the bluff will be called, and the result may be a one-sided limited nuclear war. For example, the Soviet Union might launch a counterforce strike against the United States, and the United States not respond at all. Supporters of victory feel that this possibility is greater than the possibility of limited nuclear war under victory. Since they rated the chance of limited nuclear war under victory at 10 percent, they will want to rate the chance of one-sided nuclear war under detente at at least 20 percent. Supporters of detente, of course, think that the chance is much less. But if they suppose that there is a 50-50 chance that the United States will not respond (under detente) to Soviet attack, since they rated the chance of all-out war at 0.5 percent, they must rate the chance of one sided nuclear war at 1 percent. Supporters of non-possession will present intermediate estimates.

(f) Chance of Unilateral Nuclear Attack Under Non-Possession

Suppose that the United States divested itself of nuclear weapons. What are the chances that the nation would be subjected to nuclear attack?

The supporter of non-possession argues that the chances of such an attack are slight. The most likely route to such an attack would be a war between the United States and some nuclear power, but one should expect that the government of the United States would make every effort, under the circumstances, to avoid drifting into such a war. Certainly, the supporter of non-possession believes that the chance of such an attack is less than the chance of nuclear war under detente, which he sets at 15 percent. If he feels that nuclear war under detente is twice as likely as the chance of nuclear attack under non-possession, he will set the odds of a nuclear attack against a non-nuclear United States at about 8 percent over the next 40 years. Obviously the supporters of victory and detente will set it much higher. They could say that the chances of a unilateral countervalue strike against the United States if non-possession is adopted are as high as 50 percent.

Table 5.1 Estimates of Probabilities of Nuclear War by Type of Strategy

	Victory Adopted (percent)	Detente Adopted (percent)	Non-Possession Adopted (percent)
Victory supporters			
All-out war	1	5	0
Limited war[a]	10	0	0
Counterf strike[b]	10	20	0
Counterv strike[c]	0	0	50
Detente supporters			
All-out war	15	0.5	0
Limited war	30	0	0
Counterf strike	30	1	0
Counterv strike	0	0	50
Non-possession supporters			
All-out war	30	15	0
Limited war	60	0	0
Counterf strike	60	2	0
Counterv strike	0	0	4
Extreme ranges of estimates			
All-out war	30– 1	15– .5	0
Limited war	60–10	0	0
Counterf strike	0	20– 1	0
Counterv strike	0	0	50– 4

[a] A Limited nuclear war is a two-sided counterforce war that does not escalate.
[b] A Counterforce strike (Counterf strike) is an unanswered counterforce strike.
[c] A Countervalue strike (Counterv strike) is an unanswered countervalue strike.

The casualty estimates for these disasters were:

	High	*Low*
All-out war	225 mil	153 mil
Limited war	49 mil	6 mil
Counterf strike	22 mil	2 mil (against U.S.)
Counterv strike	27 mil	4 mil (against U.S.S.R)
Counterv strike	18 mil	5 mil (against U.S.)

To calculate ranges of expected deaths, we multiply the most extreme probability estimates by the most extreme damage estimates:

For victory:
High estimate (all-out war): 30% × 225 million deaths = 67.5 million expected deaths
Low estimate (all-out war):
1% × 153 million deaths = 1.5 million expected deaths
High estimate (limited war): 60% × 49 million deaths = 29.4 million expected deaths
Low estimate (limited war): 10% × 6 million deaths = 0.6 million expected deaths
High estimate (counterf st): 60% × 27 million deaths = 16.2 million expected deaths
Low estimate (counterf st): 10% × 4 million deaths = 0.4 million expected deaths

The sum of the high estimates is 113.1 million expected deaths. The sum of the low estimates is 2.5 million expected deaths. This is the range of value associated with the victory strategy.

For detente:
High estimate (all-out war): 15% × 225 million deaths = 33.8 million expected deaths
Low estimate (all-out war): = .5% × 153 million deaths = 0.8 million expected deaths
High estimate (counterf st): = 20% × 27 million deaths = 5.4 million expected deaths
Low estimate (counterf st): =
1% × 4 million deaths = .04 million expected deaths

So the high estimate for expected deaths under the detente strategy is 39.0 million expected deaths, and the low estimate is 0.8 million expected deaths.

For Non-Possession:
high estimate (counterf st): = 50% × (18 million deaths) = 9 million expected deaths
low estimate (counterf st): = 4% × (5 million deaths) = .2 million expected deaths

In sum, the ranges of millions of expected deaths for the three policies are:

	High	Low	Mid-point
Victory	113.1	2.5	57.8
Detente	39.0	.8	20.0
Non-possession	9.0	.2	4.6

Our remaining task is to translate these ranges of expected deaths into judgments about the common good. Various methods are available for evaluating ranges of expected value. One method is: compare the worst ends of the range, and then prefer the policy that has the best worst end. Another method is to mark the mid-points of the ranges, and then prefer the policy that has the best mid-point. In the case at hand, both methods yield the same result: Non-possession (mid-point 4.6) is preferable to detente, and detente (mid-point 20.0) is preferable to victory (mid-point 57.8). Thus, if we believe that we know something about the probability of the various outcomes of nuclear weapons policies, and if we confine our attention to the death and destruction that these policies might cause, the result is that non-possession is the policy that best serves the common good of mankind.[7]

Certainly these methods of estimation are rough. Nevertheless, in a certain sense they are unprejudiced. The low estimates represent each supporter's view of the destructive tendencies of the policy he supports. The high estimates present each opponent's view of the destructive tendencies of the policies he opposes. Each range is constructed from estimates provided by all three sides. One hopes the truth lies somewhere between the extremes.

Sensitivity to Error

The judgment of the preceding section—that non-possession serves the common good better than detente and that detente serves the common good better than victory—depends on various estimates of damage and various estimates of the probability of disaster. These estimates may be mistaken: the end points may be wrong and thus the mid-points may be incorrectly placed. It is worth considering which estimates are most likely to be wrong and how far wrong these estimates are most likely to be. It is also important to consider how far wrong these estimates must be in order to tip the scales and produce a new verdict as to which policy best serves the common good.

To begin, we should note that the damage estimates are in general more reliable than estimates of the probability of war. Different estimates about the probability of war result from political disagreements about how people and national leaders will behave. Different estimates of the damage produced by nuclear war result from scientific disagreement about natural facts.

If one examines the reasoning behind the scientific estimates, one discovers that the low estimates seem to underestimate the number of deaths due to unattended sickness and untreated wounds, and overestimate the availability and effectiveness of fallout shelters. The high estimates overestimate the number of deaths from untreated wounded and sickness, but make reasonable assumptions about fallout shelters. The most probable figures, then, are at least two-thirds of the way *up* the given ranges. At that level, an all-out nuclear war will cause about 200 million deaths, a limited nuclear war will cause 35 million deaths, a counterforce strike against the U.S. will cause 15 million deaths, a counterforce strike against Russia will cause 20.7 million deaths, and a unilateral countervalue strike against the United States will cause 13.5 million deaths.

The probability estimates are far more controversial. Each side in the nuclear debate claims that its preferred strategy generates the smallest chance of nuclear war. Victory claims that the way for Americans to prevent nuclear war is to convince the Soviets that if they begin a nuclear war they are sure to lose. Detente claims that the best way for Americans to prevent nuclear war is to convince the Soviets that if they begin a nuclear war their country will be destroyed. Non-possession claims that the best way for Americans to prevent nuclear war is to stop bombarding the Soviets with threats of destruction and to deprive themselves of the tools of mischief. Each side's assessment of the probability of war will be dismissed as partisan by the other two.

One approach to assessing the probability of war is simply to list the number of different ways that a nuclear war might begin, once each of these policies is adopted. Roughly, the more ways there are for a nuclear war to begin, the more likely it is that a nuclear war will start. Table 5-2 gives a sample enumeration of causes:

Table 5.2   Possible Causes of Nuclear War, by Type of Weapons Policy

Victory	Detente	Non-Possession
1. Soviet accident	Soviet accident	Soviet accident
2. Deliberate Soviet first strike	Deliberate Soviet first strike	Deliberate Soviet first strike
3. Soviet escalation following conventional defeat	Soviet escalation following conventional defeat	Soviet escalation following conventional defeat
4. Soviet mistake	Soviet mistake	Soviet mistake
5. American accident	American accident	
6. American mistake	American mistake	
7. Deliberate American first strike		
8. American escalation after conventional defeat		

All three weapons policies are susceptible to disaster caused by a Soviet accident, a sudden Soviet strike, and a Soviet attack following a conventional defeat. Detente is susceptible, but non-possession is not susceptible, to disaster caused by a Soviet mistake, by an American mistake, or by an American or Soviet accident. Victory, but not detente or non-possession, is susceptible to disaster caused by an American first strike or by American escalation brought on by conventional defeat.[8] If we take these to be the basic routes to disaster, there are four routes to disaster under non-possession, six routes to disaster under detente, and eight routes to disaster under victory. If there is a correlation between the number of routes to war and the probability of war, the average risk assigned to victory is correct relative to the average risk assigned to detente, but the average risk assigned to non-possession may be too high relative to the average risk assigned to victory or detente.

Further reviewing the proability estimates, there are two estimates that many may feel are simply out of line. One is the assumption, by victory supporters, that there is a 20 percent chance of a Soviet counterforce attack under detente. Right now, there is no chance at all that the United States will launch a first strike at the Soviet Union, for fear of reprisals by Soviet submarines. It is even less likely that the Soviet leadership would launch a counterforce strike against the United States in the face of reprisals from less vulnerable, better equipped American submarines. The other unreasonable assumption is the assumption of victory supporters that only one-tenth of all nuclear wars will escalate to all-out war. Once the nuclear threshold is crossed, it will be very difficult for national leaders to believe that the opposing side will act with restraint. This will make it very difficult for anyone to exercise self-restraint. Given mutual fear of countervalue reprisals, it is safe to assume that at least half of all nuclear wars will escalate to all-out war. These presumptions will increase the number of expected deaths attributable to victory and somewhat decrease the number of expected deaths attributed to detente.

If we review the three policies under these assumptions, one striking point is the difference between the worst damage victory and detente might cause compared with the worst damage that non-possession might cause. The worst damage of victory and detente—all-out nuclear war—will cause 15 times as many deaths as the worst damage of non-possession—a countervalue nuclear attack on the United States. Even a limited nuclear war will kill two and a half times as many people as a unilateral countervalue attack on the United States.

It will be particularly difficult for supporters of victory to show that victory is 15 times less likely to cause disaster than non-possession. Suppose that the victory supporter sticks to his original estimate that the policy of victory generates a 10 percent chance of limited nuclear war over the next 40 years. Since we are assuming that half of all nuclear wars will be all-out nuclear wars, it follows that the victory supporter is conceding a 5 percent chance of all-out war (10 million expected deaths) and a 5 percent chance of limited nuclear war (1.6 million expected deaths) over the next 40 years. Since a countervalue strike against the United States will cause 13.5 million deaths, it follows that the supporter of victory must assume that non-possession runs at least an 86 percent chance of a Soviet first strike over a 40 year period, if victory is to cause fewer deaths than non-possession. If he assumes anything less than 86 percent, non-possession still causes fewer expected deaths than victory, using probability assumption supplied by victory supporters themselves. But I think most people would think it quite unreasonable to maintain that non-possession makes it *nearly certain* that the Soviet Union will attack the United States.

The supporter of detente may feel that he has a much easier case against non-possession. According to its supporters, detente produces only a 0.5 percent chance of nuclear war (1 million expected deaths) every 40 years. If this figure is right, then all it takes is a 7.5 percent chance that during 40 years of non-possession the Soviet Union would launch a first strike against the United States, and the number of expected deaths generated by non-possession will be greater than the number of expected deaths generated by detente. The supporter of detente may well feel that 7.5 percent is a fair estimate of the risks inherent in non-possession.

But this argument accepts partisan claims about the risks of detente at their face value. Is it really reasonable to assume that detente generates only a 0.5 percent chance of all-out war in a 40 year period? This figure implies that detente will cause an all-out nuclear war *less than once every 18,000 years.** Can we honestly believe that the balance of terror will survive 18,000 years before collapsing, even if the United States is committed to a policy of no first use and avoids a technological arms race? Even under the best of conditions, detente requires the deployment of hundreds of missiles ready to be fired at a moment's notice. The incidents that might trigger the firing of the missiles are not completely under the control of the United States. A person who thinks that such a system will have one accident in 18,000 years is an optimist indeed.[9]

Suppose that the defender of detente reassesses the problem and declares that in his guts he feels that the detente system has a 50–50 chance of making it through 1,000 years without a war. *This* figure implies a 5 percent chance of war every 40 years, and a 5 percent chance of all-out war in 40 years produces 10 million expected deaths. For non-possession to generate the same number of expected deaths, the chance of Soviet attack under non-possession must be greater than 77 percent. Is it reasonable to assign such a high probability to the chance of a Soviet first strike under non-possession? Presumably the main motive for a Soviet first strike would be the destruction of American nuclear weapons. (Destruction of strategic capability was the main motive behind American plans for pre-emptive strikes against Russia in 1948 and 1954.) But if the United States practices non-possession, it will have no nuclear weapons for the Soviets to destroy, thus eliminating the main motive for Soviet pre-emption. On what grounds, then, could anyone claim that the chance of a Soviet first strike under non-possession must be as high as 77 percent?

It appears that if detente or victory are to surpass non-possession as servants of the common good, the risks of non-possession must be substantially greater, or the risks of victory and detente must be substantially less, than any of the estimates so far presented. If the risk of Soviet attack under non-possession is *nearly certain*, or if the risk of all-out war under victory or detente is practically *negligible*, then the policy of non-possession does not serve the common good. But not many people, speaking honestly, will declare that non-possession will surely precipitate a Soviet attack, and very few people are prepared to dismiss the possibility of nuclear war under either victory or detente. Many people do feel that the chance of trouble under non-possession is greater than the chance of trouble under either victory or detente. But *if* the chance of trouble with victory or detente is less, the trouble, when it comes, is far worse, from the standpoint of the common good, than the trouble that comes from non-possession. For most estimates this tips the scales in favor of non-possession.

Since the main disaster resulting from victory and detente is the same, the conclusion that detente serves the common good better than victory is more susceptible to revision if the probability estimates are changed. The low end of the victory probability-of-disaster range was 0.5 percent. If these estimates are off by a factor of 2, victory will have a higher low point than detente. If the estimates are off by a factor of 3, then victory will have a higher mid-point than detente. This gap is much smaller, and much more likely to be bridged, than the gap between detente and victory, which could only be bridged if the consensus of estimates was off by a factor of 10.

Other Factors Relevant to the Common Good

The preceding arguments show that victory causes more expected deaths than detente, and that detente causes more expected deaths than non-possession. If we assume that the best way a weapons policy can serve the common good is to minimize expected deaths, we get the result that the common good is served by non-possession, detente, and victory, in that order. But there may be other ways that nuclesar weapons serve the common good besides minimizing expected deaths. They may possibly deter conventional wars as well as nuclear wars. They may defeat attempts at nuclear blackmail. American nuclear weapons may serve the function of containing Soviet influence around the world. All these possibilities are relevant to judgments about the common good.

(a) Preserving Conventional Peace

Many people, the present Secretary of Defense included, think that nuclear weapons have helped to preserve peace in Europe.[10] Since a conventional war against nuclear powers can escalate to a nuclear war, nations confronting a nuclear power are deterred from conventional attacks as well as from nuclear attacks. Now, since escalation occurs more easily under victory than under detente, we should assume that if nuclear weapons do deter conventional war, victory performs this function better than detente, and detente performs it better than non-possession.

First, let us consider how much better victory deters conventional war than detente. As we have already noted, the idea that the Soviets are *much* more likely to be deterred from conventional war by victory than by detente is not plausible. Whether the United States adopts victory or detente, the basic thought that will grip the mind of a Soviet leader contemplating an attack on the United States or its allies will be that such an attack could lead to nuclear destruction. All else will be in the mental background. At best, then, victory provides a marginally better deterrent to conventional war than detente. To put it in figures, we will say that victory deters conventional attack 50 percent better than detente.

Now consider the effectiveness of detente and non-possession against conventional attack. Non-possession is consistent with the possession of powerful conventional forces, so a national leader, contemplating a nuclear attack against a nation practicing non-possession still has to count his expected costs and expected benefits. The costs of conventional warfare may appear relatively trivial to Americans, who are principally concerned with the effects of nuclear war. But Europeans have seen their continents twice devastated by conventional war, the effects of which are in many cities daily before their eyes. After World War I, it took the irrational optimism of Adolph Hitler to let slip the dogs of war in Europe. Certainly no responsible European leader today would launch a conventional attack unless something as important as national survival were at stake.

To assess the chance of conventional attack properly we have to consider what might make a Soviet leader think that a conventional attack is the best route to national survival. It is difficult to imagine a Soviet leader deciding that an attack on a non-nuclear Germany is necessary to the national survival of the Soviet Union unless Adolph Hitler gets re-elected on a platform of unilateral nuclear disarmament. There is, really, only one thing in Europe that poses a threat to the survival of the Soviet Union: the nuclear weapons now in the hands of NATO and France. One could imagine, *barely* imagine, the Soviet Union attempting to wipe these weapons out with a conventional attack, hoping that, by not crossing the nuclear threshold, the United States would not use its strategic weapons in response.

If this analysis is correct, a conventional Soviet attack against a nuclear NATO is more likely than a conventional Soviet attack against a non-nuclear NATO. Nevertheless, the vast majority of writers on the subject feel that nuclear weapons are essential to NATO's security. We will acknowledge majority rule and concede that the chance of conventional attack under non-possession is higher, perhaps even several times higher, than the chance of conventional attack under detente or victory. Because of the considerations advanced here, however, we will not concede that the chance of a conventional attack under non-possession is any greater than this.

Consider what these estimates imply for the total of expected deaths under these policies. We will assume that the number of deaths to be expected in a large-scale conventional European war is 30,000,000. (This is approximately the number of Europeans who died in World War II.) Now we will multiply this number by the percentage chance of large scale *conventional* war over the next 40 years, under each of the three basic policies. What is the percentage chance of conventional war under victory? Since few experts are predicting any sort of big war in Europe under current conditions, we could set this figure as low as 2 percent. If we pick 2 percent, it follows that the chance of war under Detente will be 3 percent—50 percent higher than victory, and the chance of war under non-possession no more than 9 percent—3 times higher than detente. This gives us 0.6 million more expected deaths under victory, 0.9 million more expected deaths under detente, and 2.7 million more expected deaths under non-possession. To some degree, these figures close the gaps between non-possession and detente, and between detente and victory. But the differences in these figures are not large enough to eliminate the gaps or reverse the basic judgment that non-possession causes the fewest expected deaths and serves the common good best, at least in these terms.

(b) Nuclear Blackmail

All of the preceding discussions have equated serving the common good with minimizing the total of expected deaths. Stress on expected deaths is justifiable. The primary effect of war is death and destruction, and it is reasonable to rate weapons policies by the amount of death and destruction that they might bring into the world. But people will argue that exclusive attention to death and destruction unfairly tilts the scales in favor of non-possession. Obviously, if you have fewer weapons, you are less likely to cause death and destruction. But if you have few weapons you are more likely to be intimidated by those who have more. Supporters of victory and detente claim that the retention of nuclear weapons by the United States is needed to preserve the balance of power and to protect the United States and other nations from nuclear blackmail.

Since a nuclear response to nuclear attack is more likely under victory than under detente, a threat to use nuclear weapons is less credible against victory than against detente. So we will assume that victory provides better protection against nuclear blackmail than does detente and that detente provides better protection against blackmail than does non-possession. Most people believe that the gap between victory and detente on this score is small but that the gap between detente and non-possession on this score is large. Victory and detente, then, save the world at large from terrorizing by nuclear bullies: non-possession does not.

The threat of nuclear blackmail is often the trump card played by opponents of nuclear disarmament. But the threat is perhaps exaggerated and perhaps misunderstood. (i) Nuclear blackmail is rarely attempted. When attempted, it rarely works. Truman threatened the total destruction of Japan in the Potsdam Declaration;[11] it did not work. Since then, the explicit ultimatum has practically disappeared from the world diplomatic scene. There are, of course, implicit threats, but they fall in the general catgeory of power politics, not the sub-category of blackmail techniques. (ii) The typical case of nuclear blackmail is not really *blackmail* at all. A blackmailer wants to *compel* his victim to take some sort of action, usually to hand over money. The nuclear blackmailer wants to *deter* his victim from taking some prospective action. If this is blackmail, then the threat of jail blackmails most of us into not committing crimes. Blackmail is hardly the right word.

For victory or detente to prove that non-possession hurts the common good by leaving the world subject to Soviet blackmail, they must show that there is some action (a) that the United States *would* perform under victory or detente, (b) that the United States would *not* perform under non-possession, and (c) that serves the common good. Such actions are rare. Look at the last 35 years of the Cold War. Are there any actions that the United States would not have performed if it had given up nuclear weapons in 1945?

Perhaps the U.S. might not have thrown a naval blockade around Cuba in 1962 if it had not had nuclear weapons. It might not have bombed North Vietnam from 1964 through 1972 if it had not felt that American nuclear weapons would prevent the Soviets from taking offensive action in support of their ally. But it is difficult to argue that these actions served the common good. A world poll in 1962 would have preferred a negotiated settlement over Cuba, and many Americans feel that the bombing of North Vietnam did not serve the national interest, much less the common good. Consider the next 35 years of the Cold War. The reader is invited to propose an action which the United States might take under victory or detente, but which it would not take under non-possession, an action, furthermore, which clearly serves the *common* good. (Note that it is not permissible to submit "the liberation of Eastern Europe" as a sample act, since history has shown that this is a step that the United States will not take even under the victory strategy.) I suggest that most proposed actions actions that the United States would take under victory but not under non-possession are simply acts to extend American influence. As American tourists in Asia, Africa, and Latin America are always astonished to discover, such extension of American influence is not generally identified with the common good.

For all these reasons, the chance of successful nuclear blackmail under non-possession may be much less than is commonly believed. Furthermore, the chance of successful nuclear blackmail is not zero under either victory or detente. One reason that the United States did not respond to the Soviet invasions of Hungary, Czechoslovakia, and Afghanistan was fear of confrontation with the Soviet Union, confrontation that might somehow lead to nuclear war. To some degree, these three cases provide instances of implicit but successful nuclear blackmail against a nuclear power.

Given that successful nuclear blackmail *can* occur under victory and detente, and given that successful nuclear blackmail *might not* occur under non-possession, it is difficult to argue that the "increased risk of nuclear blackmail" posed by non-possession is a decisive reason for overruling the priority among these policies established by counting the numbers of expected dead.

(c) Containing Soviet Influence

There is little doubt that if American strategic strength wanes, the Soviet Union, at least experimentally, would attempt to extend its influence. We will assume that the extension of Soviet influence does not serve the common good any better than the extension of American influence. Supporters of victory and detente argue that retention of American nuclear weapons is needed to maintain the containment of Soviet influence that has been the dominant note in American foreign policy ever since George Kennan's long telegram arrived in the State Department in February 1946.[12]

This is hardly the place for even the rudiments of a discussion of the various strategies of containment hatched and tested by the United States since 1946. Suffice it to say that history does not exhibit the relationship between Soviet influence and Soviet strategic strength postulated by those who feel that nuclear weapons are an essential part of any viable strategy of containment. In the late 1940s, when the United States alone had nuclear weapons, the Soviets tightened their grip on Eastern Europe, took over Czechoslovakia, and gained a tremendous ally in China. In the 1950s, as SAC busily deployed 1,800 jet bombers, the Soviets crushed revolts in Eastern Europe and extended their influence in the Middle East, the Caribbean, Latin America, and South East Asia. In the 1960s, the Soviets deployed large numbers of ICBMs, lost China and endured the physical annihilation of the Communist Party in Indonesia. In the early 1970s, they achieved strategic parity and got booted out of Egypt. In the late 1970s, they deployed the MIRV, almost lost control of Afghanistan, almost lost Poland, and endured the development of independent policy in Romania. What the record shows is practically an inverse relationship between political influence and nuclear strength.

Anyone who suggests that the ebb and flow of Soviet influence is correlated with the flow and ebb of American Soviet strategic strength is presenting a fantastically simple hypothesis to explain fantastically complex phenomena, a hypothesis that seems to run against the trend exhibited in the facts. It is no wonder that Kennan for over 30 years has been trying to explain that though he called for the "containment" of Soviet influence in 1946, he never felt that containment could be achieved or even substantially assisted by the application of brute force.

Strategic and Moral Implications of Nuclear Winter

All of the estimates presented in this chapter have excluded the effects of "nuclear winter," discussed at the end of Chapter 3. But suppose that Turco, Sagan, Ehrlich and the other proponents of the "nuclear winter" hypothesis are correct, that it really is true that a 5000 megaton exchange will produce a nuclear winter, and that even a 100 megaton nuclear attack, distributed in 1000 nuclear blasts and directed against cities, will produce nuclear winter. How will this affect the comparison of victory, detente, and non-possession?

One obvious conclusion is that the argument, presented in this chapter, that detente serves the common good better than victory is considerably strengthened. The typical comparison between detente and victory holds that victory produces a bigger chance of a smaller war and detente produces a smaller chance of a bigger war. But if a "smaller war" and a "bigger war" produce approximately the same number of casualties, then victory produces a big chance of a big catastrophe and detente produces a smaller chance of the same catastrophe—a clear victory for detente.

But what about the comparison between detente and non-possession? At first sight, the claims about nuclear winter seem to favor detente. If non-possession creates a greater probability of Soviet attack than the probability of nuclear war started by *either* side under detente (a view many endorse), and if the number of casualties resulting from a one-sided Soviet attack will equal the number of casualties from a two-sided nuclear war, then the United States and the world have little to gain from non-possession.

But the case for detente is not so easy. If the Soviets know that any nuclear attack greater than 100 megatons will generate enough dust or soot to destroy the Soviet Union, then (a) they will not launch a nuclear attack, or (b) if they launch an attack, they will keep its size below the 100 megation threshold. This prediction assumes, of course, that the Soviets will behave rationally when and if they come to use nuclear weapons. Some might question this presumption of rationality, but detente also assumes that the Soviets are rational, and will behave rationally in the face of American deterrent threats.

As the facts about nuclear winter become more generally known, nations will be more and more deterred from the use of their own nuclear weapons. If so, there will be less and less need for nuclear weapons for purposes of deterrence through threats of a second strike. Mutual deterrence will be replaced by self-deterrence.

Thus, though the threat of generating a nuclear winter remains if the United States gives up nuclear weapons and the Soviet Union does not, the chance that a nuclear winter will be produced under detente is greater still. With detente we get a nuclear winter if either the United States or the Soviet Union chooses to commit suicide. Under non-possession, we get a nuclear winter only if the Soviet Union chooses to commit suicide. If we assume that the inclination of the Soviets to commit suicide is about the same as our own inclination to commit suicide, the chance of nuclear winter under detente is twice as great as the chance of nuclear winter under non-possession.

Conclusion

Unless one places unwarranted stress on the threat of nuclear blackmail, the verdict of this chapter is that non-possession serves the common good better than detente or victory. This result is not surprising. Few people are prepared to argue that American nuclear weapons serve humanity. For most Americans, it suffices that they serve the United States. This argument, couched in terms of the national interest, is not a moral argument. Americans who seek a moral defense of nuclear weapons must argue, not that American nuclear weapons serve the common good, but that the United States has a *right* to keep these weapons even if they do not serve the common good. The appeal to a *right* takes us into a new moral domain, explored in the next chapter.

Notes

1. The Gallup Poll for 11 May 1983 reported that 70 percent of the American people supported a "verifiable bilateral nuclear freeze." In May 1981, 57 percent of the public indicated in a Gallup Poll that they would vote "for nuclear disarmament" if a world-wide poll were taken on the subject of nuclear arms. This poll did *not* ask what the American people would want if the Soviet Union refused to disarm.

Lest it appear that the idea of a world-wide poll is biased against the United States, the reader should observe than an even larger majority of the world's people would favor the unilateral nuclear disarmament of the Soviet Union. (I assume that China and the Eastern European nations have no interest in being protected by the Soviet strategic deterrent.)

2. A good introduction to the general problem of choice under uncertainty is Luce and Raiffa 1957, chs. 13 and 14. See also Raiffa 1968.

3. Of course, it is still possible to have an all-out nuclear war even if the United States disarms; there might be one, for example, between the U.S.S.R. and China sometime in the future. But that war would not be a result of the American policy of non-possession.

4. For an example of near complete agnosticism about the probabilities of weapons policies outcomes consider the following remarks by James Fallows: "There has never been a nuclear war, and nobody knows what a nuclear war would mean . . .. No one knows how these weapons would preform if they were fired; whether they would hit the targets at which they are aimed; whether human society would be set back for decades, centuries as a result . . . Most strategic arguments [are] disputes of faith rather than fact." (Fallows 1981 139–40)

5. In addition to the "rough equality in magnitude" of disasters produced, Kavka lists eight other conditions that must be satisfied before the disaster avoidance rule can be applied. But he goes on to argue that all eight of these conditions are satified in the case of choice among nuclear weapons policies.

6. Various methods for generating and evaluating ranges of expected values are discussed in Rescher 1983 94–114. Rescher's ranges, however, are generated by the uncertainty of a single estimator; the ranges given here are generated by disagreements among multiple estimators.

7. The argument that non-possession produces fewer expected deaths than detente, and that detente produces fewer expected deaths than victory, is presented in Lackey 1982. For criticism see Hardin 1983 and Kavka 1983.

8. The reason that the Soviets will not attack by mistake under non-possession is that they will have nothing on their radar screens that they could misinterpret as an American attack. Detente is not open to disaster through escalation because of its commitment to "no first use."

9. The percentage chances of war were estimated for a 40 year period since "40 years" is, I believe, about as much time as people have in mind when asked about "the future." The projections forward beyond that are for heuristic purposes only; they are to be taken no more seriously than claims that a nuclear reactor will suffer a meltdown "once every 17,000 reactor years." Some of the implications of guesses about catastrophe are summarized in Table 5-3.

10. Weinberger 1982. The argument that nuclear weapons have prevented a conventional war between the United States and the Soviet Union is slightly preposterous. The United States and the Soviet Union are not traditional enemies, and ideology aside, each has almost nothing to gain from attacking the other. In the early 1960s and in the early 1980s the one non-ideological bone of contention that might have produced conventional war was forward placement of intermediate-range strategic weapons.

11. The Potsdam declaration did not mention nuclear weapons but did threaten total destruction: "We call upon the government of Japan to proclaim now the unconditional surrender of all armed forces, and to provide adequate assurances of their good faith in such action. The alternative for Japan is prompt and utter destruction." (Feis 1960.) Certainly after the fall of Okinawa the threat was credible, atomic bomb or no atomic bomb.

12. The early history of containment is documented in Etzold and Gaddis 1978. For the later history, see Gaddis 1982.

Appendix: Expected Deaths and the National Interest

In discussions of expected deaths and the common good, what primarily concerns us is the total number of expected deaths, not the nations in which different expected deaths occur. In considering the national interest, however, what concerns us are the expected deaths in the United States. Given the estimates and methods of this chapter, it is interesting to consider which weapons policy causes the fewest expected *American* deaths.

Table 5.3   Projections of War Probabilities by Time Period

Chance of War (percent)	Time Period (years)	
5	next	40 implies:
23	next	200
40	next	400
65	next	800
93	next	2000
1	next	40 implies:
5	next	200
10	next	400
18	next	800
37	next	2000
99	next	8000
0.5	next	40 implies:
2.5	next	200
5	next	400
10	next	800
23	next	2000
90	next	18000
98	next	30000

In discussions of nuclear war that take the side of national prudence, it is commonly assumed that the chance of nuclear war is substantially greater under non-possession than under either detente or victory. From this, the inference seems irresistable that non-possession is contrary to the American national interest. But if we seek what is best for the United States, we must consider not only the differing probabilities of nuclear war under the three weapons policies, but also the differing damage that wars resulting from these policies might cause to the United States.

It is, of course, possible, that a Soviet attack under non-possession would be just as devastating as a Soviet attack under detente or under victory, but this is not likely, since it would have different targets. As we have suggested, a Soviet attack under non-possession would be either a terror raid on a limited number of American cities or a counterforce raid against American conventional forces and oil supplies. If the former, as many as 15 million Americans might die. If the latter, less than 5 million Americans might die.

In an all-out nuclear war we can reasonably expect that 100 million Americans will die. In a limited nuclear war, we can expect that 22 million Americans will die. In a Soviet counterforce attack on American strategic weapons, we can expect that 15 million Americans will die. It follows that if the chance of a Soviet counterforce strike under detente is equal to the chance of a Soviet nuclear attack under non-possession, detente causes more expected American deaths than non-possession. Unless the chance of a Soviet attack under non-possession is seven times greater than the chance of all-out war under either victory or detente, victory or detente cause more expected American deaths than non-possession. Unless the chance of Soviet attack under non-possession is 50 percent greater than the chance of limited nuclear war under the victory strategy, victory causes more expected American deaths than non-possession.

Let us take some specific estimates. If we accept the estimates that we have attributed to the victory supporter of a 1 percent chance of all-out war and a 10 percent chance of limited war under 40 years of the victory strategy, we are assuming that the victory strategy causes (or, perhaps, *permits*) 3.2 million expected American deaths. Since a Soviet attack on an America practicing non-possession will cause no more than 15 million deaths, it follows that the victory supporter must claim that the chance of Soviet attack under non-possession is at least 20 percent, or else concede that victory causes more expected American deaths than non-possession.

If we accept the estimate that we attributed to the detente supporter of a 5 percent chance of all-out war under detente (a "50–50 chance of war in 800 years"), we are assuming that detente will permit over 5 million expected American deaths. It follows that supporters of Detente must claim that the chance of Soviet attack under non-possession is greater than 33 percent, or else concede that detente causes the greater number of expected deaths. Our conclusion is that unless we consider non-possession to generate a very substantial risk of Soviet attack, non-possession causes fewer expected American deaths than either victory or detente.

Now we must consider victory vs. detente. Each side claims that the other strategy poses the greater risk of all-out nuclear war. But supporters of detente attribute an additional evil to victory—the threat of limited nuclear war—and supporters of victory attribute an additional evil to detente—the threat of an unanswered Soviet counterforce strike. Since we are assuming that a limited nuclear war (which may have several stages) will kill more Americans than a single Soviet counterforce strike, it follows that unless the probability of a counterforce strike under detente is greater than the probability of a limited nuclear war under victory, victory causes more expected deaths than detente.

Is it reasonable to assume that the chance of Soviet attack under detente is greater than the chance of limited nuclear war under victory? Consider the problem from the Soviet point of view. The Soviets know that, under detente, they may "get away" with a nuclear attack, but they also know that if the United States does respond, the response will be devastating and they will lose everything. They also know that, under victory, if they launch a limited attack, they will surely lose something, but the response will be proportional and they will not lose everything. Now suppose that there is some target in the United States that the Soviets are desperately interested in destroying. (For example, suppose that their spies report that a reseach center is about to make a breakthrough in particle-beam weapons that will render their strategic systems obsolete.) If the United States practices detente and the Soviets attack the particle-beam station, they may lose nothing or they may lose everything. If the United States practices victory and the Soviets attack the particle-beam center, they will surely lose something (perhaps a research center of their own, plus something extra for damages), but they will not lose everything. It is not obvious that the Soviets will be more inclined to attack if the United States practices detente than if the United States practices victory. But unless they are so inclined, detente causes fewer expected American deaths.

6

Weapons Policies and Human Rights

A belief in human rights, by itself, does not resolve the question of which weapons policy best serves human rights. Supporters of victory, of detente, of non-possession all declare that they have the deepest respect for human rights. They all believe that their favorite policy protects human rights better than the alternatives.

The human rights primarily affected by strategic weapons are the right to self-defense and the right to life. People in the United States have a right to life and self-defense. People in the U.S.S.R. have the same rights. Supporters of victory emphasize self-defense and claim that their policy protects the American people from the Soviet threat. Supporters of non-possession emphasize the right to life and point out that their policy protects the Soviet people from annihilation by American strategic weapons. Supporters of detente claim that their policy maximizes protection for the American people while minimizing (relative to victory) the threat to the Soviet people, thus protecting both rights.[1]

In this chapter we will be primarily concerned with the right to life of people in the Soviet Union. Do American weapons policies violate this right? If they do, is there some stronger right, possessed by the American people, which justifies the violation of the rights of Soviet citizens? If there is no justification for violating these rights, is there at least a morally acceptable excuse?

Killing the Innocent

The right to life implies the right not to be killed. This is a right actually possessed only by the innocent. We pause here to note that the Soviet people are innocent, and will remain so even if the Soviet Union happens to launch a first strike against the United States. The people who allege that Soviet policy is aggressive will be the first to concede that the average Soviet citizen has no say in the formulation of that policy. Certainly the Soviet people do not have the power to demand or to prevent the launching of Soviet strategic weapons towards the United States. Regardless of what happens, the Soviet people remain innocent and retain their right to life.

Supporters of victory and supporters of detente will deny that their policies violate the rights of any citizen in the Soviet Union. The argument is elementary: no Russian, no Soviet citizen, has ever been killed by American strategic weapons. Consequently no right to life has ever been violated. When the day comes that the United States launches a first strike against the Soviet Union, or even when the day comes that the United States launches a second strike against the Soviet Union, *then* we can speak of the violations of the right to life. But surely we cannot speak of such violations of those rights *now*, when no one has been killed. [2]

This argument is commonly given, but it is flawed, (a) because it ignores the distinction between evaluating *actions* and evaluating *policies*, and (b) because it ignores the fact that we can reliably translate possible greater evils into actual lesser evils.

(a) Actions and Policies

We are concerned in this book with the evaluation of policies, not just the evaluation of particular acts of state. Particular actions take place at one point in time; policies control actual and possible actions taken at many points in time. If you argue that a particular *action* violates human rights, you must produce the person whose right has been violated. When you argue that a *policy* violates human rights, all you need show is that the policy sanctions actions that would violate human rights if they occurred. You need not show that those actions have actually happened.

For example, suppose that the Congress passed a law prescribing a 10 year jail term for any American who utters the words "Ronald Reagan is a pink ostrich." It may well be that no American ever feels inclined to utter these words and that there is no prospect of anyone going to jail for violating this law. Nevertheless, the law violates the right to free speech, because it sanctions putting someone in jail for saying "Ronald Reagan is a pink ostrich," and such imprisonment, if it occurred, would violate the right to free speech. Likewise, the policy that says "We will kill innocent people in Moscow if there is a nuclear attack on the United States" violates the right to life of people in Moscow, since if there *were* a nuclear attack on the United States, people in Moscow *would be* killed, and those killings, if they occurred, would violate the right to life of the people killed in Moscow.

(b) Risks and Evils

Most moral and legal systems are ill-equipped to deal with the moral problem of the imposition of risk. Most prefer to concentrate their efforts on risks realized, where actual damage is done and all can see it. The difference between a risk unrealized and a risk realized is perceived as tremendous, and in general people tend to absolve those who impose unrealized risks, even though the contribution of a person to the creation of a risk is often the same whether the risk is realized or not. There seems to be a deep psychological bias against the proper moral assement of unrealized risk.

To combat this bias, we introduced in Chapter 1 a device that translates a possible harm presented by a risk into an actual harm caused by a destructive act. The device suggested was something like what decision theorists call the "certainty equivalent" of a risk; that is, whatever value the victim of risk would be willing to give up in order to be completely free of the risk. In decision theory, the certainty equivalent of a risk is usually stated in monetary terms, but the certainty equivalent can be stated in non-monetary terms as well. For example, if Jones has bone cancer in his leg, and is told that he has a 50 percent chance of dying from cancer if he does not undergo an amputation, then if Jones has the amputation, losing his leg is, for *him*, the "certainty equivalent" of a 50–50 chance of dying from cancer.

Let us consider what the notion of a "certainty equivalent" for risks implies as regards the moral gravity of inflicting risks on Jones. By his choice, Jones has indicated that for him 100 percent chance of losing his leg is equivalent to a 50 percent chance of a painful death. Doesn't this imply that inflicting a 50 percent chance of a painful death on Jones, *whether he actually dies or is luckily spared*, is morally equivalent to amputating his leg? In short, we will consider, as a hypothesis, that *imposing a risk on someone is morally equivalent to inflicting on him the certainty equivalent of the risk.*

Is it reasonable to equate "imposing a risk" with "forcible seizure of the certainty equivalent of the risk?" Since the victim of the risk has indicated that he is indifferent as between accepting the risk and losing the certainty equivalent of the risk, we can say that *imposing the risk* or *seizing the certainty equivalent* subtracts equally from the victim's welfare. But to lower a person's welfare is to do him an injury. It follows that to impose a risk on someone is to injure him as much as if the certainty equivalent had been seized. If people have a right not to be injured, they have the right not to be put at risk, even if the risk draws no blood and causes no scars.

Victory and Commitments to Killing the Innocent

The human right to life implies a moral duty not to kill innocent people. Now, if a person has a moral duty to do something, he also has a moral duty not to put himself in the position of being unable to do his duty.[3] If I buy an automobile, I have a moral obligation to pay for it. It follows that I have a moral duty not to squander my money so that I am incapable of meeting the payments. If I squander my money on Monday and the payment falls due on Tuseday, then on Monday I have violated a moral duty, even though I have not *yet* failed to meet a payment. If I have a duty not to kill innocent people, I have a duty not to put myself in the position of being unable to avoid killing. If Dr. Jekyll knows that once he drinks a potion he will be transformed into the murderous Mr. Hyde, he has a moral duty not to take the potion.

The connection between this fact about duty and the victory strategy is clear. The victory strategy attempts to enhance deterrence through a strong commitment to the use of nuclear weapons. (The flexibility of victory lies not in the decision to respond or not respond, but in the variety of responses given.) Under the victory strategy, it is virtually impossible for the United States, faced with a Soviet nuclear attack or a massive Soviet conventional attack, to avoid launching a nuclear strike. This strike would in all likelihood be a counterforce strike, and a counterforce strike against the U.S.S.R. will kill between 4 and 27 million people. Thus even if no *acts* have been undertaken thus far under the victory strategy, the strategy itself has violated the duty not to put oneself into a position in which the killing of the innocent will be unavoidable.

What can the victory supporter say against this argument? He cannot deny that his strategy involves a commitment to nuclear response. What he might say is that there is an important difference between the car-buyer example (or the Dr. Jekyll example), and the commitment involved in the victory strategy. The car-buyer who squanders his money puts himself in a position in which it is *inevitable* that he will default. Dr. Jekyll, when he drinks his potion, puts himself in the position in which he knows that it is inevitable that he will murder someone. But the United States, when it adopts the victory strategy, does *not* put itself in the position in which it is inevitable that the United States will kill innocent Russians. In fact, victory supporters believe that if their policy is adopted there is very little chance of a Soviet attack and thus very little chance of an American nuclear response. The United States, then, has not really "put itself in the position" of being unable to avoid killing. Furthermore, whether or not someone gets killed depends not on what the United States does but on whether or not the Soviet Union attacks. If the Soviets know that the United States will respond and they attack anyway, then the Soviets are responsible for the killing of their own people. So, at least, argues the victory supporter.

Does lack of inevitability make for a significant difference between what the United States does when it adopts the victory strategy and what Dr. Jekyll does when he drinks the potion that turns him into Mr. Hyde? We can bring the examples closer together if we introduce an element of chance into the Dr. Jekyll case. Suppose that Mr. Hyde kills someone only half of the time before he turns back into Dr. Jekyll. *Now* when Dr. Jekyll drinks the potion, it is not inevitable that he will kill someone. Nevertheless, Dr. Jekyll still has a moral duty not to drink the potion, and there is no way to explain the existence of this duty except to say that, when he drinks the potion, he violates the right to life of the people around him.

We feel this way when there is a 50–50 chance that Jekyll will kill someone, and we probably feel the same way if he has a 1 in 10 chance of killing someone. On the other hand, if the chance is 1 in 10,000, we will find it odd to say that Jekyll is violating the rights of the people around him if he drinks the potion. The upshot is that the intrusion of chance provides an excuse only if the chance is negligible. In the last chapter, we attributed to the victory strategy a 1 in 10 chance of limited nuclear war. *This* chance is certainly not negligible.

This leaves the consideration that the American commitment to a counterstrike does not violate the right to life of Soviet citizens because if anyone gets killed, the fault lies with the Soviet leadership. The argument is odd. Suppose that I say to you, "I will kill the President if you tell me to." You tell me to, and I kill the President. *You* may bear some responsibility for what happened, especially if you know that I can be relied on to do what I say. But it hardly follows that I, who shot the President of my own free will, bear no responsibility for what I have done. Likewise, if the Soviets attack the United States and we respond with an attack that kills millions of people in the Soviet Union, the Soviets bear some responsibility for what has happened to their people, but it hardly follows that we bear none. We can *extend* blame to the Soviet leadership, but we cannot *shift* it from ourselves.

Detente and the Infliction of Risk

The victory strategy involves a commitment to the use of nuclear weapons. The detente strategy does not. The deterrent posture under detente may be pure bluff. Thus, if there is a duty to avoid irrevocable commitments to killing the innocent, detente fulfills that duty while victory does not.

Nevertheless, the detente strategy does create risks for the Soviet people. Detente requires the possession of strategic weapons, and this creates the chance that Soviet citizens will be killed by them. If the United States had no strategic weapons, there would be no chance that people in the Soviet Union would be killed by them. Does this infliction of risk violate the right to life of people in the Soviet Union?

One way of describing the risks and benefits of nuclear deterrence under detente is this: By deploying strategic weapons the United States *decreases* the chance of a Soviet attack on the United States by *increasing* the chance of an American attack on the Soviet Union. Another way of putting this is to say that through deterrence the United States decreases the number of expected American deaths by increasing the number of expected Soviet deaths. We have argued that increasing the risk of attack on Russia violates the right to life of people in the Soviet Union. Yet many Americans feel that it is morally permissible to make these threats against the Soviet people. They feel that it is morally justifiable to increase Soviet risks in order to decrease American risks. They feel that it is morally justifiable to cause expected Soviet deaths in order to save expected American lives. But *is* it permissible to cause expected deaths in order to save expected lives?

If we remove the word "expected" from the preceding sentence we are left with the question "Is it permissible to cause deaths in order to save lives?" This question has been heatedly discussed by contemporary students of ethics. At this juncture we will make a rather startling assumption, justifiable on the grounds that it seems intuitively plausible and there seem to be no strong arguments against it. We will assume that the word "expected" *makes no difference*: that the moral problem of killing a human being is the same as the moral problem of causing an expected death. The *basic* problem is whether it is ever permissible to kill an innocent human being in order to save another innocent human being. The moral problem of whether it is permissible to inflict a risk of death on one innocent human being in order to remove another innocent human being from risk of death is merely the statistical version of the basic problem. It follows that whatever opinion a person has about the basic problem of killing should determine his opinion about the statistical problem. If a person feels that it is never permissible to kill one human being in order to save another, then he should feel that it is never permissible to put one human being at risk in order to remove another human being from risk. If he feels that it is generally permissible to kill one human being in order to save another, then he should feel that it is generally permissible to put one human being at risk in order to remove another human being from risk, and so forth.[4]

There is no rule in ethics stating that every imposition of risk is a morally intolerable violation of human rights. If the risk is negligible, then the risk is excusable. If the victim of risk freely consents to the risk, then the imposition of the risk is excusable. If the person imposing the risk does so on the basis of some right that is stronger than the right of the victim not to be put at risk, then the infliction of risk is morally justifiable. We will consider all these possibilities, and other justifications for inflicting risks on the Soviets.

Arguments That The Risk Is Permissible

(a) Are the Risks of Detente Negligible?

In a modern industrial society, nearly every person every day creates risks and suffers risks. When I drive my car I create risks (hopefully, small risks), to pedestrians and other vehicles along the road. If I stand by my office window, I create risks for the people below on whom I might fall. When I light my stove, I create a small risk of blowing up the gas line and killing everybody in the building. Likewise, other people create similar risks and impose them on me. It would be an intolerable restriction on personal liberty to require people never to create risks. Most of the risks each of us creates are permissible risks, small enough to be tolerated, small enough to be absorbed without notice into the general background level of risk.

Supporters of detente might argue that the risks detente imposes on the Soviet people are so small that they are absorbed into the background level of risk. The odds that the average Russian is going to die from an American missile are minuscule (so the argument goes) compared with the odds that he is going to die from cancer, suicide, industrial accident, or other causes. Supporters of detente might compare the risks of detente with a risk imposed by a careful automobile driver who observes all the rules of the road. He might compare the larger risks raised by victory with the risks raised by a drunk driver. If so, the risks of detente are excusable risks.

Stated in qualitative terms, this argument appears to have some force, but is it really the case that the risks raised by American nuclear weapons are tolerable compared with the background Soviet levels of risk? To begin with, it is not proper to compare the risks raised by detente with the *total* background level of risk in the U.S.S.R. Much of the background level of risk is caused by natural perils that cannot be eliminated. Such natural risks are "tolerated" only in the sense that nothing can be done about them. The proper comparison is between the risks imposed by detente with the risks imposed by human hazards that could be eliminated by appropriate legislation.

What are the risks of detente to the Soviet people? In the previous chapter, we estimated the risks of nuclear war under detente at 0.5 percent to 15 percent over 40 years. According to the OTA study, a large scale nuclear attack on the Soviet Union would kill between 50 million and 100 million Soviet citizens. It follows that over 40 years, detente causes between 250,000 and 15 million expected deaths; that is, between 5,800 and 375,000 expected deaths every year. Does this quantity of risk melt into the background? Is even the low estimate of risk *negligible*?

Let us put ourselves in the position of the Soviet people. Suppose that the Soviets placed thousands of Skylab-type satellites in orbit, and that these satellites came crashing down by the hundreds killing 5,800 Americans every year. These lives could be saved by eliminating the satellite program, but the Soviets are intensely interested in continuing it. Furthermore, 5,800 deaths is a small number of deaths. More than 2 million Americans die every year. About 40,000 Americans die every year in automobile accidents alone, many of which could be eliminated by lowering the national speed limit to 40 miles per hour. "If the American government will not save thousands of its people simply by lowering the speed limit," Moscow announces, "why should the Soviet Union worry about a mere 5,800 deaths?"

One could imagine the uproar such a communication would cause. The fact is that the American people would never tolerate 5,800 Soviet-inflicted deaths, and if the United States would not consider this total negligible, it cannot expect to have a similar total of expected Soviet deaths treated as negligible.

Of course, there is one conspicuous difference between the risks imposed by detente on the Soviet people and the risks imposed by falling Soviet satellites in our imaginary example. The falling satellites, every year, cause *real* American deaths. The risks of detente cause *expected* Soviet deaths. For some reason, people find real deaths less tolerable than expected deaths. Perhaps this contributes to the impression that detente imposes only negligible risks. But it is irrational and immoral not to take expected deaths seriously. Consider the following problem. You must choose between act A and act B. If you choose A, one man out of a group of 200 will be selected by lot and killed. If you choose B, there is a 10 percent chance that all 200 men will die and a 90 percent chance that all 200 men will live. (The choice is determined by a roulette wheel.) Act A causes one expected death; act B causes 20 (10% × 200) expected deaths. Most people, confronted with the problem think that B is the morally preferable act. They reason that if they choose A, they will surely cause someone's death, while if they choose B, they have a 90 percent chance of causing no one's death.[5] But this is a mistake: A is the morally preferable act. If you do not believe this, ask the 200 men in the group. They will *all* beg you to choose A, because with A each man has *20 times* as much chance of surviving as he does with B. Obviously in this situation you have no moral warrant to ignore the unanimous wish of the people who are affected by your acts. The moral is that in problems of homicide, expected deaths cannot be ignored.

(b) Does SALT I Signify Consent to Nuclear Risk?

We will assume, then, what is generally assumed, that the risks of detente are not negligible. Next, let us consider the possible justification that the American infliction of risk is morally tolerable because the Soviet people have consented to it.

At first sight, any claim that the Soviet people have freely consented to the risk of nuclear annihilation seems absurd. Nobody *wants* to be blown up by nuclear weapons. But the fact that the Soviet people do not want to be blown up is no proof that they have not consented to the risk of being blown up. I may not *want* to pay $10,000 for a new car, but if I like a certain model, I may *consent* to paying this sum. In return for consideration, I often consent to *doing* things that I do not like to do. Now, in 1972, the United States and the Soviet Union signed a strategic arms limitation treaty that defined the maximum number of strategic launchers to be deployed by each side. In effect, each side consented to the deployment of *some* strategic weapons in return for an agreement that there would not be *more*. Since there is consent, the American imposition of risks resulting from the development of strategic weapons does not violate rights of the Soviet people.

Supporters of non-possession, I expect, will be outraged by this argument from consent. To begin with, they will point out that there are many people in the world threatened by American strategic weapons who live in countries that have not signed arms agreements with the United States: all the people in China, for example. The risk imposed on these people cannot be explained away on grounds that the risk is a consensual risk. Furthermore, a number of objections can be raised against the comparison of SALT I with the purchase of an automobile. There is a difference between free exchange and a blackmail agreement. When a contract is freely signed, both parties are better off than they would have been if the agreement had not been struck, better off in the sense that the welfare of each is higher than it was the moment before the exchange was made. When I buy the car, I want the car more than the $10,000, and the dealer wants the $10,000 more than the car. When a blackmail agreement is struck, at least one side is no better off than he was the minute before the agreement was struck. He only knows that he would be worse off if he did not accept the agreement. If I agree to pay the $10,000 in return for incriminating pictures that would otherwise be published, I am no better off the minute after I pay my $10,000 than I was the minute before I paid my $10,000. I only know that I would have been worse off if I had not paid. In short, there are coercive exchanges and non-coercive exchanges. Blackmail is a coercive exchange.[6]

In this light, let us now look at SALT I. Each nation kept roughly the number of missiles it had when the agreement was signed, so neither nation was significantly better off after the agreement was signed than before. Each nation knew that it would be worse off if it did not sign. Thus SALT I has the structure of a blackmail agreement, with the special feature of each side succeeding in blackmailing the other, each side saying "sign the agreement, or *else*." SALT I, it appears, is mutual consent derived from mutual coercion. When I was a schoolboy there was a schoolyard bully who used to punch kids in the arm. If you protested, he punched you ten times. If you said you liked it, he punched you five times. Many said they liked it. It does not follow that the bully did not violate their rights.

Several other features of SALT I call for comment. First, the agreement was binding for only five years, and legally expired in 1977. If the United States bases its right to put the Soviet people at risk on an agreement reached with the Soviet government, the failure of the U.S. Senate to ratify SALT II has left the United States with no further ground for inflicting the risk. The fact that current deployments in fact fall within SALT II limits is irrelevant; no formal, binding agreement exists to observe these limits. Second, many strategic systems were not covered by SALT I: strategic bombers, cruise missiles, intermediate range ballistic missiles, strategic bombers, to name a few. Each of these systems poses a risk of death to many people in the Soviet Union. (The largest fraction of American nuclear megatonnage, in fact, is carried on strategic bombers). Since the Soviet people have struck no agreement with regard to these systems, the risk of death posed by these systems can by no means be excused on grounds of consent. Third, no attempt was made on the Soviet side to submit SALT I to any body that could plausibly claim to express the will of the Soviet people. Since no such submission occurred, the best that can be said is that the Soviet *government* consented to take risks, not that the Soviet *people* consented to take these risks.

If we reject the argument that the Soviet people have consented to the risks that American strategic weapons have imposed on them, we are left with the imposition of the risk of death, pure and simple. Such impositions violate the right to life, even if the risk is never realized. It follows that American strategic weapons violate the right to life of people in the Soviet Union, even if worst does not come to worst, even if American strategic weapons are never used, and even if no Soviet citizen is ever killed by them.

(c) The Justification of Good Intentions

In considering the risks imposed by American strategic weapons, one excuse that readily comes to mind is that the United States intends no harm to come from its strategic weapons. The motto of the Strategic Air Command is "Peace is Our Profession," and a long sequence of Secretaries of Defense have explained to Congress and the world that the main purpose of American stragetic weapons is to preserve the peace. Thus, if war results from strategic systems, the consequence is unintended, an accident. But if it is an accident, it should be excused.

This argument, however, hinges on a confusion between two senses of "intended". In one sense, what we intend is what we desire to result from our actions; in this sense an unintended consequence is an undesired consequence. In another sense, the important sense in law, what we intend is what we foresee or what we ought to forsee as resulting from our actions. In this sense an unintended consequence is one which we did not forsee and ought not to have forseen. It is the second sense of "unintended" that provides an excuse from moral responsibility for results which I could not forsee.

Now, the risks raised by American strategic weapons are risks that *are* forseen by the American leadership.[7] Since they are forseen, the American leadership is responsible for them. True, we do not *like*, we do not *desire*, to create risks for innocent people in Russia. But these likes and preferences do not excuse us when we create the risk. Imagine that you discover that your neighbor has just installed a stock of dynamite in his basement, put a trip wire connected to the dynamite on the front door, and erected a sign saying "Danger, Dynamite" in front of his house. "If my house blows up, so will yours too," your neighbor says, "But I'm tired of burglars. Mind, I don't want to put dynamite in the basement and I don't want to blow you up, but I have a right to keep out burglars and there's only a small chance that the dynamite will blow." I doubt that you would find the fact that your neighbor *regretfully* installed the dynamite a sufficient excuse for putting you at risk. Likewise, the fact that Americans don't like nuclear deterrence does not excuse putting the Soviet population at risk.

(d) The Justification of Self-Defense

In Chapter 1, we acknowledged a right to self-defense against those who seek to violate rights. If we argue that the deployment of strategic weapons by the United States violates the right to life of people in the Soviet Union, it follows without much argument, that the deployment of strategic weapons by the Soviet Union violates the right to life of people in the United States. Since American rights are being violated, American attempts to stop, or mitigate, the violation of these rights seem justified on grounds of self-defense.

Whether or not this argument is acceptable depends on how one conceives the right to self-defense. If one believes that the right to self-defense entitles the victim to do *anything* to prevent further violation of his rights, then the right to self-defense will justify, not only nuclear deterrence, but such active steps as a counterforce first strike against the Soviet Union. Most moral philosophers who have thought about self-defense will not go this far.

Suppose that we do not attack, but simply inflict risks on the Soviets, tit for tat. There are still problems with the justification of self-defense. Self-defense, as we have defined it and as it is usually conceived, justifies the taking of steps against the *attacker* who is violating rights. It does not justify taking steps against *anyone else*. It follows that the United States has the right to inflict risks on Soviet decision makers and on Soviet strategic weapons, but not on the Soviet people. If someone threatens my life and I have no recourse, I can threaten the aggressor's life in order to escape the threat. This is legitimate self-defense. But if someone is threatening my life, I have no right under self-defense to threaten, for example, the aggressor's *son*, even if I have good reason to believe that by threatening his son, I can save my life.

If self-defense permits attacks on aggressors but on no one else, it might seem that the victory strategy could claim the justification of self-defense even if detente could not. Detente, which targets urban centers as part of the very business of deterrence, clearly is in no position to claim self-defense. But victory, which targets Soviet strategic weapons first and foremost, can claim that it is directing deadly force directly at the attacker: the Soviet leadership and the strategic weapons with which they threaten the United States.

As things *now* stand, however, it is a fact that a counterforce strike under victory would kill millions of Soviet citizens. Those who would order such a strike know this in advance. Such foreseen infliction of risk on even a single innocent person cannot be jusitified as self-defense. If I am pinned down by a sniper, I am entitled under self-defense to shoot back at the sniper. But if I see that my shots are likely to kill an innocent passer-by, then I am not entitled to shoot back at the sniper, even if I do not want to kill the passer-by and would be happier if I could devise a way to shoot the sniper without putting the passer-by at risk.[8]

There is no way, it seems, that either victory or detente can be justified by invoking the right to self-defense.

(e) The Right To Survive

Soviet strategic systems, it is often alleged, threaten the very survival of the United States. Many people, when they discuss ethics, feel that when survival is at stake the normal moral rules do not apply.[9] They feel that any steps taken to secure survival are morally justified. A person might feel that the act that saves his life runs contrary to his moral values, but he might also feel that he is "the source" of his moral values and that he cannot serve these values if he ceases to exist. Likewise, the act that helps provide security for the United States in the nuclear age may be an act contrary to American values, but many will feel that American values can only be preserved if the United States is preserved.

It is difficult, in many cases, to tell whether a person who presents this "argument from survival" is claiming that *morality is suspended* when survival is at stake or whether he is claiming that *the right to survive is the highest moral right.*

Most moral philosophers will balk at the idea that a supreme emergency could produce a *suspension* of morality. Some moral philosophers believe that moral principles are "subjective" all of the time. But *no* moral philosopher thinks that moral principles are subjective sometimes and objective at other times. Some philosophers feel that the principles of mathemathics are invented; others feel that the principles of mathematics are discovered. But no one feels that mathematics principles are at some times invented and at other times discovered. Likewise with moral principles.

This leaves the claim that the right to survive is a supreme moral right. The only way to test such a moral claim is to consider its consequences in particular cases. Does the need to survive justify *anything*? Suppose that you are on a sinking ocean liner and through carelessness have lost your life preserver. Does your need to survive justify stealing a life preserver from a small child? Suppose that someone catches you in the act of ripping the life preserver off a child. Would an impartial spectator think that what you are doing is morally justified on the ground that you need the life preserver to live? We can *understand* why someone would steal from a child in order to survive, but we do not *condone* such acts. But if the need to survive does not justify stealing the child's life preserver, there is no such thing as a right to survive. And if there is no such thing as the right to survive, it cannot be invoked as a justification for violating the right to life of people in the Soviet Union.

(f) The Right To Be Saved From Death

Suppose that you are walking along a pier and suddenly notice someone struggling in the water. There is a life ring nearby which you can throw to the drowning person at no risk to yourself. There is no doubt that it is not morally acceptable to just walk by. From such cases a number of philosophers have inferred that people have a right to be saved from death. If there is such a right, one might describe the debate about weapons strategies as a debate between those who emphasize the right of the Soviet people not to be killed and those who emphasize the right of the American people to be saved from death.

In the non-political world most people assume that the right not to be killed is a much stronger moral right than the right to be saved from death; that is, that the duty not to kill people is stronger than the duty to save them. But a number of contemporary ethical theorists have taken issue with the popular view and have postulated that the right to be saved, other things being equal, is just as strong as the right not to be killed. One argument for this radical view is the fact that if we take a pair of cases in which all elements are the same except that one case is a case of killing and the other is a case of failing to save, we seem to reach the same moral judgments about the two cases.

Here is such a pair of cases, devised by James Rachels.

[A] Jones wants to kill his wife and claim her inheritance. He sneaks in while she is bathing and forces her head under water.
[B] Jones wants to kill his wife and claim her inheritance. He sneaks in while she is bathing and discovers that she has just hit her head and slipped under the surface. He leaves the room without pulling her out.

Most people feel that what Jones does in [B] is morally as bad as what he does in [A]. But in [A] Jones violates his wife's right to life while in [B] Jones violates his wife's right to be saved. If the two acts are equally bad, the two rights are equally strong.[10]

Since a number of thoughtful and morally decent philosophers have endorsed the moral equivalence of killing and letting die, we will explore the implications of the assumption that the right to be saved is as important as the right not to be killed. One implication is that whenever we face an exclusive choice between killing one group of innocent people and failing to save another group of innocent people, the rights of the two groups cancel each other out. In such cases, the choice between the two groups cannot be made on the basis of rights.

What, then, are our moral obligations when we face choices between killing one group and letting another group die? What are our moral obligations when we face choices between imposing deadly risks on one group and relieving another group from deadly risks? If one feels that morally permissible conduct, by definition, is conduct that does not violate human rights, then one will feel that it is equally permissible to favor either group. Thus, *if* we postulate that the right to be saved is as important as the right not to be killed, and *if* we assume that the sole moral wrong is to violate human rights, it follows that it would be morally permissible to impose risks on the Soviet people in order to save the American people from risks.

This conclusion, however, is only as strong as the premise that generated it. Is the right to be saved as important as the right not to be killed? One thing that seems pretty clear is that this premise has not been demonstrated. The example of the drowned wife hardly serves as a proof. That example assumed that if two situations are morally equal and differ only in one part, that the differing parts must be morally equal. This is a little like saying that if two trucks are equally useful and differ only in one engine part, that the two engine parts must be equally useful. But that may not be so. One engine part may have many alternative uses and the other, no alternative uses. Since the examples do not succeed, the common sense view that the right to be saved is weaker than the right not to be killed still stands.

(g) The Duty of American Leaders to Protect the American People

It is implicitly assumed in many political discussions that American political leaders have a special moral duty to protect the American people.[11] It follows that they have a special duty to protect the American people from nuclear attack. If the only way the American people can be protected from attack is by increasing the chance of nuclear attack on the Soviet people, they have a duty to do that too. The American people (the argument continues) have a right to expect that their elected leaders will prefer their welfare to the welfare of the Soviet people. Any American leader who refuses to protect the American people from annihilation shirks the responsibilities of leadership and breaks his implicit promise to consider the responsibilities of his own constituents first and foremost.

The claim that American leaders have a special responsibility to take care of Americans is like the claim that parents have a special responsibility to take care of their own children. Just as we would morally censure parents who favor the welfare of other children in preference to their own, so should we censure political leaders who favor the welfare of other constituencies in preference to their own. If a building is burning with two children trapped inside, only one of which can be rescued in time, we would find it more than strange if a mother preferred to rescue someone else's child in preference to her own. Likewise, if two populations are at risk from nuclear war, it would seem more than strange if American leaders took the course of action that minimized the threat to the Soviet people (non-possession) rather than the course of action that minimized the threat to the American people (victory or detente).

Most moral philosophers are willing to concede the existence of special moral obligations, like the obligations of parents to their own children, which permit discrimination by some individuals in favor of other individuals. Most will concede that American political leaders have a special moral obligation, perhaps even a contractual obligation, to the American people. Though special moral obligations license some acts of discrimination, they do not license others. We must consider whether the special obligation falling on American political leaders entitles them to impose the risks of nuclear war on the Soviet people.

Consider the case of parental obligations. In the example of the burning house, the mother is confronted with a choice between saving her own child and saving someone else's child. Certainly we do not blame the mother if she rescues her own child, and we may even censure her if she rescues the other person's child. We certainly do not feel that she should flip a coin before deciding which child to rescue, on the ground that each child should be provided with an equal opportunity to live. It is an important feature of this problem, however, that both children are *already* at risk, and that the mother by her actions has not increased the risk to the other person's child. The relevance of these features will be manifest if we consider a case in which the children are not both at risk before the mother arrives. Suppose that the ocean liner sinks, the two children are thrown into the water, and the mother discovers that her child has no life preserver but that the other child has one. Even those who believe in the existence of the special moral obligations of parenthood will recoil from the suggestion that the mother is morally obliged, or even morally permitted, to take the life preserver from the other child and put it on her own. In this case, the other child is not already at risk; the mother puts that child at risk when she takes his life preserver. Instead of saving her own child rather than saving someone else's, she is saving her own child at the expense of someone else's. The special obligations of parenthood do not go that far.

When American leaders endorse weapons policies that put the lives of Soviet citizens at risk, are they acting like the mother who rescues her child from the burning building, or are they acting like the mother who steals a lifejacket from one child and puts it on her own? One can hardly argue that the Soviet people were *already* at risk from nuclear destruction before American decisions about nuclear weapons were made. The risk imposed on the Soviet people was created by a sequence of Presidential decisions in the United States: Truman's decision to build the Super, Eisenhower's decision to develop the ICBM, Nixon's decision to deploy the MIRV, Carter's decision to proceed with the cruise missile, and so forth. The American Presidents by their decisions did not rescue the American people from this threat while leaving the Soviet people subject to a risk that was already there. Just as the mother creates a risk when she seizes the lifejacket from someone else's child, deployments of American strategic systems create risks for the Soviet people. If special obligations will not justify seizing the lifejacket, special obligations will not justify putting the Soviet people at risk.

Some students of ethics construe special obligations, like the obligations of parenthood, as special cases of contractual obligation. On this interpretation, when parents take children into their homes, they are promising society and promising their children that they will be given special attention. Analogously, the President can be said to have special obligations to the American people because he promised them such attention when he took his oath of office.

This is not the place to decide whether special moral obligations exist *sui generis* or whether they can be derived from general moral obligations. What must be noted is that even if we interpret special obligations as examples of contractual obligations, they do not justify putting those who fall outside the contract at risk. It is a principle in law that contracts for immoral purposes are void, and it is a precept in moral philosophy that promises for immoral purposes do not bind. If every promise created a binding obligation, then every moral rule could legitimately be broken simply by making a promise to break it. Unless we are willing to accept such absurdities, the promise of the American President to protect the American people does not justify the protection of the American people by immoral means, even if such means are the only way that the American people can be protected.

One Argument That The Risk Is Not Permissible

The conservative response to our basic problem is to proclaim that it is never permissible to kill an innocent person, no matter how much good can be achieved by killing him. It follows that it is never permissible to kill an innocent person to save the life of another innocent person, or any number of innocent people. Killing an innocent person is murder, and murder should never be done, even if the heavens fall. Given our theory of risk, it follows that it is always impermissible to inflict non-negligible deadly risks.

There are a variety of arguments for the conservative view. For those who think that moral principles are ultimately the commands of God and who believe that God's commands can be discerned in the Bible, there is the injunction "Thou shalt not kill" (Exodus 20:13), which is later clarified as an explicit prohibition against killing the innocent: "The innocent and just person thou shalt not put to death" (Exodus 23:7). There is no argument, not even a suggestion, anywhere in the Bible that this injunction can be overruled in the interest of the common good or in the interest of innocent people who might be saved if murder is committed. On the contrary, in the New Testament, St. Paul repudiates the suggestion that moral laws should be overruled in the interests of society. One must not, Paul says, do evil that good might come (Romans 3:8).[12]

Second, the duty to save lives is a duty that derives from the virtue of charity, while the duty not to kill derives from the virtue of justice. Those who believe that the essence of moral conduct consists of activity in accordance with virtue usually maintain that when the virtues of justice conflict with the virtues of charity, it is charity that should give way. Generally speaking, the virtues of charity are introduced in the New Testament, and Christ himself proclaimed that the new law was not to overthrow the old: "Think not I come to destroy the law and the prophets, but to fulfill" (Matthew 5:17).

Third, there is a distinction between perfect moral duties and imperfect moral duties. Perfect duties are duties that every person has to all people at all times; imperfect duties are duties that every person has to some people at some times. The duty not to steal, for example, is a perfect duty, since at all times one must not steal. But the duty to give alms is not a perfect duty, since one is not obliged to give alms at all times to all persons. It is impossible to be charitable to every person in the world at every moment of time. When one is being charitable to some, one will neglect others, and if one extends charity to everyone, one's resources will swiftly be exhausted.

When a perfect duty conflicts with an imperfect duty, the imperfect duty should give way. The reason is that one can be sure at any particular time that one is bound by the perfect duty, but one cannot be sure that one is bound by the imperfect duty, since these do not bind at all times. By these standards, the duty not to kill is a perfect duty, and the duty to save lives is an imperfect duty. It follows that if one must choose between killing an innocent person and failing to save an innocent person, one must avoid killing, and let the innocent person perish.

Fourth, history teaches that the common good is best served by an absolute injunction against killing the innocent. If society permits the innocent to be killed in the few cases in which such killings serve the common good, people will lose their inhibitions about killing, and in short order the innocent will be slain even in cases that do not serve the common good. For example, in Nazi Germany, once the euthanasia program of 1939 established the principle that extremely retarded and similarly "useless" persons could be exterminated for the public good, it was not long before entire peoples perished to satisfy the all-consuming hatreds of the Nazi leadership. Any breach in the absolute prohibition against killing the innocent, however well intended, will only cater to the desires of people whose actions are governed by sadistic passions.

Fifth, the absolute prohibition against killing the innocent expresses to the highest degree that respect for persons that, ever since Kant, has been considered a fundamental part of ethics. If we say that a person's life can at any moment be appropriated when the common good demands it, we are saying that people are always to be used as means, not ends. It is part of the larger social contract tradition that flowed through Rousseau into Kant that people are not obliged to give up their purposes on behalf of the common good without beforehand giving their consent.

(a) Counterexamples

These are powerful arguments, derived from every major tradition in Western ethics. Nevertheless, the principle that *one should never kill an innocent person* leads to results in particular cases that run contrary to the intuitions of many people whose basic moral decency is not in doubt. There are the counterexamples to the conservative view, of which the following present a sample:

Counterexample I: The Space Plague. Most people will balk at the idea that it is permissible to kill one person to save one other person. But is it impermissible to kill one person to save ten? A thousand? the whole human race? Suppose that returning astronauts have contracted a space plague that kills 99 percent of those who contract it. The astronauts insist on landing, even though this threatens the life of nearly everyone on earth. Would it be morally wrong to shoot the spaceship down? Wouldn't it, rather, be morally irresponsible for those who could shoot the spaceship down to let it land, on the grounds that shooting it down would violate human rights? In short, when the demands of the common good are *very* great, they overwhelm the claims of human rights.

Counterexample II: The Sinking Lifeboat: The lifeboat is overloaded, as it always is in books of ethics, and unless some people are thrown overboard the lifeboat will sink and everyone will drown. Everyone's name is put into a hat, and the five whose names are drawn out are to be cast overboard. Jones rejects the idea of the lottery, but his name is put in anyway, and Jones' name is one of the five drawn out. He refuses to jump overboard, but the other passengers gang up and throw him over. Did they do wrong? After all, under the lottery Jones had the same opportunity to live as anyone else, and if his name had not been drawn, he would have profited from *other* passengers being thrown over. If you feel that it was not wrong to throw Jones overboard, then you perhaps feel that the claims of justice and fairness can override the claims of human rights.

Counterexample III: The Doomed Baby. A woman, seven months pregnant, is told that there is a medical complication. If she has an operation, she will live but the fetus will die. If she does not have an operation, both she and the fetus will die. Assume that the seven month old fetus is developed enough to have a right to life. Even so, many people feel that it is morally permissible for the mother to have the operation, on the grounds that the fetus is going to die no matter what anyone does.

Counterexample IV: The Sadistic Dictator (a) A sadistic dictator has divided seven prisoners into a group of two and a group of five. "Kill these two," he tells Jones, "or I will kill all seven."[13] Many people feel that it would be morally permissible for Jones to kill two, saving five, even though by so doing Jones violates the rights of the two. They reason that the two are going to die anyway, no matter what Jones does.

Counterexample V: The Sadistic Dictator (b) The sadistic dictator has divided seven prisoners into a group of two and a group of five. "Kill these two," the dictator tells Jones, "or I will kill these five." Many people feel that it is permissible for Jones to kill the two, reasoning that guilt for such killings falls on the dictator, not on Jones.

Counterexample VI: The Runaway Trolley. (a) A trolley has gotten loose and is careening down the tracks. If the switchman does nothing, the trolley will collide with the trolley ahead and five people will die. If the switchman throws the switch, the trolley will go on a spur, collide with another trolley, and two people will die.[14] Most people think that it is morally permissible for the switchman to throw the switch, reasoning that he is simply deflecting an already existing threat, and that by so doing he will save lives on balance.

Counterexample VII: The Runaway Trolley (b): The trolley is careening down the tracks. If the switchman does not throw the switch, the trolley will go forward and run over the switchman's son. If the switchman throws the switch, the trolley will go onto a spur and kill a stranger. Many people feel that it would be permissible for the switchman to throw the switch, reasoning that he is simply deflecting an already existing threat.

Counterexample VIII: The German Blockhouse: The Allies are pushing into Germany but encounter stiff resistance from an entrenched artillery blockhouse. In a frontal assault, 20 Allied soldiers will probably die. If the blockhouse is bombed from the air, no Allied soldiers will die, but 5 civilians living nearby will probably be killed. Many people feel that it is morally permissible to bomb the blockhouse, reasoning that the killing of the civilians is not "intentional" and that the bombing will save lives.

(b) Various Modifications of the Conservative View

It is one thing to state counterexamples. It is another thing to state general rules that indicate classes of exceptions to the conservative view. Let us assume that the conservative view is basically correct, that it is a violation of human rights to take the life of an innocent human being—except under certain specific circumstances. The exceptions that we write in can be derived from the counterexamples, as follows:

From the Space Plague Example:

> It is permissible to kill an innocent human being if by so doing, and only by so doing, a great many innocent lives can be saved. (Permission I)

From the Sinking Lifeboat:

> It is permissible to kill an innocent human being if some member in a group of innocent people must die and if the person killed has been selected for death from the group by a fair procedure. (Permission II)

From the Doomed Baby Example and the Sadistic Dictator (a):

> *It is permissible to kill an innocent human being if by so doing, and only by so doing, an innocent life can be saved and if the person killed will soon die anyway. (Permission III).*[15]

From the Sadistic Dictator (b) and Trolley (a):

> *It is permissible to kill a group of innocent human beings if by so doing, and only by so doing, one deflects a deadly pre-existing threat away from a larger group of innocent human beings. (Permission IV).*[16]

From Trolley (b):

> *It is permissible to kill an innocent human being provided that by so doing, and only by so doing, one deflects a pre-existing threat away from another innocent human being. (Permission V)*

From the German Blockhouse:

> *It is permissible to kill an innocent human being provided that his death is not intended as a means or as an end, and provided that by so doing, and only by so doing, a greater number of lives can be saved. (Permission VI)*

This last principle is an application of an important principle from Catholic moral theology, called the *principle of double effect.*

Some readers will reject all of these permissions. Some will accept some and reject others. Some will accept all. But it is doubtful that anyone who believes that there is such a thing as a right to life will propose *further* permissions. To develop more rules sanctioning the killing of innocent people would render the notion of a right to life virtually meaningless.

(c) Applying Rules About Homicide to Nuclear Risks

The conservative view states that it is never permissible to kill an innocent human being, even to save another innocent human being. The statistical or "risk" version of the conservative view states that it is never permissible to take an expected life, even to save an expected life. It follows from the conservative view that nuclear deterrence, as practiced by either victory or detente, is not morally acceptable.[17] It is like killing a Russian to save an American. But according to the conservative view, it is not morally permissible to kill a Russian to save an American. It is not even morally permissible to kill a Russian to save a great number of Americans. It is not morally permissible to kill any innocent people at all.

So says the conservative view. But what about the modifications of the conservative view, which many people accept on the basis of the counterexamples? Let us consider each in turn.

Permission I states that it is permissible to kill one innocent person in order to save the lives of a great many innocent people. The statistical version of this principle would be that it is permissible to take one expected life in order to save a *great* many expected lives. It does not appear that this permission can sanction the risks of nuclear deterrence. The victory or detente strategies do not save a *great* many more expected lives than does non-possession. As the previous chapter indicated, there is some reason to think that victory and detente save fewer expected lives than non-possession. It is hardly the case that victory or detente cause one or two expected deaths but save thousands of expected lives, along the lines of the Space Plague Example.

Permission II says that it is permissible to kill an innocent person if someone in a group must die and the person killed is selected from the group by a fair procedure. The statistical version of this principle would work as follows. Take a group of people all of whom are subject to some risk of death. Permission II would sanction increasing the risk to some of the people in the group provided that so doing would decrease the risk to others to a greater extent, and provided that those picked for increased risk have been selected by a fair procedure.

It is difficult to see how Permission II can be applied to American nuclear deterrence. Before the United States deployed strategic weapons, the Soviet population was not at risk. Thus, the Soviet people are not like the people already in the sinking lifeboat. In a sense, they have been *forced into* the sinking lifeboat by American strategic weapons. Furthermore, no "fair procedure" has been used to determine who is to be the victim of nuclear risk. American policy since 1950 has consisted allegedly in attempts to make the risk to Americans as small as possible.

Permission III permits the killing of an innocent person provided that at least one innocent life is saved and provided that the person killed is soon to die anyway. The statistical version of Permission III would permit the infliction of a given quantity of risk provided that those on whom the risks are imposed would be subjected to the same quantity of risk *anyway*. Consider how this relates to American nuclear deterrence. American strategic weapons currently inflict a certain quantity of risk on the Soviet population. Permission III says that it is permissible to inflict this risk if the Soviet population would be subjected to this risk anyway, even if the United States did not possess nuclear weapons.

There is one way that Soviet people *might* find themselves subjected to the same level of nuclear risk as they now experience even if the United States abandoned its nuclear weapons. If, after the United States abandoned its nuclear weapons, the other nuclear nations of the world beefed up their forces to the present American levels, then the Soviet people would be subject to the same risk as before. But is it likely that the other nuclear nations, in the event of American nuclear disarmament, would beef up their arsenals to American levels? The British, the French, and the Chinese have always insisted on their own nuclear forces because they have not felt confident that the United States would use its nuclear weapons to defend *them* in a nuclear confrontation with the Soviets. They have chosen their present force levels because those levels make them feel that they have an adequate deterrent against Soviet attack no matter what the United States does. It follows that they feel that those levels are adequate even if the United States abandons nuclear weapons altogether. There is little reason to think that in the event of American nuclear disarmament they would be eager to pay the huge sums needed to increase their forces to American levels. But unless it is nearly certain that they would do so—as certain as it is that the expectant mother's baby is going to die anyway, no matter what she does—then Permission III does not provide a sanction for inflicting nuclear risks on the Soviet people.

Permission IV says that it is permissible to kill some innocent people if by so doing you deflect a deadly risk from an even larger group of innocent people. Permission V neglects any reference to numbers but allows the diversion of a deadly risk from one innocent person to another. The statistical translations of these two permissions refer to the deflection, not of deadly threats, but of risks of death of varying sizes.

To some it might appear that the *deflection* of risk is precisely what nuclear deterrence achieves. The risk to the American public is created by Soviet strategic weapons (the argument goes), and the systems of deterrence bounces this risk back at the U.S.S.R. But this argument is self-defeating. If the deployment of Soviet strategic weapons *creates* a risk for the American population, then the deployment of American strategic weapons *creates* a risk for the Soviet population, and nuclear deterrence is not sanctioned by Permission IV and V, which apply only to already existing risks.

It is easy to imagine a strategic system that would satisfy Permissions IV and V. Suppose that the United States developed a force field that bounced attacking Soviet weapons back to the U.S.S.R. The weapons so bounced would kill many innocent people who would not be killed if the United States turned off its force field. According to Permissions IV and V, the United States would be violating the rights of Soviet people so killed but would be justified in so violating them. The Soviet people should direct their complaints to Soviet leaders who launched the weapons, rather than to the Americans, who bounced them in their direction, even though the Americans have the last clear chance of preventing the weapons from landing on Russia. But the system of nuclear deterrence is nothing like a force field, and the nuclear weapons that land on innocent people under the present system of deterrence will be American weapons, not Soviet weapons bounced in the reverse direction. It follows that nuclear deterrence is not sanctioned by Permission IV or V.

Permission VI, the *principle of double effect*, is sufficiently important to deserve a section of its own.

(d) The Principle of Double Effect

By far the most venerable and widely endorsed of the five suggested permission principles is the principle of double effect. The principle probably originated with Aquinas, underwent alteration in the eighteenth century, and reached canonical form in the mid-nineteenth.[18] Catholic moral theology acknowledges that in the course of doing good it is sometimes necessary to bring evil into the world. The principle of double effect says that it is permissible by action A to bring such evil into the world provided that four conditions are satisfied:

(1) Act A must not be evil in itself;
(2) Act A must also have a good effect that outweighs the evil effect;
(3) The good effect must be intended and the evil effect not intended;
(4) The evil effect must not be the means by which the good effect is achieved.

The principle is stated in terms of good and evil, not in terms of killing and saving lives. But the application of the principle to the question of killing some to save many is straightforward. Suppose that A is an act of killing the few to save the many. Conditions (1) and (2) of the doctrine of double effect are automatically satisfied. Condition (1) is satisfied because killing, unlike lying or blasphemy, is not an act that the Catholic Church classifies as "evil in itself." Condition (2) is satisfied because A is defined as an act that saves lives on balance; and this means that A, on balance, produces more good than evil. But conditions (3) and (4) are not automatically satisfied. Condition (3), applied to A, requires that the agent not intend the deaths of those he kills; he must intend only to save lives. Condition (4) requires that the deaths of those killed not be the means by which the lives of the others are saved. Obviously, in some cases of killing the few to save many, conditions (3) and (4) are not met.

Let us look carefully at conditions (3) and (4). Condition (3) says that the deaths of those killed must not be intended. What sense of "intended" is meant here? It cannot be "intended" in the sense of "foreseen" or "predicted," because in all eight counterexamples the deaths of those killed are foreseen; the switchman, for example, foresees that if he throws the switch, two people on the spur will be killed, and so forth. "Intended," then, must mean something like "desired." Suppose that act A kills the few to save the many. For condition (3) to be satisfied, the person who performs A must not desire the deaths of those he kills, but he must desire the continued life of those he saves. On this interpretation, condition (3) says that A is morally all right only if the agent would not perform A if he came to believe that A would not save lives, and only if the agent would still perform A even if he came to believe that A would kill no one. These are subjective conditions, and on occasion it may be very difficult to verify whether condition (3) has been satisfied or not. On other occasions, though, the agent's statements and behavior may provide clear evidence that (3) has been satisfied or has been violated.

The fourth condition requires that the deaths of those killed not be the means by which the saved are saved. Though the fourth condition has been little discussed in the literature, it is by far the most difficult condition to interpret, because the word "means" is terribly ambiguous. The general idea of means is something that is done or produced in order to bring about a certain result. The ambiguity in the idea of *a means* is concealed in the words "bring about." What do we mean when we say that act A (or event A) has "brought about" event B?

The answer is that at different times we mean different things. Sometimes we mean merely that A is a necessary condition for the production of B, that without A, B would not have happened. Sometimes we mean that A is a sufficient condition for B; and that given A, B was sure to follow. Sometimes we think of A as "producing" B, even though A is neither a necessary condition for B nor a sufficient condition for B. Jones wants to get rid of Smith and eventually kills him. How? He shot him with a pistol. The means Jones used to achieve his end was "a pistol" or "shooting with a pistol." But "shooting with a pistol" is neither a necessary condition nor a sufficient condition for Jones' producing Smith's death. Jones might have killed Smith some other way. And Jones might have shot him, but not fatally. All these senses of "means" must be kept in mind when attempting to apply the principle of double effect.

Now let us consider what the principle of double effect says about nuclear threat under victory and detente. We will start with condition 2, since victory and detente obviously both satisfy condition 1. If Catholic moral theology holds that killing a person is not an act which is evil in itself, it follows that inflicting a risk on a person is not an evil in itself.

(e) Double Effect and Victory

The second condition of the principle of double effect says that killing the innocent is permissible only if such killings do more good than harm. Do the good effects of victory outweigh the bad? In the previous chapter, we suggested that the good effects of victory for the United States might outweigh the bad effects of victory for the United States. But we did not suggest that the good effects of victory outweigh the bad effects of victory. *overall*. On the contrary, it seems plain that victory causes more expected deaths than it saves expected lives. But it is to *overall* good, not American good, that conditon 2 refers. If Catholic moral theology is to devise a way by which the good effects of victory outweigh the bad effects, it must introduce some spiritual sort of good effect produced by victory and it must take precautions not to make these spiritual good effects a ghostly expression of the American national interest.

The third condition of the principle of double effect requires that the evil effects of victory not be intended, in the sense of "desired." Now, the evil effect of victory is that it subjects innocent people in the Soviet Union to the risk of death. But are they *intentionally* subjected to this risk? Under victory, American strategic weapons are pointed at Soviet strategic weapons and military forces, not at the Soviet people, at least in the initial stages of nuclear war. It seems that under victory Soviet citizens are the unintended victims of risk in the same way that German civilians living beside the blockhouse are the unintended victims of Allied attack.

Nevertheless, the argument that civilians' expected deaths are unintended and undesired under victory needs to be examined carefully. The primary goal of the victory strategy is to deter nuclear attacks on the United States. The fact that a massive American counterforce attack will kill a good many Soviet civilians—sometimes called the "bonus damage" of a nuclear attack—enhances the deterrent effect of American strategy. Can it honestly be argued that American leaders do not desire this "bonus damage?"

The fourth condition of the principle of double effect requires that the evil effect not be the means by which the good effect is produced. The good effect of victory, presumably, is a reduced chance of Soviet attack. Is an increased risk to Soviet civilians the means by which the alleged good effect of victory is obtained? Certainly *some* part of the deterrent effect of victory is due to threates to Soviet weapons, not Soviet civilians. But just as certainly, *some* part of the deterrent effect of victory is due to threats to Soviet civilians, not Soviet weapons. It follows that threats to Soviet civilians are *one* means by which the good effects of victory are produced, and victory does not satisfy condition 4 of the principle of double effect.

(f) Detente and Double Effect

In the preceding chapter, we argued that non-possession causes fewer expected deaths than detente. Nevertheless, the gap in total expectd deaths between non-possession and detente is not very large. A person who claims that detente causes fewer expected deaths than non-possession is not being wildly unreasonable. Consequently we cannot say that detente for sure does more harm than good, or that detente for sure violates condition 2 of the principle of double effect. But what about condition 3?

Supporters of detente, like supporters of victory, will vehemently deny that they desire to impose risks on civilians in the Soviet Union. They will assert that under detente the United States intends to kill large numbers of Soviet civilians *if* the United States is attacked. But they point out that they do not believe that the United States will be attacked and they do not believe, therefore, that detente will kill any Soviet civilians. True, detente permits a risk that non-possession does not. But simply to permit the risk does not entail that under the policy we desire to create the risk. Perhaps on this ground we can say that detente satisfies condition 3 of the principle of double effect.

It is, in fact, condition 4 which creates the main stumbling block for the legitimization of detente. There is no question that the increased risk to Soviet citizens posed by detente is the means by which the decreased risk to American citizens is obtained. Consequently detente fails to satisfy condition 4. Since all four conditions must be satisfied before the blessing of double effect can be applied, detente is not sanctioned by this principle.

Summary of the Argument Thus Far

People in the Soviet Union, like people everywhere, have a right to life. Victory and detente impose a risk of death on people in the Soviet Union, and we argued that such impositions violate what is implied in a right to life. This imposition of risk is not excusable on the grounds that it is unintentionally (that is, accidentally) imposed; nor is it excusable on the grounds that the

Soviet people have freely consented to this imposition of risk, nor on the grounds that the risk is negligible.

The American people also possess rights, such as the right to survive and the right to special treatment by their elected leadership. But the preservation of rights does not justify everything, and we argued that American survival and the duties of American leaders towards the American people do not justify violations of the right to life of people in the Soviet Union. The right to self-defense is not applicable to nuclear deterrence, which inflicts risks on people who have not attacked or threatened the United States.

This left the possibility that there was something in the situation at large that might justify this infliction of risk. We considered, and dismissed, the argument that the Soviet people are already at risk, and the argument that the United States is merely deflecting a risk from itself towards the Soviet Union. This left the argument that this imposition of risk is a forseen but unintended (i.e. undesired) consequence of an otherwise laudable attempt to protect the American people. This argument from double effect was undercut by the fact that the imposition of risk on innocent Soviet people was one means by which this laudable end was achieved. Unless some further argument is produced, the conclusion stands that victory and detente violate human rights by putting innocent people at risk, even if the bombs are never dropped and the missiles are never fired.

Human Rights and Wartime Uses of Nuclear Weapons

In all of the preceding discussions we have been considering the risks imposed by nuclear weapons before war begins. We must now consider uses of nuclear weapons after war begins—actual explosions of nuclear weapons, not merely deterrent threats. Do wartime uses of nuclear weapons violate human rights?

Under detente, such uses will always be second strikes; that is, responses to a nuclear attack. Under victory, such uses may be either first or second strikes.

(a) First Strikes Under Victory

The commonest scenario for a first strike under victory involves NATO nuclear weapons in Europe. In this scenario, the Warsaw Pact attacks Western Europe with conventional weapons. NATO forces, unable to stem the tide, turn to tactical and perhaps to intermediate range nuclear forces in response. Studies invariably show that such uses of nuclear weapons cause large numbers of civilian casualties, not only in the Warsaw Pact nations, but also in the NATO countries. Is there a moral justification for NATO forces killing large numbers of their own civilians?

There is one obvious difference between NATO killings of NATO civilians and NATO killings of Warsaw Pact civilians. The NATO nations have voluntarily accepted nuclear weapons on their soil. Since these nations are democracies, it can be argued that the people in these countries have to some degree consented to the risks posed by their own weapons. It is the price they pay for protection from the Bolshevik horde. This argument, however, will take us only so far.[19] Human rights are individually possessed and can only be waived by the individuals who possess them: the majority cannot waive the rights of the minority. Now, it is certain that there is a substantial minority of people in NATO countries who are adamantly opposed to having nuclear weapons on their soil. It would be perverse to argue that *they* have consented to the risks posed by these weapons simply because other people in their countries have consented to the risk. What justification can be given for violating the rights of this anti-nuclear minority?

The best hope for justification seems to lie in the principle of double effect. Certainly the NATO countries do not desire to massacre their own civilians, and the killing of NATO civilians is not the means by which the Soviets are to be repulsed. The civilians just happen to be caught in the crossfire. Conditions 3 and 4 of the principle of double effect are satisfied.

But there is difficulty with condition 2, which requires that more good than harm must come from such uses of nuclear weapons before the blessing of double effect is bestowed. Will the use of tactical and intermediate range strategic weapons against a conventional invasion do more good than harm?

The main funcion of NATO nuclear weapons is to deter Soviet attack with the threat of escalation to nuclear war. If the Soviets launch a conventional attack on Western Europe, NATO nuclear weapons will have failed to achieve their primary purpose. Nor does it seem likely that they will achieve their secondary purpose of preventing Soviet conquest once the Soviet invasion begins. Should NATO use nuclear weapons against a Soviet conventional attack, the Soviets can reply with their own battlefield nuclear weapons, and there is some reason to believe that Warsaw Pact forces are far better trained in battlefield uses of nuclear weapons than NATO forces.[20] The use of tactical nuclear weapons cannot save Western Europe from conquest, except in the sense that it will make parts of Western Europe not worth conquering. Thus, it hardly seems that NATO use of nuclear weapons in these circumstances will do more good than harm.

(b) Limited Second Strikes Under Victory

A second strike under victory will be tailored to the first strike received by the United States. If the Soviet strike is a massive countervalue strike, victory calls for a countervalue strike in return. If the first strike is less massive, the response will be less massive. If the strike is a counterforce strike, the response will be a counterforce strike. We will begin with less than all-out strikes.

Suppose that the United States suffers a massive counterforce strike, killing 2 to 22 million Americans, but sparing the major American cities. If the United States launches a counter-strike with its surviving strategic weapons, 4 to 27 million Soviet civilians will die. Is there a moral justification for killing so many innocent people? Presumably the point behind such a tit-for-tat response is to demonstrate to the Soviets that every nuclear attack on the United States will provoke an appropriately painful reprisal against the Soviet Union. This will discourage the Soviets from proceeding to attack American cities.

The protection of American cities is a morally attractive goal. But we must consider carefully how American cities remain at risk after a Soviet counter-force attack. Presumably the Soviets will have some goal in mind if they launch a counterforce strike, and we can expect that the strike is accompanied by some kind of ultimatum. The ultimatum will be either just or unjust. If it is just, the United States has no grounds for not accepting it, in lieu of killing 4 to 27 million innocent people. If the ultimatum is unjust, the United States must choose between submitting to injustice, or killing 4 to 27 million innocent people. It is a standard precept of moral theory that it is better to suffer a wrong than to commit one. It follows that it is morally better for the United States to submit to the ultimatum than to commit mass murder.

Such submissions to injustice will strike many as a return to the policy of appeasement, universally regarded as having been morally bankrupt when practiced in the 1930s. But there are many differences between the appease-ments of the late 1930s and submission to injustice in lieu of a nuclear counterattack. Britain and France appeased Hitler because they were not prepared to sacrifice French and British lives for the legitimate claims of Czechoslovakia. If the United States submits to a Soviet ultimatum, it will submit because it recognizes the right to life of millions of people in the Soviet Union. In submitting, the United States would demonstrate that it is prepared to sacrifice its own interests rather than pursue those interests by murderous means. If this is appeasement, the precedent is set not by Chamberlain and Daladier but by Mohandas Gandhi. But Gandhi is not usually regarded as an appeaser.

(c) Massive Responses to Limited Strikes

The policy of detente does not tailor American responses to Soviet strikes. In order to maximize deterrence, detente calls for massive strikes in response to any nuclear attack against the United States, even a limited attack. Such attacks would kill tens of millions of innocent people.

There are, it seems, no arguments, from either morality or prudence, in support of massive responses to limited strikes. Such responses would endanger American cities by provoking the Soviets to acts of revenge. Furthermore, they are perfectly avoidable, since under detente, top deci-sion makers retain total discretion over the use of strategic systems, even in the actual event of Soviet attack. It follows that, under detente, the morally required course of action in the event of a limited strike is to not respond at all.

(d) Massive Responses to Massive Strikes

Suppose that the Soviet Union launches a massive counterforce and counter-value strike against the United States. We can assume that the Soviets will use most of their weapons in such a strike, since the likelihood of an American response is very high and there would be little point in leaving strategic weapons on the ground where they can be destroyed by an American second strike. Everything left standing in the United States is therefore relatively free of risk. Under these circumstances, is there a moral justification for proceeding with an attack on the Soviet Union, an attack which, like most nuclear attacks, will kill tens of millions of innocent people?[21]

Nothing in all of history will equal in evil what the Soviets will have done in such a massive first strike. One argument, then, for striking back, is that evildoers deserve to be punished. This argument appeals to the notions of retributive justice, so we will hold it for the next chapter, which is devoted to weapons policies and justice. Are there any arguments, besides retribution, in support of such a massive second strike?

There is only one possible excuse available to victory that is not available to detente. That is the excuse that in the event of a massive Soviet strike, it may be impossible under victory to prevent an American second strike, since under victory so many people have the actual or potential authority to launch a second strike. But this excuse of helplessness is not valid in this case, since the United States has, under victory, *put itself* into the position of not being able to stop a second strike. To accept the excuse would be like accepting the drunk driver's excuse that he could not stop because he was too drunk to find the brake.

(e) Summary

Our survey shows that the typical wartime uses of nuclear weapons violate human rights. It does not follow that all uses of nuclear weapons in wartime are immoral: there is always the possibility, much celebrated in discussions of nuclear weapons in the 1950s, of using a nuclear device against an isolated enemy ship at sea. But our task is not to evaluate isolated uses but policies for use, and on this score both victory and detente fare quite poorly compared to non-possession.

What about the moral choice between victory and detente? By and large, when it comes to actual uses of nuclear weapons, victory seems to do better on the moral scales than detente. There is, however, one means by which detente can defeat victory, and that is by exercising the option, possible under detente, of not using strategic weapons at all. Such a maneuver will not produce military victories for the United States, but it is part and parcel of detente thinking that the notion of victory in a nuclear war makes very little sense.

Connection Between War Uses and Deterrent Uses of Nuclear Weapons: The Paradox of Deterrence

Both victory and detente involve threats to Soviet cities. Detente requires threats of very destructive reprisals even in the event of limited Soviet strikes. Victory requires threats of very destructive reprisals in the event of a massive Soviet strike.

It seems clear from the preceding discussions that there is no moral warrant for proceeding with "city-busting" under *any* circumstances. But victory and detente involve threats to do just this. From this many have concluded that victory and detente are immoral policies. Isn't it immoral to threaten to perform an immoral act?

To make a point of logic, it is *not* necessarily immoral to threaten to do what is immoral. Making a threat is one act; carrying out the threat is a different act. Carrying out a threat may be quite wicked, but logic alone will not tell you it is immoral to make that threat.[22] In fact, sometimes it may be morally obligatory to threaten to do something that it would be morally impermissible to do. For example, a mother, trying to coax a child out of a burning building, may be obliged to threaten "I'll kill you if you don't jump." Nuclear deterrence, for many who approve of it, is thought to involve this type of threat. The President is morally obliged to protect the American people. The only way he protects the American people is by threatening to bomb Moscow if Washington is bombed, but it would be morally wrong to bomb Moscow if Washington were bombed. Hence (the argument goes) the President must threaten to do something that he should not do. This is sometimes called "the paradox of deterrence."

We must be careful, however, not to go too far in separating the making of threats from the act of carrying them out. True, the fact that it is immoral to do X does not imply that it is immoral to threaten to do X. But it does not follow that it is morally permissible to make any threat to do anything at any time. Sometimes the very making of a threat can be immoral. even if the threat is not carried out. The making of a threat to perform an immoral act will itself be immoral if it involves an irrevocable commitment to carrying it out. And if the immorality of carrying out the threat consists of damage to the public good, then making the threat may be immoral because it makes damage to the public good more likely.

Thus it is not the logical connection between making a threat and carrying it out that matters for moral analysis: what does matter is the *physical* connection. Those who believe that deterrent threats are morally permissible threats think that there is only a weak physical link between making a nuclear threat and carrying it out. Those who believe that deterrent threats are immoral threats believe that there is a strong physical link between making a threat and carrying it out. The key question is whether making a nuclear threat pushes the probability of carrying it out over a morally acceptable "threshold level." The general message of this chapter and the preceding is that nuclear threats are high above that threshold.

Notes

1. Since the United States is more democratic than the Soviet Union, the American people are relatively more responsible for acts of the leadership. But the cloak of secrecy that has been thrown over American strategic projects since the days of the Manhattan Project generally exempts the American people from responsibility for decisions about strategic weapons.

Whether the United States attacks the Soviet Union or the Soviet Union attacks the United States, the result will be a slaughter of the innocent on a grand scale.

2. If one insists that policies that threaten life do not violate the right to life until the moment that someone is killed, then one cannot argue that non-possession is an immoral policy because it fails to protect the American people from attack. Given this way of thinking, non-possession would only "fail to protect the American people" the moment that a nuclear attack landed on the United States.

3. The argument of this section is that the duty to respect life implies a duty to avoid commitments to killing. But even if there is a duty to avoid commitments to killing, there may be a stronger duty, the satisfaction of which *requires* commitments to killing the innocent. The argument establishes only a *prima facie* duty to avoid these commitments.

The duty to avoid "commitments to kill" requires everyone to avoid entering into situations in which it might become physically or psychologically impossible to avoid killing the innocent. In Catholic moral theology these situations are described as "near occasions of sin", and there is a special duty to avoid them.

4. Moral philosophers have said surprisingly little on the subject of risk. One exception is Robert Nozick, who develops some principles that permit infliction of risk in Chapter 4 of Nozick 1974. For commentary see Von Magnus 1982. See also Rescher 1983, and Fried 1970 ch. XI.

The argument that the right to life straightforwardly implies the right not to be threatened with the chance of death is given by Gewirth 1980. See also the argument of the Catholic bishops of Australia that careless driving violates the Fifth Commandment: "Annual Social Justice Statement for 1958," *Catholic Mind* (Nov-Dec 1958).

5. I have presented this problem to several groups of students, and they overwhelmingly favored choice is B. This exhibits the well-documented psychological tendency to avoid sure disasters: see, for example, Tversky and Kahneman 1981 453–459. This psychological tendency explains the popularity of B, but that does not show that B is either the rational or the moral choice.

6. The argument that a coercive agreement can be distinguished from a non-coercive agreement by establishing a baseline of welfare and considering whether the agreement represents a move up from the baseline is given in Nozick 1969. For a discussion of what distinguishes blackmail from a free exchange, see Murphy 1980.

7. The argument here is not that the American leadership forsees that its policies will lead to nuclear war. It is that the American leadership forsees that deployments of nuclear weapons generate a *risk* of nuclear war.

8. The right of self-defense requires that deadly force be used only against the attacker, but it does not require that the attacker be guilty, in either a legal or a moral sense. If a maniac attacks me I may justifiably kill him to save my life even though he is innocent because of his mental illness. This proviso has an interesting consequence for those who claim that American threats against the Soviet Union are innocent of ill intent. Even if they are, the Soviets are entitled to take steps in their own self-defense against them.

Another argument against the self-defense justification of nuclear deterrence is this: self-defense is permissible only against aggressors engaging in acts of aggression. Defenders of nuclear deterrence deny that American nuclear deterrence constitutes aggression. It follows that Soviet nuclear deterrence does not constitute aggression. If so, self-defense cannot be invoked to justify steps taken against Soviet strategic systems.

9. Michael Walzer, for example, argues that the laws of war are suspended in cases of "supreme national emergency." See Walzer 1977 ch 16.

10. One early presentation of the view that killing a person, as such, is morally no different than letting a person die is Bennett 1966. Rachels' example of the Drowned Wife is found in Rachels 1975. Prominent attacks on the equivalence of action and omission are Foot 1967, and Russell 1977. All of the aforementioned articles and other important contributions to the study of this problem are contained in the anthology, *Killing and Letting Die*, edited by Bonnie Steinbock (Steinbock 1980). See also Glover 1977, and Bennett 1983.

11. The idea that a role can generate special obligations not interpretable as general moral rules applied to particular circumstance is discussed by Alan Goldman in Goldman 1981. Goldman is generally critical of the idea that what are usually called "professional obligations" can override human rights.

12. The Pauline principle that one must not do evil that good may come is considered by some to be the essence of morality. See, for example, Donagan 1977.

13. The Sadistic Dictator problem is presented by Bernard Williams in Smart and Williams 1973 98.

14. The trolley problem was introduced into discussions of homicide by Philippa Foot in Foot 1967. Foot treats this problem from the standpoint of the driver and analyzes it as a conflict between killing five and killing two. By developing the case from the standpoint of the switchman, the problem is more obviously a conflict between killing two and failing to save five.

15. The notion that someone "already threatened with death" has only an attenuated right to life is developed in Montmarquet 1982.

16. The idea that *deflecting* a deadly threat is morally quite different from *creating* a deadly threat is developed in Thomson 1975.

17. The other part of American policy has consisted in efforts to contain Soviet influence. It is difficult to find a single act of policy that could be interpreted as an attempt to diminish the risks for the Soviet people, pure and simple.

18. The classic nineteenth century presentation of the principles of double effect is Gury 1874. For its history from Aquinas on down see Mangan 1949, and Connell 1967. For developments in this tradition, see Griesz 1970. The relevance of direct vs. oblique intention to the analysis of permissible and impermissible homicide is challenged by Phillippa Foot in Foot 1967. Double effect is defended in Anscombe 1961 and supported from a secular standpoint in Fried 1979 20-29. For more critical discussions see Bennett 1966 83-102, Hart 1968 Ch. V, Frey 1975 259-63 and Bennett 1981 95-117.

19. Strictly speaking, Britain and France developed their own nuclear weapons; other NATO nations accepted these weapons on their soil. One should not exaggerate the degree to which the public in these countries participated in these decisions. Matters of national security in Western European nations are generally less available for public discussion than in the United States. Nevertheless, polls and recent elections generally exhibit majority approval.

20. Data showing Soviet superiority in the battlefield use of nuclear weapons is given in Douglass and Hoeber 1981.

21. The problem of whether it is morally permissible for the United States to strike back after everything on the American side has been destroyed was raised as early as 1947 in Theodore Sturgeon's brilliant science-fiction story, "Thunder and Roses," published in *Astounding* in November 1947 and anthologized in Gunn 1979.

22. Kavka (1978) finds the mistake of assuming that intending to perform a wrongful act is itself a wrongful act in Abelard, Aquinas, Butler, Kant, Bentham, Sidgwick, and Anthony Kenny.

7

Weapons Policies and the Concept of Justice

Justice, Fairness, and Consistency

In Chapter 1, we noted that there is an essential connection between justice and fairness, and that there is an essential connection between fairness and consistency. Fairness requires that we judge similar cases similarly and different cases differently. It requires that we not judge our own case differently from the case of others. It requires that we do not expect others to accept burdens that we are not willing to accept ourselves. The cases of consistency that we considered all applied to the conduct of individuals. But the conduct of nations must maintain a similar consistency if it is to be fair.

Throughout this book we have confined our attention to the United States and the Soviet Union. In this chapter we will do the same. The difference is that in this chapter we will try to imagine ourselves, looking down at the United States and the Soviet Union "from above." We will demand that whatever conduct each nation approves in itself, it must approve in the other, and that whatever conduct it condemns in the other, it must also condemn in itself.[1]

Is Unilateral Nuclear Disarmament Unfair?

Many people feel that the possession of nuclear weapons by the United States is fair so long as the Soviet Union continues to possess them. It is only fair (the argument goes) that we possess them if they possess them; it is fair for us to inflict risks on their people if they inflict risks on our people, and so forth. From these claims the argument is advanced that it would be unfair for the United States to voluntarily divest itself of nuclear weapons.[2]

This argument, however, confuses how we are treated by others with how we treat ourselves. If there were a world government that had the power to seize the nuclear stockpiles of any nation, then it would be unfair for that government to seize the stockpile of the United States without seizing the stockpile of the Soviet Union (assuming that the United States had been behaving legally up to that point). It does not follow that it would be unfair for the United States to give up its nuclear weapons *voluntarily*. It would be unfair for the government to *impound* $100 from my bank account in order to support famine relief; it does not follow that it would be unfair for me to take $100 from my bank account and voluntarily send it off to famine relief. Voluntary non-possession is not unfair.

Possession and Fairness

The United States possesses nuclear weapons and does not condemn itself for possessing them. Moral consistency requires, then, that the United States not condemn other nations for the mere possession of nuclear weapons. Moral consistency also requires that the United States take no coercive steps to deprive other nuclear nations of their nuclear stockpiles and no coercive steps to prevent other nations from acquiring them. (It does not require that the United States *assist* other states in the development of nuclear arms.)

Does moral consistency require any more than this? Many philosophers think not. But other philosophers feel that moral consistency requires more. One of these is Kant.

According to Kant, one tests the moral consistency of policies by testing them according to a supreme moral principle, which he called the Categorical Imperative:

> *Act only according to that maxim by which you can at the same time, will that it should become a universal law. [Kant 1785 39]*

The word "will" has proved a stumbling block for interpreters, but after several years of meditation on this text, I have decided that there is no harm in interpreting the term "will" to mean "wish." On this interpretation it follows that Kant is saying that fairness requires that each person act only as he could wish every person to act. Supporters of non-possession, who wish all nations to forego nuclear weapons, certainly pass Kant's test. Anyone who wishes that the United States be the sole possessor of nuclear weapons, does not.

Consistency: Victory and Detente

One way of characterizing the overall difference between victory and detente is that detente seeks only to deter nuclear attack. Victory seeks not only to deter nuclear attack but also to win a nuclear war should one break out. To win a nuclear war, taking the formulation given by Caspar Weinberger in 1983, is "To deny the enemy his political and military goals and to counterattack with sufficient strength to terminate hostilities at the lowest possible level of damage to the United States and its allies." (Weinberger 1983 32.)

If the United States adopts detente, it must not object to other nations practicing detente against it. Furthermore, according to the categorical imperative, it must not even wish that other nations practice something other than detente. Is it possible for the nation to have these wishes? There seems to be no logical obstacle. Detente is a purely deterrent policy, and if the United States seeks to so defend itself, there is no reason in the world why it should not wish that the other nuclear nations defend themselves in exactly the same way. Indeed, there is every reason for the United States, if it practices detente, to prefer that the other nations practice detente. To use Kantian language, detente can be willed to be a universal law.

But with victory, it is a different matter. Victory attempts to manipulate the behavior of opposing states with credible threats, to deter conventional attacks with nuclear strikes, and in the event of war to deny the opponent his political and military objectives. It is quite impossible for the United States to wish that other nations practice victory against it, attempting to manipulate United States behavior with credible threats, deterring U.S. conventional attacks with nuclear strikes, and seeking to deny the political and military objectives of the United States. Thus the victory strategy dictates that the United States do unto other nations what it would not be willing to have done unto itself. The victory strategy cannot be made a universal law.

Kant's interpretation of moral consistency leads to the result that non-possession and detente are consistent policies, but victory is not. Accordingly, victory is unfair and immoral, unless there are decisive arguments in its favor derived from human rights or the common good. In previous chapters these arguments were not forthcoming. Kant's message is so severe, and the verdict of the categorical imperative so decisive against victory, that we should spend some time considering whether we should accept it.

Even in nuclear war, Colin Gray assures us, victory is possible. (Gray 1979, 1980) And if victory is possible, Barry Goldwater asks us, why not victory? What is so terrible about the United States seeking to obtain its political and military objectives? Isn't the categorical imperative just another example of philosophical confusion? If the categorical imperative were the correct standard of fairness, then any competition in which not everyone is a winner would be unfair. But this is absurd. If the categorical imperative is the correct standard of moral intention, then it would be immoral to intend to enter any profession unless you also wished everyone in the world to enter that profession. But *that* is absurd. Why should we worry about results reached by reasoning from so strange a premise?

Since the categorical imperative is simply the philosopher's version of the Golden Rule, and since the Golden Rule has been presumed for 2,500 years to have some bearing on the moral evaluation of conduct, students of ethics will not so easily accept Barry Goldwater in place of Kant. True, the Golden Rule is inconsistent with personal egoism and the nationalistic doctrine of reasons of state, but this should not surprise us, since egoism and nationalism are not moral doctrines but rejections of morality.

Let us look at the alleged absurdities of the categtorical imperative. On one interpretation, it would seem that Kant is saying that a person cannot choose to be a barber unless he wants everyone else in the world to be a barber as well. But a better interpretation of what Kant is saying is that if you are going to be a barber you should not resent it if others want to be barbers too, and that if you *cannot help* resenting that others are going into the occupation that you choose, your choice of occupation is immoral. Nor does it follow from the categorical imperative that all competitions that discriminate winners from losers are unfair. What Kant is saying is that it is not morally acceptable for a person to enter a contest determined that *he* be the winner, *no matter what*. It is perfectly acceptable for a person to enter a contest wishing that the best person win and determined to test if he is that person. And what goes for persons, goes for nations.

There is another morally relevant difference between competitive contests and political conflicts. A beauty contest is not unfair to the losers, even if nature has discriminated in its distribution of beauty, since all the losers freely entered the contest. But nations very rarely freely enter into international conflicts. More often than not, the conflict is forced upon them. It is one thing to lose a contest that one has freely entered, another thing to lose a contest that one was forced to play. In general, competitive games are an inappropriate moral model for international affairs. It is a misfortune, then, that the language of international affairs is saturated with vocabulary, metaphors, and attitudes of the world of sporting contests and games of chance.

The public world is not a world in which all wishes have equal moral status. Wishes that cannot be multiply realized—like the wish for world domination—are not, by Kant's standard, morally acceptable. Only wishes that can be multiply realized, like the wish for political independence, meet the test of moral consistency. To the extent that victory seeks to establish American dominance, victory embodies morally unacceptable wishes. To the extent that detente provides the American leadership only with means to influence other nations in ways that the United States could itself tolerate being influenced, detente passes the test of moral consistency.

The Veil of Ignorance Test

Kant's test of the universalizability of wishes is but one test invented by philosophers to check the fairness of policies. Another test, also devised in the eighteenth century, is to define a fair policy as one that would be approved by a perfectly impartial spectator. In Chapter 1, we suggested that an impartial spectator is a spectator trapped behind a veil of ignorance, deprived of the knowledge of his own identity. When he passes judgment on a policy, he knows only that he is *one* of the persons affected by the policy, but he does not know *which* person he is. He must assume that it is equally probable that he is any one of the persons affected by the policy, for better or worse.

Let us consider what such an impartial spectator might say about American weapons policies. Because of the pervasive effects of fallout, everyone in the world is affected by American weapons policies. So we must imagine that our impartial spectator considers it equally likely that he is anyone in the world. We assume, furthermore, that this spectator knows the basic facts about population distribution; he knows, for example, that the United States has 6 percent of the world's population; he assumes, accordingly, that there is a 6 percent chance that he is an American. We will assume, furthermore, that the impartial spectator knows, as well as anyone, what the effects of the three policies might be and the probability of these effects. Assuming that he seeks to protect his own interests, which weapons policy should he choose?

The Harvard philosopher John Rawls suggests that the policy that the impartial spectator should prefer is the policy that *guarantees* that he will not fall below a certain minimum (Rawls 1971). What minimum? Clearly, the highest possible minimum that he can obtain within the constraints of the veil of ignorance. To find this minimum the impartial spectator considers how each person in the world fares under the three policies and chooses the policy in which the worst off person is better off than the worst off person under the other two policies. We might call this the *minimax principle*, applied to recipients.[3]

Why should we accept the special relationship Rawls claims to exist between the minimax principle and the idea of justice? There is no hope in getting an answer from the theory of rational decision, since in that theory there are many principles of rational choice besides the minimax principle. The truth is that we want our impartial spectator to be fair—to be fair to *everybody*. If he is to be fair to everybody he cannot select a policy in which some people are pushed down in order that others can be pushed up, even if only a few are pushed down and the impartial spectator is willing to gamble that he is not among those few. Thus the choices of a person behind the veil of ignorance do not *constitute* fairness; they are guided by ideas of fairness, in particular by the idea that fairness requires that no one be exploited. Thus the need to be fair *to everyone* yields the minimax rule.

Let us now apply the *minimax rule for recipients* to our three weapons policies. It seems clear that the worst off people under American non-possession are people in the U.S. and the worst off people under detente and victory are people in the U.S.S.R. Now, because of the substantial possibility of limited nuclear war under victory, there is a greater chance that someone in the U.S.S.R. will be killed by victory than that someone in the U.S.S.R. will be killed by detente. Since the most endangered person is more endangered under victory than detente, the minimax principle prefers detente over victory. This leaves us the choice between non-possession and detente.

Many people believe that non-possession poses a greater risk of nuclear war than detente. If so, it follows that the most endangered person in the United States faces more risk under non-possession than the most endangered person in the Soviet Union faces under detente. Since the minimax rule for recipients prefers the policy in which the most endangered person is least endangered relative to the most endangered person under other policies, the minimax principle favors detente over non-possession.

A little meditation on non-possession and detente will explain why the impartial spectator comes out against non-possession. The standard view is that non-possession involves a large risk of a (relatively!) small disaster, while detente involves a small risk of a large disaster. Should the United States, (*per impossibile*), switch from detente to non-possession, some Americans would bear an increased risk of death in order that some Russians bear a decreased risk of death. Behind the veil of ignorance, the impartial spectator knows that there is a *chance* that he might be one of these exploited Americans. For this reason he favors detente over non-possession.

What might supporters of non-possession say about the impartial spectator's endorsement of detente? First, they might challenge the popular view that non-possession imposes a higher risk of death on some Americans than detente; they might argue that the United States without nuclear weapons is in fact safer than the United States with nuclear weapons. Second, they might argue that all the impartial spectator has shown is that it would be unfair to *impose* non-possession, and that from this it does not follow that it would be unfair if the United States *voluntarily* adopted it. The basic rules of justice, so derived, are mainly useful in justifying coercion, like the coercion of the tax system or the criminal justice system. Thus they are relevent to the choice between victory and detente, since victory and detente are coercive policies that impose risks on unconsenting Soviet citizens. They are not relevent to the choice between detente and non-possession, provided that we interpret non-possession as a voluntarily adopted policy.

Moral Consistency and Force Deployments

The principles of fairness demand that a nation desist from acts that it criticizes in others, and from criticizing acts that it continues to do itself. We have already noted that fairness requires that nations that possess nuclear weapons desist from criticizing the development of nuclear weapons by other states. Now we will consider how the requirements of fairness dictate criticisms of weapons policies beyond simple possession.

The choice of weapons with which a nation maintains its national security has been traditionally regarded as an internal matter, and nations have been loathe to criticize the development of new types of weapons by opponents provided that the new weapon does not violate signed treaties or the provisions of international law. Since international law has not formally banned nuclear weapons, official criticism of nuclear weapon developments by opposing nations has been subdued. But when it comes to deployments, things are different. Let us review the controversy surrounding three hotly debated force deployments, checking the arguments for moral consistency.

(a) The Cuban Missile Crisis

The United States did more than merely criticize the Soviet Union for placing medium range nuclear missiles in Cuba in 1962. The United States intercepted Soviet ships on the high seas and presented the Soviet Union with a choice between removing its missiles or having them blown into thin air. In his letter of 26 October, from which we quoted earlier, Khrushchev protested to Kennedy:

> You have stationed devastating rocket weapons in Turkey, right next to us. How then does recognition of our equal military possibilities tally with such unequal relations between our great states? . . . Do you believe that you have the right to demand security for your country and the removal of such weapons that you qualify as offensive while not recognizing that right for us? (Kennedy 1969 166)

Is there an answer to Khrushchev's claim of unfair treatment?

It does no good to say that the United States was really protesting a change in the status quo, while not disturbing the status quo itself. The United States had *already* disturbed the status quo by introducing nuclear weapons and missiles into Europe. The United States was continuing to disturb the status quo by deploying Minuteman and Polaris in large numbers, even after spy satellites revealed that the Soviet ICBM program had stalled after the deployment of two dozen or so missiles.

Nor does it do any good to object that the intentions of the United States in introducing nuclear missiles into Europe were purely defensive while the intentions of the Soviets in introducing MRBMs into Cuba were at least partially offensive. First, nobody knows exactly why the Soviets introduced missiles into Cuba, but it is a sure bet that they were not intended for a first strike against the United States. Certainly the Soviets do not intend suicide any more than we do. Second, given the revelations, courtesy of the Freedom of Information Act, of a number of plans for offensive nuclear strikes against the Soviet Union, plans that might have become operational if a few people had said yes rather than no, American intentions for nuclear weapons in Europe surely cannot be characterized as *purely* defensive. Third, in questions about the fairness of actions and policies, it is actions that matter, not the intentions behind the actions. Surely the protest that a certain policy is in fact unfair cannot be answered with the observation that it was intended to be fair.

It seems, then, that Khruschev's challenge went unanswered in 1962. Kennedy could have provided himself with a fair response and a fair policy by agreeing to remove American missiles from Turkey in conjunction with the removal of Soviet missiles from Cuba. But he refused to do this.[4] The main argument for the Cuban quarantine of 1962 was reasons of state.

(b) SALT I and New Soviet ICBMs

In 1972 the SALT I interim agreement limited the Soviet Union to 1607 ICBMs; the United States got 1,054. In the Vladivostock agreement of November 1974, the United States and the Soviet Union restricted themselves to 1,320 MIRVed missiles apiece. Through the 1970s both sides adhered to the launcher restrictions and the restrictions (such as they were) on MIRVs. But in the 1970s the United States retained its Minuteman II and Minuteman III missiles, while the Soviet Union introduced a new generation of ICBMs, the SS-17, SS-18, and SS-19. These excelled their predecessors in reliability and accuracy. Since the agreement gave the Soviets more

ICBMs than it did the Americans, it was soon observed that the new generation of Soviet ICBMs created a disproportion between American land-based missiles and Soviet land-based missiles. The Soviet ICBMs could take out all American ICBMs in a first strike while the Americans could not take out all Soviet ICBMs in a first strike. By 1976, citizens' groups were charging that SALT I was unfair to the United States, and these arguments, combined with patriotic appeals, led to intense American opposition to President Carter's various arms reduction proposals.

Were the Soviet deployments of the SS-17, the SS-18, and the SS-19 *unfair*? To approach this question, we must ask whether the Soviet Union objected in those years to any analogous deployments by the United States. If the Soviet Union, for example, had protested, the development of the MX missile, a charge of moral inconsistency could successfully be lodged. But the Soviet Union did not protest the development of the MX missile, nor does it seem likely that the Soviets will protest the deployment of the MX when it comes on line in 1987.

Were the protests lodged by American civilian groups in the late of 1970s fair? The argument of the protestors was that the Soviet Union had taken unfair advantage of SALT by immensely improving its land-based missiles within the numerical limits set by SALT I and the Vladivostock accords. But it must be observed that in its own way the United States was improving its strategic arsenal within the limits of SALT I and Vladivostock. The MK-12A warhead for Minuteman and the cruise missile for the B-52 both "improved" those launchers without violating the negotiated limits. Anyone who simultaneously supported the development of the cruise missile, the MX, the MK-12A warhead while denouncing the new generation of Soviet missiles would be guilty of moral inconsistency.

(c) The Pershing II

In the late 1950s and early 1960s the United States deployed Thor and Jupiter intermediate-range ballistic missiles in Europe, and the Soviets deployed their own IRBMs—the SS-4 and the SS-5. The Jupiter and Thor were soon obsolete, and NATO removed them by the mid-1960s. The SS-4s and the SS-5s were kept on, but in 1977 the Soviet Union began replacing them with SS-20s, which were more accurate, more reliable, and carried multiple warheads. As deployments of the SS-20 proceeded, NATO became alarmed, and in 1979 NATO decided to introduce 464 ground launched cruise missiles (GLCMs) and 108 Pershing II intermediate-range ballistic missiles into Europe. From December 1979 on, and from Brezhnev to Andropov, the Soviets have denounced the introduction of these new missiles as dangerous innovations which threaten the strategic balance in Europe. Is it fair for the Soviets to protest the deployment of the Pershing II while deploying the SS-20? Are they morally consistent when they object to the NATO cruise missile?

The Soviets' strong suit is that the SS-20 simply replaces SS-4s and SS-5s, while the Pershing II is a new missile, not a substitute. But if the SS-20 is not new because it merely replaces the SS-4 and SS-5, then the Pershing II is not new because it merely replaces the Thor and the Jupiter C. If the United States had left its Thors and Jupiters on their pads instead of removing them, then the Pershing II would be replacing them just as the SS-20 replaces the SS-4 and SS-5. (We could call the Pershing II the Jupiter D). The Soviets may be right that the introduction of the Pershing II is dangerous and destabilizing, but if this is true, then the introduction of the SS-20 is dangerous and destabilizing as well. It is not morally consistent to approve the one and condemn the other.

But the ground launched cruise missile is another matter. Though the idea of the cruise missile is as old as the German V-1, the *terrain contour matching guidance systems* on the new cruise missiles have, in effect, created a new type of weapon, one that presents the Soviets with unsolved problems of detection and defense. The Soviets have no comparable missile and apparently have no plans to build comparable missiles. The Soviet complaints about the cruise missile, though obviously self-serving, are not hypocritical or morally inconsistent. And when the Soviets argue that the cruise missile is destabilizing and presents them with a choice between losing second strike capacity or converting to "launch-on-warning" and other dangerous modes, what they say might even be true.

Justice and Risks to the Third World

In Chapter 4, the case was made that nuclear war will not extinguish the human species. This optimism, however, was tempered by the observation that an all-out nuclear war would destroy Western civilization, and that Europe and America after a nuclear war might never again assume positions of world power. Furthermore, an all-out nuclear war will have devastating effects even on nations that are not directly involved. These "third party" victims of nuclear war are cause for moral reflection. The Soviets have built up their nuclear arsenal mainly to protect Soviet citizens; the Americans have built up their arsenal mainly to protect American citizens. Though the populations of the superpowers are burdened with nuclear risks, each population gains the benefits of deterrence, such as they are. The people of the Third World gain none of the benefits of deterrence but are forced to shoulder some of its burdens. They live, as it were, downwind from the nuclear arsenals of the superpowers, picking up the pollution but none of the profits.

In Chapter 1, we suggested that the essence of injustice consists of attempts to seize benefits while passing burdens on to others. The American people and the Soviet people (it seems) are seizing the benefits of deterrence while passing the risks to third parties. Thus nuclear weapons systems certainly do inflict an injustice upon *them*.

This argument differs from the argument, offered in the preceding chapter, that American strategic systems violate the rights of innocent people.

That argument referred to the rights of Soviet citizens as well as the rights of people in the Third World. Though American strategic systems do violate the rights of Soviet citizens, it is not *unfair* that they be the ones whose rights are violated, because they are obtaining a similar benefit from Soviet weapons and passing on a similar risk to innocent people in the United States. If we blur the distinction between a people and their government, it seems quite fair that risks be imposed on those who impose risks. It would be hypocritical for the American people to complain about the fairness of risks inflicted by the Soviets, so long as their government inflicts similar risks, and it would be perhaps as hypocritical for the Soviet citizens to complain about the fairness of risks imposed by Americans so long as their own government continues to inflict similar risks. But there is no hypocrisy in the complaints of citizens in the Third World about the risks imposed by the nuclear arsenals of the superpowers, for they are not inflicting similar risks on anyone.

The Unresolved Problem of Compensatory Justice

One branch of justice that commands little attention nowadays on the international scene is compensatory justice. The general idea of compensatory justice is that if limb or property is damaged, restitution must be made or compensation must be paid.[5] Compensatory justice is mainly a subject for civil law, but it is also often invoked by winners against losers after the conclusion of war. It motivated, or at least rationalized, the reparations clauses in the Versailles Treaty in 1919. The connecting link between nuclear weapons policies and the principle of compensatory justice is the issue of risk. It follows from the principle of compensatory justice that justice requires that those who inflict risks must be prepared to pay compensation if worst comes to worst. It follows that the United States can legitimately inflict risks on the Soviet Union only if the United States is prepared to pay compensation if worst comes to worst.

The United States, for example, must be prepared to pay compensation in the event of an unintentional nuclear strike on the Soviet Union. But everyone knows that even an unintentional nuclear strike involving one or two bombs could do terrible damage if those bombs happened to land on cities. One might wonder if the United States is even capable of paying compensation and damages in the event of unintended nuclear catastrophe. Ten million dead, for example, at compensation of $100,000 per person, comes to $10 trillion, and if we open the field of compensation damages to include all collateral damage caused to private property by an intentional first or second strike, the figure for compensation will be clearly out of reach. To permit the United States to cause such risks without being able to pay compensation if worst comes to worst is as unfair to other nations as it would be unfair to other drivers to allow someone to drive a very fast and dangerous car on the nation's roads without automobile insurance, and without the financial resources to make good in the case of an accident.

Nuclear Risks and Future Generations

A nuclear war, as we have said, will not extinguish humanity, but an all-out war would impoverish future generations. From the long term effects alone, it follows that nuclear war is contrary to the common good, and that even fractional increases in the risk of nuclear war are contrary to the common good. But what about fairness? Are the risks raised by the three basic weapons policies fair risks to inflict on future generations?

(a) The Veil of Ignorance Again

In considering the distributions of nuclear risks among nation-states we employed the services of a judge whose verdicts were made impartial by enforced ignorance of his own nationality. In seeking impartial verdicts about the distribution of nuclear risks between generations, we might employ a judge whose verdicts are rendered impartial by enforced ignorance of the century in which he lives.[6] Such a judge will look most unfavorably on acts in one generation that have short-run benefits but impose risks on many succeeding generations. The explosion of the first atomic bomb, which took place the night after Leo Szilard went through hurried calculations to check whether the bomb would blow up the world, for example, might have been disapproved by a judge who did not know the century in which he lived. Imagine such a judge looking at our three basic weapons policies.

The worst risk of non-possession is a unilateral nuclear attack on the United States followed by a substantial American concession to some hostile nuclear power, presumably the Soviet Union. What would be the long-run effects of such an attack? The physical destruction, we might expect, can be repaired, if the attack is as limited as we have every right to expect it to be. The main long-term effects will probably be political: possibly a larger portion of the world will come under Communist domination and a smaller portion of the world may enjoy the standard civil liberties of contemporary Western democracies. This will be a great tragedy for the people who lose their liberties, but it will not be a global catastrophe. Most of the people in the world today do not enjoy these liberties, and it is not likely that a substantially larger fraction of the world's population will come to enjoy civil liberties because the United States chooses to practice victory or detente. Military force, by and large, does not determine where civil liberties flourish. They require special historical, social, and economic circumstances and are hardly exportable, especially by force of arms. And if long established civil liberties come to be regionally suppressed by military force, the suppression is often brief (for example, France 1940-44) and is as likely to come from the right as from the left.[7]

The most serious risk associated with victory and detente, of course, is all-out nuclear war. Of the long-term effects, the miscarriages, birth defects, and cancers produced by increased radiation levels have already been mentioned, as well as the losses in the arts and sciences and in global resources. But the most pervasive effects may be social and political. The social chaos caused by nuclear war and the problems of supplying food, clothing, and shelter to a post-nuclear population is sure to result in a lengthy period of military dominance. It is hardly likely that the civil liberties of Western democracies will emerge unscathed once the military become accustomed to ruling and once people become accustomed to accepting such rule.

The upshot is that the *worst* long term possible effect of non-possession is just *one* of the long term possible effects of victory and detente, while victory and detente have other long term negative effects that non-possession does not have. It follows that a judge ignorant of what century he is living in would favor non-possession over victory and detente. As between victory and detente, he would simply favor the policy that produces the lowest risk of all-out war. Victory supporters and detente supporters, to be sure, each claim that their favored policy causes the least risk of nuclear war. But after some analysis in Chapter 5 we decided that the greater risk of nuclear war lay with victory. Thus the impartial spectator supports detente over victory. This is one argument that victory unfairly throws risks towards the future while seizing benefits in the present.

(b) The Common Heritage of Mankind

No generation starts afresh; each inherits most of its knowledge, values, social organization and institutions—in short, civilization—from the past. It is elementary justice that what one generation inherits from the past it should pass on to the next generation. It is unfair to receive and not to give, if one is capable of giving at all.

What each generation passes on, the next generation holds in trust. To initiate an all-out nuclear war with a first strike or to contribute to an all-out nuclear war with a second strike, violates the trust of *past* generations. Each past generation *could* have destroyed its own contribution to the common stock, could have destroyed its discoveries the way Kafka intended Max Brod to destroy his manuscripts. But the past pioneers in the arts and sciences did not destroy their discoveries, and since they did not destroy them when they had the chance, it is hardly likely that they intended them to be destroyed several centuries later on.

Nor are they likely to sympathize with policies that produce a risk, even a small risk, of all-out nuclear war, regardless of how useful politically those risks might be to the nations of the West. Brought to the twentieth century in Wells' time machine, the artisans who built the great cathedrals of the twelfth century would have little interest in the Cold War quarrel between the one-party rule favored in the East and the two-party rule favored in the West. They would not be upset by the suppression of certain rights and liberties that they never enjoyed, nor would they be surprised or upset by the appropriation of surplus labor by the owners of the means of production. To risk the cathedrals of Chartres or Amiens or Reims or Paris for military position in *these* quarrels would strike them as offensive to their hopes and to their faith.

The contributions of past generations are intended for future generations.

For the present generation to disrupt this transmission, or even to risk disruption, seizes the inheritance of the future and sins against the intended recipients. It is one thing to risk one's own life and property for a personally favored political end. It is quite another thing to risk someone else's property, held under fiduciary obligations, for one's favored political end. Weapons policies that raise this risk are therefore unfair to both past and future generations even if no particular person is wronged by them.

How might supporters of victory, which seems to be the prime offender in this regard, reply to charges of violated fiduciary obligations? They will of course deny that their policy is intended to produce nuclear war or that the risks of victory are greater than the risks of detente. But beyond these standard objections they might argue that victory also intends to preserve a legacy from the past: the legacy of sacrifices that has kept the United States politically independent and free from intimidation by foreign powers. They might argue that victory is necessary for the containment of Communist influence, that the nation as a whole has been committed to containment since the late 1940s, that 50,000 Americans died to prevent the spread of Communist influence in Korea and 50,000 more died to prevent the spread of Communist influence in South East Asia. Many of these men who gave their lives might not have been prepared to give them if they were convinced that the cause for which they died would be abandoned by a future generation of Americans, a generation more concerned with nuclear risks than the spread of Communist influence.

Is there any moral difference between the supporters of non-possession, who are trying to keep faith with the builders of Chartres, and the supporters of victory, who are trying to keep faith with Americans who died in Korea and Vietnam? The tie between the past and the future exists in both cases. The builders of Chartres intended their building to be an ongoing monument to faith. Those who died in Korea and Vietnam intended that future generations of South Koreans and South Vietnamese be free of Communist party rule. But perhaps there is a difference between the ways the alternative policies threaten the goals laid down by past generations. The connection between victory and detente and the preservation of Chartres is clear: Chartres will not survive an all-out nuclear war. On the other hand, the connection between non-possession and the goals of the wars in Korea and Vietnam are not so clear. Certainly the supporters of non-possession are not advocating anything inconsistent with the general policy of containment. Non-possession only repudiates pursuit of the policy of containment with nuclear weapons and nuclear threats. Is the pursuit of containment with nuclear weapons and nuclear threats the goal for which Americans died in Korea and in Vietnam? Not at all: the freedom to inflict nuclear threats was not an issue in either of those wars. Hence it cannot be argued that giving up the freedom to inflict nuclear threats betrays a goal for which past generations of Americans fought and died.[8]

Notes

1. In the usual situation, justice is dealt by a judge adjudicating between two parties. On the international scene there are no judges but only disputing parties. Nevertheless we can demand that the disputing parties judge each other as consistently as a fair judge would.

2. Notice that only if the United States disarms can it demand disarmament by other states. It can, however, request disarmament, and on the nuclear front this request has often been honored. We have, for example, the 1967 Treaty of Tlatcloco, which bans nuclear arms in Latin America.

3. The reader might think that the impartial spectator, seeking to benefit himself, will choose the policy that yields the highest average welfare. But if he does that, he will simply choose the policy that best serves the common good, as defined in Chapter 5. Unless we are willing to accept a theory that identifies the just society with the happiest society, we must give the judge behind the veil of ignorance some other standard than simple maximization of expected value.

4. Adlai Stevenson made this suggestion, and also suggested trading in the American base at Guantanamo Bay in return for removal of the missiles. Robert Kennedy wrote: "There was extremely strong reaction from some of the participants to this suggestion, and several sharp exchanges followed. The President, although he rejected Stevenson's suggestion, pointed out that he had for a long period held reservations about the value of Jupiter missiles in Turkey and Italy, and some time ago had asked the State Department to conduct negotiations for their removal." (Kennedy 1969 50)

In view of this excellent opportunity for a fair exchange in which the United States would lose nothing and the Soviets would be spared humiliation, the President's later comment is remarkable: "If anybody is around to write after this, they are going to understand that we made every effort to find peace and every effort to give our adversary room to move. I am not going to push the Russians an inch beyond what is necessary." (Kennedy 1969 127.)

5. In the usual claim for damage, fault must be shown. But this rule would not apply in the case of nuclear accidents. The owner of high explosives is liable for damages caused by the detonation of his explosives even if the explosion was not his fault.

6. The notion of using the veil of ignorance to secure impartial judgments of intergenerational justice is suggested by Rawls himself in Rawls 1971 Ch. 44.

7. The cases of suppression of liberties by the *left* that are sure to be suggested as counterexamples are Poland and Czechoslovakia. But it is debatable whether these nations, both of which had experienced long periods of foreign domination, had a "long established" tradition of civil liberties.

8. The reader may have been surprised that we made no mention of the long term effects of nuclear war in our discussion of weapons policies and human rights. Certainly it is commonly claimed that nuclear war violates the rights of future generations. But in truth there is no coherent logical argument that nuclear war violates the rights of people in future centuries. The reason is that a nuclear war will affect patterns of sexual encounter, sexual activity, and cell fertilization. Thus if there is a nuclear war in the twentieth century, every person living in the twenty-seconded century is a person who would never have existed had there been no nuclear war. Those particular people are not worse off than they would have been had there been no nuclear war, since if there had been no nuclear war, they would not have existed. But if there is no way that a nuclear war would have made these particular people worse off, there is no way that a nuclear war could have violated their rights. This argument seems to have been invented by Derek Parfit and was presented by him in lectures at Oxford around 1971. Its first publication is Parfit 1983. For commentary see Glover 1977 and Norton 1982.

8

Weapons Policies and the Laws of War

The Just War Theory

The just war theory outlined in the first chapter described the permissible occasions for using military force, and the permissible ways in which that force can be used.[1] Since the just war theory focuses on actual uses of force, it is not particularly suited for judging the creation of risks that are not realized or for judging the making of threats that are not carried out. It follows that the theory is not well designed for the evaluation of nuclear deterrence. Nevertheless, numerous authors since 1945 have sought to apply the just war theory to the various types of nuclear deterrence, and so will we. Our main object will be to judge whether it would be permissible under the just war theory to use or threaten to use nuclear weapons as victory and detente prescribe.

Right Authority

One of the oldest conditions for permissible war is that permissible war can only be initiated by a competent authority. In its patristic and medieval settings, this rule was used to distinguish legitimate wars waged by states and empires from private wars and feuds waged by individuals, families, nomadic tribes, and gangs of bandits. Since, in the modern era, only states can afford the instruments of war, the focus of discussions of competent authority has shifted to the question whether the public leader that inaugurates the fighting is duly authorized to begin the war.

In the American context, the Constitution (Article I, Section 8) gives Congress the power "to declare war . . . and make rules concerning capture on land and water." But the Constitution (Article II, Section I,) also declares that "The President shall be the Commander in Chief of the Army and Navy of the United States." The intent of the framers is clear: the Congress decides whether or not the United States will go to war; the President conducts the war that Congress declares. Declarations of war were normal procedure in the eighteenth century. Since the United States enjoyed the protection of great distance in space and time from any hostile powers, no harm was foreseen in requiring the President to obtain from Congress a declaration of war before commencing military action.

American participation in World War II was, of course, preceded by a declaration of war. But after that war and after the introduction of nuclear weapons, it was not clear that solemn declarations of war served a useful role in the law of war. If declarations of war set the stage for total wars like World War II, perhaps declarations of war were no longer desirable. It was perhaps better to fight the Korean conflict as a UN police action than as a full-fledged declared war between the United States and Communist China. Likewise, the Cuban quarantine was undertaken without a declaration of war and without Congressional approval, although top congressional leaders were informed of the President's decision before it was announced. Since the Congressional reaction to the presence of Soviet missiles in Cuba was even more belligerent than Kennedy's (Kennedy 1969 53), lack of Congressional initiative was perhaps for the best.

The same, perhaps, could be said of the war in Vietnam, likewise fought without Congressional declaration. If the United States was to be involved in Indochina at all, it was perhaps better that no formal declaration was requested, since a formal declaration might have provoked an all-out contest of wills between East and West. The Johnson and Nixon administrations tried to meet the Constitutional problem by arguing that Congress had in fact approved the war by voting the money with which it was fought. The Congress never accepted this argument, and drove the point home with the War Powers Resolution of 1973 (passed over Presidential veto), which required the President to:

1. Consult with Congress before introducing U.S. armed forces into "hostilities or into situations where imminent involvement in hostilities is clearly indicated by the circumstances."
2. Report within 48 hours to Congress, in cases where U.S. forces are introduced into hostilities or situations where combat is imminent, in the absence of a declaration of war, regarding the circumstances, constitutional authority, and "estimated scope and duration of the hostilities or involvement."
3. Terminate any commitment of U.S. forces to combat or imminent combat situations, where there is no declaration of war, within 60 days, unless Congress either extends the 60-day period or grants a formal request from the President for an additional, final, 30 days, based on "unavoidable military necessity respecting the safety of United States Armed forces. [O'Brien 1981 386].

The constitutionality of the War Powers Resolution has never been tested. Nevertheless it is the law until overturned, and the Presidents since 1973 have not sought to overturn it.[2] Given the Constitution and the War Powers Resolution, does the President have due authority to use nuclear weapons against a conventional attack (as victory prescribes)? Does the President have due authority to launch a strategic second strike (as detente may call for)?

In the case of conventional Warsaw Pact assault on Western Europe, the President will probably not have the time to consult Congress authorizing a nuclear response. If the Warsaw pact invasion is so overwhelming that tactical nuclear weapons are under consideration, time will be short. If the invasion is not so overwhelming, then the odds are that nuclear weapons will not be authorized at all. In the case of a strategic second strike, the opportunity for Congressional consultation is even more circumscribed. Time will be very short; the members of Congress may be dead, and even if they are alive, the President will be airborne and will have more on his mind than Congressional debates.

If the President is to use nuclear weapons with due authority, that authority must come from an implied approval, granted in advance by Congress. During the Vietnam era, this alleged "implied approval" consisted of majority votes for war appropriations. Obviously Congress has also authorized the purchase of strategic weapons. Do these votes give the President his constitutional *quid pro quo*?

There is one important difference between the Vietnam votes and the strategic weapons votes. The Vietnam votes were votes to finance military *operations*. The strategic weapons votes were votes to *develop*, *deploy*, and *maintain* strategic weapons, but *not* votes to finance nuclear use. One cannot infer from these votes how the Congress expects the President to use these weapons. It is safe to say that Congress expects these weapons, at a minimum, to establish deterrent threats. But this does not determine *which* deterrent threats are authorized or what the Congress expects the President to do if deterrence fails.

The fact of the matter is that no President has announced a full-fledged strategic policy, and the Congress has never debated strategic policy as such. There have been sporadic rebellions (for example, the ABM revolt in 1969, and the MX revolt in 1983), but in the end the Congress has always given in to the President, and major strategic innovations—the atomic bomb, the hydrogen bomb, tactical nuclear weapons for NATO, the introduction of MIRV, the development of the cruise missile—have gone through with a minimum of Congressional probing into strategic implications. We cannot, then, infer from Congressional debates or votes any guidelines for the use of nuclear weapons by the President.

Some might argue that in the absence of authorization the President must act to preserve national security. But the President is not directly charged under the Constitution with this responsibility, and it is not clear that the American people would approve of a President who placed considerations of national security above all else, including legality and morality. Furthermore, there is a range of opinion about what comes within the scope of national security. It seems that unless the President manages to observe the rules of the War Powers Resolution, he cannot use nuclear weapons with the "due authority" required by the just war theory.

Right Cause

In the just war tradition, *right cause* is restricted to self-defense and recovery of rights. Furthermore, the tradition requires that the use of force be proportional to the gravity of the threat or the importance of the rights violated.[3] Do the uses of nuclear weapons proposed by victory and detente meet these tests?

(a) Proportionality, Self-Defense, and Deterrence

In the just war theory, the permissibility of using force in self-defense is axiomatic. The paradigm case of self-defense, however, involves an attack that poses an intentional and imminent threat of death. In the area of nuclear deterrence, there is no intentional or imminent threat of death. What we have in the case of nuclear deterrence is a risk of attack, and the problem of proportionality consists in determining what size risk it is permissible to inflict in response to a small risk of an attack that may be unintentional. Let us call the high risk of death in standard self-defense Condition (1), and the intentional character of the attack in standard self-defense situations Condition (2). Consider how our ideas about self-defense change when conditions (1) and (2) are attenuated. Suppose, for example, that A is trying to kill B, but that B knows that A has only a 10 percent chance of success, even if B does not defend himself. Is B then justified in killing A? Most people who are not pacifists think so. But now suppose that A is trying to kill B but that B knows that A has only a 0.01% chance of success. On this assumption is B justified in killing A? Most people think not.

Now suppose that A is not trying to kill B, but merely engaging in some otherwise legitimate activity that has the effect of imposing on B a 10 percent risk of death. Suppose, for example, that the risk is caused by A's attempting to defend himself against attack by C. Is B then justified in killing A? What if the risk A inflicts on B is 1 chance of death in 100? In 1,000? Most people draw the line at 1 in 100 or less.

The moral of these inquiries seems to be that under self-defense one is entitled to inflict a greater risk than the risk one suffers, but not a *much* greater risk, especially if the risk is inflicted by a person who is not deliberately trying to cause one's death. Generalizing to the case of risks inflicted by groups on other groups, it follows that if group A inflicts a certain number of expected deaths on group B, proportionality permits group B to inflict a greater number of expected deaths on A to remove themselves from risk, but not a *much* greater number of expected deaths. In the case of risks inflicted without intent to kill, we will assume that it is permissible to inflict 10 times as much risk in return. In the case of risks inflicted with intent to kill, we will assume that it is permissible to inflict 100 times as much risk in return.

With this in mind, consider detente and victory. If we confine our attention simply to loss of life, we calculated in Chapter 4 that victory produces 57.8 million expected deaths, detente produces 19.5 million expected deaths, and non-possession produces 4.6 million expected deaths. If we consider a proportionate response to inflict no more than 10 times as much risk as is suffered, then the response of detente to the Soviet threat is proportionate, the response of victory is not. But if we permit the proportionate response to inflict 100 times as much risk as if suffered, then both victory and detente inflict proportionate risks.

(b) Self-Defense, Proportionality and War Uses of Nuclear Weapons

At the strategic level, victory envisages a limited, flexible, "tit for tat" response to nuclear attacks. Even if the "tit" is substantially larger than the "tat," the thrust of the victory strategy is to provide a measured response. Thus we can assume that strategic responses under victory do meet the proportionality test.

Unfortunately, victory also prescribes nuclear responses to conventional attacks, since it condones "first use." The use of nuclear weapons in response to any conventional attack, however strong, is a significant escalatory step; indeed, it is the threat of such an escalatory step that is supposed to prevent the conventional assault from beginning. It is not unreasonable to consider such an escalatory response to be a disproportionate response. If so, the "first uses" envisaged under victory violate the just war theory's requirements of proportionality. Even self-defense cannot justify such escalatory steps.

Detente, by contrast, permits only conventional responses to conventional attacks. At the level of tactical and theater operations detente does not violate the canon of proportionality. But at the strategic level, detente postulates a massive response to *any* nuclear attack on the United States, and this implies massive responses to small nuclear attacks. Though a massive nuclear response to a small nuclear attack does not cross the dividing line between conventional weapons and nuclear weapons, such responses are disproportionate responses. As might be expected, massive retaliation in any guise violates the canon of proportionality.

(c) Redress for Rights Violations

Though the just war theory countenances the use of violence for the redress of rights violations, detente forbids the use of nuclear weapons except in the case of nuclear attack. We can thus dismiss detente as a strategy for redress of grievances; it operates strictly for self-defense.

Since victory, however, permits first use of nuclear weapons, victory permits the use of nuclear weapons for the redress of rights violations. But in the real world it is difficult to imagine situations in which it would be reasonable to use nuclear weapons, or to make nuclear threats, in order to obtain redress of rights. Would it have been reasonable to make nuclear threats against North Korea after the seizure of the Pueblo? The result could only have been the slaughter of the crew. Would it have been reasonable to make nuclear threats during the Iranian hostage crisis? Obviously not. And even if we could imagine a case in which it would be prudent to use nuclear weapons to obtain redress of rights, it is hardly likely that such a use would meet the canon of proportionality. So far as the just war theory is concerned, it would seem that the use of nuclear weapons for redress of grievances is a closed option.

Right Intention

In the development of just war theory, the requirement of *right intention* has played a double role. First, right intention requires that one maintain at all times a morally proper attitude towards one's opponents. In modern times, the rule requires that one recognize at all times that one's opponents are human beings possessed of natural moral rights. Second, right intention requires that the prosecution of the war be guided by morally acceptable long-range values, which one seeks to preserve while pursuing the maintenance of self-defense and the redress of grievances.

(a) Right Attitude

Charitable attitudes towards the opponent are difficult to maintain under the pressures of war. The war that began as a war against the Germans and the Japanese soon became a war against the "Krauts" and the "Japs," and this brutalization of attitude towards all Germans and all Japanese led straight to Dresden, Hiroshima, and Nagasaki. Since the Soviets have rarely attacked Americans since 1945,[4] no such brutalization of attitude seems to have set in regarding the peoples of the Soviet Union, who are regarded by most Americans with a certain patronizing sympathy. Though the Soviet leaders are generally disliked in the United States, hatred of Stalin, Khrushchev, Brezhnev, and Andropov did not exceed in virulence the hatred many Americans exhibited towards Presidents Johnson and Nixon during the war in Vietnam. None of the details of victory and detente seems motivated by hatred of the Soviet people. It is dislike of Communist doctrine and fear of Soviet government intentions, not dislike of particular individual acts, that has fueled support for the cold war in the United States. Neither victory nor detente, then, exhibits attitudes contrary to the rule of right intention.

(b) Right Values

Victory and detente are instruments of the cold war, and the long-range values for which the cold war is waged, are, presumably, democratic civil liberties and the system of unplanned enterprise. As the cold war drags on, the just war theory can inquire how the strategies of victory and detente affect the maintenance of these long-range values.

The problem that immediately obtrudes itself in this context is the problem of maintaining democratic control of military instruments the details of which must be kept secret. If the United States chose to fight the cold war with several million M-1 rifles, there would be little need for secrecy since it is neither possible nor necessary to keep the rifle designs secret. Detente and victory, however, rely on technology that must be kept secret if it is to fulfill its function. Victory, by definition, requires secret technological innovations to assure that Soviet weapons can be overcome and defeated in a nuclear exchange. Detente, while not requiring the same level of technical secrecy, requires the maintenance of secrecy about deterrent intentions, plus a modicum of technological secrecy to deny the opponent a breakthrough in offense.

Ever since the Manhattan Project disrupted the free flow of scientific information in the United States, there has existed an unresolved tension between the free society, which nuclear weapons are supposed to defend, and the secrecy with which those weapons are enshrouded. In the 40 plus years since the initiation of the Manhattan Project, the American people have witnessed and tolerated, in the name of national security, the foundation and immense growth of the CIA and the NSA, the witch-hunts of the 1940s and 1950s, the massive domestic espionage of the 1960s and 1970s, and the steady growth of secret research departments in the Pentagon. The result is that the American people for some time have had two governments, one visible and accountable to the people, the other invisible and accountable to almost no one. (The immense size of the invisible government can be estimated by adding up the sums attached to the classified sections of the federal budget). Nuclear weapons, of course, are not solely responsible for the growth of the American invisible government. But they are partially responsible. If the rule of right intention requires that policies be judged by their long-run effects on the values that the policies are supposed to serve, detente to some degree and victory to a greater degree violate the rule of right intention. Both these policies present the real possibility that the United States could win every deterrent battle and yet lose the cold war, since both these policies may corrupt American values from within as much as the acts of the Soviet Union could corrupt those values from without.[5]

Necessity

The just war theory requires that force be used by states only as a last resort, after all peaceful means have been exhausted. Since it is reasonable to consider nuclear threats a "use of force," we will apply the rule of necessity to wartime explosions of nuclear weapons and to nuclear deterrence.

(a) Deterrence and Necessity

Is nuclear deterrence as practiced by victory and detente an act of last resort? Deterrence, at a given level of armament, can be called an act of last resort only if every attempt to reduce armaments below that level (while maintaining second-strike capacity) has failed. So victory and detente will satisfy the requirement of necessity only if combined with vigorous and sincere efforts to achieve arms control. Since our inquiry is conceptual we need only ask: can victory and detente be combined with sincere and vigorous attempts at arms control?

In the case of detente, there seems to be no problem: it is part of the idea of detente to reduce force deployments to the lowest levels consistent with the maintenance of the American deterrent. The real problem is whether victory can be combined with vigorous steps toward arms control. There is no motive, in the victory strategy, to reduce levels of American arms unless the Soviets agree to reduce them even more than the Americans do. This is not a very likely prospect. Furthermore, the victory strategy is committed to continuous qualitative improvements in American strategic arms, and it is quite impossible to combine qualitative improvements with qualitative arms control.

(b) War Uses and Necessity

We can say with some confidence that nuclear weapons would not be exploded under the victory strategy except as a last resort. In the event of a Warsaw pact invasion of Western Europe, it is highly unlikely that the National Command Authority would release nuclear weapons unless it were apparent that NATO forces stood to suffer an imminent and total defeat.[6] By contrast, the massive strikes programmed by detente could hardly qualify as "necessary," since if it is ever required to launch a second strike, the detente strategy will already have failed. Here as elsewhere, the rules of just war favor detente over victory *before* nuclear war starts, and favor victory over detente *after* nuclear war starts. In this case, the rule of necessity is that the deterrent uses of nuclear weapons under detente are permissible, and that deterrent uses under victory are impermissible; that wartime uses under detente are impermissible, and that wartime uses under victory are permissible. It is no wonder that debate about the propriety of various weapons policies has been so long unresolved.

Chance of Victory

The rule of necessity requires that force be *necessary* before it may be used in service to a just cause. The chance-of-victory rule requires that it be *sufficient*. According to the chance-of-victory rule, force may not be used, even in a just cause, unless there is some reasonable chance that justice will be achieved.

Obviously it is impossible to apply the chance-of-victory rule without referring to the goal of the policies tested by the rule. The goal of detente is to deter a strategic nuclear attack on the United States. The goal of victory is to deter strategic nuclear attacks on the United States, to deter nuclear and conventional attacks on the United States or its allies, and to win a nuclear war should one ever begin.[7] Is there a reasonable chance that detente and victory can achieve these goals?

Many reasonable people believe that detente will deter strategic nuclear attacks on the United States. Many reasonable people believe that victory will deter strategic nuclear attacks on the West and conventional attacks against American allies. Let us assume, then, that both policies have a reasonable chance of accomplishing their deterrent functions.

When we consider the wartime aspects of these policies, however, the picture is much less clear. Suppose that there is a strategic nuclear attack on the United States, large or small. In response to such a strike, detente calls either for inaction or for a massive counter-strike against the attacker. What would such a counter-strike accomplish? Obviously it cannot deter a strategic attack on the United States, since that attack has already occurred. There is no reasonable chance that such a strike would recover rights or bring redress. Thus, given the chance-of-victory rule, a second strike under detente would not satisfy the rules of just war.

Now consider victory as it operates in wartime. Victory prescribes the use of tactical nuclear weapons in response to a conventional attack on the United States or its allies, for example, in the course of an invasion of Western Europe. Is such an escalatory step likely to produce success? No one is going to launch an attack on the United States or its Allies without a serious motive and without the resolve to press through to the end. Thus, if NATO responds to a conventional attack with tactical nuclear weapons, in all probability its Eastern opponents will respond with tactical weapons of their own, neutralizing any temporary military advantage and devastating the nations of Western Europe in which the battle is raging. If NATO escalates to theater nuclear weapons, the Warsaw Pact will too, and so on up the escalatory ladder. There is no route to victory here, no reasonable chance of success.

Victory also prescribes measured counterforce strikes in response to limited strategic strikes against the United States or its allies. The purpose of these limited responses is to deter further strategic attacks. Is this strategy likely to succeed? Supporters of victory are convinced that it will succeed. But there are two obstacles that must be overcome. First, there is a technical question as to whether the policy can be carried out. If the limited strike hits American command and control centers, the ability of the United States to carry out an intelligent and measured counter-strike may be severely compromised. Second, there is a real question whether the Soviets will interpret an American counter-strike of any sort as an attempt to bring an end to hostilities. The Soviets may have already decided that if the United States chooses to respond at all, the response signifies the beginning of a protracted nuclear war between the superpowers. The American limited counter-strike will thus generate a limited counter-counter-strike, and so on back and forth until both sides lose the ability or the will to keep the war limited. It is of course *possible* that a limited counter-strike will bring an end to a limited nuclear war. But it cannot be said that such a result is probable. Whether counterforce nuclear warfare satisfies the chance-of-victory rule is a matter for debate.

Discrimination

The *rule of discrimination* requires that civilians not be objects of *direct* and *intentional* military attack. They *may* be objects of indirect or unintentional attack.[8]

(a) Discrimination and Detente

Numerous authors have charged that detente sins against the rule of discrimination. The plan of detente is to deter strategic attack by threatening a painful counter-strike against the attacker, including attacks on his cities and industry. This makes enemy civilians direct and intentional objects of threatened attack. What can supporters of detente say in their own defense?

They might argue, first, that the just war theory itself is not the last word about the morality of war; that its rules are not applicable to conditions of modern warfare; and in particular, that it is not applicable to the problem of finding protection against weapons against which no physical defense is possible. Second, they might claim that even if the just war theory were the last word about morality in war, detente does *not* violate the rule of discrimination, because:

(i) Though detente requires that implicit threats be made against Soviet cities, it does not require that these threats be carried out. The deterrent effect of detente is as much achieved by the ambiguity of American response as by the formation of a definite American intention to launch the second strike.

(ii) Detente does not involve the intention to attack Soviet cities, since there is every reason to believe that deterrence will succeed, that the Soviet Union will never launch a first strike, and that the United States will never launch a second strike. To say that detente *intends* to blow up Soviet cities because it generates a small chance that those cities will be struck is like saying that the American criminal justice system intends to put innocent men in jail because there is always a chance that juries will convict innocent men.

Arguments (i) and (ii) will not bowl over the opponents of detente. First of all, detente cannot *guarantee* that there will be no second strike. It merely provides the physical means for calling off the second strike. Whether or not there will be a second strike under detente depends upon a decision freely reached by the President and the Secretary of Defense. Second, the argument that under detente the United States does not intend to attack Soviet cities because there is little likelihood that this attack will take place confuses *intentions* with *expectations*. Suppose that Jones forms an intention to strangle the first girl he meets wearing a dress with purple and pink polka dots. Even if Jones does not believe he will ever meet such a girl and even if the chances that he will strangle such a girl are small, it is nonetheless true that he has formed a murderous intention. Likewise the expectation that detente will not lead to the mass slaughter of civilians does not prove that detente involves no intention to slaughter civilians.

If such counter-arguments succeed, supporters of detente must fall back on the contention that the just war theory is an archaic doctrine, too old to handle the moral problems of the nuclear age. Certainly the thinkers from Augustine on down who developed the just war theory rarely considered weapons against which physical defense was simply impossible. Nevertheless, the rule of discrimination and the idea of noncombatant immunity lie at the very core of just war thinking, and to discard the principle of noncombat-ant immunity will be viewed by many as an ethically dangerous move. The next step after the rejection of noncombatant immunity is the adoption of some notion of collective responsibility, and the next step after that is a massacre of the likes of Hiroshima and Dresden. Unless some new argument emerges, we will assume that nuclear deterrence as practiced under detente sins against the rule of discrimination.

(b) Victory and Discrimination

The victory strategy dictates measured responses to strategic attacks. At least in the initial stages of nuclear war, it prescribes counterforce responses to limited nuclear attacks. Because of this thrust towards counterforce targeting, victory seems to satisfy the rule of discrimination in a way detente does not.

But two problems must be addressed before we can certify that victory entirely satisfies this rule. First, victory requires countervalue strikes at *some* point in the escalatory ladder. Second, in a nuclear war, the counter-force strikes prescribed by victory may kill the millions of civilians who live near military targets. In neither case does it appear that victory is making a maximum effort to respect noncombatant immunity.

(i) Victory prescribes measured responses to strategic attacks. In response to counterforce attacks, victory prescribes counterforce attacks. But in response to countervalue first strikes, victory may be forced to prescribe countervalue attacks if no counterforce target of suitable value can be found. If the Soviets should destroy New York, there may be no military target in the Soviet Union as valuable to the Soviets as New York is to the United States. If a target of lesser value is struck, the Soviets may conclude that they have "won" the exchange. To prevent this conclusion, victory may have to prescribe an attack on Leningrad. This will presumably deter the Soviets from further attacks on American cities, since they will not want Moscow to share Leningrad's fate. Supporters of victory may argue that in most nuclear wars things will never go this far: that the Soviets will learn at the lower stages of the escalatory ladder that each strike against the United States only produces a more painful counterstrike against the Soviet Union. But this answer is no better than the answer of the supporters of detente when they protest that under detente it is very unlikely that Soviet cities will ever be struck. In both cases, the *intention* to attack is present, even though the occasion for the attack may never come.

(ii) In Chapter 4, we estimated civilian losses in a large scale counterforce attack on the Soviet Union at 4 to 27 million dead. Various NATO exercises in the 1950s and 1960s showed that the use of tactical nuclear weapons against a Warsaw Pact attack would produce several million civilian casualties in the nations so defended. Victory prescribes such counterforce strikes and tacti-cal uses. How can victory be said to discriminate soldiers from civilians?

The immediate answer is that in such attacks the deaths of civilians are not the *object* of the attack. Since they are not the object, the deaths are not intended, and if they are not intended, they do not violate the rule of discrimination.

Many critics have objected that there is something bizarre in the idea that the deaths of civilians are "unintended" when such deaths are forseeable and certain to occur. But, as we have seen, "unintended" can mean either "unforeseeable" or "undesired." When the rule of discrimination says that unintended civilian deaths are permissible, the word "unintended" has been traditionally interpreted as "undesired." Given this interpretation, we must describe the collateral civilian deaths resulting from counterforce attacks as unintended. As such, they do not violate the rule of discrimination.

The large number of civilian deaths resulting from counterforce attacks will continue to disturb many. But the number of civilian deaths is not a problem for the rule of discrimination, which is not concerned with *how many* civilians die but with the manner of their death. The problem of the number of civilian deaths is a problem for the *rule of proportionality*, to which we now turn.

Proportionality

The rule of proportionality requires that nations fighting for a just cause use the least destructive military means consistent with the successful prosecution of the war.

(a) Deterrent Uses of Nuclear Weapons

Once again the choice between detente and victory seems to be a choice between a small risk of a large disaster (detente) and a larger risk of what might be a smaller disaster (victory). Both victory and detente take as their main goal the deterrence of strategic attacks on the United States; supporters of both think that they have adopted the most efficient and least destructive means to that goal. There is no way to assess these competing claims except by developing a measure that considers both the risk of disaster and the size of the disaster when it comes. In this book that measure has been the total of expected deaths. According to Chapter 5, victory causes more expected deaths than detente. Thus the rule of proportionality favors detente (in its deterrent mode) over victory (in its deterrent mode).

(b) Wartime Uses and Proportionality

In the event of a strategic attack on the United States, detente prescribes either a massive response or inaction. The goal of any second strike is to deter further strategic attacks on the United States. Obviously, in many cases a limited response is at least as likely to deter further attacks as a massive response. Consequently, the massive second strike programmed by detente *fails* the test of proportionality. Once the apparatus of detente is set up, the only permissible option in the event of strategic attack is inaction.

The case of victory is more complicated. On the strategic level, victory prescribes limited responses to limited attacks. In the attempt to avoid provoking the opponent into irrational strategic spasms, victory asks for the smallest strike consistent with making the opponent regret the initial attack. Such responses, usually counterforce responses, pass the test of proportionality.

But victory also involves the use of tactical nuclear weapons in response to conventional attacks. One can argue that such uses violate the canon of proportionality because these weapons do more damage than the conventional weapons that would be used in their place. True, many cities in Europe and Japan were devastated by "conventional" explosives in World War I and World War II. But tactical nuclear weapons, with their intense heat and radiation in addition to standard blast effects, do much more damage than conventional weapons assigned to the same military task. Furthermore, it cannot be argued that tactical nuclear weapons were introduced into the U.S. Army and into NATO forces for the purpose of keeping down collateral damage. They were introduced into NATO forces because the leaders of NATO countries were not inclined to match the size of the conventional forces of the Warsaw Pact. In effect, the NATO governments traded increased risks to civilians in the future for decreased military burdens in the present. Since this policy does not seek to minimize damage in the course of military operations, it violates the canon of proportionality.[9]

Christian Judgments: Ramsey on Nuclear War

The just war theory laid out in Chapter 1 and in the preceding sections represents a consensus from many sources. There is no *official* just war theory, and each author has his own idea about what that just war theory is or should be. Consequently, it would be useful to consider, in addition to the preceding analyses, what several prominent writers have said about the just war theory and nuclear war. In ecumenical spirit, we will examine one Protestant source—Paul Ramsey, and one Catholic source—the National Council of Catholic Bishops.

In the late 1950s, with the dizzying expansion of SAC and limitless verbal belligerence of the Secretary of State, numerous writers took up their pens and published criticisms of strategic policy. Most stressed that the policy of massive retaliation failed to serve American interests. A minority pointed out the moral defects of massive retaliation. Of the moral analyses, perhaps the most influential was Paul Ramsey's *War and the Christian Conscience*, published in 1961.

Ramsey began by noting that Christians must behave according to the dictates of love—love for all people, including Russian people, since Christ died to save them, too. A massive nuclear attack on Soviet Union cities is directly contrary to this ethic of love.

> To press the button in counter-retaliation will also be the most unloving deed in the history of mankind, only exceeded by those who, for the sake of some concern of theirs, cause the little ones to stumble and fall into hell. I had rather be a pagan suckled in a creed outworn, terrified at the sight of hands made impure by any

shedding of blood, than a skillful artisan of technical reason devising plans to carry out such a deed. [Ramsey 1961 170]

Presuming throughout that if an act is wrong it is wrong to intend to do it under any circumstances, Ramsey argued that it is immoral to intend, to plan, or to prepare for such massive attacks on the Soviet Union, even if such an attack is a second strike, and even if such preparations make it less likely that a Soviet attack will occur.

What policy, then, should a Christian support? He should *not* support movements for the abolition of nuclear weapons, or movements for the cessation of nuclear tests, both popular among Christians at the time. He should not support nuclear disarmament because: "It is the use of weapons, and their planned use, not weapons themselves, which may be immoral" (Ramsey 1961 226), and because Christians must be prepared to use force, even nuclear force, in order to establish justice and to protect the weak from oppression. He should not oppose nuclear testing since through nuclear testing it may be possible to create more discriminating nuclear weapons, ones that have some other primary purpose than the mass slaughter of enemy civilians. What the good Christian *should* support is counterforce nuclear warfare. "Counter-forces warfare—the modern term for the just conduct of war—is the only kind of warfare in which just or merciful men can ever engage without a direct violation of those moral norms in terms of which they know they are ultimately judged." (Ramsey 1961 306)

Small wonder, then, that Ramsey hailed Secretary McNamara's June 1962 "flexible response" speech as a major step towards moral sanity. In 1965 Ramsey complained bitterly that "Hardly any of the leaders of religions and public opinion stepped forward to support the most significant change (or suggestion of change) in military policy in two decades of the nuclear age" (Ramsey 1968 212).

Now that McNmara had allegedly brought nuclear weapons within the ambit of just war, Ramsey was content to recommend refinements of the McNamara policy. In 1965 he suggested (a) that the United States and its allies further increase flexibility of response by substantially increasing expenditures for conventional armaments, (b) that the United States announce that it will never use strategic nuclear weapons first and that it will only use tactical nuclear weapons to repel invasion from the territory of the United States or the territory of its allies; (c) that the threat of escalation to strategic countervalue war should be replaced with the threat of escalation to strategic counterforce war; and (d) cities should be ruled off-limits to strategic attack (Ramsey 1968 235–45).

Points (a) and (b) are at least compatible with the victory strategy; (c) and (d) are not. Defenders of detente will quickly point out that (c) and (d) deprive the United States of the main deterrent to attacks on American cities: threats of reprisal in kind against Soviet cities. But Ramsey proposed that the United States continue to make countervalue threats while secretly resolving not to carry out the threats. In short, Ramsey proposed counterforce targeting and countervalue threats and argued that countervalue threats are permissible provided that they are sheer bluff.

The idea of combining pure bluff with what was essentially the victory strategy was original but not very practical. Within a year, Ramsey retracted the idea for two reasons:

First, one's real intentions not to go to such use will be found out, and the bluff will fail to deter; and, second, even if our top political and military leaders were pure in heart, they must count on thousands of men in missile silos, planes and submarines to be conditionally willing, under some circumstances, to become murderers. [Ramsey 1982]

With countervalue threats expunged, Ramsey was left with the victory strategy shorn of the highest level of escalatory retaliation. Since then, he has confined himself to supporting counterforce weapons, like the ABM, and to denouncing any regressions towards countervalue targeting. Considerations of strategic stability and expected deaths, the notion that weapons like the ABM might substantially increase the chance of nuclear war, play no role in his arguments.

What can we say of Ramsey's contributions? Some might find that Ramsey has twisted the just war theory towards victory by over-emphasizing the rule of discrimination and underemphasizing the rule of proportionality. Others might find that Ramsey has applied the just war theory correctly but that by so doing revealed how inadequate that theory is to deal with problems of nuclear deterrence. For Ramsey's insistence on the connection between the wrongfulness of X and the wrongfulness of intending X, his connection of intention with desire rather than with foreseeability, leads to the rather bizarre result that it is morally preferable to kill 10 million people unintentionally than one million people intentionally, even when the 10 million deaths are perfectly foreseecable.[10] Whether this result is consistent with Christian charity is debatable. Surely the 9 million additional civilians who might have been saved but who end up as "collateral damage" might find it quite unloving. If this is Christianity, it is a Christianity in which concern for purity of heart outruns concern for the objective result.

Christian Judgments: The Catholic Church on Nuclear War

While Ramsey concentrated first and last on the issue of discrimination, the Catholic Church focused initially on the issue of proportionality. Even before the nuclear age began, the immense physical destructiveness of modern weapons prompted Pope Pius XII to pronounce, in his 1944 Christmas message: "The theory of war as an apt and proportional means of solving international conflicts is now out of date." But in the 1948 Christmas message this unqualified rejection of the just war theory was modified into a condemnation of aggressive total war, which is a sin, and offense, and outrage . . . a crime worthy of the most severe national and international sanctions."

In *Pacem in Terris* (1963) Pope John XXIII condemned aggressive war but approved defensive war, specifying that defensive wars are proportionate wars against injustices being perpetrated, not wars to right standing wrongs:

"In an age such as ours that prides itself on atomic energy it is contrary to reason to hold that war is now a suitable way to restore rights which have been violated."[11]

These pronouncements left open the means by which self-defense could be pursued, and set the stage for the *jus in bello* arguments of Vatican II. The central document relating to warfare is the Pastoral Constitution entitled *Gaudium et spes*. Preliminary versions of *Gaudium et spes* were in circulation in 1964. The November 1964 draft came out boldly for non-possession:

> The controversies that may perchance arise between nations must not be settled by force and arms, but by treaties and agreements. Although, after all the aids of peaceful discussion have been exhausted, it may not be illicit, when one's rights have been unjustly hampered, to defend those rights against such unjust aggression by violence and force, nevertheless the use of arms, especially nuclear weapons, whose effects are greater than can be imagined and therefore cannot be reasonably regulated by men, exceeds all just proportion and therefore must be judged before God and man as most wicked. Every honest effort therefore must be made, so that not only nuclear warfare may be solemnly proscribed by all nations and alliances as an enormous crime, but also that nuclear arms or others of like destructive force may be utterly destroyed and banned.[12]

Needless to say, this draft paragraph exploded like a bombshell in the Catholic community, provoking intense debates all through 1964. When the final draft of *Gaudium et spes* was issued in 1965, the paragraph condemning possession had disappeared. Instead, the Council declared: "Any act of war indiscriminately aimed at the destruction of entire cities or of extensive areas along with their populations is a crime against God and man himself. It merits unequivocal and unhesitating condemnation." (Abbott 1966 294/80.)

This statement is by no means a condemnation of the possession of nuclear weapons. It only condemns indiscriminate use. It also seems to permit nuclear weapons uses that kill large numbers of civilians and devastate large areas *provided* that the weapons are not *aimed* at achieving these results—an apparent reference to the intention with which the weapons are used. Unfortunately the document did not spell out with any precision what was meant by "aimed," nor did it provide any guidance as to what constitutes a proper policy of nuclear deterrence. But as the strategic situation appeared increasingly stable through the 1960s, *Gaudium et spes* seemed morally acceptable and politically agreeable: it gave the leaders of state the weapon they wanted, requiring merely the promise that they would be properly used. The promise was easily provided, since fulfillment of the counterforce promise was consistent with developing the new generation of strategic weapons. Thus matters rested, until the arrival of Ronald Reagan prompted renewed interest among Catholics in the morality of weapons policies.

The National Council of Catholic Bishops had issued occasional pronouncements on the problems of nuclear war, but the Reagan administration's apparent endorsement of nuclear war-fighting options led them to examine the issues anew. An ad hoc committee on war and peace was formed to draft a pastoral letter, the second draft of which was presented to the bishops in November 1982. The second draft, which endorsed the movement to freeze nuclear weapons arsensals, caused a furor and prompted intense opposition from the Reagan administration. A slightly watered down version, not specifically endorsing the freeze, was adopted by the bishops in May 1983. Despite the revisions, the third draft of the pastoral letter leans as much towards detente as the policies of the Reagan administration have leaned towards victory.

The motivating spring of the bishops' argument is the notion of proportionality:

> Once we take into account not only the military advantages that will be achieved by using this means, but all the harms reasonably expected to follow from using it, can its use still be justified? Do the exorbitant costs, the general climate of insecurity generated, the possibility of accidental detonation of highly destructive weapons, the danger of error and miscalculation that could provoke retaliation and war—do such evils or others attendant or indirectly deriving from the arms race make the race itself a disproportionate response to aggression? Pope John Paul II is very clear in his insistence that the right and duty of a people to protect their existence and freedom is contingent on the use of proportionate means. [National Council 1983 34].

Given these destructive powers, the prospects for keeping nuclear war confined are dubious:

> Recent talk about winning or even surviving a nuclear war must reflect a failure to appreciate a medical reality: Any nuclear war would inevitably cause death, disease and suffering of pandemonic proportions and without the possibility of effective medical intervention. That reality leads to the same conclusion physicians have reached for life-threatening epidemics throughout history: Prevention is essential for control. Today the possibilities for placing political and moral limits on nuclear war are so infinitesimal that the moral task, like the medical, is prevention: As a people we must refuse to legitimate the idea of nuclear war. (National Council 1983 42).

Notice the fact that many of these effects are unintended plays no role in the argument. Now, *if* we accept moral responsibility for unintended but foreseeable damage and *if* we believe that nuclear war, once it starts, cannot be kept limited, what policies should Catholics support? The bishops (a) reaffirmed the Vatican II denunciation of counter-population bombing, even in response to a first strike; (b) denounced counterforce nuclear retaliation, if such retaliation results in disproportionate civilian casualties; (c) called for a renunciation of the "first use" of nuclear weapons of any kind and in any circumstances; (d) severely limited the permissible occasions for limited nuclear retaliation, even if nearby civilians are not endangered; (e) found nuclear deterrence of any sort legitimate only if connected with serious attempts at arms control; and (f) deplored the development of weapons that might suggest preparations for an American first strike (National Council 1983 59–60). All of these suggestions are consistent with a detente strategy in which counter-city attacks are bluffed; most of them are inconsistent with a victory strategy.

The bishops' conclusions in 1983 are strikingly at variance with the conclusions reached by Ramsey in 1965. By emphasizing discrimination and propriety of intention, Ramsey out-Catholics the Catholics and ends up endorsing victory. By emphasizing proportionality and accepting responsibility for collateral damage, the bishops partially jettison the rule of double effect and end up endorsing detente. Clearly the bishops in 1983, unlike Ramsey in 1965, give special moral weight to the tremendous incidental damage to be expected from limited nuclear exchanges. And the bishops see more clearly than Ramsey that the problem of regulating nuclear weapons is more like regulating potentially irresponsible automobile drivers than regulating potential murderers.

Nevertheless, there is a certain inconsistency between the bishops' ringing denunciation of most uses of nuclear weapons and their endorsement of nuclear deterrence. First of all, if we are morally responsible for foreseeable collateral damage, then we are morally responsible for raising the risk that foreseeable collateral damage will occur. Second, if we are going to accept deterrence at all, we might as well accept it in its most effective version, and its most effective version involves threats against countervalue targets, which are ruled out. The bishops' ambivalence towards deterrence is summarized in this remarkable statement:

> "As clearly unsatisfactory as the deterrent posture of the United States is from the moral point of view, use of nuclear weapons by any of the nuclear powers would be an even greater evil" (National Council 1982 317).

This comes remarkably close to rejecting the traditional Pauline principle that one must not do evil that good may come.

The Legality of Nuclear Weapons: Possession

The sources of international law are (a) decisions and judgments of international bodies; (b) agreements and treaties signed among nation states, and (c) the customary behavior of nations. Though judgments about what is legal do not necessarily indicate what is moral, law is a civilizing force, and there is a presumption that what is illegal is also immoral. Thus it is worth considering what international law might say or imply about the legality of non-possession, detente and victory.

Very little evidence exists that the possession of nuclear weapons by nation states is illegal. Certainly there is no general custom that nations refrain from the development of nuclear weapons, and no treaty exists that declares any and all uses of nuclear weapons to be illegal. Nevertheless, there are four indications of a modest thrust in the direction of criminalizing nuclear weapons.

(i) On 24 November 1961, the General Assembly of the United Nations adopted a resolution declaring that:

> The use of nuclear and thermonuclear weapons would bring about indiscriminate suffering and destruction to mankind to an even greater extent than the use of those weapons declared by the aforementioned international declarations and agreements to be contrary to the laws of humanity and a crime under international law. [Yearbook 1961 30–31]

The resolution passed by a vote of 55 to 20, with 26 abstentions, the Soviet Union voting for the resolution, and the United States voting against.

Unfortunately for partisans of non-possession, a General Assembly Resolution of this sort has little legal force. At best, such resolutions are evidence of international custom, but the vote in this case was so badly split that the resolution can hardly be said to constitute evidence of general custom or universal sentiment.

(ii) On 17 June 1925 in Geneva, various plenipotentiaries signed the Protocol for the Prohibition of Poisonous Gasses and of Bacteriological Methods of Warfare, which read in part:

> The use in war of asphyxiating, poisonous, or other gasses, and of all analogous liquids, materials, and devices, has been justly condemned by the general opinion of the civilized world. The prohibition of these weapons and methods shall be universally accepted as part of International Law. [Friedman 1972 I 454]

Two obstacles exist to interpreting the 1925 Protocol as implying the illegality of American possession of nuclear weapons. First, the protocol does not mention nuclear weapons as such. Second, the United States Senate, then and now, has refused to ratify the 1925 protocol even though two American representatives at the conference signed it.

To be sure, nuclear weapons are not chemical or biological weapons. But the Geneva Protocol prohibits not only chemical and biological weapons but also "all analogous materials and devices," and nuclear weapons are certainly analogous to chemical and biological weapons in the crucial aspect that they poison territory and cause sickness in human beings.[13]

Though the United States has not ratified this convention, most nations in the world have, giving the protocol some force in international law. Furthermore, the United States and the Soviet Union on 10 April, 1972, signed an agreement to destroy all stocks of toxic and bacteriological weapons. The signing of this agreement accepts the general implication of the Geneva Protocol that nations simply should not possess bacteriological weapons. But if nations should not possess bacteriological weapons because they operate by causing sickness, logical consistency would seem to demand that weapons that cause radiation sickness should not be possessed as well.

(iii) Numerous proposals have been put forward over the years to prohibit nuclear weapons in certain geographical zones. Two of these suggestions have been incorporated into international agreements. In 1959 the United States and other nations signed an agreement resolving that "Antarctica shall be used for peaceful purposes only . . . Any nuclear explosions in Antarctica and the disposal of radioactive waste material shall be prohibited" (Keesing 1971 328).

In 1968, 21 Latin American nations at Tlateloco, Mexico, signed an agreement that "The contracting parties undertake . . . to prohibit and prevent in their respective territories (a) the testing, use, manufacture, or acquisition of any nuclear weapons, (b) the receipt, storage, installation, deployment, and any form of possession of any nuclear weapon" (Keesing 1971 332–44). The United States is not a signatory to the Treaty of Tlateloco, but has ratified the first protocol, which recognizes the denuclearization of Puerto Rico, the American Virgin Islands, and the Panama Canal Zone, and the second protocol, in which the parties were asked to respect "the status of the denuclearization of Latin America" and "not to use or threaten to use nuclear weapons against the contracting parties of the Treaty."

The United States has not responded with equal warmth to all suggestions of nuclear free zones. In the late 1950s, for example, the United States rejected the Rapacki Plan for the denuclearization of Germany and Poland. But some nuclear free-zones have been established, and there is reason to hope that there will eventually be more. In these zones, any use of nuclear weapons by the consenting parties will be criminal as well as immoral.

(iv) There have been a great many wars since 1945, and quite a few of them (Korea, Sinai, Vietnam, Afghanistan) have involved states that possess nuclear weapons. Nevertheless, since 1945 no nuclear weapon has been used in war. In many cases the reason for avoidance was absence of military advantage, but even in the presence of possible military advantage, nations have shunned the use of nuclear devices. After these many years avoidance has become the norm.

The custom of avoidance does not demand non-possession as such, but it does condemn *all* uses of nuclear weapons. A custom so long observed begins to develop legal force: it functions not so much like the criminal law of states but like civil or tort law, which is largely unwritten but nevertheless effective.[14] Unfortunately, if the custom of avoidance ever breaks down, the resulting war will probably turn the international order into such a shambles that no one will be left with the ability to prosecute violators, or take action against them. Crime and justice will both perish together.

The Legality of Nuclear Weapons: Use

There are no treaties or conventions in international law that specifically discriminate legal uses of nuclear weapons from illegal uses of nuclear weapons. Those who would discriminate legal from illegal uses must reason by analogy, using the line drawn between legal and illegal uses of conventional arms. Let us begin by noting for the record that international law, the 1907 Hague Convention, for example, does distinguish between legal and illegal uses of weapons, even by nations fighting a just war: "Article 22: The right of belligerents to adopt means of injuring the enemy is not unlimited" (Friedman 1972 318).

What principally concerns us in considering legal limits on nuclear weapons use is the degree to which the just war ideas of proportionality and discrimination have been incorporated into the body of international law.

First, proportionality. International law does incorporate the idea that the use of force must be limited by the value of the object defended and kept to the minimum necessary to achieve justice. But international jurists and lawyers have made no deep attempt to apply the notion of proportionality to the use of nuclear weapons. One distinguished student of international law, Ian Brownlie, did argue in 1963 that the use of nuclear weapons against a conventional attack violated the rule of proportionality (Brownlie 1963 263), but he reached this conclusion by philosophical reasoning about the qualitative difference between nuclear weapons and conventional weapons, not by reference to the sources of international law. Other scholars have argued that proportionality requires that nuclear weapons be used only after conventional weapons have failed (for example, Singh 1959 132–36). Once again the argument is more a proposal about what the law should be than an analysis of what the law is. Declaratory military practice by states that possess nuclear weapons leans in the direction of first use, with the reservation that "first use" is to be directed, "against aggression," whatever that is.

The principal basis, however, for declaring that certain uses of nuclear weapons are illegal, lies in those provisions of international law that attempt to embody the rule of discrimination. Attempts to do this, as Chapter 1 showed, date from the nineteenth century. Article XXV of the 1907 Hague Convention specified that "The attack or bombardment, by whatever means, of towns, villages, dwellings, or buildings which are undefended is prohibited" (Friedman 1982 318). Article XXVII demanded that all necessary steps be taken to avoid the bombardment of buildings dedicated to religion, arts and science, and so forth. Nevertheless, the march of technology through the century constantly increased the damage that could be done from a distance, and millions of civilians died from air or artillery bombardment in World War II.

The Fourth Geneva Convention of 1949 attempted to erect some legal defenses for civilians in time of war, but the bulk of the Fourth Convention is devoted to explicating civilian rights in occupied territories, and no explicit attention is paid to problems of bombardment. This omission was rectified by the First Protocol attached to the Fourth Geneva Convention, drafted on 8 June 1977. The pertinent provision is article 51:

1. The civilian population and individual civilians shall enjoy general protection against dangers arising from military operations. To give effect to this protection, the following rules, which are additional to other applicable rules of international law, shall be observed in all circumstances.
2. The civilian population as such, as well as individual civilians, shall not be the object of attack. Acts or threats of violence the primary purpose of which is to spread terror among the civilian population are prohibited.
3. Civilians shall enjoy the protection afforded by this Section, unless and until such time as they take a direct part in hostilities.
4. Indiscriminate attacks are prohibited. Indiscriminate attacks are:
   (a) those which are not directed at a specific military objective;
   (b) those which employ a method or means of combat which cannot be directed at a specific military objective; or
   (c) those which employ a method or means of combat the effects of which cannot be limited as required by this Protocol: and consequently, in each such case, are of a nature to strike military objectives and civilians or civilian objects without distinction.
5. Among others, the following types of attacks are to be considered as indiscriminate:
   (a) an attack by bombardment by any methods or means which treats as a

single military objective a number of clearly separated and distinct military objectives located in a city, town, village or other area containing a similar concentration of civilians or civilian objects;

and

(b) an attack which may be expected to cause incidental loss of civilian life, injury to civilians, damage to civilian objects, or a combination thereof, which would be excessive in relation to the concrete and direct military advantage anticipated.

6. Attacks against the civilian population or civilians by way of reprisals are prohibited.[15]

The language of Article 51 is straightforward, and had this protocol been in effect in 1944 and 1945, many of the bombing operations of both the Allies and the Axis nations would have been illegal. The article also has implications for strategic nuclear bombing. Clearly, indiscriminate countervalue attacks of the Hiroshima sort are illegal according to Article 51. This leaves, however, two crucial items the legality of which is not explicity determined: (a) deterrent nuclear threats, and (b) counterforce nuclear strikes.

(a) Deterrent Threats and Article 51

As regards deterrent threats, the text is difficult. Paragraph (2) of Article 51 specifically forbids threats aimed at the civilian population. This would seem to rule out the sort of countervalue threats that we have associated with the detente strategy. On the other hand, the same paragraph describes the forbidden threats as "threats of violence the primary purpose of which is to spread terror among the civilian population." Deterrent threats under detente and victory do not seem to be threats the primary purpose of which is to spread terror among the civilian population. The primary purpose of deterrent threats under detente is to convince the leadership on the opposing side not to launch a strategic attack on the United States. Terrorization of the civilian population is at most an incidental effect of deterrence, and if the Soviet people have been terrorized by American deterrent threats, their behavior hardly shows it. So far as Article 51 is concerned, deterrent threats, even countervalue deterrent threats, are not obviously illegal.

(b) Counterforce Attacks and Article 51

Counterforce attacks are intended to strike military targets. At first sight, then, counterforce attacks do not seem to qualify as the "indiscriminate" attacks forbidden by Article 51. As clause 4(a) requires, counterforce attacks are directed at military objectives; and, as clause 4(b) requires, they can be directed at military objectives. But clause 4(c) might be taken to forbid even counterforce nuclear attacks. Clause 4(c) forbids means of warfare that release effects that "cannot be limited." The fallout released in strategic bombings cannot be limited, and the radioactive elements released by strategic weapons will harm an unlimited number of future generations. Furthermore, Paragraph 5, clause (b), forbids counterforce attacks on "mixed" targets, that is, attacks that hit two military targets with one bomb, when civilians reside between the targets. Though this author has not seen the Single Integrated Operational Plan currently in force, there is reason to think that some of the targeting plans aim to destroy military targets in heavily populated areas. Any such attack that destroys two targets with one bomb violates Paragraph (5).

(c) The American Attitude Towards Article 51

The United States signed the First Protocol to the Fourth Geneva Convention in 1977. But while it signed the Protocol with gratifying speed, the United States attacked a remarkable proviso to its approval: "The United States understands that the rules established by this Protocol were not intended to have any effect on and do not regulate or prohibit the use of nuclear weapons."[16]

The wording of the American proviso makes it appear that the United States is merely noting a consensus achieved among the authors of the Protocol. But such an interpretation is strained. The convention is designed to afford protection to civilians from methods and weapons that may injure them. Nuclear weapons fit into this category, perhaps preeminently. Furthermore, Article 49 of the Protocol explicitly applies the Fourth Convention to methods of bombardment. Clearly the Protocol has straight-   . forward application to bombing with nuclear weapons, and it would be bizarre to deny that these applications exist. The American proviso, then, cannot be interpreted as representating an uncontroversial view of the Protocol. What it represents is a unilateral attempt to disregard the Protocol's obvious implications for American strategic policy. What the American proviso implies is that the United States wants to consider nuclear weapons as a unique class of weapons, to which the established body of international law does not apply. It denies all reasoning by analogy from conventional weapons to nuclear weapons. But if reasoning by analogy is denied, then the natural development of international law will be disrupted, since reasoning by analogy—inference from case to case—is essential to all jurisprudence.

The American view that nuclear weapons are special weapons has a discomfiting implication for supporters of victory and detente. If the illegality of certain uses of nuclear weapons cannot be established by reasoning by analogy from illegal uses of conventional weapons, it follows that the legality of certain uses of nuclear weapons cannot be established by reasoning from analogy from the legal uses of conventional weapons. The United States may be prepared to argue that every use of every weapon is legal until international law says otherwise, but a presumption of innocence in favor of nuclear weapons is a little strange. In international law, there is a general presumption against war, and it would seem to follow that there should be a general presumption against new and immensely destructive means of war. If there is a presumption against the legality of nuclear weapons, and if reasoning by analogy is denied, then no use of nuclear weapons is permissible in the eyes of international law. From the standpoint of logical clarity, it would be better all around if the United States dropped its proviso and ratified the First Protocol as it stands.

Nuclear Reprisals

International Law over the centuries has recognized the right of states in certain cases to undertake military reprisals, and the use of reprisals is countenanced in both the Army's 1956 *Field Manual of Land Warfare* and the Air Force's 1976 manual *International Law—The Conduct of Armed Conflict and Air Operations.* Here is the Air Force definition of reprisal:

> Reprisals in war are commission of acts which, although illegal in themselves, may, under the specific circumstances of the given case, become justified because the guilty adversary has himself behaved illegally, and the action is taken in the last resort, in order to prevent the adversary from behaving illegally in the future.[17]

The manual lays down eight conditions for the use of reprisals.

1. They must respond to grave and manifestly unlawful acts.
2. They must be for the purpose of compelling the adversary to observe the law of armed conflict. Reprisals cannot be undertaken for revenge, spite, or punishment. Rather they are directed against an adversary in order to induce him to refrain from further violations of the law of armed conflict.
3. There must be reasonable notice that reprisals will be taken.
4. Other reasonable means to secure compliance must be attempted.
5. A reprisal must be directed against the personnel or property of an adversary.
6. A reprisal must be proportional to the original violation. Although a reprisal need not conform in kind to the same type of acts complained of (bombardment for bombardment, weapon for weapon), it may not significantly exceed the adversary's violation either in violence or effect. Effective but disproportionate reprisals cannot be justified by the argument that only an excessive response will forestall futher transgressions.
7. It must be publicized.
8. It must be authorized by national authorities at the highest political level and entails full state responsibility. [O'Brien 1981 68]

Given all these restrictions, we can ask whether or not the use of a nuclear weapon could be justified as a reprisal against a prior illegality.

Clearly the notion of reprisal could not be invoked to justify a massive response to a massive attack. After a massive attack, there is little chance of a further attack, first, because the opponent's arsenal will probably be depleted; second, because there will be little left in the United States worth destroying. It should be noted that the Air Force manual requires that reprisals be undertaken only if they will deter future illegalities.

The sort of attack that might be justified under the principle of reprisals is the more limited countervalue or counterforce attack. In the late 1950s Leo Szilard proposed a system of "city-exchanges"—reprisals intended to limit nuclear war.[18] In Szilard's scheme we announce that if New York is destroyed, Leningrad will be destroyed, if Cleveland is destroyed, then Kiev is destroyed, and so forth.

Now, if the Soviets attack *one* American city, or *one* American military installation, there is a clear possibility that they will attack others. A reprisal in these circumstances meets the requirement that reprisals can be undertaken only to deter future crimes. But it is doubtful that the other rules of the Air Force manual could be followed in the case of a limited nuclear exchange. If the United States, for example, observes the requirement of "reasonable prior notice," the opponent can reply with a notice of his own that American reprisal will be met with a definite counter-reprisal. Futhermore, under the pressure of time, it is hardly likely that explorations of "other reasonable means of obtaining compliance" can be carried out.

In addition to these points of detail, there is a deeper objection to the use of nuclear weapons for reprisals against the enemy. Though reprisals have a time-honored status in international law, their moral status is dubious.[19] If reprisals have a moral basis at all, it lies in the right to self-defense. In previous discussions of self-defense, we noted that self-defense was not permissible if innocent bystanders are threatened by the act of self-defense, *even if those innocent by-standers are not made direct objects of attack*. For example, it is not permissible to shoot an attacker if the shot must travel through the body of an innocent bystander, even though the bystander in such a case is not a direct object of attack. Thus the rules of international law, which (nowadays) specify that civilians cannot be the "object" of reprisals are, from the moral point of view, too weak: according to the principles of morality, civilians should not even be *indirect* victims of acts of reprisal. Since the explosions of nuclear weapons will almost certainly injure civilians, nuclear weapons cannot be employed in morally legitimate reprisals.

Notes

1. Just war analyses of nuclear deterrence can be divided into Protestant, Catholic, and secular contributions. Perhaps the outstanding contributions from the Protestant side are Potter, n.d.; Ramsey 1961, Ramsey 1968; and Ramsey 1973. On the Catholic side, see Murray 1959; Clancy 1967; and Stein 1961. In the secular tradition, see Rapaport 1964; Green 1966; and Walzer 1977 ch. 17.

2. Since 1973, the Presidents have submitted five reports in compliance with the War Powers Resolution. Ford reported to Congress after the evacuation of Da Nang, Pnom Penh, and Saigon in April 1975, and after the Mayaguez "rescue" in May 1975. Carter reported after the failed attempt to rescue the hostages in 1980. In the Mayaguez case, Mike Mansfield reported that Congress had only been "informed, not consulted" beforehand and that the 48 hour deadline had been missed. Carter neglected to consult with Congress before the Iranian rescue attempt. None of these incidents involved nuclear weapons.

3. The idea that one should not fight unless one has something worth fighting for looks simple on the surface. But when one tries to compare the losses incurred by fighting with the gains expected by winning, one finds oneself comparing values from very different categories: the freedom lost if one does not fight with lives lost if one does, etc. The problem of incommensurable values makes the canon of proportionality very difficult to apply. For a Catholic analysis of proportionality and just cause, see John Courtney Murray, "Theology and Modern War," in Nagle 1960 60. For an argument that the just war rule of proportionality is so vague that it is worse than useless, see Robert W. Tucker in Osgood and Tucker 1967 301–2 n.

4. From 1950 to 1962 the Soviets attacked American planes at least 33 times, usually killing the American crews. See "Another Incident—The U.S. Aircraft and the Ten Year Record," *The New York Times* (17 July 1960); and Bamford 1982 137 and 179. Since most of these were attacks

on American spy planes, the American people learned little of them. But even in the case of highly publicized incidents, such as the Soviet downing of the Korean commercial airliner 007 in September 1983, hostility has been directed at the Soviet leadership, not the peoples of the Soviet Union. Anti-Communist ideology brutalizes the image of the Soviet leaders while softening the image of the Soviet people.

5. If the cold war is being fought to preserve "free" or unplanned enterprise, one can ask to what extent the Pentagon, which might be described as the world's second largest socialist economy, has corrupted the American system of free enterprise. Certainly the government's rescue of Lockheed set the stage for the rescue of Chrysler, and so forth.

6. My view that NATO will not use tactical and theater nuclear weapons except as a last resort may be excessively generous. Possibly NATO contingency plans call for the use of tactical nuclear weapons immediately upon invasion. And there is always the chance of unauthorized use by commanders who must use them or lose them.

7. In the case of the victory strategy, I am defining "victory" as the preservation of American independence and American values. I do not count as a "victory" the result that more Russians are dead than Americans are dead.

8. In addition to the works of Ramsey cited in note 1 above, studies attempting to apply the rule of discrimination to the facts of modern weapons include, among the Catholics, John C. Ford, "The Hydrogen Bombing of Cities" (in Murray 1959 98–103) and O'Brien 1967. For criticisms of the success of the efforts at reconciliation, see Robert Tucker in Osgood and Tucker. 1967 290-322.

9. The reader will have noticed that "proportionality" comes up twice in just war theory, once in the *jus ad bellum* (the injury must be severe enough to justify the use of force) and one in the *jus in bello* (only the minimum force needed to repair the injury must be used). The two conditions are logically independent.

10. I am assuming that the deterrent effect of the 1 million intentional deaths is precisely the same as the deterrent effect of 10 million unintentional deaths.

11. The statements of Pius XII and John XXIII, and many other Catholic documents relevant to the issue of this book are collected in *Peace and Disarmament: Documents of the World and the Roman Catholic Church Council of Churches* (Geneva and Rome, 1982).

12. An early draft of paragraph 25 appeared in the *The New York Times* 12 October 1964. The final wording appeared in the *The New York Times* 10 November 1964.

13. The argument that all uses of nuclear weapons violate the Hague and Geneva Conventions forbidding poisonous weapons is developed by Schwarzenberger 1958, 26–39. Schwarzenberger considers the argument that nuclear weapons are poisonous to be the only good argument that uses of nuclear weapons are contrary to international law. Michael Akehurst (1982 232) rejects the argument on the grounds that "fallout is only a side effect to nuclear weapons, whereas poisoning is the main effect of using poison gas." This distinction between main and side effects, however, is irrelevant. If an atomic device were (somehow) encased with germs that caused disease, there is no question that everyone would consider the device contrary to the Hague and Geneva Conventions, even if the resulting illnesses were only a minor part of the bomb's effect.

14. For the argument that international law functions more like tort law than criminal law see Rubin 1983.

15. Diplomatic Conference on Reaffirmation and Development of International Humanitarian Law Applicable in Armed Conflicts; Protocol Additional to the Geneva Convention of 12 August 1949 and Relating to the Protection of Victims of International Armed Conflicts. Protocol I, Part IV, Chapter II, Article 51. Text reprinted in the *American Journal of International Law*, 1978, p. 478.

16. Ibid., p. 404.

17. This is the definition given by U.S. attorneys in the war crimes trials, U.S. vs. Ohlendorf (1950), quoted in O'Brien 1981 383.

18. Szilard seems to have been one of the first to grasp the strategic difference between counterforce and countervalue warefare and one of the first (and one of the few) to boldly assert that threats of countervalue warfare are more likely to produce stable peace. See Szilard, 1955 297–307. Szilard pursued the ruthless logic of countervalue warfare, and described his "cities-exchange" system for limiting escalation, in Szilard 1961 407–412.

19. For what is perhaps an unduly sympathetic view of reprisals. see Walzer 1977 207–11.

9

Steps Toward Disarmament

The Role of Moral Criticism

Recently I participated in a three-day conference on morality and strategic policy. The conference was attended by high-level military personnel, civilian advisors to agencies of government, renowned stratègists, and academic specialists in defense issues. After several hours of floundering in moral argument, a well-known authority on international relations remarked in exasperation: "What's the use of moral discussions? They don't generate policy options."

The distinguished scholar was right: moral codes don't tell you what to do. They tell you what you *can't* do. The development of strategic options is a job for specialists; and the moral critic is not a specialist.

It is the job of the moral critic to tell the politicians and the experts when they have crossed over the line, when they have suggested something that simply ought not to be done. At that point, the moral critic intervenes and tells the experts: "You cannot do that, because that is wrong." If the expert asks what should be done, the moral critic simply replies, "You must think of something else."[1]

As near as can be inferred from the annual reports of Caspar Weinberger, the American policy currently in force is close to what we have been calling the victory policy.[2] We have found that the victory strategy is not morally satisfactory. It does not serve the common good. It is not undertaken in obedience to special moral duties. It seems to violate human rights. It violates the categorical imperative and the golden rule. It sins against the just war requirements of proportionality and necessity. Even though it can be broadly characterized as "defensive" policy, it is a policy designed primarily to advance American interests, at least in the short run. But it is not a policy which advances American interest in accordance with moral principles. The United States must give it up. In the ensuing section, we will consider what is involved in giving up victory, and whether, as many believe, it would be a disaster for the United States.

From Victory to Detente

Let us for the moment put non-possession aside and consider the option of changing American strategic policy from victory to detente.[3] The aim of detente is to prevent American involvement in nuclear war. It seeks to deter deliberate strategic attack by threatening the attacker with sure destruction. At the same time, it seeks to minimize the chance of accidental nuclear war, to diminish the chance that nuclear war will result from escalation, and to prevent American leaders from being tempted into adventures that could lead to nuclear war. To get from victory to detente would require *at least* the following 11 changes in American strategic policy:

(a) Elimination of Fixed Base ICBMs

Under detente, the United States is pledged to not using nuclear weapons first. Thus the United States must anticipate that if nuclear war breaks out, its opponent will attack first. This attack will in all probability be a counterforce attack. To maintain its capacity for assured retaliation, the United States must eliminate strategic weapons that are not likely to survive a first strike.

It follows that the United States should eliminate all fixed base ICBMs: all its Titan and all its Minuteman missiles.[4] No issue has agitated strategic discussion more in the last 10 years than the vulnerability of American fixed-base ICBMs. The problem can be solved and the controversy ended simply by eliminating the fixed-base ICBMs. To many readers, such a drastic step is hard to imagine. But for previous generations it was hard to imagine the elimination of the battleship. From the standpoint of detente, fixed ICBMs are like old sea battleships; easy targets that attract enemy fire.

(b) Elimination of the FB-111 and B-52 Bomber Force

At any given time the United States can keep only a fraction of its strategic bombers aloft. The B-52s and FB-111s caught on the ground during a first strike are more vulnerable than fixed base ICBMs. One must expect, then, in the event of a Soviet first strike, that only a fraction of American strategic bombers will participate in a second strike. These bombers will encounter the heaviest air defense systems that the world has yet seen. There is a real question whether the planes can reach their targets. What is more, the Soviets may believe that their air defenses are sufficient and believe that American planes will not get through. To the extent that the Soviets have faith in their air defenses, the American strategic bombers fail to fulfill their deterrent role—even if they can in fact penetrate Soviet defenses.[5]

(c) Elimination of the Trident Submarine

The United States is currently phasing out its Polaris submarines, cutting back its fleet of Poseidon submarines, and replacing the Poseidons with the new Trident. Trident is superior to Poseidon in many respects, but it is inferior to Poseidon in one crucial respect: there are fewer of them. Thus each Trident carries a large fraction of the submarine based deterrent, making the deterrent more vulnerable. Since the invulnerability of the deterrent is an essential part of the detente strategy, it makes sense *not* to replace Poseidon with Trident.[6]

Step (c), combined with steps (a) and (b), would reduce the current American "strategic triad" to a "strategic monad." Deterrence would be achieved through a fleet of Poseidon submarines armed with MIRVed Poseidon missiles. With the elimination of fixed base ICBMs and strategic bombers, the Air Force would lose its strategic role; the tactical, non-nuclear part of the Air Force, however, would be retained.

In addition to these changes, detente would require:

(d) Withdrawal and Elimination of Tactical Nuclear Weapons

The United States currently stocks 20,000 or so tactical nuclear weapons. These weapons play no role in deterring strategic attack on the United States, but they do increase the chance that the United States will become involved in a nuclear war through a process of escalation. More than any other sort of nuclear weapons, they pose a risk of unauthorized use. Under detente, the entire stock of tactical nuclear weapons would be withdrawn and destroyed.[7]

(e) Elimination of New Counterforce Weapons

Unlike victory, detente does not seek qualitative superiority over the Soviets. Furthermore, detente avoids counterforce targeting, in the belief that such targeting encourages the opponent to use his nuclear weapons before he loses them. It follows that a switch from victory to detente would require the cancellation of new or current weapons with pronounced counterforce capacity. The highly accurate and very powerful MX missile, and the ultra-accurate cruise missile, would both be cancelled. (The Trident D-5 missile would be cancelled along with the Trident).[8]

(f) Announcement of a "No First Strike" Pledge

Detente by definition is committed to the use of strategic weapons only in the event of a nuclear attack on the United States or its allies. In the interests of stability, detente indicates that the United States should publicly announce a commitment to "no first use."

Leonid Brezhnev made such a pledge on behalf of the Soviet Union in July

1982. The United States need not take the Brezhnev promise at face value. It suffices that the Soviets know that the United States will be more irritated by Soviet first use *after* the Brezhnev pledge than before the pledge. This increases the probability of American retaliation if the pledge is broken. An American pledge would provide a similar step towards strategic stability.[9]

(g) Negotiation of a Comprehensive Test Ban Treaty

Whether or not the United States cancels its new generation of counterforce weapons, supporters of detente will demand that the United States enter into negotiations for a comprehensive ban on tests of nuclear weapons. (Current treaties permit underground tests of weapons up to a power of 150 kilotons.) Each of the superpowers knows by now that whatever one side develops, the other will duplicate. A comprehensive ban on nuclear weapons testing reduces the chance of destabilizing the balance and frees both sides from the expensive treadmill of the qualitative arms race.[10]

(h) Negotiation of a Treaty for the De-Militarization of Outer Space

The United States and the Soviet Union each spend about $10 billion yearly to explore the strategic uses of outer space. Many futuristic space-based systems are under discussion, but in the near term the only weapon likely to emerge is the anti-satellite device, or ASAT. The Soviets have been developing a missile-borne ASAT; the Americans have been working on a canister sized ASAT dropped from an F-15 fighter. (Sewall 1983)

Detente is interested in weapons that facilitate and guarantee a second strike. There is no way that an ASAT weapon can facilitate a second strike. American ASATs cannot protect American satellites; they *can* blind an enemy to a forthcoming surprise attack. Detente has no use for surprise attacks, and thus no use for ASAT weapons. But since the Soviet ASAT impedes the ability of the United States to detect a Soviet first strike on its way, prudence under detente calls for a bilateral rather than a unilateral renunciation of ASAT weapons.

(i) Cessation of Production of Fissionable Materials for Weapons

The United States currently possesses tens of thousands of nuclear weapons. If the proposals of the preceding sections are adopted by the United States, the result will be an immense warhead surplus, since there will be many more warheads than vehicles to deliver them. In these circumstances, it would be in the national interest for the United States to announce that it has ceased production of fissionable materials for weapons. This announcement could be followed by a call for other nations to follow suit. President Nixon used this "cut first, negotiate second" approach in 1969 when he announced the unilateral destruction of the American stockpile of biological weapons. The result was a multilateral treaty banning biological weapons, signed in 1972. If unilateral American cuts in the production of fissionable materials lead to a multilateral agreement to cease production, the dangers of nuclear proliferation could be much more easily contained.

Much of the fissionable material contained in surplus American nuclear weapons could be converted into nuclear fuel for nuclear power plants. Such a conversion would transform a dangerous or useless resource into a useful one. Furthermore, by increasing the supply of nuclear fuel, the proposed conversion would diminish the demand for uranium reprocessing procedures which, as we noted, generate as a byproduct plutonium usable in nuclear weapons. By cutting demand for reprocessing, a ban on the production of fissionable materials would reduce the possibilities for nuclear terrorism and adventurism in nations currently addicted to reprocessing and to nuclear power.[11]

(j) Replacement of MIRV Missiles with Single Warhead Missiles

In retrospect, it now appears that MIRV was the great technical innovation of the 1970s. The placing of many warheads on a single missile led to an explosive increase in the number or warheads of both sides. By installing MIRVs on ICBMs and SLBMs the Air Force and the Navy got "more bang for the buck." But they paid a strategic price. With more warheads on each missile, each missile is more valuable to its possessor and more threatening to its opponent. This increases the desire of the opponent for pre-emptive attack, and increases the desire of the possessor to fire off the MIRVed missiles before they are caught under sea or on the ground. For this reason, MIRVed missiles magnify the chance of nuclear war and make nuclear war worse when and if it comes. Accordingly, detente requires that the United States replace all of its MIRVed missiles with single-warhead missiles. If the United States retains any land-based ICBMs, they must be single-warhead ICBMs. Likewise, its strategic submarines must forgo MIRV. Such changes would require the development of a new generation of strategic missiles, but this is one qualitative change that would be welcomed by supporters of detente.[12]

(k) Introduction of a New Fleet of Strategic Submarines

If the United States reduces its strategic triad to a strategic monad, it is imperative that strategic submarines serve the purposes of deterrence. We have already noted that the new Trident submarines do not serve deterrence as well as the older Poseidons, partly because there will be fewer of them, and partly because of their immense size. Whether or not the United States introduces Trident, it should consider, in the interests of deterrence, the development of a new fleet of strategic submarines that would be smaller than Poseidon and would not carry MIRVed missiles. If the experts decide that the United States needs 600 SLBMs for the purposes of assured retaliation, these 600 missiles would be better placed on 75 submarines carrying 8 missiles each, rather than on 38 submarines carrying 16 each. The more submarines there are under the seas, the more invulnerable the American deterrent.[13]

Doubtless some people in the Navy will be displeased with the image of a strategic naval force consisting of many small boats rather than a few majestic ones. But such reactions have nothing to do with morality or prudence. A more serious problem is that a proliferation of strategic submarines increases the number of persons with the discretion to fire nuclear weapons. The discretion that strategic submarine commanders now have to launch nuclear weapons would have to be cut back in the era of mini-submarines.

Objections to the Switch to Detente

The cuts mentioned in steps (a) through (k) in the preceding section would eliminate about 90 percent of American strategic weapons. Most of the steps proposed are unilateral steps, steps taken by the United States whether or not other nuclear states reciprocate. Many will object to such deep and detailed cuts. There are two principal objections, one based on prudence, one based on moral considerations.

The *prudential objection* is that such a step would put the United States in peril, because it would leave the Soviets with more weapons than we have. The objection assumes that if nation A has more weapons than nation B, than nation A has some military advantage over B. That assumption may have held true in the pre-nuclear age. But supporters of detente will deny that it holds true now. They will point out that the inferior nation—the United States in this case—continues to possess under detente an invulnerable fighting force more powerful than all the armies in all the world before 1945. True, the strategic forces of detente are less flexible and can do less than the strategic forces under victory. But in the nuclear age, the ability to do less might not be such a bad thing, even from the prudential point of view.

For this book, the *moral objection* is the more disturbing: "If the United States cuts back unilaterally, the Soviets will have no incentive to cut back. But the common good of the world is better served by mutual cuts in which the United States agrees to withdraw its weapons if and only if the Soviet Union does too. American weapons are bargaining chips in serious negotiations for world disarment."

This objection deserves the most careful consideration. Throughout this book, we have presented numerous criticisms of the possession of nuclear weapons by the United States. Obviously these same criticisms apply to the possession of nuclear weapons by the Soviet Union. At a minimun, possession of nuclear weapons by the Soviet Union does not serve the common good, and it violates human rights by putting the lives of innocent people at risk. If the United States can take steps to encourage the Soviets to disarm, such actions serve the common good and help the people whose rights are violated. Certainly these are morally worthy goals. But (so the argument goes) the United States cannot achieve these goals unless it retains its weapons as bargaining chips in negotiations with the Soviets.

There are, however, numerous assumptions behind the call for the retention of weapons as bargaining chips.

(i) The argument assumes that if the United States cuts back unilaterally, the Soviet Union will not decrease its arsenal *at all*. There is some reason to hope that this will not be so. Strategic weapons cost money to build and maintain. With a manifest decline in the American threat, economic pressures alone may force the Soviets to make corresponding cuts.

Supporters of victory will object that the Soviet Union in the past has not shown restraint when the United States has shown restraint. For example, the United States held its ICBM force constant from 1968 to 1972, but the Soviets from 1968 to 1972 showed no corresponding restraint in the development of their ICBM force. But this argument is not overpowering. First, the fact that the Soviets did not show restraint in the face of *mild* American restraint does not prove that they will not show restraint in the face of *substantial* American reductions. Second, the Soviet ICBM buildup from 1968 to 1972 can be viewed as an attempt to obtain overall parity in missile *launchers* (ICBMs plus bombers, in which the U.S. had a substantial lead). Once having reached rough parity in launchers, the Soviets deployed no further strategic launchers even though SALT I permitted them to deploy more bombers. There is no evidence that the Soviets intend to perpetually increase the size of their strategic forces even in the face of substantial American cuts.

(ii) The argument presumes that if the United States insists on mutual steps, serious mutual nuclear disarmament will occur. This may be unduly optimistic. Certainly the record of negotiations for mutual disarmament is not very encouraging. It took 27 years for the superpowers to get to SALT I, and SALT I did not force the United States to give up any missile that it intended to build, nor did it stop the Soviets from building more missiles than they already had. (The Vladivostock accords in 1974 allotted each side more missiles than it ever hoped to build).[14]

The reasons for these failures—distrust, suspicion, a refusal to place the common good above the national interest, and an exaggerated fear of appearing to have been swindled at the bargaining table, are likely to persist on both sides in the decades ahead, especially if the United States continues to wage an ideological war against Russia. If so, there is no great chance that talks between the superpowers will lead to substantial reductions in strategic arms. There is even less reason to believe that the total of cuts in strategic arms that might be achieved by such bilateral negotiation would be greater in quantity than the total of cuts that the United States could achieve unilaterally by the adoption of detente.

This is a point not often noticed by proponents of the need for "bargaining chips." If the total risk to the world is roughly proportional to the quantity of strategic arms in the world—a proposition that seems reasonable—then the common good is best served by the policy that produces the greatest reduction, regardless of who does the reducing. Suppose that the Soviet Union and the United States can give up eight units of strategic weapons without losing second-strike capacity, and that the Soviets will only agree to give up two units of strategic weapons if the United States gives up two units. On these assumptions, which seem fairly realistic, the common good is better served by unilateral nuclear disarmament (eight units reduction), than by bilateral nuclear disarmament (four units reduction). For bilateral disarmamant to produce force reductions the equal of unilateral disarmament, the Soviet Union and the United States must each agree to accept one-half or more of the reductions the United States would unilaterally implement if it unilaterally adopted detente. Since no multilateral negotiations since the 1920s have produced significant reductions in force levels, there is no reason to believe that the Soviets and the Americans, placed at a bargaining table, could achieve 51 percent or more of the American cuts mandated by detente.

(iii) Given the frequency with which the "bargaining chip" argument is cited as a justification for new strategic weapons, it is remarkable how few examples can be provided of cases where the bargaining chips have actually produced overall reductions in the total of nuclear arms in the world. One example is swiftly supplied, but it seems to be the only one: many people believe that the development of the "thin" American ABM in the late 1960s prodded the Soviets into the ABM Limitation Treaty of 1972.

The ABM case is certainly worth examining. Would the Soviets have refused the ABM treaty if the United States had not started to build its own ABM? Given the inscrutability of the Kremlin, such claims about Soviet intentions are always a shot in the dark. Possibly the Soviets would have stopped building their ABM even if there had been no SALT talks. But *once in* the SALT talks, the Soviets wanted *something* in return for a limitation on their ABM. It does *not* follow that the only thing that they would have accepted in return for a Soviet ABM limitation was a limitation on the new American ABM. Indeed, the logical thing to ask in return for a limitation on one's own ABM is a reduction in offensive missiles on the other side—not a reduction in the opponent's defensive systems. It simply cannot be shown that the Soviets would have gone on to build an immense ABM system if the United States had not started to build its own.

There is a general presumption among ethical theorists that one should worry about one's own morals first and only secondarily worry about the morals of others. In terms of strategic arms, this presumption implies that one should worry about the risks raised by one's own stockpile first, and only afterwards, worry about the risks raised by the stockpiles of other states. From the prudential point of view, the United States should focus its attention on the risks of Soviet weapons. From the moral point of view, it should focus its attention on the risks of American weapons. Of course, in reducing its stockpile, the United States should take care not to increase the overall levels of danger in the world. But there is no strong argument that detente increases overall levels of risks. Indeed, many supporters of detente feel that detente does not even increase the level of risk to the United States. If so, the switch to detente is morally required *and* prudentially acceptable.

Detente Plus City Avoidance

Suppose that, by some magic, the eleven proposals described above were all adopted by the United States. The B-52s, the ICBMs, the MIRVed missiles, the small tactical weapons and the big strategic submarines, all disappear. In their place sail one hundred strategic submarines, armed with single-warhead SLBMs. Is this posture morally satisfactory?

One feature of detente that has disturbed many critics is that detente countenances countervalue second-strike targeting. If the one hundred strategic submarines are committed to maximizing deterrence, their single warhead missiles will be aimed at civilian occupied areas. The submarines are not committed to bombing civilian targets; there is always the possibility that the President will refuse to order the second strike. But this possibility will not reassure morally scrupulous Americans who fear that millions of innocent people may be killed in their name. For the President may order the second strike. Or he may be dead and unable to prevent it.

The assurance that morally concerned people demand is a guarantee that the President will never bomb enemy cities with nuclear weapons.[15] Technically, this guarantee can be obtained by crossing off the National Strategic Target List all strategic targets that are in or near cities. Steps should be taken to make it very difficult to return these targets to the list during periods of international crisis. Politically, however, it will be very difficult to obtain this targeting guarantee. Although a resolution of Congress could legally bind the President not to target cities, such a resolution would almost certainly be defeated on the grounds that divulging part of the targeting plan would damage American security. A more acceptable route would require negotiation of a "no cities" pledge with the Soviets, but the verification of Soviet intention and targeting capacities would be a formidable task. Given these facts, it seems unlikely that a "no cities" posture could be imposed on an unwilling President. A willing President, however, could impose it on himself, and then pass it on to his successors with something of the authority of a *fait accompli*.

If the United States adopts detente but refuses to target cities, what should it target? One thing is clear: it should not target Soviet strategic weapons. Under detente, the United States is committed to using nuclear weapons only in the event of a first strike. If the Soviet first strike is massive, there is no point in targeting Soviet strategic weapons, since they will all have been launched. If the Soviet first strike is limited, there is no point in targeting Soviet strategic weapons since the Soviets under these assumptions will have a surplus of strategic weapons (compared to the United States). They would not mind losing a few in order to obtain whatever they hope to achieve by launching a first strike.

Nor should the United States target Soviet command and control centers. Many of these centers are located in or near cities. Furthermore, if Soviet command structures are disrupted, the result may be the release of all remaining Soviet strategic weapons in one mighty spasm—not the desired cessation of hostilities.

What about targeting Soviet troop concentration, to the extent that such concentrations can be found outside cities? Detente-plus-city-avoidance would countenance such targets provided that such troops are engaged in an unprovoked attack on Western Europe and provided that the Soviets have already used nuclear weapons first. But if the Soviets have launched a *strategic* attack—large or small—against the United States, then Soviet ground troops are as innocent of the attack as are the residents of Soviet cities. If Soviet cities are to be spared on moral grounds, it would follow, in these circumstances, that concentration of Soviet troops should not be struck either.

It seems, then, that the logical targets for detente-plus-city-avoidance are the targets usually classified as "econcomic": railroads, highways, bridges, dams, power stations, power lines, oil lines, oil fields, and oil refineries. The Soviets have no surplus of these targets. Many of them, when struck, will be lost forever. Others can be restored only after considerable effort. Routing a railroad around a radioactive site is much more difficult than routing it around a TNT crater.

Let us suppose, then, that the missiles aboard an American fleet of strategic submarines are all assigned to such economic targets. Three questions must be asked about this policy, which is neither detente nor victory but some combination of the two. Is it stable? Will it deter? Is it morally acceptable?

(a) Stability

Detente-plus-city-avoidance is stable in a number of important respects. Like any version of detente, it cuts down on strategic forces and therefore cuts down on the possibility of accidents. It presents no threat to enemy weapons, eliminating enemy interest in pre-emptive strikes or launch-on-warning postures. In limited nuclear wars, its avoidance of enemy command and control centers and enemy cities produces the best chance that limited nuclear wars will not escalate to all-out wars.

(b) Deterrence

Under detente-plus-city-avoidance, the United States gives up *assured destruction*, if "assured destruction" implies the destruction of Soviet cities. But if it gives up assured destruction, and the capacity to knock out Soviet weapons, how can it deter Soviet attack?

The answer is that it will deter as all American policies deter—by vague threats of horrible reprisal. Details of American targeting policy under detente-plus-city-avoidance remain secret, just as targeting details now are secret. The Soviet leaders may suspect that the United States will not strike Soviet cities, but there is too much at stake for the Soviets to gamble that this is so. Then as now, they must assume that a nuclear attack on the United States will produce their own destruction. Even if they launch a limited first strike and receive in return a limited strike on (say) Soviet oil fields, they have reason to believe that if they go one step further, Moscow and Leningrad may be struck. As ever, the uncertainty of what will happen after nuclear weapons are used is the strongest deterrent to first use.

(c) Morality

Detente-plus-city-avoidance is perhaps the most morally palatable of those strategies that retain the basic idea of deterrence: the idea of preventing nuclear attack by threatening a nuclear counterattack. By reducing the chance of war to detente levels and by reducing the destructiveness of nuclear war to victory levels, the number of expected deaths produced by detente-plus-city-avoidance will be lower than the number produced by either victory or detente. Indeed, the number of expected deaths produced by detente-plus-city-avoidance may be lower than the number produced by non-possession. Furthermore, Detente-plus-city-avoidance, like simple detente, satisfies the basic canon of justice; if we practice it, we could tolerate its being practiced by the other side.

But the fact that detente-plus-city-avoidance serves the common good without violating the standards of justice does not prove that it is morally acceptable. Detente-plus-city-avoidance is still committed to nuclear deterrence, which requires that the United States put the lives of millions of Soviet citizens at risk. In the case at hand, a precision strike aimed solely at Soviet oil refining capacity would kill 1 to 1.5 million people, more than all the Americans killed in all the wars since the American Revolution. Anyone who has accepted the argument of Chapter 6 that inflicting a risk is morally equivalent to inflicting an injury will feel moral pressure to go beyond the policy of detente-plus-city-avoidance.

From Detente to Non-Possession

The move to detente from the present status quo would require major cutbacks in American strategic weaponry. Nevertheless, in three senses the policy of detente does not constitute unilateral nuclear disarmament: first, the United States would continue to possess nuclear weapons; second, the United States would continue to seek to deter attack through threats of counterattack; third, the United States would retain second-strike capacity: the ability to inflict unacceptable damage on any attacker who dares to launch a nuclear first strike against the United States.[16]

All three of these conditions are abandoned under the policy of non-possession. Under non-possession the United States would no longer possess nuclear weapons, make nuclear threats, or possess second-strike capacity. Many people in the world, and some in the United States, hope for the day when peace between the superpowers can be preserved without recourse to nuclear threats. But hope is not enough. The details must be filled in as to how this hope might be realized.

It might appear that the starting point for the study of proposals for nuclear disarmament is the set of arms-control agreements already negotiated by the superpowers, particularly SALT I and SALT II. That would be a mistake. SALT I and SALT II are arms-control agreements, not disarmament agreements: they seek to provide the superpowers with a balanced and hopefully stable repertoire of armaments. Disarmament is not the intent of SALT, and no extension of the SALT process could eventuate in non-possession by either or both of the nuclear superpowers. To find proposals that lead towards non-possession, one must go back to the days before arms-control supplanted disarmament as the responsible liberal hope regarding nuclear weapons. This takes us back to 1946, to the early schemes for the internationalization of atomic weapons.

Internationalization of Nuclear Weapons

(a) Early Proposals

From the earliest days of the Manhattan Project, persons closely associated with the development of atomic weapons believed that the development of nuclear weapons was inconsistent with the traditional prerogatives of national sovereignty. The scientists who felt this way assumed (a) that the "atomic secret" could not be kept; (b) that peace between nations cannot be indefinitely maintained by mutual deterrence and the balance of power; and (c) that there is no feasible defense against atomic attack. In this view, continued insistence on national sovereignty must lead to a nuclear arms race and nuclear catastrophe. Perhaps the majority of scientists working on the Manhattan Project felt that the sole route to future peace was some form of internationalization of atomic energy and atomic weapons.[17] To these scientists, the appropriate political instrument for dealing with atomic energy and weapons would be the newly formed United Nations.

After Hiroshima, the views of American scientists began to register on the American government. On 7 January, 1946, Secretary of State Byrnes appointed a committee, chaired by Undersecretary Acheson, to report on international aspects of atomic energy. This committee appointed a five member Board of Consultants, including J. Robert Oppenheimer and David Lilienthal. After six grueling weeks, the board presented its report, which was endorsed by the Committee and forwarded to Byrnes. The "Acheson-Lilienthal Report" called for the establishment of:

> An international agency conducting all intrinsically dangerous operations in the nuclear field, with individual nations and their citizens free to conduct, under license and a minimum of inspection, all non-dangerous, or safe, operations.
>
> The international agency might take any one of several forms, such as a UNO Commission, or an international corporation or authority. We shall refer to it as Atomic Development Authority. It must have authority to own and lease property, and to carry on mining, manufacturing, research, licensing, inspecting, selling, or any other necessary operations.
>
> The proposal contemplates an international agency with exclusive jurisdiction to conduct all intrinsically dangerous operations in the field. This means all activities relating to raw materials, the construction and operation of production

plants, and the conduct of research in explosives. The large field of non-dangerous and relatively non-dangerous activities would be left in national hands.[18]

Neither Byrnes nor Truman endorsed the Acheson-Lilienthal Report. Without consulting any of the atomic scientists, Truman appointed financier Bernard M. Baruch to present *some* plan for international control of atomic energy to the United Nations. Described by Acheson as a person whose "reputation as a wise man was without foundation in fact and entirely self-propagated,"[19] Baruch presented his own official set of proposals to the United Nations on 14 June 1946.

Like the Acheson-Lilienthal proposals, the Baruch proposals called for the establishment of an international agency for the development of atomic energy. But the Baruch proposals differed from the Acheson-Lilienthal plan in several important respects. Baruch spelled out a timetable for the implementation of internationalization, and in Baruch's timetable other nations accepted restrictions on production of fissionable materials before the United States internationalized its stockpile of nuclear weapons. Second, Baruch proposed a set of sanctions for violations of the rules for internationalization, and insisted that these sanctions remain exempt from veto by the participating parties.

Neither of these provisions was acceptable to the Soviet delegation. Rather than accept a plan that left the United States with nuclear weapons on hand while depriving the Soviet Union of its ability to build them, the Soviets proposed that the United States give over its atomic bombs first, after which the arrangements for the control of fissionable materials could be completed. Second, the Soviets insisted on retaining their veto, which they viewed as their only defense against Western majorities in the General Assembly and the Security Council.

Discussions dragged on through 1946. The atmosphere of negotiation was progressively chilled by the deepening cold war, and the United States government hardly set a positive tone by continuing to manufacture atomic bombs and by setting two of them off in the summer of 1946. By 1947, when the Soviets began presenting plans for general and complete disarmament, the situation was irremediable. Remarkably, Truman's hope that the Soviets would accept the Baruch terms persisted until 1949.[20] Then Truman gave up on internationalization and issued orders for development of the thermonuclear weapons.

Four years later, Stalin was dead, Truman was gone, and both superpowers had the superbomb. With the world stunned and terrified by the size of the new weapons, the British and French submitted a new disarmament plan calling for a "no first strike" pledge, reductions in conventional arms, termination of nuclear weapons production, and the establishment of a control agency to inspect possible production. To everyone's astonishment, on 10 May, 1955, the Soviet Union accepted the substance of the British-French proposals. The Soviets called for the establishment of an international agency to "establish control at large ports, at railway junctions, on main motor highways, in aerodromes, to exercise control including inspection on a continuing basis and to have permanently in all States its own staff of inspectors having unimpeded access at all times to all objects of control."[21] This was close to what the United States had been demanding in the way of international control since 1946. But now it was 1955; NATO was committed to introducing tactical nuclear weapons, and Dulles had announced the policy of massive retaliation. At Geneva in July 1955, Eisenhower proposed that Soviet disarmament agreements be monitored by American overflights. The Soviets, recognizing that these overflights would provide the Strategic Air Command with maps needed to mount a successful atomic offensive, countered with a proposal for ground inspection posts. On 29 August, 1955, the United States announced:

> In view of these facts which have been set forth, the United States does now place a reservation upon all of its pre-Geneva substantive positions taken in this Sub-Committee or in the Disarmament Commission or in the United Nations on these questions in relationship to levels of armaments pending the outcome of our study jointly or separately of inspection methods and control arrangements and of review together of this important problem.[22]

The "moment of hope" was over.[23] The age of the ICBM was about to begin. Each superpower had proposed and each had rejected an agreement for the international control of atomic weapons. There was to be no disarmament, and the only thing left was deterrence.

New Steps Towards Internationalization

The Acheson-Lilienthal Plan was *not* a plan for an international agency that possessed atomic weapons: a world policeman with an atomic nightstick. As Oppenheimer explained, it called for the establishment of an agency that would control fissionable materials, thus preventing nuclear weapons from coming into being. By 1983, of course, the hope of preventing stocks of nuclear weapons from coming into being is vain: they are already here. Any proposal for non-possession-through-internationalization must recognize that internationalization requires collection of nuclear weapons by an international agency.

(a) Warheads

Currently, the International Atomic Energy Agency (IAEA) keeps track of radioactive materials used in nuclear power plants. Given this experience, the IAEA is the logical repository for nuclear weapons transferred under a new program of internationalization. The IAEA could either simply store the weapons, or could attempt to circulate diluted quantities of the fissionable materials in the weapons to nuclear power plants.

The United States, in years past, has made proposals for the transfer of fissionable weapons materials to civilian use. These proposals have foundered for lack of multilateral response. The United States could revive its earlier proposals, or it could proceed with the transfer on a unilateral basis. Such a unilateral initiative could remind the world that there are other options available than the present mixture of national sovereignty and nuclear terror.

Nevertheless, we must recognize that such transfers of warheads, whether multilateral or unilateral, address only a small part of the nuclear disarmament problem. There is plenty of plutonium in the world, and it would not be difficult, given an increase in world tensions, for "disarmed" states to start up manufacture of new nuclear warheads. In the age of nuclear scarcity, control of bombs and warheads seemed more important than control of delivery systems. In the present era of nuclear plenty, control of delivery systems is more important than control of warheads. Thus the ultimate step towards non-possession requires the internationalization, not just of warheads, but of strategic systems. What follows is a sequence of steps leading to this result. There may well be other sequences.

(b) Transfer of Information about Strategic Systems

In 1955, as part of the "Open Skies" proposal, President Eisenhower suggested that the United States and the Soviet Union swap blueprints of their respective strategic systems.[24] The Soviets rejected Eisenhower's suggestion, not least because the Soviets had no planes that could reach the facilties on the American maps while the United States had a fleet of B-47's that could reach the facilities on the Soviet maps. But nowadays it is possible for the Soviets to reach everything in the United States. Perhaps it is worth considering a revival of Eisenhower's suggestion.

Some will argue that the revelation of American "secrets" would be a grave breach of national security and would work to the disadvantage of the United States. Such fears are exaggerated. If the United States is truly committed to launching *only* a second strike, then the revelation of details about American capabilities would only serve to enhance American credibility. The main reason to keep one's strategic weapons and plans secret is to prevent the opponent from becoming aware of one's ability or intention to launch a first strike.

(c) Establishment of a Unitary Communications Post

Presently there is only a single communications link between the strategic systems of the superpowers: the "hot line" that connects the White House to the Kremin. The hot line teletype is of course better than nothing, but it has its weaknesses. In particular, it only links the political leaders of the superpowers, not the military men who might have a clearer picture of what is actually going on.

Thus, in addition to the hot line, the United States should set up a post, manned by American and Soviet personnel and linked directly with the warning systems of the two countries. The creation of such a communications post would, by itself, reduce the chance of accidental or unintended nuclear war. But the establishment of such a command center would also serve as a step towards internationalization, since the placement of international observers in the post would provide the world community with daily information about the operations of the two major strategic systems. And with such knowledge should come power.

(d) Transfer of the Keys

As time passes, the superpowers will become accustomed to the presence of international observers in the unitary communications post and the observers will become increasingly sophisticated in their study of superpower strategic systems. At some point, international observers should begin to move from the communications post into the two command centers of the two strategic systems. Gradually the competence of these observers will improve, so that eventually they will be able to control and operate the strategic systems themselves. At this point, the national operators should be progressively replaced by international operators. In dual key systems, the international operators will have one key. When the international operators are in place, the national operators should step back and the controlling links to the national leadership should be broken. Instead of two strategic systems pointed at each other, there will be one strategic system, pointed at nothing at all. The balance of terror will have been dissolved.

(e) Unilateral Internationalization?

All of the preceding steps have been envisaged as multilateral steps, taken simultaneously by the United States and the Soviet Union. But sometimes it is difficult to get the Soviets to agree. If they do not agree to swap blueprints or to set up a unitary communications post, is there any point in taking these steps unilaterally?

Perhaps there is. Regardless of Soviet participation, if American strategic facilities were gradually internationalized, the prestige of the International Atomic Energy Agency would be increased and the moral position of the United States would be enhanced. Furthermore, we could expect that nuclear weapons under international control would only be used in the event of a grave breach of world peace—not in the service of American national interests, should the pursuit of American interests be detrimental to world peace. For these reasons, unilateral internationalization, though not as attractive as bilateral internationalization, is still desirable from the moral point of view.

Moral Aspects of the Internationalization of Nuclear Weapons

Suppose that somehow or other the two major strategic systems come under the control of the IAEA. If so, the staff of the International Atomic Energy Agency will end up with far more power than was even envisaged for an international nuclear agency under the Acheson-Lilienthal plan. With power comes responsibility, and the question must be raised what the IAEA would do with its new power. One possibility would be to use this power to set up a world government, with the military force of the IAEA at its disposal.

Under this plan, there would still be nuclear weapons in the world, and still the possibility of their use. The difference would be that nuclear weapons would no longer be part of national arsenals for use in war; they would be part of the police power of the new world state, used to enforce world law, suppress insurrections, and prevent civil wars.

Any new world government would be sorely tempted to retain, and perhaps to use, the atomic police club. Retention of nuclear weapons would give the world government the preponderance of firepower against any rebel party, and the threat of nuclear punishment by the world government could prevent civil wars from ever getting started.

But our study of the moral challenges confronting the use of nuclear weapons under present conditions should lead us to reject the idea of a world police force armed with nuclear weapons. The same problems of proportionality and discrimination that make the use of nuclear weapons in war immoral should also lead us to recognize the immorality of using weapons to enforce world law. The nuclear response will never be proportional to the threat, and large numbers of innocent people will be killed by the world police. In present times, in countries that retain capital punishment, innocent people are occasionally killed by order of the courts. But at least in such cases, the victim is (hopefully) subjected to due process of law, and the dead are at least thought, with some reason, to be guilty. Atomic police operations would kill people whom by process of law we know to be innocent. That sort of killing no just judicial system can tolerate.

So there is no morally permissible use of strategic weapons after all strategic systems have been internationalized. In enforcing world law, the police force of the world state must stay within the moral law. They cannot do this if they are equipped with nuclear weapons. The strategic systems, once internationalized, must be dismantled. Instead of a police force armed with nuclear weapons, what the world state needs is a warning system and a special force to detect and seize clandestine nuclear devices.

Conventional Weapons in a Post-Nuclear World

In surveying schemes for international control, we have considered two possibilities: (a) the United States unilaterally transfers its strategic systems to international control; (b) the nuclear powers multilaterally transfer their strategic systems to international control. Suppose that the international authority that has assumed control of strategic systems does not intend to use them to preserve the peace or enforce international law. What steps might the United States take to preserve the peace after it gives up its nuclear weapons?

(a) Even if the United States unilaterally transferred its nuclear weapons to international control, by no means would the United States be disarmed. There would still be the Army, Navy, Air Force, and Marines. The question is whether the military services, shorn of nuclear weapons, could defend the

United States in a world in which other powers still possess nuclear weapons.

One thing is certain. If the United States gives up its nuclear weapons, it could not protect its people against an all-out nuclear attack. But this is not a devastating criticism. The United States cannot protect the American people against all-out nuclear attack *now*. Under present conditions, with the victory strategy, all the United States can do is try to persuade the Soviets, with threats and blandishments, not to attack the United States. Presumably, under non-possession, the United States would rely more on blandishments and less on threats as instruments of persuasion. Skeptics may say that such blandishments have no hope of protecting the United States. But there is a whole psychological literature devoted to showing that rewards for good actions are at least as effective in controlling behavior as are punishments for bad actions. In the long run, the carrot controls behavior far better than the stick.

One would hope that the United States, practicing non-possession, would become skillful in manipulating Soviet behavior through the system of rewards. But, like any system, the system of rewards might fail, and the consequences of failure are serious. In this context, it is vital to look once more at the question of defense against ballistic missiles. If the United States gives up its present missile systems, then all the research and resources currently devoted to the development of offensive missile systems can be transferred over to the problem of defense against ballistic missiles. Perhaps such research would produce a defense against missile attack, perhaps it would not. This much is clear: the development of such a defense against ballistic missiles would *not* be destabilizing. Ballistic missile defense is destabilizing only if the development of ballistic missiles defense by country A deprives its opponent B of needed second-strike capacity against it. If the United States had no missiles, it could not launch a first strike.

(b) If the nuclear powers jointly give up their nuclear weapons, they will still retain formidable arsenals of conventional arms. Some have suggested that nuclear disarmament will increase the chance that conventional wars will occur since nation states will no longer be deterred by the thought that wars can go nuclear. On this view, nuclear disarmament would make the world safe for non-nuclear war. But those who argue that nuclear disarmament increases the chance of conventional war *and* that conventional wars can be as devastating as some nuclear wars refute their own case. Conventional wars, like World War I, can be as devastating as a small scale nuclear war. But this fact provides a deterrent to conventional war just as the thought of nuclear holocaust provides a deterrent to nuclear war. True, the thought of a conventional holocaust will not provide a guarantee aganst conventional war. But the thought of nuclear holocaust will not provide a guarantee against conventional war either.

Fear of Disarmament: Reflections on the Cult of Strength

The switch from victory to detente and the move from detente to non-possession each require tremendous cuts in American strategic systems.

During the hostage crisis in Iran and after the Soviet invasion in Afghanistan, the American people were hostile to any demands for cuts in defense. Ronald Reagan campaigned successfully in 1980 on a pledge to build a "strong America." A "strong America" sounds like a good thing. A "weak America" sounds like a bad thing. If strong is necessarily good and weak is necessarily bad, then the recommendations of this chapter are a bad thing.

The Reagan campaign assumed that strength is necessarily a good thing. But the acquisition of strength, like anything else, can have good consequences and bad consequences. There are bad things that can come with strength, especially when "strength" derives from the power of nuclear weapons. A strong America can be a dangerous America, dangerous to the world, and dangerous to herself. At numerous points in this book we noted how the American search for strength has generated risks to innocent parties, risks which the United States has no moral right to inflict.

Nevertheless, many people are seized with fear at the prospect of being weak in a world of the strong. Thus, many Americans fear the prospect of living in a nation that has no nuclear weapons when other nations have them. Since this fear influences their evaluation of defense policies, it must be addressed. But since we are dealing here with emotions as much as thoughts, we must address it on a personal level, putting philosophical arguments aside.

I live in New York, a city in which there are about 1,600 homicides every year. Almost all New Yorkers fear being attacked on the streets, and many New Yorkers, especially older people, allow this fear to control the pattern of their daily lives. As one reads the daily reports of murders and muggings, as one realizes that the police are capable of apprehending only a small fraction of violent criminals, the desire develops to take steps towards one's own self-protection. For many people, a logical step towards their own self-protection is the acquisition of a handgun, which in their view cuts the criminals on the streets down to size.

People who have an interest in acquiring a handgun for their own self-defense have a clear picture in mind of the kind of circumstances in which handguns might save them. They see themselves under attack or about to be attacked; they see themselves flourishing the handgun; they see the attacker scared off or struck down. Since they believe that use of a gun in self-defense is morally permissible, they consider the acquisition of a handgun to be a step that is in their self-interest and breaks no moral law.

But there are hidden moral dimensions to the acquisition of a handgun. The situation in which one uses the handgun against a mugger is easily imagined. Less easily imagined are the other ways in which the handgun might be used. To begin with, there might be an accident: the gun purchaser might shoot himself or shoot someone else, thinking the gun not loaded. He might believe that he is under attack when he is not under attack, and shoot an innocent person by mistake. He might use the gun to commit suicide, a suicide that might not have been committed if the gun had not been available, or which might not have been successful if other methods had been attempted. He might use the gun in self-defense, but the self-defense might not succeed. Worse still, his attempt to use the gun in self-defense might provoke his attacker to use more force than he otherwise might have used. The gun purchaser might even become a killer himself, shooting the gun off in the middle of an argument or giving way to some overpowering passion for revenge. In addition to all this the gun might be stolen and do mischief in someone else's hands.

When one speaks about such things to people that buy hand-guns for self-protection, one receives assurances that these things will never happen with *this* particular gun. Such things only happen to other people, people who are careless, people who lack skill and self-control. But the same assurance has been provided by the other people, people whose loaded guns go off by accident, or who use guns to commit suicide, or who fire off guns in fits of passion.

True, the gun purchaser does not intend to bring about these results. He does not imagine that these results will occur, and he honestly believes that they will not happen. Yet this sort of thing happens every day. The gun purchaser must acknowledge that if they happen to other human beings, they can happen to him. If he is fair, he will admit if others can shoot themselves by accident, he can too. And if others lose control of themselves or misplace their guns, so can he. For he is human, too.

The statistics show that if a person acquires a handgun, it is far more likely that an innocent human being will be killed with it than that a murder will be stopped by it.[25] If we adopt an ethics of self-scrutiny, we will be led to accept responsibility, not only for the foreseen and intended consequences of our acts, but for consequences that we do not foresee but that statistics tell us are probable. In this case, if we study the statistics and realize that the purchase of a gun is far more likely to do harm than good, then we will recognize that it is morally irresponsible to acquire a gun.

In this case, the morally responsible decision is also the safe decision. Gun owners are the principal victims of their own guns. One may not *feel* safer without a handgun, but one *is* safer, and the statistics show it. If a person has bad luck, he might blunder into a situation in which he would be better off with a handgun: there is no denying that. But the number of such situations is far less than the number of situations in which he will learn, usually too late, that he would have been better off without a gun.

The ethics of self-scrutiny proposed here for judging personal choices can also serve as an ethics of national self-scrutiny for judging strategic choices. Like the city dweller thinking about muggers, the United States discovers itself in a world populated with powerful opponents, and desires to take steps in its own self-protection. For the supporter of victory, security for the United States requires that we have bigger guns than the opponent; for the supporter of detente, security requires that we have guns of the same size. In either case, the supporters of nuclear weapons are gripped by a mental picture showing how the possession of weapons prevents attack: somewhere in Moscow there is a man who would like to destroy the United States, who is about to give the order to destroy the United States, but who is stopped from doing so by the thought of American retaliation. With this scene vividly illuminated in the foreground, the entire background of unintended and unforeseen results—results which we know may happen but which we hope will not happen—fades into darkness. The ethics of self-scrutiny demands that the United States assume responsibility for these unintended risks. Once *all* the effects are brought into view, the judgment of what is morally acceptable may be radically changed.

It is, of course, *possible* that strategic weapons will prevent attack on the United States. It is possible that a handgun will prevent a mugging. But one is not likely to be mugged in the first place, and if one is mugged, the handgun may be of no help. Likewise, the United States might not be attacked if it had no strategic weapons, and it may be attacked even if it does have strategic weapons. For the ethics of self-scrutiny, the acquisition of strategic weapons by a sovereign state is as indefensible as the purchase of a handgun by a private citizen. For the logically proper moral accusation to make against nuclear deterrence is not that it is malevolent, but that it is morally irresponsible.

Notes

1. The sort of moral criticism that limits itself to a simple principled "nay" is well exhibited in Ramsey 1973.

In most cases, the experts will find other options in short order. When President Kennedy rejected, on moral grounds, proposals for an air attack on Cuba in October 1962, new alternatives were forthwith laid on the table. See Kennedy 1969 49.

2. The fact that the victory strategy is not merely confined to defending the United States but to the ultimate truimph of American influence is intimated in Weinberger's *Annual Report to Congress* for fiscal year 1983:

> For the long term our prospects are bright, provided we take prudent advantage of the great assets of the Free World—the resilience of democratic nations, the productivity and innovativeness of capitalism, the vigor of free societies. As President Reagan said, "the West won't contain Communism, it will transcend Communism." To transcend in peaceful competition, the United States and our allies need a long-term strategy that will build on our strengths with determination and persistence . . .
>
> For the natural strength of free societies to prevail in the long run, our defense strategy must do two things. First, it must bring to a halt the further expansion and consolidation of the Soviet military empire . . . Second, our strategy must see to it that the productivity and technological creativity of free societies are not exploited to make good the chronic deficiencies of the communist system.
>
> The Soviet leaders must know full well by now that their central planning system is fatally flawed. But their system cannot be reformed without liberalizing Soviet society as a whole.
>
> In the nuclear age, more than in any other period in human history, military strategy must be the servant of national policy, a policy that is the ultimate trustee of the nation's interests. [Weinberger 1982a 22]

It appears that Weinberger has here instituted a goal that even Paul Nitze rejected in NSC-68: the erection of a *cordon sanitaire* around Russia and the exertion of constant pressure, in the hopes that someday such pressure would bring down the Communist system.

3. All of the recommedations in this section could be characterized as "steps towards strategic stability." For more formal assessments of what makes for strategic stability, see Grotte 1980, 213–39; and Legault and Lindsey 1974.

4. The Boston Study Group recommended eliminating all but 100 land-based ICBMs in Boston Study Group 1978 78.

5. If detente called for air-launched cruise missiles, a certain number of B-52s would be retained as cruise missile launchers. But detente need not call for cruise missiles.

6. There *is* a small chance that Poseidon submarines will become vulnerable in future decades. The best estimates at present, however, indicate that they will remain invulnerable through the next century. If the Poseidons do become vulnerable, the United States will be aware of this fact long before the Soviets, since American research into anti-submarine warfare is far ahead of Soviet research. Given sufficient warning, steps could be taken to retain an invulnerable deterrent. See Wit 1981.

7. Robert McNamara called for a 50 percent reduction in tactical nuclear weapons in Europe, in McNamara 1983. The argument presented by McNamara, however, clearly implies that *all* NATO tactical nuclear weapons should be eliminated. A partial and more bi-lateral approach to the elimination of tactical nuclear weapons in Europe is presented in Blechman and Moore 1983.

8. One way of measuring the counterforce capacity of a missile is to devise an index that is a function of the accuracy of the missile and the intensity of its explosive charge. Such a measure, called the "k" or kill factor, takes the two-thirds power of the explosive charge and divides it by the square of the accuracy of the missile. The k-factors for present and planned systems are:

ICBMs		SLBMSs	
Minuteman II	$k = 9$	Poseidon C-3	$k = 2$
Minuteman III	$k = 34$	Trident C-4	$k = 12$
MX	$k = 204$	Trident D-5	$k = 24$

The cruise missile has an astounding k-factor of 1,305. Thus, in all categories, the new American missiles exhibit tremendous upward leaps in counterforce capacity.

9. The Soviets will certainly have reason to expect a stronger American reaction if they use nuclear weapons after a "no first use" pledge than before it. They will remember that Jimmy Carter's unexpectedly strong reaction to the Soviet invasion of Afghanistan was due to Carter's feeling that Brezhnev had lied to him about Soviet intentions in Afghanistan. On "no first use," see Gottfried 1983.

10. New technologies make verification of a Comprehensive Test Ban Treaty verifiable in ways that may satisfy American suspicions without being unacceptable to Soviet claims of territorial sanctity. See Sykes and Evernden, 1982.

11. Some of the details of a ban on the production of fissionable material for weapons are presented in Epstein 1980. In 1978 Paul Warnke suggested that the United States begin negotiations for such a treaty. The fate of this suggestions is chronicled with gusto by Brzezinski in his memoirs:

In early 1978, Vance and Warnke even proposed to the President that the United States initiate immediate negotiations with the Soviets on a production cutoff of fissionable materials for weapons. Since responsibility for nuclear weapons production rested with the Department of Energy, I forwarded the Vance-Warnke proposal to Secretary James Schlesinger for comment. As I had expected, Schlesinger produced a blistering memorandum, criticizing the proposal for lacking even the most basic supporting analysis and warning that it would prompt questions regarding U.S. stability and resolve. With his aid, I was able to nip this in the bud. [Brzezinkski 1983 316–17]

12. The wisdom of switching from multi-warhead missiles to single warhead missiles is acknowledged in the long range plans of President Reagan's Commission of Strategic Forces (The Scowcroft Commission):

The commssion believes that a single-warhead missile weighing about 15 tons (rather than the nearly 100 tons of MX) may offer greater flexibility in the long-run effort to obtain an ICBM force that is highly survivable, even when viewed in isolation, and that can consequently serve as a hedge against potential threats to the submarine force.

The commission thus recommends beginning engineering design of such an ICBM, leading to the initiation of full-scale development in 1987 and an initial operating capability in the early 1990s. The design of such a missile, hardened against nuclear effects, can be achieved with current technology. It should have sufficient accuracy and yield to put Soviet hardened military targets at risk. During that period an approach toward arms control, consistent with such deployments, should also seek to encourage the Soviets to move toward a more stable

ICBM force structure at levels which would obviate the need to deploy very large numbers of such missiles. The development effort for such a missile need not and should not be burdened with the uncertainties accompanying a crash program; thus its timing can be such that competitive development is feasible. [Scowcroft 1983]

13. The suggestion for a new fleet of mini-submarines each carrying a few missiles was one of the options under discussion as a basing mode for the MX. In 1967, the Defense Department's own Institute for Defense Analyses studied the mini-sub option in its comprehensive "Strat-X" study. Although the analysis was favorable, the Pentagon proceeded with the Trident (See Scoville 1981 99). Scoville recommends the mini-sub idea, though not mini-subs carrying the MX.

14. One book emphasizing the difficulties of the arms control process and superpower duplicity in this area is Myrdal 1976.

15. The proposals in this section may sound like a simple resurrection of the "no cities" strategy announced by Secretary McNamara in June of 1962. But the so-called "no cities" policy was not a policy to *never* strike cities. It was a strategy to strike cities only if American cities were struck (see Halperin 1962). The policy proposed here is that Soviet cities not be struck even if American cities are struck. The recommendations regarding targeting are a not wholly effective guarantee that such a city-avoidance policy will stick. For an informative history of American nuclear targeting policy, see Ball 1983.

16. The shift of interest from disarmament schemes to arms-control schemes is exhibited in the articles in Brennan 1961.

17. The history of the early schemes for internationalizing atomic weapons is given from the Atomic Energy Commission point of view of the atomic scientists in A.K. Smith 1965. An extremely critical view of Bernard Baruch's role is given in Herken 1982 151–70. A more sympathetic view of Baruch is in Wohlstetter 1979 55–62.

18. Lilienthal et al., 1946 558–559.

19. Acheson 1969 154.

20. On 14 July, 1949, Truman told his advisors, "I am of the opinion that we'll never obtain international control." (Rosenberg 1983 22.)

21. Bechhoefer 1961 292.

22. Bechhoefer 1961 311.

23. The "moment of hope" phrase is from Noel-Baker 1958 30.

24. Bechhoefer 1961 302–04.

25. Statistics regarding the effects of gun possession are notoriously difficult to assess, but the basic claims asserted here are upheld in Newton and Zimrig 1969. For a dissenting view, see Kleck and Bordua, 1982.

Bibliography of Works Cited

Abbott, M., S.J., ed. 1966. *Documents of Vatican II*. New York: American Press.

Abrams, Herbert, and von Kaenel, William. 1981. "Medical Problems of Nuclear War." *New England Journal of Medicine* 305:20 1226–32.

Acheson, Dean. 1969. *Present at the Creation*. New York: W. W. Norton.

Adams, Sherman. 1961. *Firsthand Report: The Story of The Eisenhower Administration*. New York: Harper & Row.

Adomeit, Hannes. 1982. *Soviet Risk Taking and Crisis Behavior*. London: Allen & Unwin.

Allais, M. 1953. "Le Comportement de L'Homme Rationnel Devant le Risque:

Critique des Postulats et Axiomes de L'ecole Americaine." *Econometrica* 21 (October).

Amster, William. 1956. "Design for Deterrence." *Bulletin of the Atomic Scientists* 12 (May).

Anderson, David A. 1976. *Strategic Air Command: Two-Thirds of the Triad*. New York: Scribner's.

Anscombe, Elizabeth. 1961. "War and Murder." In *Nuclear Weapons: A Catholic Response*, ed. Walter Stein. London: Merlin.

Arkin, William, and Pringle, Peter. 1983. *S.I.O.P.: The Secret U.S. Plan for Nuclear War*. New York: W.W. Norton.

Armacost, Michael. 1969. *The Politics of Weapons Innovation: The Thor-Jupiter Controversy*. New York: Columbia Univ. Press.

Arnold, H. H. 1946. "Air Force in the Atomic Age." In *One World Or None*, ed. Dexter Masters and Catherine Way, pp. 26–33. New York: McGraw Hill.

Arrow, Kenneth. 1951. *Social Choice and Individual Value*. New York: John Wiley.

Austin, John. 1961. "Negligence." In *Freedom and Responsibility*, ed. Herbert Morris. Stanford: Stanford University Press.

Axelrod, Robert. 1980a. "Effective Choice in the Prisoner's Dilemma." *Journal of Conflict Resolution* 24:1.

———. 1980b. "More Effective Choice in Prisoner's Dilemma." *Journal of Conflict Resolution* 24:3.

———. 1984. *The Evolution of Co-operation*. New York: Basic Books.

Baier, Kurt. 1958. *The Moral Point of View*. Ithaca: Cornell University Press.

Bailey, Sidney. 1972. *Prohibitions and Restraints in War*. Oxford: Oxford Univ. Press.

Bainton, R. H. 1960. *Christian Attitudes Towards War and Peace*. Nashville: Abingdon Press.

——. 1969. *Erasmus of Christendom*. New York: Scribner's.

Baker, John C., and Berman Robert P. 1982. *Soviet Strategic Forces: Requirements and Responses*. Washington, D.C.: Brookings Institute.

Ball, Desmond. 1975. *Deja Vu: The Return to Counterforce in the Nixon Administration*. California Seminar in Arms Control and Foreign Policy.

——. 1979. *Can Nuclear War Be Controlled?* London: Institute for Strategic Studies.

——. 1980a. *Politics and Force Levels: The Strategic Missile Program of the Kennedy Administration*. Berkeley: Univ. of California Press.

——. 1980b. "Soviet ICBM Deployment." *Survival* 22:4

——. 1981-82. "U.S. Strategic Forces: How Might They Be Used?" *International Security* 7:3 (Winter).

——. 1983. *Targeting for Strategic Deterrence*. London: Institute for Strategic Studies.

Ball, George. 1983. "Deterrence, Thresholds, and the Real World." *Proceedings of Senior Conference* XXI. West Point. Xeroxed.

Bamford, James. 1982. *The Puzzle Palace*. Boston: Houghton Mifflin.

Barnard, Chester I. 1945. See Lilienthal et al.

Beard, Edmund. 1976. *Developing the ICBM*. New York: Columbia Univ. Press.

Bechhoefer, Barnard G. 1961. *Postwar Negotiations for Arms Control*. Washington, D.C.: Brookings Institute.

Bennett, Jonathan. 1966. "Whatever the Consequences." *Analysis* 26: 83–102.

——. 1981. "Morality and Consequences" in *The Tanner Lecturers on Human Values, vol. II*; ed. Sterling M. McMurrin, pp. 45–85. Cambridge: Cambridge University Press.

Bentham, Jeremy. 1793. *An Introduction to the Principles of Morals and Legislation*, ed. L. Lafleur. New York: Oxford University Press, 1948.

Bernstein, Barton J. 1976. "The Week We Almost Went to War." *Bulletin of the Atomic Scientists* 32.

——. 1980. "The Cuban Missile Crisis: Trading the Jupiters in Turkey?" *Political Science Quarterly* 95.

Bertram, Christian, ed. 1981. *Strategic Deterrence in a Changing Environment*. London: Institute for Strategic Studies.

——. 1981. "Implications of Theater Nuclear Weapons for Europe." *Foreign Affairs* 60:2.

Best, Geoffrey. 1979. "Restraints on the Law of War Before 1945." In *Restraints on War*, ed. Michael Howard. New York: Oxford University Press.

——. 1970. *Humanity in Warfare*. New York: Columbia University Press.

Bethe, Hans, and Garwin, Richard. 1968. "Anti-Ballistic Missile Systems." *Scientific American* (March).

Bindschedler-Robert, D. 1970. *The Law of Armed Conflicts*. New York: Carnegie Endowment for International Peace.

Black, Edward. 1973. "Hegel on War." *The Monist* 57:4 (October).

Blechman, Barry M., and Kaplan, Stephen S. 1978. *Force Without War: U.S. Armed Forces as a Political Instrument*. Washington, D.C.: Brookings, Institute.

Blechman, Barry M., and Moore, Mark R. 1983. "A Nuclear Weapons Free Zone in Europe." *Scientific American*. (April).

Born, Max. *Einstein's Theory of Relativity*. 1924. London: Methuen, 1924.

Boston Study Group. 1978. *Winding Down: The Price of Defense*. San Francisco: W. H. Freeman.

Bracken, Paul. 1983. *The Command and Control of Nuclear Weapons*. New Haven: Yale University Press.

Braun, Ernest, and Macdonald, Stuart. 1978. *Revolution in Miniature: The History of the Impact of Semiconductor Electronics*. Cambridge: Cambridge University Press.

Brennan, Donald, ed. 1961. *Arms Control, Disarmament, and National Security*. New York: Braziller.

———. 1969. "The Case for Population Defense." In *Why ABM?* ed. John Holst and William Schneider. New York: Pergamon Press.

———. 1969. "The Case for the ABM" in Center 1969.

Brewer, Garry D., and Blair, Bruce. 1979. "War Games and National Security." *Bulletin of the Atomic Scientists* (June).

Broad, William J. 1982. "Rewriting the History of the H-Bomb." *Science* (19 Nov) 769–72.

Brodie, Bernard. 1945. *The Atomic Bomb and American Security*. New Haven: Yale University Press.

———. 1959. *Strategy in the Missile Age*. Princeton: Center for International Studies, Princeton University Press.

———. *Escalation and the Nuclear Option*. Princeton: Center for International Studies, Princeton University Press.

———. 1973. *War and Politics*. New York: Macmillan.

Brodie, Bernard; Corbett, Percy; Fox, T. R. and Wolfers, Arnold. 1946. *The Absolute Weapon*. New York: Harcourt, Brace.

Brown, Harold. 1979. *Report of the Secretary of Defense Harold Brown to the Congress on the FY 1980 Defense Budget* (25 January). Washington, D.C.: U.S. Government Printing Office.

Brownlie, Ian. 1963. *International Law and the Use of Force by States*. New York: Oxford University Press.

Brundage, J. A. 1969. *Medieval Canon Law and the Crusader*. Madison: University of Wisconsin Press.

Brzezinski, Zbigniew. 1983. *Power and Principles: Memoirs of the National Security Advisor 1977–1981*. New York: Farrar, Strauss, & Giroux, 1983.

Buchan, Alastair, ed. 1966. *A World of Nuclear Powers*. Englewood Cliffs: Prentice Hall.

Bueno de Mesquita, Bruce. 1981. *The War Game*. New Haven: Yale University Press.

Bundy, McGeorge; Kennan, George F.; McNamara, Robert S.; and Smith, Gerard. 1982. "Nuclear Weapons and the Atlantic Alliance." *Foreign Affairs* 60.4 (Spring).

Burns, Arthur Lee. 1959. "Disarmament or the Balance of Terror." *World Politics* 12:1.

Burt, Richard. 1977. "The SS-20 and the Euro-Strategic Balance." *World Today* (February).

Carter, Barry. 1974. "Nuclear Strategy and Nuclear Weapons." *Scientific American* (May).

Cave Brown, Anthony, ed. 1978. *Dropshot: The United States Plan for War with the Soviet Union in 1957*. New York: Dial Press.

Center for the Study of Democratic Institutions, ed. 1969. *Anti-Ballistic Missile: Yes or No?* New York: Hill & Wang.

Cicero, Marcus Tullius. *De Officis*, trans. Walter Miller. New York: Putnam, 1928.

———. *On the Commonwealth*, trans. G. H. Sabine and S. B. Smith. Indianapolis: Bobbs-Merrill, 1976.

Clancy, William, ed. 1961. *The Moral Dilemma of Nuclear Weapons*. New York: Council on Religion and International Affairs.

Clark, Ian. 1982. *Limited Nuclear War: Political Theory and War Conventions*. Princeton: Center for International Studies, Princeton University Press.

Clark, Ronald W. 1980. *The Greatest Power on Earth*. New York: Harper & Row.

Cochran, Thomas B., Arkin, William M. and Hoenig, Milton M. 1984. *Nuclear Weapons Databook*, Vol. I. Cambridge, Mass.: Ballinger.

Cockburn, Andrew. 1983. *The Threat: Inside the Soviet Military Machine*. New York: Random House.

Committee for the Compilation of Materials on Damage Caused by the Atomic Bombs. 1981. *Hiroshima and Nagasaki: The Physical, Medical, and Social Effects of the Atomic bombings*. New York: Basic Books.

Connell, F. J. 1967. "Double Effect, Principle of." *New Catholic Encyclopedia*. New York: McGraw Hill.

Cook, Fred J. 1964. *The Warfare State*. New York: Collier Macmillian.

Cox, Arthur Macy. 1982. *Russian Roulette: The Superpower Game*. New York: Times Books.

Craig, William. 1967. *The Fall of Japan*. New York: Dial Press.

Curie, Marie. 1910. *Trait de Radioactivité*, Paris: Gautier-Villais.

Dando, Malcom, and Newman, Barrie. *Nuclear Deterrence*. Tunbridge Wells: Castle.

Davis, Lynn Etheridge. 1981. "Limited Nuclear Options: Deterrence and the New American Doctrine." In *Strategic Deterrence in a Changing Environment*, ed. Christoph Bertram. London: Institute for Strategic Studies.

Degrasse, Robert W. 1983. *Military Expansion and Economic Decline*. New York: Council on Economic Priorities.

Dockrill, Michael, and Paskins, Barrie. 1979. *The Ethics of War*. Minneapolis, University of Minnesota Press.

Donagan, Alan. 1977. *Theory of Morality*. Chicago: University of Chicago Press.

Dougherty, James. See Nitze et al. 1979.

Douglas, Joseph D., and Hoeber, Amoretta M. 1981. *Conventional War and Escalation: The Soviet View*. New York: Crane, Russak.

Dunnigan, James F. 1983. *How To Make War*. New York: William Morrow.

Dworkin, Ronald. 1978. *Taking Rights Seriously*. Cambridge, MA: Harvard, University Press.

Dyson, Freeman. 1979. *Disturbing the Universe*. New York: Harper & Row.

Ehrlich, Paul *et. al.* 1983. "Long Term Biological Consequences of Nuclear War." *Science* (23 December).

Einstein, Albert. 1916. *Relativity: The Special and General Theory*. New York: Crown Publishers, 1961.

Eisenhower, Dwight D. 1963. *Mandate for Change*. New York: Doubleday.

Ellsberg, Daniel. 1960. "The Theory and Practice of Blackmail." In *Bargaining: Formal Theories of Negotiation*, ed. Oran Young. Urbana: University of Illinois Press, 1975.

———. 1981. "A Call To Mutiny." In *Protest and Survive*, ed. E. P. Thompson and Dan Smith. New York: Monthly Review Press.

Enthoven, Alain C., and Smith, K. Wayne. 1971. *How Much Is Enough? Shaping the Defense Program 1961–1969*. New York: Harper & Row.

Epstein, William. 1979. "Nuclear Terrorism and Nuclear War." In *The Dangers of Nuclear War*, ed. Franklin Griffiths and John C. Palanyi. Toronto: University of Toronto Press.

————. 1980. "A Ban on the Production of Fissionable Material for Weapons."
  Scientific American (July).
Etzold, Thomas, and Gaddis, John Lewis, eds. 1978. *Containment: Documents on
  American Policy and Strategy 1945–1960.* New York: Columbia University Press.
Evernden, Jack. See Sykes and Evernden 1982.
Fallows, James. 1981. *National Defense.* New York: Harper & Row.
Feinberg, Joel. 1973. *Social Philosophy.* Englewood Cliffs: Prentice-Hall.
Feis, Herbert. 1966. *The Atomic Bomb and the End of World War II.* Princeton:
  Princeton Univ. Press.
Feld, Bernard. 1976. "The Consequences of Nuclear War." *Bulletin of the Atomic
  Scientists* (June).
Feldman, Fred. 1978. *Introductory Ethics.* Englewood Cliffs: Prentice-Hall.
Fleming, D. F. 1961. *The Cold War and its Origins.* Garden City: Doubleday.
Foot, Philppa. 1967. "The Problem of Abortion and the Principle of Double Effect."
  Oxford Review; also in Rachels 1975.
Ford, John C. S. J. 1944. "The Morality of Obliteration Bombing." In *War and
  Morality,* ed. Richard Wasserstrom. Belmont: Wadsworth 1970.
Foster, G. 1982. "The Effect of Deterrence on the Fighting Ethic." In *Nuclear
  Deterrence,* ed. Malcom Dando and Barrie Newman. Tunbridge Wells: Castle.
Franck, J., et. al. 1945. *A Report to the Secretary of War.* In Smith, Alice Kimball, *A
  Peril and a Hope,* Appendix B. Chicago, University of Chicago Press, 1965.
Freedman, Lawrence. 1981. *The Evolution of Nuclear Strategy.* New York: St.
  Martins Press.
Frei, Daniel. 1983. *Risks of Unintentional Nuclear War.* Totowa, N.J.: Allanheld,
  Osmun.
Frey, R. G. 1975. "Some Aspects of the Doctrine of Double Effect." *Canadian
  Journal of Philosophy* 5.
Fried, Charles. 1970. *An Anatomy of Value.* Cambridge, Mass: Harvard University
  Press.
————. 1978. *Right and Wrong.* Cambridge, Mass: Harvard University Press.
Friedberg, Aaron L. 1981. "A History of U.S. Strategic Doctrine." In *Strategy and
  the Social Sciences,* eds. Amos Perlmutter and John Gooch. London: Frank Cass.
Friedman, Leon, ed. 1972. *The Laws of War.* New York: Random House.
Gaddis, John Lewis. 1972. *The United States and the Origins of the Cold War.* New
  York: Columbia University Press.
————. 1982. *Strategies of Containment: A Critical Appraisal of Postwar American
  National Security Policy.* New York: Oxford University Press.
Gaddis, John Lewis and Etzold, Thomas. See Etzold and Gaddis 1978.
Gallois, Pierre. 1961. *The Balance of Terror: Strategy for the Nuclear Age.* Boston:
  Houghton Mifflin.
Gandhi, Mohandas. 1961. *Non-Violent Resistance.* New York: Shocken.
Gansler, Jacques. 1980. *The Defense Industry.* Cambridge, Mass.: MIT Press.
Garwin, Richard, and Bethe, Hans. 1968. "Anti-Ballistic Missile Systems." *Scientific
  American* (March).
George, Alexander, and Smoke, Richard. 1974. *Deterrence in American Foreign
  Policy: Theory and Practice.* New York: Columbia University Press.
Gewirth, Alan. 1980. "Human Rights and the Prevention of Cancer." *American
  Philosophical Quarterly* (April).
Gilpin, Robert. 1962. *American Scientists and Nuclear Weapons Policy* Princeton:
  Center for International Studies, Princeton University Press.
Glasstone, Samuel, ed. 1977. *The Effects of Nuclear Weapons.* 3rd ed. Washington,
  D.C.: U.S. Atomic Energy Commission.

Glover, Jonathan. 1977. *Causing Death and Saving Lives*. London: Penguin.
Glover, Trudy. 1979. "What Shall We Do About Future People?" *American Philosophical Quarterly*.
Goldman, Alan. 1981. *The Moral Foundations of Professional Ethics*. Totowa, N.J.: Rowman & Littlefield.
Goldwater, Barry. 1962. *Why Not Victory?* New York: McGraw Hill.
Gooch, John. See Perlmutter and Gooch 1981.
Gottfried, Kurt and Kendall, Henry W. 1984. "No First Use of Nuclear Weapons" *Scientific American* (March).
Gray, Colin S. 1977. *The Geopolitics of the Nuclear Era*. New York: Crane, Russak.
———. 1979. "Nuclear Strategy: The Case for a Theory of Victory." *International Security* (Summer).
———. 1981. *The MX ICBM and National Security*. New York: Praeger.
———. 1982. *Strategic Studies and Social Policy*. Lexington: University of Kentucky Press.
———. 1982b. *Strategic Studies: A Critical Assessment*. Westpoint: Greenwood Press.
Gray, Colin S., and Payne, Keith. 1980. "Victory Is Possible." *Foreign Policy* (Summer).
Green, Philp. 1966. *Deadly Logic*. Columbus: Ohio State University Press.
Griesz, Germain G. 1970. "Towards Consistent Natural Law Ethics of Killing." *American Journal of Jurisprudence* 15.
Grotius, Hugo. *De Juri Belli ac Pacis Libri Tres*, trans. Francis Kelsey. New York: Oxford University Press, 1925.
Grotte, Jeffrey H. 1980. "Measuring Strategic Stability with Two-Strike Nuclear Exchange Models." *Journal of Conflict Resolution* 24:2.
Groves, Leslie. 1962. *Now It Can Be Told*. New York: Harper & Row.
Gulley, Bill. 1980. *Breaking Cover*. New York: Simon & Schuster.
Gury, J. P. 1953–54. *Compendium Theologiae Moralis*. Ed. Tommaso Ioria. Naples: M. d'Auria.
Hahn, Otto. 1970. *My Life*, trans. Ernest Kaiser and Eithne Wilkins. London: Macdonald.
Haldeman, H. R., with diMona, Joseph. 1978. *The Ends of Power*. New York: Times Books.
Halloran, Richard. 1982. "Pentagon Draws Up First Strategy for Fighting a Long Nuclear War." *The New York Times* (30 May).
Halperin, Morton. 1962. "The 'No Cities' Doctrine." *New Republic* (8 October).
———. 1962. *Limited War in the Nuclear Age*. New York: Wiley.
Hardin, Russell. 1983. "Unilateral vs. Multi-lateral Disarmament." *Philosophy and Public Affairs* (Summer).
Hare, R. M. 1973. *Applications of Moral Philosophy*. New York: Oxford University Press.
Hart, H. L. A. 1968. *Punishment and Responsibility*. New York: Oxford University Press.
Harvard Nuclear Study Group. 1983. *Living With Nuclear Weapons*. Cambridge, Mass.: Harvard University Press.
Healy, Edwin F. S. J. 1960. *Moral Guidance*. Chicago: Loyola.
Hegel, G. W. F. 1802. *Natural Law*. trans. T. M. Knox. Philadelphia: University of Pennsylvania Press, 1975.
———. 1820. *Philosophy of Right*. trans. T. M. Knox, New York: Oxford University Press, 1952.
Herken, Gregg. 1980. *The Winning Weapon*. New York: Alfred A. Knopf.

Hersey, John. 1946. *Hiroshima*. New York: Alfred A. Knopf.

Hewlitt, Richard, and Anderson, Oscar. 1962. *The New World 1939/46: A History of the Atomic Energy Commission*, vol. 1. University Park: State University of Pennsylvania Press.

Hobbes, Thomas. 1651. *Leviathan*, ed. Michael Oakeshott. New York: Collier, 1962.

Hoeber, Amoretta. See Douglas and Hoeber 1981.

Hoffman, Stanley. 1981. "NATO and Nuclear Weapons." *Foreign Affairs* 60:2.

Holloway, David. 1983. *The Soviet Union and the Arms Race*. New Haven: Yale University Press.

Holst, Johan J., and Nerlich, Uwe, eds. 1977. *Beyond Nuclear Deterrence*. New York: Crane Russak.

Holst, Johan J., and Schneider, William, eds. 1969. *Why ABM?* New York: Pergamon Press.

Hoopes, Townsend. 1973. *The Devil and John Foster Dulles*. Boston: Little, Brown.

Howard, Michael. 1979. *Restraints on War*. New York: Oxford University Press.

Hughes, G. Philip. 1978. "Cutting the Gordian Knot: A Theater Nuclear Force for Europe." *Orbis* (Summer).

Ikle, Fred. 1973. "Can Nuclear Deterrence Last Out the Century?" *Foreign Affairs* 51:2.

Institute for Strategic Studies. *The Military Balance*. London: Institute for Strategic Studies. Yearly.

Intriligator, Michael D. 1968. "The Debate Over Missile Strategy." *Orbis*.

———. 1967. *Strategy in a Missile War: Targets and Rates of Fire*. Berkeley: University of California Press.

Jeffries, Zay *et al.* 1944. *Prospects on Nucleonics* (18 November) In Smith, Alice Kimball, *A Peril and a Hope*, Appendix A. Chicago: University of Chicago Press, 1965.

Johnson, J. T. 1981. *Just War Tradition and the Restraint of War*. Princeton: Center for International Studies, Princeton University Press.

Kahan, Jerome H. 1975. *Security in the Nuclear Age: Developing U.S. Strategic Arms Policy*. Washington, D.C.: Brookings Institute.

Kahn, Herman. 1960. *On Thermonuclear War*. Princeton: Center for International Studies, Princeton University Press.

Kahneman, David and Tversky, Amos. 1979. "Prospect Theory: An Analysis of Decision Under Risk." *Econometrica* 47:2.

———. 1981. "The Framing of Decisions and the Psychology of Choice." *Science*. (30 January)

———. 1982. "The Psychology of Preferences." *Scientific American* (January).

Kant, Immanuel. 1785. *Foundations of the Metaphysics of Morals*, trans. Lewis White Beck. New York: Bobbs-Merrill, 1959.

———. 1793. *On the Old Saw: It May Be Right In Theory But It Won't Work In Practice*, trans. E. B. Ashton. Philadephia: University of Pennsylvania Press, 1974.

———. 1795. "Perpetual Peace." In *On History*, trans. Lewis White Beck. New York: Bobbs-Merrill, 1963.

Kaplan, Fred. 1978. "Enhanced Radiation Weapons." *Scientific American* (May).

———. 1983. "Cruise Missile: Wonder Weapon or Dud?" *High Technology* (February) 26–34.

———. 1982. "Russian and American Intentions." *Atlantic Monthly* (July).

———. 1983. *The Wizards of Armageddon*. New York: Simon & Schuster.

Kaplan, Morton A. 1959. *The Strategy of Limited Retaliation*. Princeton: Center for International Studies, Princeton University Press.

————, ed. 1973. *Strategic Thinking and its Moral Implications*. Chicago: University of Chicago Press.

Karas, Thomas. 1983. *The New High Ground: Strategies and Weapons of Space Age War*. New York: Simon & Schuster.

Katz, Arthur M. 1982. *Life After Nuclear War*. Cambridge, Mass.: Ballinger.

Kaufmann, William. "The Requirements of Deterrence," Memo #27. Princeton: Center for International Studies, Princeton University Press, (November).

————, ed. 1956. *Military Policy and National Security*. Princeton: Princeton Univ. Press.

————. 1964. *The McNamara Strategy*. New York: Harper & Row.

Kavka, Gregory. 1978. "Some Paradoxes of Deterrence." *Journal of Philosophy* (June).

————. 1980. "Deterrence, Utility, and Rational Choice." *Theory and Decision* 12.

————. 1983. "Doubts About Unilateral Disarmament." *Philosophy and Public Affairs* (Summer).

Keen, M. H. 1965. *The Laws of War in the Middle Ages*. Toronto: University of Toronto Press.

Keesing's Research Service. 1971. *Disarmament Negotiations and Treaties 1946–1971*. New York: Scribner's.

Kennan, George, F. 1982. "On Nuclear War," *New York Review of Books* (23 January).

————. 1982. "NATO and Nuclear Weapons," See Bundy et al. 1982.

Kennedy, Robert F. 1969. *Thirteen Days*. New York: Signet.

King, James. 1957. "Nuclear Weapons and Foreign Policy II: Limited Annihilation." *New Republic* (15 July).

Kinnard, Douglas. 1977. *President Eisenhower and Strategic Management: A Study in Defense Politics*. Lexington: University of Kentucky Press.

Kissinger, Henry. 1957. *Nuclear Weapons and Foreign Policy*. New York: Harper & Row.

————. 1961. *The Necessity for Choice*. New York: Harper Brothers.

————. 1979a. *White House Years*. Boston: Little Brown.

————. 1979b. "NATO: The Next Thirty Years." *Survival*. (Nov./Dec.).

————. 1982. *Years of Upheaval*. Boston: Little Brown.

Kleck, Gary, and Bordua, David. 1982. "The Assumptions of Gun Control." *Federal Regulation of Firearms*. United States Senate Committee on the Judiciary. Washington, D.C.: U.S. Government Printing Office.

Kolko, Gabriel. 1968. *The Politics of War: The World and United States Foreign Policy 1939–1945*. New York: Random House.

Kolko, Gabriel, and Kolko, Joyce. 1972. *The Limits of Power*. New York: Harper & Row.

Krosney, Herbert. See Weissmann and Krosney 1982.

Lackey, Douglas. 1975. "Ethics and Nuclear Deterrence." In *Moral Problems*, ed. James Rachels. New York: Harper & Row.

————. 1982a. "A Modern Theory of Just War." *Ethics* (April).

————. 1982b. "Missiles and Morals: A Utilitarian Look at Nuclear Deterrence." *Philosophy and Public Affairs* (Summer).

————. 1983. "Disarmament Revisited." *Philosophy and Public Affairs* (Summer).

————. 1984. "The Intentions of Deterrence." In *Nuclear Weapons and the Future of Humanity*, ed. Avner Cohen and Steven Lee. Totowa, N.J.: Allenheld, Osmun.

Lapp, Ralph. 1969. *International Herald Tribune* (6 March).

Legault, Albert, and Lindsey, George. 1974. *The Dynamics of the Nuclear Balance*. Ithaca: Cornell University Press.

Leghorn, Richard S., Col. 1955. "No Need to Bomb Cities To Win War." *U.S. News and World Report* (28 January).

Leitenberg, Milton. 1981. "Presidential Directive 59 and American Nuclear Weapons Targeting Policy." *Journal of Peace Research*.

Lens, Sidney. 1970. *The Military Industrial Complex*. Philadelphia: Pilgrim Press.

————. 1977. *The Day Before Doomsday*. Boston: Beacon Press.

Liddell-Hart, B. J. 1960. *Deterrence Or Defense?* New York: Praeger Publishers.

Lifton, Robert Jay. 1968. *Death in Life*. New York: Harper & Row.

Lilienthal, David; Barnard, Chester I., Oppenheimer, Robert. Thomas, Charles A., and Winne, Harry A. 1945. *A Report on the International Control of Atomic Energy*. Department of State Publication 2498 (16 March). Washington, D.C.: Superintendent of Documents.

Lindsay, George. See Legault and Lindsay 1974.

Little, I. M. D. 1950. *A Critique of Welfare Economics*. Oxford: Oxford University Press.

Locke, John. 1690. *Two Treatises of Government*, ed. Thomas I. Cook. New York: Hafner, 1973.

Luce, R. Duncan, and Raiffa, Howard. 1957. *Games and Decisions*. New York: John Wiley.

McCormick, R. A. 1967. "War, Morality of." *New Catholic Encyclopedia*. New York: McGraw Hill.

McPhee, John. 1975. *The Curve of Binding Energy*. Cambridge, Mass.: Ballantine.

McNamara, Robert S. 1962. Commencement Address at the University of Michigan at Ann Arbor (16 June). Excerpts. *The New York Times* (17 June).

————. 1965. *Statement of the Secretary of Defense Before the House Armed Services Committee* (18 February). Washington, D.C.: Superintendent of Documents.

————. 1968. *The Essence of Security*. New York: Harper & Row.

————. 1983. "The Military Role of Nuclear Weapons: Perceptions and Misperceptions." *Foreign Affairs* 62:1.

Mandelbaum, Michael. 1979. *The Nuclear Questions: The United States and Nuclear Weapons 1946–1976*. Cambridge: Cambridge University Press.

Mangan, Joseph T. S. J. 1949. "A Historical Analysis of the Principle of Double Effect." *Theological Studies* 19.

Martin, Lawrence. 1967. *Strategic Thought in the Nuclear Age*. Baltimore: Johns Hopkins.

Masters, Dexter, and Way, Katherine, eds. 1946. *One World Or None*. New York: McGraw Hill.

Maxwell, Neville. 1973. "The Chinese Account of the 1969 Fighting at Chenpao." *China Quarterly* (Fall).

Melman, Seymour. 1974. *The Permanent War Economy: American Capitalism in Decline*. New York: Simon & Schuster.

Melzer, Yehuda. 1975. *Concepts of Just War*. Leiden: Sijthoff.

Mill, John Stuart. 1861. *Utilitarianism*. Garden City: Doubleday, 1961.

Montmarquet, James A. 1982. "Doing Good: The Right Way and Wrong Way." *Journal of Philosophy* (August).

Moore, G. E. 1912. *Ethics*. Oxford: Oxford University Press.

Moore, Mark R. See Blechman and Moore 1983.

Morgenstern, Oskar. 1959. *The Question of National Defense*. New York: Random House.

Morgenthau, Hans. 1949. *Politics Among Nations*. New York, Alfred A. Knopf.

Murphy, Dervla. 1982. *Nuclear Stakes*. New York: Ticknor & Fields.

Murphy, Jeffrie G. 1980. "Blackmail: A Preliminary Inquiry." *The Monist* (April).

Murray, John Courtney. 1959. "Theology and Modern War" *Theological Studies* 20: 40–61.

Myrdal, Alva. 1972. "The Game of Disarmament." *Impact of Science on Society* 22:3.

———. 1976. *The Game of Disarmanent: How the United States and Russia Run the Arms Race.* New York: Pantheon.

Nagel, Thomas. 1979. "Ruthlessness in Public Life." In *Mortal Questions,* Cambridge: Cambridge University Press.

———. 1980. "The Limits of Objectivity." *Tanner Lectures on Human Value,* vol. 1. Salt Lake City: University of Utah Press.

Nagle, W. J., ed. 1960. *Morality and Modern War.* Baltimore: Helicon.

Narveson, Jan. 1967. *Morality and Utility.* Baltimore: Johns Hopkins.

———. 1965. "Pacifism: A Philosophical Analysis," *Ethics* 75: 259–71. Reprinted in Wasserstrom 1970.

National Academy of Sciences. 1975. *Long-Term Effects of Multiple Nuclear Weapons Detonations.* Washington, D.C.: National Academy of Sciences.

National Council of Australian Catholic Bishops. 1958. "Social Justice Statement for 1958." *Catholic Mind* (November-December).

National Council of Catholic Bishops ad hoc Committee on Peace and Disarmament. 1982. "The Challenge of Peace: God's Promise and our Response." *Origins* 12:20.

———. 1983. *The Challenge of Peace: God's Promise and Our Response* (3 May). Washington, D.C.: National Council of Catholic Bishops.

Newhouse, John. 1973. *Cold Dawn: The Story of Salt.* New York: Holt, Reinhart, & Winston.

Newton, George D., and Zimrig, Franklin E. n.d. *Firearms and Violence in American Life.* Washington, D.C.: Superintendent of Documents.

Nitze, Paul. 1976a. "Assuring Strategic Stability in an Era of Detente." *Foreign Affairs* 54:2.

———. 1976b. "Strategic Stability." *Foreign Affairs* 54:3.

———. 1977. "Deterring Our Deterrent." *Foreign Policy* 25.

Nitze, Paul; Dougherty, James, and Kane, Francis X. 1979. *The Fateful Ends and Shades of SALT.* New York: Crane, Russak.

Nixon, Richard M. 1970. *U.S. Foreign Policy for the 1970's: A New Strategy for Peace.* Washington, D.C.: Office of the White House Press Secretary (18 February).

———. 1978. *RN: The Memoirs of Richard Nixon.* New York: Grosset & Dunlap.

Noel-Baker, Philip. 1958. *The Arms Race: A Programme for World Disarmament.* London: Stevens & Son.

Norton, Bryan G. 1982. "Environmental Ethics and the Rights of Future Generations." *Environmental Ethics* (Winter).

Nozick, Robert. 1969. "Coercion." In *Philosophy, Science, and Method,* ed. Sidney Morgenbesser et. al. New York: St. Martin's Press.

———. 1974. *Anarchy, State, and Utopia.* New York: Basic Books.

Nussbaum, Arthur. 1954. *Concise History of the Law of Nations.* New York: Macmillian.

O'Brien, William V. 1967. *Nuclear War, Deterrence, and Morality* Westminister: Newman.

———. 1981. *The Conduct of Just and Limited War.* New York: Praeger Publishers.

Office of Technology Assessment (U.S. Congress). 1979. *The Effects of Nuclear War.* Totowa, N.J.: Allanheld, Osmun, 1980.

Osada, Arata, ed. 1959. *Children of the A-Bomb,* trans. Jean Dan and Ruth Sieben-Morgen. Tokyo: Uchida Rokakuho.

Paolucci, Henry, ed. 1962. *The Political Writings of St. Augustine*. Chicago: Regnery.

Parfit, Derek. 1983. "Energy Policy and the Further Future." In *Energy and the Future*, ed. Douglas Maclean. Totowa, N.J.: Rowman & Littlefield.

Parmentola, John. See Tsipis and Parmentola 1977.

Paskins, Barrie. See Dockrill and Paskins 1979.

Peeters, Paul. 1959. *Massive Retaliation*. Chicago: Regnery.

Perlmutter, Amos, and Gooch, John, eds. 1981. *Strategy and the Social Sciences*. London: Frank Cass.

Peterson, Jeannie, ed. 1983. *The Aftermath: The Human and Ecological Consequences of Nuclear War*. New York: Pantheon Books

Phillipson, Coleman. 1911. *The International Law and Custom of Ancient Greece and Rome*. London: Macmillian.

Pipes, Richard. 1977. "Why the Soviet Union Thinks It Could Fight and Win a Nuclear War." *Commentary* (July).

Podhoretz, Norman. 1976. "Making the World Safe for Communism." *Commentary* (April).

Polmar, Norman. 1982. *Strategic Weapons: An Introduction*. New York: Crane, Russak.

Potter, Ralph. n.d. *The Moral Logic of War*. Philadelphia, United Presbyterian Church.

Potter, William C. 1982. *Nuclear Power and Nonproliferation*. Cambridge: Oegeschlager Gunn & Hain.

Praeger, Robert J., ed. 1976. *Detente and Defense: A Reader*. Washington: American Enterprise Institute.

Quester, George. 1970. *Nuclear Diplomacy: The First Twenty-Five Years*. New York: Dunellen.

———. 1973. *The Politics of Nuclear Proliferation*. Baltimore: Johns Hopkins University Press.

Rachels, James, 1975a. "Active and Passive Euthanasia," *New England Journal of Medicine* 242: 78–80.

———, ed. 1975. *Moral Problems*. New York: Harper & Row.

Raiffa, Howard. 1968. *Decision Analysis: Introductory Lectures on Choices Under Uncertainty*. Reading, Mass.: Addison-Wesley, 1968.

Raloff, Janet. 1983. "Beyond Armageddon." *Science News* 12.

Ramsey, Paul. 1961. *War and the Christian Conscience*. Durham: Duke University Press.

———. 1968. *The Just War*. New York: Scribner's.

———. 1973. "A Political Ethics Context for Strategic Thinking." In *Strategic Thinking and Its Moral Implications*, ed. Morton Kaplan. Chicago: University of Chicago Press.

———. 1982. Letter. *Newsweek* (5 July).

Ranft, Bryan. 1979. "Restraints on War at Sea Before 1945." In *Restraints On War*, ed. Michael Howard. New York: Oxford University Press.

Rapaport, Anatol. 1964. *Strategy and Conscience*. New York: Harper & Row.

Rawls, John. 1975. *A Theory of Justice*. Cambridge, Mass.: Harvard University Press.

Reagan, Ronald. 1983. Speech on Defense Policy. 22 March. *The New York Times* (23 March).

Rescher, Nicholas. 1983 *Risk*. Washington, D.C.: University Press of America.

Ridenour, Louis N. 1946. "There Is No Defense." In *One World or None*, eds. Dexter Masters and Katherine Way, pp. 33–39. New York: McGraw Hill.

Roherty, James M. 1970. *Decisions of Robert Ɔ. McNamara*. Coral Gables: University of Miami Press.

Rose, John P. 1980. *The Evolution of U.S. Army Nuclear Doctrine*. Boulder: Westview.

Rosenberg, David Alan. 1979. "American Nuclear Strategy and the Hydrogen Bomb Decision." *Journal of American History* 66.

―――. 1981. "A Smoking Radiating Ruin at the End of Two Hours: American Plans for Nuclear War with the Soviet Union 1954–1955." *International Security* 6:3 (Winter).

―――. 1982. "U.S. Nuclear Stockpile 1945–1950." *Bulletin of the Atomic Scientists* 38 (May).

―――. 1983. "The Origins of Overkill: Nuclear Weapons and American Strategy, 1945–1960." *International Security* 7:4 (Spring).

Rosenfeld, Stephen A. 1977. "A Hawkish Argument with Holes." *Washington Star* (8 July).

Rostow, Eugene, 1979. "The Case Against SALT II." *Commentary* (February).

Rowen, Henry. 1979. "The Evolution of Strategic Nuclear Doctrine." In *Strategic Thought in the Nuclear Age*, ed. Lawrence Martin. Baltimore: Johns Hopkins University Press.

Rubin, Alfred P. 1983. "Nuclear Weapons and International Law." In *Proceedings of Senior Conference*, XXI. West Point. Xeroxed.

Russell, Bertrand. 1910. "The Elements of Ethics." *Philosophical Essays*. New York: Simon & Schuster, 1968.

―――. 1959. *Common Sense and Nuclear Warfare*. New York: Simon & Schuster.

―――. 1961. *Has Man A Future?* New York: Penguin.

Russell, Bryce. 1977. "The Relative Strictness of Positive and Negative Duties." *American Philosophical Quarterly* 14:2.

Russell, F. H. 1975. *The Just War in the Middle Ages*. Cambridge: Cambridge University Press.

Russell, Ruth B. 1958. *A History of the United Nations Charter*. Washington, D.C.: Brookings Institute.

Russett, Bruce. 1983. *The Prisoners of Insecurity*. San Francisco.

―――, ed. 1972. *Peace, War, Numbers*. Beverley Hills: Sage, 1972.

Rutherford, Ernest, and Soddy, R. 1903. "Radioactive Change." *Philosophical Mazagine* 6:5.

―――. 1904. *Radio-activity*. Cambridge: Cambridge University Press.

Ryan, C. C. 1983. "Self-Defense and the Possibility of Killing." *Ethics* 93:3.

Sagan, Carl. 1983. "Nuclear War and Climatic Catastrophe." *Foreign Affairs* 62/2, Winter.

Sapolsky, Henry M. 1972. *The Polaris System Development*. Cambridge, Mass.: Harvard University Press.

Scheer, Robert. 1983. *With Enough Shovels: Reagan, Bush and Nuclear War*. New York: Random House.

Schell, Jonathan. 1982. *The Fate of the Earth*. New York: Alfred A. Knopf.

Schelling, Thomas. 1960. *The Strategy of Conflict*. Cambridge, Mass.: Harvard University Press

―――. 1982. "Thinking About Nuclear Terrorism." *International Security* 6:4.

Schilling, Warner. 1961. "The H-Bomb Decision: How to Decide Without Actually Choosing." *Political Science Quarterly* 77.

―――, ed. 1973. *American Arms and a Changing Europe*. New York: Columbia University Press.

Schindler, Dietrich, and Toman, Jiri. 1970. *The Laws of Armed Conflict*. Leiden: Sijthoff.

Schlesinger, James R. 1974. *Report of the Secretary of Defense James R. Schlesinger on the FY 1965 Defense Budget and the FY 1975–1976 Defense Program* (4 March). Washington, D.C.: Superintendent of Documents.

————. 1975. *Report of the Secretary of Defense James R. Schlesinger on the FY 1976 and the Transition Budget, the FY 1977 Authorization Request and the 1977–80 Defense Program* (5 February), Washington, D.C.: Superintendent of Documents.

Schrader-Frechette, K. S. 1980. *Nuclear Power and Public Policy*. Boston: Reidel.

Schwarzenberger, George. 1955. *The Legality of Nuclear Weapons*. London: Stevens & Son.

Scowcroft, Brent, et al. 1983. "Report of the President's Commission on Strategic Forces" (excerpts). *The New York Times* (12 April).

Scoville, Herbert. 1981. *MX: Prescription for Disaster*. Cambridge, Mass.: MIT Press.

Sen, A. K., and Williams, Bernard, eds. 1982. *Utilitarianism and Beyond*. Cambridge: Cambridge University Press.

Sewell, Sarah B., et al. 1983. "Militarizing the Last Frontier: The Space Weapons Race." *The Defense Monitor* (September).

Sherwin, Martin. 1975. *A World Destroyed: The Atomic Bomb and the Grand Alliance*. New York: Alfred A. Knopf.

Sigal, Leon. 1983. "Towards Stable Deterrence in Europe: Implications of No First Use for NATO's Force Posture." *Proceedings of Senior Converrence*, XXI West Point, Xerox).

Singer, J. David, and Small, Melvin. 1972. *The Wages of War 1816–1965: A Statistical Handbook*. New York: John Wiley.

Singh, Nagendra. 1959. *Nuclear Weapons and International Law*. London: Stevens & Son.

Small, Melvin. See Singer and Small 1972.

Smart, J. J. C. and Williams, Bernard. 1973. *Utilitarianism: For and Against*. Cambridge: Cambridge University Press.

Smith, Alice Kimball. 1965. *A Peril and a Hope*. Chicago: University of Chicago Press.

Smith, Dan. See Thompson and Smith, eds. 1981.

Smith, Gerard K. See Bundy, McGeorge.

Smith, R. Jeffrey. 1983. "The Search for a Nuclear Sanctuary." *Science* (1 July and 8 July).

Smith, Wayne K. See Enthoven and Smith 1971.

Smoke, Richard. 1977. *On War: Controlling Escalation*. Cambridge, Mass.: Harvard University Press.

Smyth, Henry Dewolf. 1945. *Atomic Energy for Military Purposes: The Official Report on the Development of the Atomic Bomb Under the Auspices of the United States Government*. Princeton: Center for International Studies, Princeton University Press.

Soddy, F. 1909. *The Interpretation of Radium*. London: John Murray.

Solberg, Carl. 1973. *Riding High*. New York: Mason & Lipscomb.

Solomon, Norman, and Wasserman, Henry. 1983. *Killing Our Own*. New York: Delta Books.

Sorenson, Theodore. 1965. *Kennedy*. New York: Harper & Row.

Sowards, J. Kelly. 1975. *Eramus*. Boston: Twayne.

Stein, Walter, ed. 1961. *Nuclear Weapons: A Catholic Response*. London: Merlin.

Steinbock, Bonnie, ed. 1980. *Killing and Letting Die.* Englewood Cliffs: Prentice Hall.

Steinbrunner, John. 1978. "National Security and the Concept of Strategic Stability." *Journal of Conflict Resolution* 22.

——. 1981–1982. "Nuclear Decapitation," *Foreign Policy* 45.

Stopel, Jan. 1982. "Dutchman Not Favor Unilateral Disarmament But Fearful of Nuclear War." *The Gallup Report* (January).

Stockholm International Peace Research Institute. *Handbook of World Armaments and Disarmament.* Yearly.

Sturgeon, Theodore. 1978. "Thunder and Roses." In *The Road to Science Fiction,* ed. James Gunn. New York: New American Library.

Suarez, F. 1944. *Selection from Three Works of Suarez,* trans. G. L. Williams, A. Brown, and J. Waldron. Oxford: Oxford University Press.

Sullivan, Roger, et al. 1979. *Civil Defense Needs of High Risk Areas of the United States.* Arlington: Systems Planning Corporation.

Sykes, Lynn R., and Evernden, Jack. 1982. "Verification of a Comprehensive Test Ban." *Scientific American* (October).

Szliard, Leo. 1955. "Disarmament and the Problem of Peace," *Bulletin of the Atomic Scientists* 11:8.

——. 1960. "How To Live With the Bomb and Survive." *Bulletin of the Atomic Scientists* 16:2.

——. 1961. "The Mined Cities." *Bulletin of the Atomic Scientists* 17:12.

——. 1968. "Reminiscences." In *Perspectives in American History*, ed. Gertrude Weiss Szilard and Kathleen R. Windsor. Cambridge, Mass.: Harvard University Press.

——. 1972. *The Collected Works of Leo Szilard: Scientific Papers.* Eds. Bernard Feld and Gertrude Weiss Szilard. Cambridge, Mass.: MIT Press.

Taton, Rene, ed. 1960. *Science in the 20th Century.* New York: Basic Books.

Taylor, Maxwell. 1969. *Precarious Security.* New York: W. W. Norton.

Taylor, Theodore B. See Willrich, ed. 1974.

Teller, Edward, and Brown, Allen. 1962. *The Legacy of Hiroshima.* Garden City: Doubleday.

Terry, Henry T. 1915. "Negligence." In *Freedom and Responsibility*, ed. Herbert Morris. Stanford: Stanford University Press: 1961.

Thompson, E. P. and Smith, Dan, eds. 1981. *Protest and Survive.* New York: Monthly Review Press.

Thomson, Judith Jarvis. 1975. "Killing, Letting Die, and the Trolley Problem." *The Monist* (April).

Tolstoy, Leo. 1890. *The Kingdom of God Is Within You.* Trans. Leo Weiner. New York: Noonday, 1966.

——. 1909. *The Law of Love and the Law of Violence.* Trans. Mary Tolstoy. New York: Holt, Reinhart, & Winston, 1971.

Tooke, Joan D. 1965. *The Just War in Aquinas and Grotius.* London, S.P.C.K.

Toynbee, Philip. 1959. *The Fearful Choice.* Detroit: Wayne State University Press.

Tsipis, Kosta. 1981. "Laser Weapons." *Scientific American* (December).

Tsipis, Kosta, and Parmentola, John. 1977. "Particle Beam Weapons." *Scientific American* (April).

Tsipis, Kosta, and Fetter, Steven. 1981. "Castastrophic Releases of Radioactivity." *Scientific American* (April).

Tucker, Robert W. 1960. *The Just War.* Baltimore: Johns Hopkins University Press.

——. 1967. *Force, Order, and Justice.* Baltimore: Johns Hopkins University Press.

Turco, R. P., Toon, O. B., Packerman, T. P., Pollack, J. B., and Sagan, Carl. 1983. "Nuclear Winter: Global Consequences of Multiple Nuclear Explosions" Science, 23 December.

United Nations. Yearbook of the United Nations. New York. Yearly.

United States Arms Control and Disarmament Agency. 1975. The Effects of Nuclear War (April). Washington, D.C.: Superintendent of Documents.

United States Congress, House Committee on Science and Astronautics. 1961. A Chrononlogy of Missile and Astronautic Events. Washington, D.C.: U.S. Government Printing Office.

United States Congress, Office of Technology Assessment. 1979. The Effects of Nuclear War. Totowa, N.J.: Allanheld, Osmun, 1980.

United States Department of the Air Force. 1976. International Law: The Conduct of Armed Conflict and Air Operations (17 November). Washington, D.C.: Department of the Air Force.

United States Department of State. Foreign Relations of the United States. Washington, D.C. Cited by year and volume.

United States Senate, Committee on the Judiciary. 1982. Federal Regulation of Firearms (May). Washington, D.C.: U.S. Government Printing Office.

Vitoria, Francisco. 1532 De Indis et de jure belli relectiones. Ed. Ernest Nys. Washington, D.C.: Carnegie Institute 1917.

Viner, Jacob. 1946. "The Implications of the Atomic Bomb for International Relations." Proceedings of the American Philosophical Society XC:1.

Van Der Meer. 1961. Augustine the Bishop. New York: Harper & Row.

Von Magnus, Eric. 1982. "Risk, State and Nozick." Midwest Studies in Philosophy VIII.

Walkowicz, T. F. 1955. "Counterforce Strategy," Air Force (February).

Walters, Leroy, Jr. 1971. Five Classic Just War Theories: Aquinas, Victoria, Suarez, Gentili, and Grotius. Ph.D. Dissertation, Yale University.

Walzer, Michael. 1977. Just and Unjust Wars. New York: Basic Books.

Warrender, J. H. 1975. The Political Philosophy of Thomas Hobbes. New York: Oxford University Press.

Watt, Donald Cameron. 1979. "Restraints on War in the Air Before 1945." In Restraints on War, ed. Michael Howard. New York: Oxford University Press.

Weinberger, Caspar W. 1982a. Report of the Secretary of Defense Casper W. Weinberger to the Congress on the FY 1983 Defense Budget (31 January 1982). Washington, D.C.: U.S. Government Printing Office.

———. 1982b. Shattuck Lecture: Remarks by the Secretary of Defense to the Massachusetts Medical Society (19 May). New England Journal of Medicine 307:12.

———. 1983. Report of the Secretary of Defense Caspar W. Weinberger to the Congress on the FY 1984 Budget, FY 1985 Authorization Request, and the FY 1984–88 Defense Program (1 February). Washington, D.C.: U.S. Government Printing Office.

Weissman, Stephen and Herbert Krosney. 1982. The Islamic Bomb. New York: Times Books.

Wells, Donald A. 1967. The War Myth. New York: Pegasus.

Wells, Samuel F., Jr. 1981. "The Origins of Massive Retaliation," Political Science Quarterly 96.

Wells, H. G. 1914. The World Set Free. London: Macmillian.

Westmoreland, William. 1976. A Soldier Reports. New York: Doubleday.

Wiesner, Jerome and York, Herbert. 1964. "National Security and the Nuclear Test Ban." Scientific American (October).

Wit, Joel S. 1981. "Advances in Anti-Submarine Warfare." *Scientific American* (February).

Williams, Bernard. See Smart and Williams 1973.

Williams, Granville. 1953. "Recklessness." In *Freedom and Responsibility*, ed. Herbert Morris. Stanford: Stanford University Press, 1961.

Willrich, Mason. 1974. *Nuclear Theft: Risks and Safeguards*. Cambridge, Mass: Ballinger.

Wohlstetter, Albert. 1959. "The Delicate Balance of Terror." *Foreign Affairs* 37:2.

————. 1974a. "Is There a Strategic Arms Race?" *Foreign Policy* 15.

————. 1974b. "Rivals But No 'Race'" *Foreign Policy* 16.

————. 1975. "Optimal Ways to Confuse Ourselves," *Foreign Policy* 20.

————. 1976a. *The Spread of Military and Civilian Nuclear Energy: Predictions, Premises, and Policies*. Los Angeles: Pan Heuristics E-1.

————. 1976b. "Spreading the Bomb Without Breaking the Rules." *Foreign Policy* (Winter).

Wohlstetter, Albert, et al. 1979. *Swords From Plowshares: The Military Potential of Civilian Nuclear Energy*. Chicago: University of Chicago Press.

Wolfe, Thomas W. 1979. *The SALT Experience*. Cambridge, Mass.: Ballinger.

World Council of Churches. 1982. *Peace and Disarmament: Documents of the World and the Roman Catholic Church Council of Churches*. Geneva and Rome.

World List of Nuclear Power Plants. 1981. *Nuclear News*.

Yanella, Ernest J. 1977. *The Missile Defense Controversy: Strategy, Technology and Politics 1955–1972*. Lexington: University of Kentucky Press.

Yergin, Daniel. 1977. *Shattered Peace: The Origins of the Cold War and the National Security State*. Boston: Houghton Mifflin.

York, Herbert. 1976. *The Advisors: Oppenheimer, Teller, and the Superbomb* San Francisco: W. H. Freeman.

————. 1976. "Military Technology and American Security." *Scientific American* (August).

————. 1970. *Race to Oblivion*. New York: Simon & Schuster.

Young, Oran, ed. 1975. *Bargaining: Formal Theories of Negotiation*. Urbana: University of Illinois Press.

Zuckerman, Solly. 1982. *Nuclear Illusion and Reality*. New York: Viking.

Index